Doing the Work of Reference: Practical Tips for Excelling as a Reference Librarian

Doing the Work of Reference: Practical Tips for Excelling as a Reference Librarian has been co-published simultaneously as *The Reference Librarian*, Numbers 72 and 73 2001.

Doing the Work of Reference: Practical Tips for Excelling as a Reference Librarian

Celia Hales Mabry
Editor

Doing the Work of Reference: Practical Tips for Excelling as a Reference Librarian has been co-published simultaneously as *The Reference Librarian*, Numbers 72 and 73 2001.

Routledge
Taylor & Francis Group
New York London

First published by

The Haworth Information Press ®.10 Alice Street, Binghamton, NY 13904-1580 USA

The Haworth Information Press ®. is an imprint of The Haworth Press, Inc., 10 Alice Street, Binghamton, NY 13904-1580 USA

This edition published 2013 by Routledge

Routledge
Taylor & Francis Group
711 Third Avenue
New York, NY 10017

Routledge
Taylor & Francis Group
2 Park Square, Milton Park
Abingdon, Oxon OX14 4RN

Routledge is an imprint of the Taylor & Francis Group, an informa business

Doing the Work of Reference: Practical Tips for Excelling as a Reference Librarian has been co-published simultaneously as *The Reference Librarian*, Numbers 72 and 73 2001.

Cover design by Thomas J. Mayshock Jr.

Library of Congress Cataloging-in-Publication Data

Doing the work of reference : practical tips for excelling as a reference librarian / Celia Hales Mabry, editor.

p. cm.
Co-published simultaneously as The reference librarian, nos. 72 and 73, 2001.
Includes bibliographical references and index.
ISBN 0-7890-1322-3 (alk. paper) – ISBN 0-7890-1323-1 (pbk. : alk. paper)
1. Reference services (Libraries)–United States. 2. Academic libraries–Reference services–United States. I. Hales-Mabry, Celia. II. Reference librarian.

Z711 .D65 2001
025.5'2777–dc21

2001039146

Doing the Work of Reference: Practical Tips for Excelling as a Reference Librarian

CONTENTS

ABOUT THE EDITOR

Celia Hales Mabry, PhD, is Reference/Instruction Librarian and Bibliographer at the University of Minnesota Libraries, Minneapolis, where she has worked since 1986. Dr. Mabry edited *Philosophies of Reference Service* (The Haworth Press, Inc., 1997) and wrote *The World of the Aging: Information Needs and Choices* (American Library Association, 1993). She lives in St. Paul with her husband Paul D. Mabry, a neuroscientist at the University of St. Thomas. E-mail: *c-hale@tc.umn.edu*.

Introduction

Celia Hales Mabry

The topic of this publication drew a great deal of interest from librarians across the U.S.; I received over 150 abstracts for consideration. As I learned that there would be a significant time delay before the volume would be published, I mostly eliminated technologically-oriented topics, knowing that what was relevant in 1999-2000 would no longer be cutting edge when the publication came out. What remained, though, was a great sample of perennial issues in reference librarianship, those timeless topics that recur through the years and demand our attention. I am particularly pleased with the quality of the articles in this publication. The authors worked through various drafts with great diligence, and I do hope that you, too, are pleased with the result.

I have worked to provide a logical progression in the topics covered. First, our keynote is provided by Charles R. Anderson, whose name will be well-recognized by reference librarians for his "The Exchange," published in *The Reference and User Services Association Quarterly* (formerly *RQ*) for many years. He is the only individual whom I am singling out for special recognition, but there are many unsung heroes in the remaining authors. I hope that this publication will lead many authors to publish again and again in their remaining years as professionals.

Orientation is always a challenge for reference librarians, whether new to the field or whether they are moving from a different job responsibility. The suggestions are indeed quite "practical" (as our

[Haworth co-indexing entry note]: "Introduction." Mabry, Celia Hales. Co-published simultaneously in *The Reference Librarian* (The Haworth Information Press, an imprint of The Haworth Press, Inc.) No. 72, 2001, pp. 1-3; and: *Doing the Work of Reference: Practical Tips for Excelling as a Reference Librarian* (ed: Celia Hales Mabry) The Haworth Information Press, an imprint of The Haworth Press, Inc., 2001, pp. 1-3. Single or multiple copies of this article are available for a fee from The Haworth Document Delivery Service [1-800-342-9678, 9:00 a.m. - 5:00 p.m. (EST). E-mail address: getinfo@haworthpressinc.com].

subtitle requested), and there are three articles that give varying viewpoints to this topic. The authors are Teresa Portilla Omidsalar, Margo Young, Susan Sykes Berry, Erica W. Reynolds, Angela Locknar, and Scott Vine. A recurring theme is that the new reference librarian must take responsibility for her orientation, whether or not a formal orientation program is in place.

Many articles could fit the heading of "On the Desk," but I selected three that are particularly germane to that category. The authors are Maggie Leonicio, Brian Quinn, Susan E. Beck, and Nancy B. Turner. All picture a reference librarian who, with a smile, helps his library users with good humor and also is a team player who does not conflict with his co-workers.

"Our Challenges" presents three articles of diverse topics that suggest that we are presented with difficulties that cry for solution. The authors are Frederick R. Reenstijerna, Patricia J. M. Rodkewich, JoAnn DeVries, and Peggy Keeran. This is the only section that specifically addresses the technological challenges, and the manner in which this issue is discussed suggests to me that it will still be relevant when our volume is published.

There is a flow of practical tips in the next seven articles, and a progression that I hope will appear logical. The theme is that we need to do good work in our primary function–reference desk service. Mark Y. Herring offers a word of caution in saying to us that he has observed a decline in a good general liberal arts preparation for reference librarians in recent years; he also offers some suggestions for remedying perceived lacks if you yourself know that the questions sometimes challenge basic knowledge that somehow your college education did not provide. James Morris-Knower approaches the common problem of being a science librarian with a liberal arts background, and offers some very astute recommendations of how to handle the very difficult subject matter; the fact that reference librarians historically have not had a science background will lead many of you to identify with his descriptions. Finally, we take a look at five articles, "Getting Some Assistance for Ourselves," that offer ways of building knowledge that might be lacking as well as looking to files at the reference desk and student workers who might take off some of the pressure. The authors in this section are Elaine Coppola, Susan Gangl, Jacqueline Borin, Karla J. Block, Julia A. Kelly, and Kierstin C. Hill.

The next heading, "Looking at Our Users," offers diverse articles by Sandra Jenkins, and Deborah Stanley and Natasha Lyandres. It is illustrative in this section that the practical tips are about such diverse topics; the same trend replays throughout the book.

In "Reaching Out," Catherine Cardwell, John Cruickshank, David G. Nowak and Sarah Reneker Andeen look beyond the walls of the library to determine what we might do to expand our influence. Again, the topics are diverse and the ideas practical and replicable in other settings.

Instruction is still a prevalent concern in libraries, especially academic, today. Many libraries are opting to become "teaching libraries," and this trend is noted in articles by Naomi R. Sutherland, C. M. Winters, Joan E. Conger, Tracy L. Hull, and Kelley A. Lawton. The focus in all of these pieces is upon ways to keep the interest of the students who are our captive audience.

Finally, we look to our profession to see how we might better serve it. Gary W. White, Sarah Brick Archer, Candace R. Benefiel, Jeannie P. Miller, Pixey Anne Mosley, and Wendi Arant-Kaspar offer variations on the theme of professional service, service that, well-documented, is so important to success in our own careers. Concluding with this theme turns us outward even as we look inward to see just what our particular talents might be by way of service.

Once again, as in 1997, I wish to single out Bill Katz for a particular nod of thanks. He is ever-supportive, ever the consummate professional, with a low-keyed handling of the editorship of the overall series that makes his direction a pleasure to have. We in librarianship have a gem in this man.

My own work at the University of Minnesota's Wilson Library went on, despite many e-mails with questions to my authors and prospective authors, and many drafts. I wish to thank my colleagues, all of whom are my friends as well, for recognizing the value of scholarly contribution even as we do our everyday work. And my husband, Paul Mabry, provides the stable home background that allows me not only to produce, but to do so with great joy.

THE KEYNOTE

Reference Librarianship: A Guide for the 21st Century

Charles R. Anderson

SUMMARY. Changes in the practice of Reference Librarianship as well as some practical and philosophical traits for success in this field in the 21st Century are discussed. There are brief summaries of specific elements of technological change that quite likely will have major impacts on library service delivery and some discussion of historical trends that have or have not prepared the field of librarianship to meet the demands of service in the coming decade. *[Article copies available for a fee from The Haworth Document Delivery Service: 1-800-342-9678. E-mail address: <getinfo@haworthpressinc.com> Website: <http://www.HaworthPress.com> © 2001 by The Haworth Press, Inc. All rights reserved.]*

KEYWORDS. Futurology, reference services, public libraries, academic libraries, technology, computers in libraries, World Wide Web, Internet, digital reference

---

Charles R. Anderson is currently President of *the-indexer.com*, an indexing and library consulting organization. He has served as editor of "The Exchange," *RQ* (now *RUSQ*) for the past fifteen years.

Address correspondence to: Charles R. Anderson, P.O. Box 15642, Seattle, WA 98115-0642 (E-mail: anderson@the-indexer.com).

[Haworth co-indexing entry note]: "Reference Librarianship: A Guide for the 21st Century." Anderson, Charles R. Co-published simultaneously in *The Reference Librarian* (The Haworth Information Press, an imprint of The Haworth Press, Inc.) No. 72, 2001, pp. 5-19; and: *Doing the Work of Reference: Practical Tips for Excelling as a Reference Librarian* (ed: Celia Hales Mabry) The Haworth Information Press, an imprint of The Haworth Press, Inc., 2001, pp. 5-19. Single or multiple copies of this article are available for a fee from The Haworth Document Delivery Service [1-800-342-9678, 9:00 a.m. - 5:00 p.m. (EST). E-mail address: getinfo@haworthpressinc.com].

Historically, librarianship has been a relatively stable career field. While many practitioners may have come to the field after one or more prior careers, once a librarian, many people tended to remain one for the remainder of their professional lives. Although this pattern may change in the future, it still behooves new entrants as well as current employees to consider carefully whether their chosen career path is something they will be comfortable following for the next 30-40 years. For this reason, the more aware you become of possible changes, at least in the near (5-10 years) future, the more likely it is that you will be happy with your choice of professions.

At no other time since the beginning of the public library movement in the United States has the profession faced so many profound challenges and opportunities. Perhaps there is some significance to the congruity of dates between the burgeoning of public libraries in the 1890s and the transformation of libraries that is taking place in the 1990s. The well-known Pogo cartoon with the caption, "We are faced with insurmountable opportunities" could be taken as a motto for library service today.

For example, consider the following trends or factors in library service in the 90s:

- Libraries' version of the "baby boomer" bulge that resulted from the large influx of MLS librarians after perceived serious shortages of librarians in the early 1960s, many of whom are now within a decade of retirement.
- Increasing uncertainty among support staff about the future prospects of employment in a world of self-service checkouts and outsourced technical processing (with a concomitant attractiveness and complications of unionization efforts).
- Ethical and practical concerns from an increasingly more intimate relationship between commercial enterprises and free public libraries (viz. Microsoft's *Libraries Online* project).
- Threats of obsolescence if we do not transform ourselves into an electronic village.
- Fears of obsolescence in the reference area if we do successfully become completely *wired*, and our users are able to access the world of information through the Internet without our intervention.

- Budgets that do not keep pace with inflation and become more and more skewed towards automation at the expense of "traditional" library materials.
- Near-complete uncertainty about near-term technological developments that will affect how libraries function.
- Frequently confused understandings of the true market factors that drive our service. *(What does the public really want–other than more of everything?)*

We can look at every one of these trends as an opportunity or as a coming disaster depending upon our individual orientation. Objectively, libraries in the U.S. probably intersect with these (and other) trends at different points of a continuum. There are libraries on the sharpest of cutting edges. Other libraries have made a conscious decision to stay away from the sharp edges of technology completely. Most libraries fall somewhere between these extremes.

The field of Librarianship has a long and illustrious history. Since the beginning of formal libraries with recognized professional librarians, the primary role of the librarian has been to serve as an intermediary between stored information and people who can use that information. A fundamental belief of librarians is that their training and mindset give them a special capability of organizing knowledge so that it can be retrieved easily and passed on to others. This belief is now subject to challenges in ways that could not have been conceived even five-ten years ago.

Few would argue that the beginning of major changes in libraries in the 20th Century came with various technological advances. For example, the introduction of the typewriter in library work made such things as the catalog card economically possible. Another turning point was the introduction of the first Xerox copier in libraries in 1962. Certainly the beginnings of computerized library catalogs can be considered a major turning point in library service and librarianship.

As the rate of published information increased over the last several decades of the 20th Century, librarians continued to improve various schemes for organizing information. When computers became a major part of library service, the complexities for librarians and the problems of organizing knowledge increased enormously. The real change came only in the closing years of the 20th Century. The turning point–the paradigmatic shift that will define librarianship in the 21st Century–

came when libraries jumped on the "Information Superhighway," and began adding public access terminals connected to the Internet. The extremely rapid development of the Web, in particular the increasingly sophisticated search engines that developed, changed the way the public used libraries and raised enormous problems for librarians. Many of these problems were not immediately recognized, especially by library administrators. Reference librarians found themselves in increasingly stressful situations, attempting to deal not only with new information sources but new equipment hardware and software, with little training or previous experience in either sources, hardware, or equipment.

The problems faced by the profession go far beyond simple questions of how to train reference librarians to install new software or deal with crashed hard disks. The problems are philosophical in nature and must be understood in philosophical terms if one is to understand the changes that are taking place as we enter the 21st Century. Anyone considering a career in librarianship must understand these philosophical changes if she is to be happy and successful in a new career. The change in focus for librarians is quantitatively and qualitatively different than any previous change in the field.

To give you a frame of reference, consider two quotations. The first is by the 20th Century futurist, David Burrus, author of the well-known "Rules of Technology." As Burrus noted in his first Rule, "If it works, it's obsolete" (Burrus, 1993). The second quotation, variously attributed, reads, "The future isn't what it used to be." In the incredibly fast-changing world of the first decade of the new millennium, many institutions will need to predict and solve tomorrow's problems today. This need will be particularly critical for organizations involved in the information industry. Coping with the coming changes will mean that we have to move away from the historical library method of crisis management, that is, tending to deal with problems only when they arise.

It has become painfully obvious over the past ten years that most library professionals–despite numerous conferences, "Initiatives," and "Goals statements" generated by the various library associations–were only partially successful in understanding and planning for the vast changes taking place in society and the world of information. This is apparent in many areas: from the types of buildings that libraries continue to design and build, through the cries for training and more training that come from working librarians, to the types of curricula that many library schools still offer. Although a number of non-library authors described these potential changes, many librarians somehow managed to ignore or downplay the implications.

For example, Kevin Kelly, another futurist of the 90s, cites a seminal work by Jay David Bolter. Bolter pointed out how rigidly planted was the concept of *text* as being something firmly fixed in the pages of a printed work.

> The conceptual space of a printed book is one in which writing is stable, monumental, and controlled exclusively by the author. It is the space defined by perfect printed volumes that exist in thousands of identical copies. The conceptual space of electronic writing, on the other hand, is characterized by fluidity and an interactive relationship between writer and reader. (Kelly, 1994)

Kelly and Bolter believe that the technology of knowledge shapes the very way we think and in turn the way we think the world is organized.

"Different technologies allow certain ways of thinking and make other ways difficult. An oral tradition, in pre-historical times, built a knowledge base that was fluid, incorporating all sorts of interruptions, questions, and parenthetical introductions. A quill pen required more control over the thought that went into producing a page. A printed work, to be widely disseminated, needed even more editorial control. Once in print, information took on an intrinsic reality and authority" (Anderson, 1998).

In libraries the permanence and authority of print has some intrinsic corollary to a perceived need for such things as "Collection Development Policies." While these policies ostensibly serve as a guide for acquiring library materials, they also serve a political purpose, i.e., they provided some backup if the need for a public explanation regarding particular material ever arose. In some public libraries, particularly the larger and better-funded ones, the collection development policy became so broad that anything was fair game to acquire regardless of particular local need or value to society in general of particular items. In the name of Intellectual Freedom, a number of libraries may have managed to remove themselves from understanding the basic needs of their users, creating new difficulties in areas such as public support and funding.

Additionally, this "buy as much of everything published as we can afford" philosophy proved to be a good demonstration of the economic principle called the Pareto or 80/20 Principle, which states that a small number of causes is responsible for a large number of effects. In other words, it is fairly typical to find that in libraries following this unselective way of acquiring materials, approximately 80 percent or more of the circulation tends to come from approximately 20 percent or less of the collection–leaving rational taxpayers to wonder about the wisdom of such a broad scale acquisition policy. This is just one example of how libraries may have fallen short in becoming aware of, and responding to, the increasingly segmented needs of their clients. As selectivity in selection decreases, the utility of the material selected for specific client groups probably decreases.

Another example of library insularity is the difficulty that librarians have faced coming to terms with the provision of digital, on-line information sources, particularly the proper relationship of these external sources to the in-library "catalog." Since this internal catalog accesses a static, linearly arranged collection, it has been very difficult for many librarians to accept the proposition that Web access is just as important (but no more important) than access to locally-held materials. This leads inevitably to conflicts between the desires of the more computer-literate users and the print-oriented librarians.

The introduction of hypertext on electronic networks stimulates "another way of thinking: telegraphic, modular, nonlinear, malleable, cooperative" (Kelly, 1994). It has taken a number of years, and some painful episodes, for many libraries to recognize that a collection development policy for electronic networks is an oxymoron. Attempts to fit dynamic information into a static, 20th Century mold are inherently prone to failure.

One factor which makes it difficult for some libraries to adapt quickly to the changes in information delivery is inherent in the way that many libraries are administered. Library directors, as a general rule, tend not to be extremely mobile. Once in a leadership position, many tend to stay until retirement. A perfectly natural bent toward hiring senior administrators in their own image can lead to an administrative-level staff that finds it very difficult to understand or accept the changed information environment. New employees in the library field will need to be prepared for the possibility that it may be many years before librarians trained in the 1990s rise sufficiently in organizations to have any real impact on how new technology is developed, acquired, and supported.

The above may explain why so many librarians in the 1990s had so much trouble adapting to information service in an on-line, electronic environment. For centuries, the word *Library* meant a collection of written materials surrounded by walls. We are accustomed to thinking in terms of tangible objects–a page, a tape, a video. We think in terms of specific locations–a room, a floor, an aisle, a stack. Most of all, we think of Certainty. A reference book classified 016.7 yesterday will be classified 016.7 tomorrow, next week, next decade (barring occasional revisions of Dewey!). A reference librarian will always find a certain answer by going to a certain spot in the collection.

However, the operative word for electronic information networks–or, to use the popular term, the Cybrary–is not Certainty. It is Ambiguity–a difficult concept for most people and most certainly a difficult mode of operation for reference librarians.

The new electronic library collections are not tangible; they are existential–existing only as bits, states of electrical charges, either on or off. The collections are constantly changing, mutating, growing, adapting to the environment. The collections have a lot in common with living organisms. Like living organisms, predictability of behavior is uncertain. The path to particular pieces of information may change constantly (Anderson, 1996).

The last five years' movement towards a holistic view of the broad spectrum of human knowledge means that successful reference librarians in the 21st Century will need backgrounds that are broader than even the legendary Renaissance Man. Librarians need to constantly keep updating their basic skills and knowledge as "specialists in generalities," while also mastering the complex searching capabilities of medical, legal, and other specialists. The library profession will need to employ individuals who are capable of meeting the challenges of the coming decades. A primary trait of the new librarian will be curiousity–people who are above all curious and eager to learn new things and who are self-starters.

If your background is highly specialized, you probably will not want to choose librarianship as a career. The libraries of the 21st Century will need specialists in generalities. Daniel Burrus identified some particular characteristics that can be applied to success in reference librarianship (Burrus, 1993).

- Optimistic about the future
- Open to alternatives
- Good at turning innovative ideas into practical solutions
- Adventurous, with multiple interests
- People who take action and make things happen
- Full of commitment to what they're doing
- Nonconformists

Both for those now in the field and for those seriously considering making a career of librarianship–that is, entering into a career which may last for the next 30 or 40 years–it is important to become aware of some particularly significant technological developments looming on the near-time horizon. Some of these developments which have been identified in numerous articles are: high performance networking, neural networks, virtual reality, high-definition imaging with miniaturized displays, artificial intelligence programs, and nanotechnology.

HIGH PERFORMANCE NETWORKING AND NEURAL NETWORKS

Advances in networking and artificial intelligence technology may lead to the use of neural networks in library information services. A major feature of neural networks is built-in learning capability. Among other applications, a neural system will be able to track and analyze how the public interacts with the library information services. From this data will come rich new levels of management information that will predict such things as peak use times and future needs for types and quantities of materials in each branch–tailored very specifically to local demand. This process will be akin to the Marketing-on-Demand (MOD) impetus by manufacturers. Another way to conceptualize this approach is Market Segmentation–fine tuning library collections and access to remote information sources to deliver needed information to ever-finer sub-sections of users.

The adaptive capabilities of neural networks will enable the system to respond rapidly to changing public needs–faster than any human "current awareness" system or in-house staff manipulated "push" attempts.

One major benefit from these neural networks will be the more efficient use and allocation of staff. Library administrators made some primitive attempts at staff forecasting in the past, usually at great cost in dollars and staff time, with little beneficial results. It is not too difficult to imagine a program, perhaps named DISTAFF (Dynamic Interactive System-wide Technical Analysis for Staff Forecasting), as a part of the neural network. DISTAFF could provide far superior information on staff availability and utilization, including up-to-the minute tracking of sick leave, vacation, meeting and training responsibilities, etc. Based on continually revised data and on past experience, including the capacity to learn, DISTAFF could predict, among other things, when and where substitute staff is needed. The real-time attendance reporting data that feeds into the system from the individual library staff check-in points can easily generate the information needed to produce the payroll each month.

To use this kind of new technology will require considerable training, especially of managers and supervisors, in using this new system. The system will require a much higher order of technological involvement on the part of our managers than their experience in the past.

VIRTUAL REALITY, HIGH-DEFINITION IMAGING WITH MINIATURIZED DISPLAYS, AND ARTIFICIAL INTELLIGENCE PROGRAMS

Although the term *virtual reality* now has a somewhat quaint, outdated sound, librarians in the future will probably remember it as a major factor in the transition from the physical library to the electronic library. In the early 90s, the capabilities of virtual reality were barely realized due to the cumbersome requirements of the technology. A recent market development has been the invention of a miniature video receiver, capable of high-definition imaging, built into a pair of glasses and capable of projecting an extremely legible heads-up display of text and graphics. An obvious library application would be to extend Internet connections to an on-line library to an individual wearing this kind of heads-up display, or at least to a wireless Personal Digital Assistant.

When this type of interface is popularized and coupled with artificial intelligence technologies to customize information delivery, it could well impact the typical information needs of many library users. For example, document delivery, at least, does not need any sort of human interface. As the public accesses our system through direct satellite links, they can order electronic or paper copy delivered to their home or office.

NANOTECHNOLOGY

Of all the new technologies that began to come to fruition in the 1990s, nanotechnology, or molecular engineering, probably has been the major area ignored by library literature. Nanotechnology requires manufacturing tolerances at dimensions of nanometers–billionths of a meter, or roughly between the size of an atom to the wavelength of light. This developing technology is pointed towards the ability to manipulate atoms to build extremely tiny machines, called *assemblers* which, when replicated many times on a molecular level, could theoretically produce any desired product, in a very short time. Some of the capabilities foreseen in the 1990s were a tape storage system with ten billion gigabytes of information per cubic centimeter and the computational power of ten billion Cray computers in the size of a sugar cube.

Richard Fenyman pointed out in 1959 that, "In the year 2000, when they look back at this age, they will wonder why it was not until 1960 that anybody began to seriously move in this direction" (Hanssen, 1991). Fenyman was a bit optimistic. However, once some basic developments such as the scanning tunneling microscope were in place, the technological rate of change accelerated tremendously. By 1994, *PC Magazine* was predicting an estimated time of arrival for nanotechnology between 2010 and 2020, which probably will turn out to be pessimistic (*PC Magazine,* 1994).

One turning point that seems to have persuaded many scientists and engineers to begin taking these possibilities seriously was a somewhat trivial experiment. In 1990 IBM engineers used a scanning tunneling microscope to spell out the IBM logo with xenon atoms on a nickel surface (Eigler, 1990). This convinced skeptics that molecular manipulation was indeed possible. However, until very recently, the general public largely ignored the possibilities as the millennium end grew near.

Unfortunately, it seems that the full impact of this new technology is still a mystery to most of the public (and many librarians). The central techniques of the Industrial Revolution involved the use of many special purpose machines to create the complex inventions of the age. Only now in retrospect can we understand the full significance of the changes in society these inventions produced. Nanotechnology will allow people to use a general purpose machine controlled by digital data, operating on bulk, inexpensive materials, to build anything in a very short period of time, including a replica of the machine itself. The economic and social consequences of this invention will be enormous. Eric Drexler, a 20th Century engineer and one of the gurus of the field, claimed that nanotechnology would bring about the greatest turning point in the history of life on earth. One of the best collections for a technical introduction to the subject is *Prospects in Nanotechnology: Toward Molecular Manufacturing,* edited by Markus Krummenacker and James Lewis.

This report is not the place to delve deeply into the various applications of nanotechnology. However, just to theorize about one specific area, consider how the entire process of book creation and distribution might change if the entire contents of a work could be contained in something the size of a period on this page–and viewed or printed at will. We are getting close enough to the point where nanotechnological innovations will begin reaching the marketplace to make it worthwhile for leaders in the library profession to at least begin grappling with what the coming changes in society caused by nano machines will mean for the future existence of the library.

WHERE ARE WE GOING FROM HERE?

People often tend to assume change always will be gradual and phased in over time. This mindset leads to postponing action under the premise that there is insufficient data to make rational decisions about the future. However, while much of the process of change in society has indeed taken place over centuries, there do exist examples of radical, almost overnight, change.

For example, at least from the time of the Persian mail service that inspired the motto of the U.S. Postal Service until the invention of the telegraph, the speed of written communication was (with a few limited exceptions such as smoke signals and mirrors) limited to how fast a horse could run. In a few years' time, the telegraph raised communication capabilities to near light speed, with numerous sudden impacts on economic and social life.

Before 1945, the energy that could be gotten from matter was limited to a few thousand energy units per gram. The atomic bomb released billions of units of energy per gram of material. Again, society witnessed an extremely rapid change that sprung its results on us nearly overnight. While initial steps towards nanotechnology have been relatively slow, once the nanotech assemblers are in general production, the experts expect that future new products will arrive in a matter of days. Compare this to the average development time of a new product in the past, where it often took years from invention to working device to tooling up for factory production and eventual distribution. This rapidity of product development will undoubtedly affect libraries just as it does the rest of society.

ORGANIZATIONAL IMPACTS

Changes such as those briefly discussed above will undoubtedly furnish some of the greatest challenges libraries and librarians have ever faced. As one author pointed out:

> Librarians are a curious enigma. Librarians have a long history of dealing with change, but in a schizophrenic way. They cling to the past, and yet they are often the heaviest users of technologies, such as computing and telecommunications resources. (Penniman, 1992)

This schizophrenia has been clearly evident over the years as libraries and librarians have struggled to adapt to the many changes in how libraries work. We now can see clearly how accurate Penniman was when he went on to postulate that the central issue to be faced by librarians involved *control*–who controls access to information and information technology–the system or the user? Each time that libraries have run into trouble in accommodating a new piece of technology, problems with employees have arisen because managers and line staff were unwilling to accept technologies that diminished their areas of control. In earlier methods of information dissemination, because of the supposed skills of librarians in organizing knowledge, they became de facto "gatekeepers," and this is a role that some are finding difficult to give up. It is essential that library administrators recognize that "when we deal with issues of change, we are dealing with strategic social issues, not technological ones" (Burrus, 1993). Successfully meeting the challenges of social change requires "a brand of leadership that is opportunistic, entrepreneurial, and able to change direction rapidly with the changing needs of its customers" (Burrus, 1993). An administration of this nature must then have the trust and respect of all employees to ensure buy-in to the same characteristics for ultimate success.

We have some evidence that early fears of replacement of professional librarians by robotic *PDA*s (Personal Digital Assistants) and "Push" technology are groundless. *Forbes* noted in an article in 1999 that "nearly one-quarter of library schools once in existence have shut their doors, most since the 1970s. Fewer than 5,000 degrees in Library Science were awarded in 1993, down 30% from 20 years before." However, the article went on to point out that "Digital-savvy librarians are being wooed not just by public or university libraries, but by companies to set up and manage Web sites and on-line research centers."

The same sort of fears of career obsolescence existed in the 1980s, when secretaries worried about being replaced by word processors operated by managers. However, as we know, the earlier three classifications of secretaries–receptionist, secretary, and executive secretary–were soon replaced by at least 18 different specializations, such as transcription specialist, administrative assistant, statistical typist, office manager, etc. Similarly, we will see the development of many more specialties in the library, as our reference staff become intermediaries between the Cybrary and users to meet advanced information needs in many diverse fields–medicine, law, business, the social sciences, and the humanities. Moreover, in a world of ever-increasing specialization by professionals, librarians may well be the only ones who can provide a nexus between professions. The new library "specialists" will need to perform the almost impossible task of remaining *au courant* with many fields. This is a daunting challenge but an invigorating one if the new librarians in the 21st Century can rise to meet it.

How will these and other changes affect new students entering the field? If, after considering some of the implications of the above scenarios and doing your own investigation of the current and projected job market for librarians, you are determined to enter this profession, the following are some basic steps to take. If you are already a working librarian, it will still be helpful to follow numbers three through five.

1. Research carefully the program of study and the background of the faculty at any accredited MLS (Master of Library Science) program that you are considering. Do not assume, just because the name of the program includes the words "Information Sciences," that the curriculum and faculty are actually prepared to teach and graduate students for jobs in the 21st Century. Do some library research, checking for publications by faculty members, how recently they received a Ph.D., and memberships (do they belong to the American Society of Information Science and other technologically oriented associations, or just the American Library Association?).
2. Talk to managers of reference service departments in libraries in the geographic area of the library school. Ask them about their experiences with graduates from the school. Explain that you are not asking for personnel information, just their candid impressions about how well the school prepared people for jobs in their library. Ask them for recommendations about programs. Unless the library is very small, talk to reference managers–not administrators.
3. Try to stay abreast of current developments in the areas described above as well as other new technologies. Spend some time imagining how new technologies might impact the way libraries carry out their roles.
4. Go to Library Board meetings in your area. Observe whether there is any discussion of new technology.
5. Finally, keep in mind that whatever the field of librarianship looks like today, it probably will look considerably different in five years. Be certain that you will be comfortable beginning, or staying, in a field that, unlike the experiences of your predecessors of 30-40 years ago, is in the midst of constant ferment and development.

REFERENCES

Anderson, Charles R., "The Exchange," *RQ* 35 (Summer, 1996), 458-459.

Anderson, Charles R., "The Exchange," *RUSQ* 37 (Spring, 1998), 253.

Burrus, *TechnoTrends* (New York: HarperBusiness, 1993), pp. 210, 353.

Bolter, Jay David, *Writing Space: The Computer, Hypertext, and the History of Writing* (Lawrence Erlbaum Associates, 1991). Cited by Kevin Kelly in *Out of Control* (Reading, MA: Addison-Wesley, 1994), p. 463-464.

Eigler, D.M., and E.K. Schweizer, "Positioning Single Atoms with a Scanning Tunneling Microscope," *Nature* (1990): 524-26.

Drexler, Eric. *Engines of Creation.* New York: Doubleday (1986).

Hansson, Per Anders, "Nanotechnology: Prospects and Policies," *Futures* (October, 1991): 849.

PC Magazine (February 8, 1994): 32, "How Far Out is Nanotechnology?"

Penniman, W. David, "Walking Your Talk: Why Information Managers Are Not High-Tech," in *Artificial Intelligence and Expert Systems: Will They Change the Library?* eds. F. W. Lancaster and Linda C. Smith (Urbana, IL: University of Illinois, 1992), pp. 267-269.

THE ORIENTING FUNCTION

Orientation to Reality

Teresa Portilla Omidsalar
Margo Young

SUMMARY. Reference librarians who are new to an organization need to participate in a systematic orientation program as soon as possible regardless of whether they are experienced or not. A well-planned orientation program helps new librarians provide better and more efficient service for their patrons; and facilitates identification with the organization that they have joined. The need for such orientation programs has no significant relevance to the degree of the librarian's previous experience. Experienced librarians need orientation more than training, though they may also need some training specific to changes in their duties and work location. *[Article copies available for a fee from The Haworth Document Delivery Service: 1-800-342-9678. E-mail address:*

Teresa Portilla Omidsalar and Margo Young are both affiliated with the John F. Kennedy Memorial Library, California State University, Los Angeles (CSULA), 5151 State University Drive, Los Angeles, CA 90032-8300. Teresa Portilla Omidsalar has been User Services Librarian at CSULA since 1997 and Margo Young has been Associate University Librarian since 1998 (E-mail: Omidsalar: tomidsa@calstatela.edu; Young: myoung3@calstatela.edu).

[Haworth co-indexing entry note]: "Orientation to Reality." Omidsalar, Teresa Portilla, and Margo Young. Co-published simultaneously in *The Reference Librarian* (The Haworth Information Press, an imprint of The Haworth Press, Inc.) No. 72, 2001, pp. 21-32; and: *Doing the Work of Reference: Practical Tips for Excelling as a Reference Librarian* (ed: Celia Hales Mabry) The Haworth Information Press, an imprint of The Haworth Press, Inc., 2001, pp. 21-32. Single or multiple copies of this article are available for a fee from The Haworth Document Delivery Service [1-800-342-9678, 9:00 a.m. - 5:00 p.m. (EST). E-mail address: getinfo@haworthpressinc.com].

KEYWORDS. Orientation, training, reference librarians, academic libraries, motivation, mentoring, socialization, new employees

How does orientation fit into the overall professional development and training picture of librarians? Orientation is often considered part of the overall training and is, in fact, the most common type of training provided by organizations. Ninety-two percent of organizations claim to provide some type of new employee orientation (Tyler, 1998). Orientation focuses primarily on attitude or motivation and is thus unique. Training deals with the development of knowledge, skills and attitudes and emphasizes the development of skills. In other words, "Training answers the *what* and the *how* while orientation answers the *why.*" *What* is the goal of the organization and *how does* the employee's role fit in it? (Wehrenberg, 1989). Orientation explains why things are done in a certain way within the institution. Answers to these questions require knowledge of the organizational culture and the work ethic of particular institutions.

Orientation, also called induction, is defined as "the process of familiarizing new employees with whatever is necessary for them to feel at home and to understand and perform their duties efficiently . . . it is the beginning of a fusion process leading to the integration of company and employee goals and needs." The goal of orientation is primarily socialization and an orientation program should be designed to develop a particular attitude about work and the worker's role (St. John, 1980). Socialization is a broader concept than orientation: "socialization focuses on how individuals learn the beliefs, values, orientations, behaviors, skills and so forth necessary to fulfill their new roles and function *effectively* within an organization's milieu" (Ashforth, 1996). Thus, socialization deals both with knowledge to function and with the fit between an organization and an individual.

While an individual is becoming socialized to a new organization, there are two types of orientation occurring: formal (planned and officially conducted by the company) and informal (unplanned and unofficially conducted by fellow workers). While the informal orientation is inevitable, management can set the tone and direction of the formal orientation. The individual observes the activity of the workplace and compares her observations of actual practice with the expectations that have been outlined. "Perceptions of congruence between the organizationally stated requirements and observed activity in the workplace are developed and a personal decision is then made as to how he or she will react to the expectations of the new workplace" (George, 1986). In other words, the individual makes a psychological or mental contract with the organization and performs in a manner consistent with this contract. Depending on his impressions, he becomes a productive member of the organization or passes into what has been called "the lost workforce," i.e., those who either leave the organization or fall into the habit of doing only the absolute minimum.

WHY IS ORIENTATION IMPORTANT?

Orientation is important for a variety of reasons. One of the most important is retention of employees and helping them develop commitment to the new organization. "Attitudes developed during the first few days contribute greatly to the subsequent work ethic adopted . . . Assuming that new employees already have an awareness of what is expected from them can be an expensive mistake" (McDougle, 1982). Evidence suggests that orientation programs increase retention of professionals. Texas Instruments reported that their "early career turnover rate has dropped by 40 percent since we put in our new orientation program," while Corning Glass Works reported a 17 percent decrease in separations with three or less years of service. Corning reported that "the most lasting impressions about an organization are formed early, within the first 60-90 days. These impressions, if poor, lead people to look around for other jobs–maybe not right away, but sometime during the first three years" (McGarrell, 1983). Retention obviously prevents incurring re-recruitment costs. Since the cost of recruiting can be one-third of an employee's first year salary, retention is fiscally desirable (Lindo, 1993).

Orientation can help sustain motivation and productivity. Aligning an individual's goals with the organizational goals is an essential purpose of orientation. Orientation programs should make new employees feel that their work is important, that they are making a valuable contribution to the organization, and that others recognize their contributions (Woodard, 1989).

ORIENTATION PROGRAMS IN ACADEMIC LIBRARIES

With the radical changes in the delivery of information and the fiscal demands placed upon academic libraries, it is crucial that libraries invest adequate time, money, and energy in developing and implementing orientation programs; they should regularly assess the usefulness of these programs.

A search of the literature shows that whereas there are numerous articles about newly graduated librarians, how to teach specific reference skills, such as interviewing and question negotiation, reference desk training, and mentoring individuals, there is relatively little available on orientation programs for both new and experienced librarians. Older literature outlines orientation and training programs in considerable detail, but anecdotal evidence suggests that implementation of such programs is either not as widespread as it should be or as it used to be. One possible reason may be the fiscal restraint placed upon academic libraries during the 1980s and early 1990s. It is only recently that libraries have begun to hire. Further, new librarians graduate with many new technical skills that many experienced librarians lack. This gap of knowledge often means that neither the new nor the experienced librarians benefit from the knowledge of the other.

New librarians really have not learned all they need to know in library school (Walker, 1990). As in any profession, much in the practice of librarianship comes with experience and is learned on the job. Recent graduates may be easier to orient and train because they have not developed poor work habits that may be difficult to modify. By contrast, an experienced librarian who assumes a new position in new surroundings may require more time for "re-learning" and altering past practices.

Reichers, Wanous, and Steele (1994) state that experience allows for a quicker adjustment and suggest experienced workers come with mental maps that help them discriminate between important and unimportant information. In addition, these mental maps help determine which aspects of the workers' prior knowledge are relevant to the new surroundings. Relevant experience typically means less surprise and consequently less anxiety. New workers can be divided into four categories based on their amount of previous experience and its relevance to the new job. These are: neophytes, initiates, converts and veterans. Neophytes, with no relevant experience, need to receive both job and organization knowledge. They are prone to considerable anxiety.

Thus, programs designed for neophytes need to reduce anxiety first and emphasize content second. Classroom instruction, on-the-job training and buddy systems are components of such programs. Initiates, with some relevant experience and knowledge, should be evaluated in order to determine the level of their knowledge. Training can then be focused on appropriate topics. Converts have considerable irrelevant experience and need access to experienced people who can help them determine what part of their past experience is relevant and what part of it is irrelevant. Converts may need rituals to help in "divestiture" of their past experience and "investiture" in the new organization. Veterans with lots of relevant experience require relatively little socialization or training but may do best with access to colleagues who can answer specific questions (Reichers, 1994). Our experience suggests that assuming a veteran needs no training or orientation can leave the veteran with gaps in local knowledge. One way of customizing a program is to divide a program into modules. IBM's orientation has three components: on-boarding (getting "signed up"), competencies (job training), and foundation skills (values, norms and methodologies) (Ganzel, 1998).

Orientation programs should not be voluntary. All librarians (and library assistants) who are new to an institution, regardless of their previous experience, need to participate.

ROLE OF THE ADMINISTRATION IN ORIENTATION PROGRAMS

The success of a library orientation program depends on the strong support of the library's administration. Such support lends legitimacy to the program. The library administration should provide a general overview, in which the library's mission, goals, and strategic direction are emphasized. The administration can also provide leadership by ensuring that the orientation program is headed in the right direction, and that it is not bogged down by too many bureaucratic details. The administration should see to it that the program remains flexible so that it can be changed or revised with ease and speed.

THE ROLE OF THE COORDINATOR

In the case of reference librarians, the AUL for Public Services or the Coordinator of the Reference Department should be in charge of overseeing the orientation schedule for the new librarian. In a team-based organization it would be appropriate for the team leader to coordinate the orientation.

The orientation should include weekly meetings between the coordinator and the new librarian. These weekly meetings provide an opportunity for mutual feedback and constructive criticism and may include discussion of the different styles and methods of supervision exercised in the library. Throughout the orientation, the coordinator can focus on the actions necessary to meet library goals. Furthermore, she can also discuss the standards by which the new librarian will be evaluated. Newly hired persons are more receptive because they are in the "learning mode" during the orientation period (Wogaman, 1992). Faculty status for librarians brings with it considerable discretion on how their work is accomplished and courses are delivered; therefore, it is particularly important to use this orientation period to influence and guide the librarian with faculty status.

No one person should do all of the orientation and training. Sharing responsibility for the orientation will allow staff members to share their expertise and will give the new librarian the opportunity to spend time and get acquainted with each staff member.

CONTENT OF THE ORIENTATION

According to Walter St. John (1980), employees need specific information in three areas:

- Technical aspects of the job;
- Company standards, expectations, norms, traditions, policies, etc.;
- Social behavior.

While much of the content of an orientation is intuitive, it is easy to miss the obvious. Sometimes it is not knowing the small things that make the new librarian feel overwhelmed and not part of the organization. We recommend beginning with a checklist such as that of the Ohio Library Association's Basic Reference Task Force (Off to a Good Start, 1990). It is important that the members of the organization buy into it. We suggest that a small committee made up of members from different departments or units work together to develop the components of the program. Shea suggests listing "the 10 easiest tasks performed in the work group . . . and . . . 10 tasks the new employee might face in the new environment which were probably done differently in his or her old job" (Shea, 1982). Once a draft checklist is created it should be circulated to all staff for input. It would be particularly useful to consult the staff members last hired. They should be asked to identify the orientation and training components which would have been useful to them. You may discover that your previous orientation/training program was poorly organized, too brief, too superficial, or lacking in other areas. The checklist may include the length of time to be spent on individual items, and may also include the names of the individuals with whom the librarian must meet.

The new librarian should also get a packet of information which includes policies, forms, or any other material that librarians and staff use regularly. Information may also be presented through the Web. At the CSULA library the orientation checklist refers to the Library's Intranet where many of the library's forms and policies are stored electronically.

By the end of the orientation the new librarian should have a clear understanding of the goals, objectives, policies, procedures, and expected behavior of members of that organization (Stabler, 1987).

The following Table 1 outlines material that should be covered in the orientation. There are a variety of ways that the components could be arranged, but it is important to differentiate between those components which must be covered on the first day (on-boarding, to use IBM's terminology) from those which are part of the orientation process or the skills training. In addition, the table differentiates the needs of neophytes, initiates, converts and veterans. The depth at which the topics are covered and the rate of the orientation should be individualized based on the librarian's experience and rate of absorption.

SCHEDULING THE ORIENTATION

How soon after the librarian's starting date should the orientation program begin? We agree with those who say right away, even as early as the first day of work (Wogaman, 1992). We believe that an early orientation program helps the new librarian to feel that there is a plan for his training and he may depend upon the immediate support of the organization. The orientation checklist should be given to the new

TABLE 1

	On-board	Foun-dations	Compe-tencies	Neophyte	Initiate	Convert	Veteran
Personnel Items							
Hours of work, Absence reporting, Vacations	X			Day 1	Day 1	Day 1	Day 1
Review of compensation procedures: pay periods, direct deposit, time sheets	X			Day 1	Day 1	Day 1	Day 1
List of company holidays	X			Day 1	Day 1	Day 1	Day 1
List of fringe benefits	X			Day 1; Review later	Day 1; Review later	Day 1; Review later	Day 1; Review later
Insurance plans (health, dental, life, vision, disability)	X			Day 1; Review later	Day 1; Review later	Day 1; Review later	Day 1; Review later
Copies of required forms (e.g., travel, conference, absence)		X		Day 1; Review later	Day 1; Review later	Day 1; Review later	Day 1; Review later
Union contract		X		Day 1	Day 1	Day 1	Day 1
Sources of information (e-mail address, one card, telephone, supplies, parking)	X			Week 1	Week 1	Week 1	Day 1-2
The Job & Expectations							
Retention, tenure and promotion guidelines		X		Week 1	Week 1	Week 1	Day 2-3
Copies of performance evaluation forms, dates and procedures		X		Week 1	Week 1	Week 1	Day 2-3
Job description and duties; performance expectations		X		Week 1	Week 1	Week 1	Day 2
List of on-the-job training opportunities			X	Month 1	Week 2	Month 1	Week 2
The Organization							
Introduction to colleagues	X			Day 1	Day 1	Day 1	Day 1
Organization Chart		X		Week 1	Week 1	Week 1	Day 1-2
Where and how individual fits in	X			Day 1-2	Day 1	Day 2-3	Day 1
Telephone numbers and locations	X			Day 1	Day 1	Day 1	Day 1
Computer accounts and policies, use of software applications	X	X		Day 1	Day 1	Day 1	Day 1
Map of the facility and tour (outlining idiosyncrasies); location of keys; office set up; mail pick up, delivery and policies	X			Day 1-2	Day 1-2	Day 1	Day 1
Emergency and accident prevention procedures; ergonomics	X			Week 1	Day 2-3	Week 1	Day 2-3
Overview of the organization (university, library, department); important organization publications		X		Month 1	Week 1-2	Week 1	Week 1
Acronyms and definitions	X			Week 1	Day 1	Week 1	Day 1

	On-board	Foun-dations	Compe-tencies	Neophyte	Initiate	Convert	Veteran
Strategic plan, mission, vision, goals, objectives and actions		X		Month 1	Week 1-2	Month 1	Week 1-2
Introductions to administrators	X			Month 1	Month 1	Month 1	Month 1
Job Specific							
Information about how to use PC, printers (how to fix jams, how to install cartridges, how to add paper), fax, copiers, telephone (on and off campus, transferring, long distance, voice mail greeting, pick up messages, send messages, distribution lists), ordering supplies	X		X	Month 1-2	Month 1-2	Month 1-2	Month 1-2
Primary reference tools (print and on-line) and their locations			X	Month 1-6	Month 1-4	Month 1-6	Month 1-3
Specific job goals and descriptions (and job-specific training and how to schedule it), e.g., how to prepare a B1, how to book an instruction room, how to prepare a handout, format standards; collection development policy, selection procedures, donations, new subscription requires, selection tools			X	Month 1-12	Month 1-6	Month 1-6	Month 1-3

librarian, and its contents should be discussed with him, on the first day of work.

The orientation schedule should be flexible enough to allow for variation in learning. New librarians should be given enough time to learn to use the library's voice mail and e-mail systems, organize their work area and digest the mass of new information included in orientation (Wogaman, 1992).

Adults learn best by doing. Therefore, new librarians should take major responsibility for their own orientation by ensuring that all of the points on their checklists are covered during the process.

PEER MENTORING: WHERE DOES IT FIT?

In a mentoring program the new librarian is either assigned a person to work with or selects one himself. An orientation program does not preclude having a mentoring component. This usually works well for librarians who have faculty status and need guidance in preparing tenure and promotion documentation. It is also helpful in introducing the new librarian to academic governance. Most new librarians need to know about departmental committees, library committees, and campus committees (Walker, 1990).

The buddy system is similar to mentoring in that two new employees are paired and go through orientation and training together. This works particularly well if the two have similar work habits and learning styles. A variation on this model involves pairing a new librarian with an experienced librarian who supports the novice through the orientation process and facilitates involvement in professional organizations. The experienced member of the pair should be a colleague, not a supervisor. Yet another alternative is to pair a new librarian with two different experienced colleagues over a period of weeks or months. This exposes the new librarian to a variety of styles. In addition to the two buddies, the mentor is important for longer-term support.

AFTER THE ORIENTATION

Skill competencies need to be addressed after the orientation. The amount of skills training required will vary depending on the individual's experience. Skills assessment should be undertaken to determine where training should be focused. Articles about training for the reference desk abound. Even professionals cannot afford to neglect reference desk training and reeducation. This training should include:

- learning the library's dominant philosophy of reference;
- careful study of the reference collection and any other heavily used collections;
- learning about resources available on campus or locally;
- learning the library's web site, catalog, and databases;
- learning local reference desk policies and procedures (e.g., telephone reference, etc.);
- reference interviewing skills, and more.

One approach to ensure further training occurs is to have the employee create a personal action plan (with the guidance of the coordinator) which lists future training needs in order of importance. Such a plan should have a time frame (Prytherch, 1986). This approach places considerable responsibility on the new employee and that increases her ownership of the program and thus her motivation. It also individualizes the program to ensure its relevance. One concern with group orientation is that it may lead to steady, but not innovative, performance (Ashforth, 1996). The personal action plan individualizes the next step and thus encourages innovation.

CONCLUSION

Developing an orientation program forces those who participate in it to think through the objectives of the training, the rationale behind existing procedures, and the justifications behind certain policies. Additionally, it makes the participants aware of areas in which the library is lacking procedures, policies, etc. (Stabler, 1987).

In conclusion, we agree with others who argue that the time required to plan and deliver an orientation pays off through increased productivity and quality of work, independence and job satisfaction (Wogaman, 1992). "New librarians will feel more welcomed to the staff and quickly become engaged in helping the library meet its goals" (Birdseye, 1991). While orientations are certainly time-consuming, their long-term benefits justify the expenditure.

REFERENCES

Ashforth, Blake E. and Saks, Alan M. (1996), "Socialization Tactics: Longitudinal Effects on Newcomer Adjustment," *Academy of Management Journal* 39 (February), 149-178.

Birdseye, Catherine and Misner, Joyce (1991), "*AL* Asides–Idea: The Grand Tour," *American Libraries* 22 (January), 17.

Flion, Isle A. and Pepermans, Roland G. (1998), "Exploring the Relationship between Orientation Programs and Current Job Satisfaction," *Psychological Reports* 83 (August), 367-370.

Ganzel, Rebecca (1998), "Putting Out the Welcome Mat," *Training* 35 (March), 54-62.

George, R. Thomas (1986), "First Impressions: How They Affect Long-term Performance," *Supervisory Management* 31 (March), 2-8.

Lindo, David K. (1993), "Orientation Express," *Office Systems* 10 (November), 64-67 .

McDougle, Larry G. (1982), "Orientation of New Employees: Implications for the Supervisor," *Supervision* 44 (April), 3-5.

McGarrell, Edmund J., Jr. (1983), "An Orientation System that Builds Productivity," *Personnel* 60 (November/December), 32-41.

"Off to a Good Start: A Checklist for the Training of New Reference Librarians." (1990), *Ohio Libraries* 3 (January/February), 6-7.

Prytherch, Ray (ed.) (1986), *Handbook of Library Training Practice.* Aldershot, England: Gower.

Reichers, Arnon E., Wanous, John P., and Steele, Karen (1994), "Design and Implementation Issues in Socializing (and Resocializing) Employees," *HR Human Resource Planning* 17 (1), 17-25.

Shea, Gordon F. (1982), "Supervising New Employees," *Training and Development Journal* 36 (January), 50-56.

St. John, Walter D. (1980), "The Complete Employee Orientation Program," *Personnel Journal* 59 (May), 373-378.

Stabler, Karen Y. (1987), "Introductory Training of Academic Reference Librarians: A Survey," *RQ* 26 (Spring), 363-369.

Tyler, Kathryn (1998), "Take New Employee Orientation off the Back Burner," *HR Magazine* 43 (May), 49-57.

Walker, Lois (1990), "All I Really Needed to Know I Didn't Learn in Library School," *North Carolina Libraries* 48 (Winter), 258-259.

Wehrenberg, Stephen B. (1989), "Training: Skill and Motivation Divide Training and Orientation," *Personnel Journal* 68 (May), 111-113.

Wogaman, Mariol R. (1992), "Training Newly Appointed Reference Librarians," *C & RL News* 1 (January), 8-9.

Woodard, Beth S. (1989), "A Selective Guide to Training Literature for the Reference Librarian/Trainer," *Reference Services Review* 17 (2), 41-51.

"I Got the Job! Now What Do I Do?": A Practical Guide for New Reference Librarians

Susan Sykes Berry
Erica W. Reynolds

SUMMARY. New reference librarians should not expect to be passive participants in their orientations. As evidenced in current literature, few libraries are able to provide the time and resources needed to fully orient and train their staff. Therefore, librarians should take an active role in planning and implementing their own training. This article provides tips for developing a self-training plan for new reference librarians. *[Article copies available for a fee from The Haworth Document Delivery Service: 1-800-342-9678. E-mail address: <getinfo@haworthpressinc.com> Website: <http://www.HaworthPress.com> © 2001 by The Haworth Press, Inc. All rights reserved.]*

KEYWORDS. New librarians, reference librarians, orientation, self-training

Congratulations! You made it through graduate school, the job search process, and arduous interviews, and now that you have your

---

Susan Sykes Berry is Instruction and Reference Librarian, Health Sciences Library, University of Missouri-Kansas City, 2411 Holmes Street, Kansas City, MO 64108 (E-mail: sykesberrys@umkc.edu). Erica W. Reynolds is Research Associate, Research PreAward Services, University of Missouri-Kansas City, 5315 Rockhill Road, Kansas City, MO 64110 (E-mail: reynoldse@umkc.edu).

[Haworth co-indexing entry note]: "'I Got the Job! Now What Do I Do?': A Practical Guide for New Reference Librarians." Berry, Susan Sykes, and Erica W. Reynolds. Co-published simultaneously in *The Reference Librarian* (The Haworth Information Press, an imprint of The Haworth Press, Inc.) No. 72, 2001, pp. 33-42; and: *Doing the Work of Reference: Practical Tips for Excelling as a Reference Librarian* (ed: Celia Hales Mabry) The Haworth Information Press, an imprint of The Haworth Press, Inc., 2001, pp. 33-42. Single or multiple copies of this article are available for a fee from The Haworth Document Delivery Service [1-800-342-9678, 9:00 a.m. - 5:00 p.m. (EST). E-mail address: getinfo@haworthpressinc.com].

start date, it's time to relax, right? Wrong! But you knew that already. Actually, up to now, you've had it easy. Years of traditional education have provided you with someone to tell you what classes to take, what to study, and when projects should be completed. But now, you are in charge of your education. And, for the most part, as a new reference librarian you will be largely responsible for your own orientation to reference work, to your library, and to your organization.

An extensive orientation is not typical of most libraries (Wogaman, 1992). Many new reference librarians before you have felt their orientation incomplete (Blenkinsopp, 1992). Depending on the size of your library or organization, you might attend an organizational-wide orientation sponsored by human resources. Additionally, your supervisors and colleagues will most likely provide instruction regarding policies, procedures, and collections. However, some librarians have started providing reference services their first day on the job (Stabler, 1987). Also, if you are the first librarian in a new position or if you go to a library where you are the only librarian, who will be training you? Further, even with the most extensive orientation you are best suited to diagnose your personal information and instructional needs.

SKILLS NEW LIBRARIANS NEED

In planning your orientation, look for strategies to improve your skills in reference work as well as learning about your organization. The curricula of each library school varies greatly, and new librarians may not have had the benefit of an in-depth reference course (Bauner, 1990). Maybe your reference classes focused exclusively on materials and you have not studied reference interviewing or communications theories. Ruth Bauner surveyed academic and public librarians "to ask them to list the most important items of information or abilities they find they need to teach the entry level librarian" (1990). Her study revealed that entry level librarians have much to conquer. According to Bauner, academic and public reference librarians seem to value different skills, but overall the following information or abilities were needed (the topics are listed in descending order as reported from the survey): (1) reference interviewing techniques; (2) technological skills; (3) knowledge of policies, procedures, and department philosophy; (4) interpersonal interests and skills; (5) knowledge of reference sources; (6) knowledge of frequently used reference sources; (7) teaching skills; (8) orientation to service; (9) search strategy skills; and (10) cataloging and classification information (1990).

Are you overwhelmed yet? Don't be. Remember that while you will always need to know more, you probably know a lot more about reference sources and information than your patrons do, and they will be grateful for your assistance. Re-channel your anxiety about not knowing enough into energy to plan your own orientation. Your self-orientation should include the following six topics: (1) languages specific to your library; (2) electronic resources; (3) print materials; (4) collection organization; (5) people (patrons and peers); and (6) long-term learning goals.

LANGUAGES OF YOUR LIBRARY

Your first goal is to learn the languages of your library. Language includes the terminologies specific to the disciplines covered by your collection. Read through the tables of contents in your discipline-specific textbooks. If you don't understand words, look them up.

Learning languages also includes the titles, processes, and structures unique to your institution; for example, most universities have deans, provosts, departments, and tenure. Most hospitals have an ICU, JCAHO, chief of staff, head nurse, and infection control. Further, every library utilizes acronyms and expressions which are specific to the organization; for example, SOM instead of school of medicine or MERLIN for the local library catalog. Create a list of organizational-specific acronyms. This list will be a beneficial tool to any future librarians.

In order to familiarize yourself with the institutional and organizational-specific languages, utilize artifacts. Organizational charts are an obvious choice, but also look at listings of committees in your organization. Notice the names and purposes of the committees. Who are the members? If possible, ask for minutes or policy statements from different committees. You don't need to memorize anything; you don't even need to read much. Just scan. Understanding what topics are of importance and who is involved in the important issues will help you to understand the institutional and organization-specific processes and structures. If such a list of committees doesn't exist, ask a few colleagues to name as many committees they can think of. This exercise will also provide insight into the visibility of your organization's committees.

Other artifacts you might utilize are old informational or marketing videos. While your library or organization may have discontinued their use, even outdated videos and films will provide insight into institutional history and culture. In addition, if your organization currently uses some form of promotional video for your patrons, ask to view it as well.

ELECTRONIC RESOURCES

A second aspect in your self-orientation is to discover and familiarize yourself with the electronic resources of your library. Larger libraries will have so many databases that a goal of learning to search effectively every database in your library may not be an attainable goal in the first few months. Remember that you are self-orienting and you need to prioritize your goals. Academic libraries often have hundreds of databases to choose from, but most patrons will only regularly utilize two or three. Talk to your colleagues to determine the most utilized databases and become familiar with them. For example, you will need to know Medline for a medical library; if you are in an academic library, you might need to learn ERIC, Dissertation Abstracts, or Science and Technology Index first. While you do not need to be an expert researcher in every database in the first week, you should have access to a list of all the databases available to your patrons.

As your self-constructed orientation progresses, look for more electronic resources like web sites and listservs helpful to your patrons and to yourself as a reference librarian. For example, for your patrons, you might want to know the addresses for governmental information. For yourself, look for listservs which will help you in your new position. Libref is a listserv specifically for reference librarians. Your library might already have a listing of reference links either on your web page or shared between librarians. Ask your colleagues, and again, if such a list doesn't exist, start one.

Think of learning your electronic resources (and print resources for that matter) as a process. For example, in your first few months as a reference librarian you will learn which resources are available, learn to use them at a basic skill level, and learn to teach them to others. As you gain experience, you will learn more advanced searching techniques and be able to teach these skills to your patrons as well.

While you need to familiarize yourself with all the common policies and procedures of your institution, one of the first policies to understand completely is your institution's Internet use policy. If you have patron-use computers with Internet access, you will need to know what is allowed and how you should handle conflicts. Talk to your superior to ensure you are interpreting the Internet policy in the same manner.

Another area in which electronic resource questions occur are the technical computer questions; for example: Do you offer a word processing program? Can you fix the printer? Can I save to the disk drive? Can I access this from home? You will need to know the answers to these and similar questions, and you need to know who the patrons can call for computer assistance. (At this point, many experienced reference librarians are laughing, "What do you mean who do you call for computer assistance? I am the computer assistance!") If you are the person your patrons will turn to for technical questions, be prepared to answer those needs as well.

Finally, although you have already investigated your library's web page during your job search, web pages are constantly updated, and you will need to know all the information available to your patrons through the web.

PRINT MATERIALS

Despite the explosion in electronic resources, many reference questions are still best answered with books. Investigating the printed materials available in your library is a necessary component of your orientation strategy. Make sure you are intimately acquainted with the books in your ready reference collection. Remember the treasure hunts we all did in reference class? Practice in your reference collection with a treasure hunt. If there is not a treasure hunt created for your library, ask your colleagues to help you write one, and then practice it. Ask your colleagues which books are requested most often. Are they requested by their title, or by description? For example, where is the green book? Or, ask your colleagues to create a top ten list of their favorite reference books.

COLLECTION ORGANIZATION

A fourth and important aspect of your orientation plan should be understanding your collection's organization. Nothing is more embarrassing than being unable to locate items in your own library. Spend time investigating the variables of your own catalog. Can you search by keyword? Can you use Boolean searching? Can you limit to a specific location or collection? How do you save results? How do you print them? Further, find out if your circulation system and on-line public access catalog (OPAC) are using the same computer program. If they are different, will you ever use the circulation system? Is there a staff mode of your OPAC? How do you determine if a journal is at the bindery? How do you determine if a material is checked out? How do you place a hold on an item? Once you become comfortable with your electronic catalog, you will be more confident helping patrons.

The classification scheme is a main component of understanding your collection's organizations. Nonetheless, cataloging curriculums vary among graduate schools and many schools do not cover specialized classification schemes (for example, National Library of Medicine). It is even possible that you made it through graduate school without memorizing Library of Congress or Dewey. It is OK if you accepted your new position without a good working knowledge of the classification scheme which your library uses. Now that you're a reference librarian, however, you need to know how your collection is organized. Look up books and find them on your shelves. Read up on your classification scheme in your old library texts. Make flash cards or list the general headings and their subjects. Unless cataloging is part of your job duties, you don't need to get out your AACR2, but you do need to be able to tell patrons that political science books are in JK if you're in LC or 320 if you're in Dewey.

Once you locate an item in your catalog, how do you know where it is physically located in your library? Although it may seem remedial to practice searching for and locating materials, many patrons believe finding books is the main job of a librarian. If you are unable to help them find a book on the shelf, they may be reticent to ask you for more advanced assistance. Similarly, be sure to locate all the equipment needed to utilize your collection. For example, are all the copiers in one place or scattered throughout the library? Where are your microfiche machines? Do you know how to use the equipment?

Finally, once you've familiarized yourself with your collection's organization, be aware of any local practices or strange idiosyncrasies specific to your library. For example, dissertations for a specific discipline may not be kept at your library but in the department. A special collection that is in the library may be present but not cataloged. All materials prior to a certain date may be in long-term storage. These practices specific to your library can not be learned in graduate school. Give yourself time to learn, and keep asking questions.

PEOPLE (PATRONS AND PEERS)

A fifth goal in your orientation is to begin to develop working relationships with the people in your library: your peers and your patrons. Regarding your peers: It is an unfortunate reality in many libraries that "peers" only refer to those employees with similar educational backgrounds and job descriptions. Of course, these unnecessary schisms between library employees only erect barriers to service and collegiality. Therefore, when we discuss peers, we refer to everyone you work with in your library, and, for that matter, anyone who works in libraries or informational organizations with whom you can network and share information.

In order to start learning from your peers, ask to shadow them in their daily work. Regardless of the shadowing time you arrange, try to get a full picture by either shadowing multiple people doing the same task or setting up observations during different hours. Shadowing will also allow you more contact with different people and provide a chance to form the working bonds you will need to do your job effectively. No one can work in a vacuum, and the people in your library will be invaluable in accomplishing your goals.

Overall, your peers will be your most valuable learning resource. Nofsinger and Lee discuss the roles that senior librarians can play in a new librarian's orientation to the profession (1994). Seek out experienced librarians who are willing to share their expertise. If you do not know where something is, or if you are unsure of an answer, ask your peers. You don't need to reinvent the wheel for every answer; benefit from the knowledge your peers have already gained.

In addition to your co-workers, seek out peers outside your library. For example, if you are the social science reference librarian, find other social science reference librarians from other universities in town with whom to interact. Find out what professional organizations are available in your field and join them. Attend the annual meeting of the American Library Association or another national organization. Often associations will offer funding opportunities to alleviate the expenses of the national meetings for new librarians. For more personalized networking, join the local branches of national organizations. The local or regional branches offer more chances to publish and join committees or hold offices. Also, local meetings are usually less expensive to attend.

If peers are your best source for information, your patrons run a close second. The more you learn from and you know about your patrons, the more your services and skills will improve. If you are in a public library, read local newspapers and demographic studies of your area to learn about the people of your community and how they spend their time and money. Demographic information is available through local organizations, like the Chamber of Commerce, and on the U.S. Census WWW page. Further, be sure to check the Internet for local information. Most cities now have one or more web sites devoted to local information.

Patron information is just as valuable if you are working in an academic or special library. You need to learn the titles and hierarchies of your organization as well as be familiar with the vocabulary of your patrons. Get to know your patrons by volunteering for committees and participating in organizational events. Call the faculty in your area of expertise and find out more about what they do. Think about services you could provide them. Discover the people with power in your organization. Remember that power comes in many forms, and often the people with whom you need to talk do not necessarily have formalized power. Who are the people who get things done? What are the favorite topics and projects of those people? Proactively increasing your interactions with patrons will help you become a better librarian.

Most importantly, learn from your patrons. If your patrons are specialists or have particular interests in a subject area, they could know more about information sources in that discipline than you do. Do not be threatened by patrons' knowledge of information sources. View patrons as partners rather than as people you pontificate to.

LONG-TERM LEARNING GOALS

Now that you have enough to do for the next three years, we have one final goal for you: Never quit learning. Just when you think you are comfortable in your new role, something is sure to come up and shake your newfound confidence. Don't let new discoveries rattle you; smart people know that they will never know everything. Recognize that information is forever expanding and keep learning. Read articles for inspiration and ideas. Scan tables of contents of journals in your field, and the fields of your patrons. Sign up for classes and workshops. Take advantage of local and national library network training sessions. Look for classes outside traditional library subjects. Take an advanced public speaking class or a class focusing on non-verbal behavior to improve your presentations and your referencing interviewing. Or, if your library's collection is focused on a specific field, take classes in the disciplines of your patrons. Take advantage of the resources in your own library (videos on computer programs, introductions to specific disciplines, etc.). Visit other libraries to see what they are doing. Try to see your library in the eyes of a new patron. Think about how you could serve that patron better. Simply observe your library as a whole. Performing a field study of your own library can help you form a quick summary of library traffic patterns, the questions patrons ask, and generally help you understand the ambiance of your library. How do staff members act towards patrons? How do they act towards each other? Record your thoughts and ideas to improve your library's service. In thinking about your continuing education, be sure to include the informal (conducting your own field study of your library) and the formal (attending classes).

CONCLUSION

Accepting a position as a new reference librarian can be overwhelming. After all, a reference librarian is the person with all the answers. It is a daunting task when you feel you only have questions. In order to become that person with the answers, focus on learning your library's languages, electronic resources, printed materials, collection organization, people (patrons and peers), and plan your own long-term learning goals. Your first step is to take control of your own orientation.

BIBLIOGRAPHY

Bauner, Ruth E. (1990), "Reference Ready Beyond the M.L.S.," *The Reference Librarian* 30, 45-58.

Blenkinsopp, Heather (1992), "How's the Water? The Training of Reference Librarians," *The Reference Librarian* 38, 175-81.

Nofsinger, Mary M. and Lee, Angela S.W. (1994), "Beyond Orientation: The Roles of Senior Librarians in Training Entry-Level Reference Colleagues," *College and Research Libraries* 55 (March), 161-70.

Stabler, Karen (1987), "Introductory Training of Academic Reference Librarians: A Survey," *RQ* 26 (Spring), 363-9.

Wogaman, Mariol R. (1992), "Training Newly Appointed Reference Librarians (At Oregon State University)," *College and Research Library News* 1 (January), 8-9.

Now What? Starting Your First Professional Academic Reference Position

Angela Locknar
Scott Vine

SUMMARY. Moving from graduate school into an academic reference position can be a difficult transition. A new environment, a variety of new people and the challenge of meeting expectations can quickly become overwhelming. This article reviews the pertinent literature and relates the relevant experiences of two reference librarians during their first three years in professional positions. Topics addressed include: reference service, collection development, committee work, relating to faculty and colleagues, professional development and understanding set procedures while striving to be innovative in the workplace. *[Article copies available for a fee from The Haworth Document Delivery Service: 1-800-342-9678. E-mail address: <getinfo@haworthpressinc.com> Website: <http://www.HaworthPress.com> © 2001 by The Haworth Press, Inc. All rights reserved.]*

KEYWORDS. Librarianship, reference, public service, college and university librarians, new professional

---

Angela Locknar is Science Librarian, Engineering and Science Library, Carnegie Mellon University, Wean Hall, 5000 Forbes Avenue, Pittsburgh, PA 15213-3890 (E-mail: locknar@andrew.cmu.edu). Scott Vine is Public Services Librarian, Johns Hopkins University, School of Advanced International Studies, Bologna Center, Via Belmeloro 11, 40126 Bologna, Italy (E-mail: svine@jhubc.it).

The authors would like to thank Tracey Depellegrin-Connelly for her patient and insightful readings of the early drafts of this article.

[Haworth co-indexing entry note]: "Now What? Starting Your First Professional Academic Reference Position." Locknar, Angela, and Scott Vine. Co-published simultaneously in *The Reference Librarian* (The Haworth Information Press, an imprint of The Haworth Press, Inc.) No. 72, 2001, pp. 43-50; and: *Doing the Work of Reference: Practical Tips for Excelling as a Reference Librarian* (ed: Celia Hales Mabry) The Haworth Information Press, an imprint of The Haworth Press, Inc., 2001, pp. 43-50. Single or multiple copies of this article are available for a fee from The Haworth Document Delivery Service [1-800-342-9678, 9:00 a.m. - 5:00 p.m. (EST). E-mail address: getinfo@haworthpressinc.com].

In the summer of 1996, we were hired into entry-level librarian positions at Carnegie Mellon University. We came from two different library schools, and each of us had some pre-professional library experience. One of us held a second master's degree. Though we have worked at the same university since then, we have had separate workplaces, distinct subject areas, and varying clientele. During our first three years of employment, we have separately observed and learned a number of best practices not touched on in library school (Anderson, 1997).

Although we could focus on any number of topics in this article, we have tried to discuss responsibilities that may come up in almost any academic reference setting. While the areas mentioned below are fairly broad, we also mention smaller, more specific topics that might arise in your first professional experience. We hope this article gives you, the beginning academic reference librarian, a good head start on moving forward in your workplace.

REFERENCE SERVICE

The manner in which reference service works is, of course, individual to the institution. But there is almost always a paper and digital collection, a service point or Reference Desk, and a clientele with questions. In a smaller library, or smaller department in a library, shelving books is a great way to learn about the collection. You will not only see what items are circulating (which helps with collection development, the next topic), but you will learn where things are located in the library. Shelving items also indicates to library users that you work in the library, and you will often be asked reference questions while you shelve. Shelving in the reference area will also be a good indicator as to what is used (and what questions patrons are asking). You will become more familiar with the reference tools, and will be able to locate these heavily used items more quickly when you know where they are found on the shelves.

Learning the digital collection can be more of a task. Today, even smaller libraries have dozens of commercial databases and digitized collections. One great way to hone your searching skills–and learn to use the digital collection–is assisting with interlibrary loan requests. Ask your interlibrary loan office if there are any requests that you can help with–they will likely be grateful for the help. You will practice searching your library catalog and learn which journal titles or book series your library owns. You can verify the citations using databases, indexes and abstracts, or other periodical reference tools such as *Ulrich's International Periodical Directory.*

If you do not have time to shelve or help with ILL requests, just investigate your surroundings at the reference desk. Be curious. Open drawers. Read handouts. Look at frequently used bookmarks on the reference desk computer. If you do not know what something is or how to use it, ask your colleagues. Pay attention to how they answer questions and approach interactions with library users. When you have time away from the desk, ask a colleague if you can shadow them, to see their reference style and how they use the tools available.

Clientele also vary from place to place, but have similar needs. Most people with a question are grateful to see a friendly face, as opposed to that rather unfortunate librarian stereotype. Be approachable, listen to what people say and try to help. It sounds simple, and it works. If you haven't been asked in graduate school to read William Katz's *Introduction to Reference Work,* take a look at it now. If you have read it in school, read it again once you have a job. Katz's advice will come to mean more to you from this perspective.

Finally, if you are not sure in a given situation how much to help someone, err on the side of service. This is possibly the best advice either of us have received as beginning reference librarians. A library user will not return to the person or place that gave them little time or effort. It's almost always better to give someone too much help, or too much information, than to not provide enough.

COLLECTION DEVELOPMENT

Because you will probably get very little hands-on experience with collection development in library school, this area is often a challenge for the new librarian. Some librarians will be asked to collect for one subject area, or will only collect monographs or journals, but not both. Sometimes you will find yourself in charge of three or four collection areas, or one in which you do not have an extensive background.

The best way to approach collection development is to get to know the academic departments and their needs. Visit the departmental web pages and review the research being done, meet faculty and discuss materials with them, and talk to colleagues who work in reference to see what areas are asked about most frequently. It may be helpful to devise a spreadsheet or document of keywords or phrases that are prevalent in your subject areas. You can use this list as a reference tool when you are ordering so you do not have to research the department every time you order. If you review and update this list each semester, your collections will remain relevant and topical.

Another good idea is to look at the academic societies in your subject areas. For example, for collection development in Materials Science, looking at publications by the American Society for Metals, the Materials Research Society or other societies will help you to see what materials are available. Another great tool for collection building is Interlibrary Loan. Ask the ILL staff if you can see statistics that describe topic areas that people from various academic departments request. This will indicate areas in which the collection is lacking. If a book or journal is requested often in a given time period, you should investigate its cost and availability so that you can add it to your collection.

COMMITTEE WORK

In many university settings, governance and departmental decision-making is managed by a set of committees. Participation on a committee will not only introduce you to the way larger decisions are made within the organization, but also allow you to work with people in other departments. Make your interests known, and volunteer. Don't join just library-oriented committees, but look around for campus or university committees. This can help with the process of getting to know faculty and establishing yourself as a useful resource on campus. You can also create valuable ties for collaboration on future projects.

Try to work your interests into committee or group participation; for example, many people are interested in web design and authoring, and academic libraries often have editorial boards that manage their web presence. Library instruction, often a requirement in reference positions, is also a popular effort that can introduce you to many faculty and students, and offers practice speaking to groups of people. Other examples of committee work include search committees, collection development groups, and organizational groups working on specific goals, such as the school's curriculum, or diversity.

As a new librarian and employee, you may not know how things have been "done in the past." This might seem like a hindrance, but there are times when it can be a blessing. Sometimes committees become stagnant over time, and your participation can bring a fresh perspective. Ask questions of those who have been in the same role. Do not be afraid to voice your opinion. You will never learn or grow in your position if you go along with what everyone else says all the time. However, try to learn which people in what areas are open to new ideas, and work with them (Drury, 1996). Most importantly, don't become a constant source of friction within the organization.

RELATING TO FACULTY

If, as a bibliographer, you are also asked to play a liaison role between the library and specific academic departments, you will need to do more than develop and maintain the collections in those areas. To learn more about the people working in your assigned academic departments, visit their web pages, or look through departmental brochures or packets. Ask your head of reference or supervisor about the possibility of getting invited to a faculty meeting. If this can not be scheduled, arrange meetings with the academic department head. Ask them what they expect from you, how best to reach faculty (remember, not all faculty read e-mail), and what they need from the libraries. When working at the reference desk, keep an eye out for faculty or students, and introduce yourself. This can be easier if you are helping them with a question, or filling out an interlibrary loan request, and you see what department they are from. If you are working on a reference question with someone, just ask which department they are from. Get to know your regular users and solicit their advice when necessary.

Learn the faculty's research terminology. Meet the graduate students, administrative assistants and secretaries, because they are often the people who work most closely with faculty. If invited, attend faculty social gatherings. Make yourself known as a person to count on in the libraries. Take action on issues that they bring up, and try to demonstrate your usefulness. You will find that this not only widens the circle of people you interact with, but is also helpful in gathering references for future job searches.

For instructional purposes, find out from colleagues or old files which faculty members were active in using a librarian to teach library instruction. Approach those faculty, introduce yourself and ask how you can help their students learn more about library research. Information sources are changing and developing rapidly these days, and it is difficult for a faculty member to keep up with tools in their own area of research. Most faculty will be thankful to have someone help them show their students how to locate and evaluate quality sources of information.

PROFESSIONAL DEVELOPMENT

Although it is easy and necessary to focus on your immediate responsibilities, joining national associations, such as the American Library Association or the Special Libraries Association, can help you understand the profession. Once you have become a member of a larger national organization, take advantage of the many divisions and sections within the large group. Join those that are relevant to your interests or your library, such as the Association for College and Research Libraries (ACRL) or the Library and Information Technology Association (LITA). Attending national conferences and trying to meet your colleagues from other institutions takes some effort, but these are great opportunities to see what other people are working on and get new ideas for your library. Local organizations can help you to network within your more immediate community. Listservs such as *libref-l* and *colldev-l* are also great ways to hear of new writing and research opportunities. Ask your colleagues about listservs in various areas of library research, such as *cheminf-l* for chemical information topics.

ADDITIONAL IDEAS

If you are replacing someone in the organization, do not automatically toss everything they have accumulated, because some items might have informational significance. Look for notes left from the previous person about the history of the libraries' relationship with academic departments. Look for hints concerning the way this person practiced collection development or instruction. You do not have to repeat what the previous person did, but this may give you some ideas about where to start, or whom to ask to learn more.

You will meet many people in your new position, and some of them will make an effort to get to know you as a colleague and a person. Take your time, get to know people, and look around for someone to act as a mentor, or advisor. Having open and honest discussions with a person you trust goes a long way toward relieving some of the pressures of a new job. A mentor does not have to be your immediate supervisor, or anyone above them. Another librarian with more experience in the organization and profession can be very helpful.

CONCLUSION

As you can see, there is much to get used to in your first academic reference position. The challenge of meeting your own and others' expectations can often be overwhelming (Fischer, 1997). In addition, the geographic reality of finding a good first job may place you in a completely new environment. Try not to allow these changes to add up to too much. Maintaining a balance between your professional and personal life and keeping things in perspective is possibly the best thing you can do for yourself and your new employer.

When you have settled in and have learned the basics, involve yourself in a few projects or committees. Although you should focus on what interests you, opportunities will arise in the workplace and new professional interests will develop out of them. Give yourself some time to grow into the position. After observing for a bit, you will be able to perceive the organization's needs, and see the opportunities to fill them. Finally, be flexible and allow yourself the room to be innovative and creative while at the same time understanding and working within your new organization's traditional procedures.

REFERENCES

Anderson, James (1997), "Didn't you learn that in library school?: Expectations of library directors for job applicants," *Mississippi Libraries* 61 (Winter), 87-8.

Bowden, Virginia Massey, Olivier, Evelyn Riche (1995), "The first professional position: Expectations of academic health sciences library employers," *Bulletin of the Medical Library Association* 83 (April), 238-9.

Drury, Claire (1996), "How to win friends: Induction strategies for librarians in a new job setting," *Library Association Record* 98 (June), 306-7.

Fischer, Susan (1997), "Taking the first job/avoiding stress," *Current Studies in Librarianship* 21 (Spring/Fall), 4-13.

Katz, William A. (1997), *Introduction to Reference Work.* New York: McGraw-Hill.

Shontz, Priscilla K., Bullington, Jeffrey S. (1998), "Tips for new librarians: What to know in the first year of a tenure-track position," *College and Research Libraries News* 59 (February), 85-88.

Wainscott, Vicki L. (1996), "I'm in heaven now or six months in hell: How to thrive as a new department head," *The Unabashed Librarian* 101, 27-8.

Walker, Lois (1990), "All I really needed to know I didn't learn in library school: New professional's first few months on the job," *North Carolina Libraries* 48 (Winter), 258-9.

"ON THE DESK"

Going the Extra Mile: Customer Service with a Smile

Maggie Leonicio

SUMMARY. Even though every library, whether research, academic, public, special, or school will tailor their service to accommodate the specific needs of their customers or community, a common thread–our attitude toward customer service–bonds all librarians. How can we improve our desire to serve with a smile? Does a smile make a difference in customer service? What are some libraries doing to motivate their employees? How can we help one another on the job? This article will explore these and other related questions. Today's libraries are competing with a variety of information sources, some of which are easily available to the user through the Internet. In order to help preserve our most valued asset–our customers–libraries need to incorporate a well-de-

Maggie Leonicio is Reference Librarian and President, InfoResearch, Inc., a self-publishing and research consulting firm, P.O. Box 207, Oak Hill, FL 32759 (E-mail: netmaster17@juno.com).

The author wishes to thank the libraries in Florida which replied to her questionnaire. Your assistance in preparing this article was invaluable.

[Haworth co-indexing entry note]: "Going the Extra Mile: Customer Service with a Smile." Leonicio, Maggie. Co-published simultaneously in *The Reference Librarian* (The Haworth Information Press, an imprint of The Haworth Press, Inc.) No. 72, 2001, pp. 51-63; and: *Doing the Work of Reference: Practical Tips for Excelling as a Reference Librarian* (ed: Celia Hales Mabry) The Haworth Information Press, an imprint of The Haworth Press, Inc., 2001, pp. 51-63. Single or multiple copies of this article are available for a fee from The Haworth Document Delivery Service [1-800-342-9678, 9:00 a.m. - 5:00 p.m. (EST). E-mail address: getinfo@haworthpressinc.com].

veloped, quality customer service program in their operational plan and budget.

KEYWORDS. Quality, customer service

"Leaders in Service With Innovation and Style" was the theme for the 76th Annual Florida Library Association Conference, held in St. Augustine, Florida, May 4-7, 1999. As I attended the various workshops and presentations, I could not help but feel a great sense of pride in our profession of librarianship. The keynote speaker, Ms. Eugenie Prime, delivered a very motivating presentation on library leadership with innovation and style. Her speech suggested that we need to articulate the vision, build a coalition around the vision, link with operational plan and budget, and nurture the vision. Reflecting on Ms. Prime's presentation, I was motivated to put a name to that vision and have called it *Quality Service*. I left the conference imbued with a spirit of leadership, with passion and a sense of shared vision.

Even though every library, whether research, academic, public, special, or school will tailor their service to accommodate the specific needs of their customers or community, a common thread–our attitude toward customer service–bonds all librarians. How can we improve our desire to serve with a smile? Does a smile make a difference in customer service? What are some libraries doing to motivate their employees? How can we help one another on the job? This article will explore these and other related questions.

Today's libraries are competing with a variety of information sources, some of which are easily available to the user through the Internet. In order to help preserve our most valued asset–our customers–libraries and librarians need to share a vision. If *Quality Service* is our vision, how do we build a coalition around it?

QUALITY CUSTOMER SERVICE PROGRAMS

A formal or organized quality customer service program is the first step that libraries need to take to make a successful transition in facing the challenges and demands of the new millennium. Libraries can no longer operate under the old myth held by some that because we are public institutions, we are exempt from a continual appraisal of our operations. In fact, the old myth that there is something inherently good in our services, so therefore we should not bother with changes of attitudes, or we should not be held accountable for the quality of service we provide, is no longer applicable. There are always those who will resist change. Nevertheless, we can begin building that bridge now.

As change permeates the information field, libraries must redefine their missions, goals, objectives and planning and marketing processes, i.e., the way they do business (Weingand, 1997). Creative planning and taking a proactive stance to the challenges that these changes bring to our profession, will determine a preferred future, rather than just merely reacting to events. Recognizing the power of the customer in an era in which ideas are the medium of exchange is the underlying philosophy of quality service. This philosophy highlights the importance of the customer's power, and securing each customer's repeat business is the goal.

Quality of customer service is a culture of shared values in a library organization. When the employees work in a cultural environment where quality of service is the spiritual essence of its purpose, the library customer will ultimately be the beneficiary. Organizational culture has a profound effect on staff morale and interaction with customers. Every organization has a spiritual essence, and libraries are no exception. Enthusiasm, *esprit de corps,* and high morale are states of being that are desirable in any enterprise.

In order to summarize the several suggestions found in the library literature of books and journal articles on planning and implementing a formal customer service program, I created a descriptive acronym to show that quality customer service requires a T.E.A.M. effort among management, employees and customers. The T.E.A.M. strategy to building, enrolling and committing individuals to the vision of quality service includes the following basic four ingredients: (1) "T" for Training, training, and more training; (2) "E" for Employee recognition and rewards; (3) "A" for Attitude with leadership and passion; and (4) "M" for Motivation stemming from the library's managed culture of shared values.

The T.E.A.M. approach strategy to service attempts to describe a positive framework for quality service. When these inputs are in place, they will nurture the vision of quality service through a positive library image, satisfied customers, increased funding and support, more cost-effective operations, plus a motivated and empowered staff. When management styles foster and encourage employee leadership, the beneficial ripple effect will extend beyond the staff to the library's customers through quality service.

"T" FOR TRAINING, TRAINING, AND MORE TRAINING

While I was working on my masters, I had an opportunity to visit libraries in different towns and counties. Only then did I realize how a patron feels when she walks into a library. Frustration, vulnerability, uncertainty and disorientation were only a few of the feelings I experienced as I approached the Reference Librarian for help. My experiences and observations taught me that not all libraries offer the same quality level of customer service.

How can we help one another on the job to deliver quality service? A very effective way is through training. The notion of continuous quality improvement is a perpetually moving target (Weingand, 1997). Identifying strengths and limitations is the first step toward setting achievable goals and objectives. An ongoing employee training program creates an organizational environment that allows and encourages staff to know more, do more, and contribute more. This sense of responsibility and involvement in the library's success creates confidence and commitment to the library's mission, its goals and objectives.

William Davidow places the responsibility for quality service squarely on management's shoulders:

> Leaders of companies that produce outstanding service incessantly pronounce their beliefs and back up their words with actions, often dramatic ones that become corporate legends. Their goal is to nurture a service culture that will shape employee behavior more effectively than rules and regulations can. They make service everyone's business and empower staff to make on-the-spot decisions in the customer's interest. (Davidow, 1989)

Training that is endorsed and nurtured by administrative support will ultimately contribute to the development of solid relationships between employees and customers. Creative problem-solving attitudes are developed through training that is optimistic and viewed as a challenge. This is an opportunity that can lead to better customer service. Through a creative training program that offers continuous improvement, the staff will emerge and grow more confident in their skills, know how to manage conflicts, become decision makers, feel a sense of responsibility, commitment and belonging to the organization, and most importantly, believe in the library's mission, goals and objectives.

"E" FOR EMPLOYEE RECOGNITION AND REWARDS

A goal of continuing improvement in quality service that is both recognized and rewarded will contribute to the values, attitudes, and beliefs that mold the way employees perceive themselves, their customers, and their work.

Giving abundant praise, recognition, and awards will contribute to the development of library organizational champions and leaders. Directors and supervisors, as well as other staff members, need to recognize that quality customer service is a shared commitment. Enthusiastic and happy employees will reflect their satisfaction by making customers feel happy. All employees are essential to the success of the library's goals.

According to the popular Maslow's hierarchy of needs, the final level of self-actualization emerges when the other needs are largely satisfied. At this level, the needs are for job enrichment, opportunity, growth, education, creativity and the opportunity to take on a challenge with risk, innovations and employee involvement in solving problems. If the library can meet the self-actualization needs of the employees, the library or employer benefits because the employee is productive, motivated, enthusiastic and fulfilled (Walters, 1994).

Employees need to feel they are a part of the library's process and success. Rewarding employees who uphold quality service as a goal creates a very positive environment in the work force. When the goals and the vision of the library have been communicated clearly, individuals have a concrete reason for working harder and staying focused. A library that takes care of its employees will contribute to the improvement of everyone's performance, and ultimately, the beneficiary will be the customer.

Rewards do not have to be monetary; in fact, most employees enjoy a sincere day-to-day word of appreciation coming from one of their own staff members or a supervisor. It is this kind of attitude that promotes originality and creativity. It is important to make the recognition and reward a timely and personal matter; for example, a personal note to an individual thanking her for her exemplary service will recognize that extra effort when it is seen. An employee is a human resource who needs constant appreciation. Formal and informal ways of recognition need to be in place.

Supervisors and administrators are encouraged to participate actively in celebrating the process. They, too, need to be aware that their outstanding skills as managers and leaders can and will be recognized by other employees and peers. Everyone should feel included in the process of recognition and rewards. Recognizing the commendable performance of a member of management sets a good example for lower-level employees.

If locating sources of funding to provide incentives and awards for employees is a problem, partnerships with local businesses can be created. Business organizations and local clubs in your community can become your best allies when they join your efforts; for example, one way is to get your "Friends of the Library" organizations or local charity clubs involved in the process. These volunteer groups can help acquire donations from local restaurants, theaters, cruises, and other sources. Be imaginative.

"A" FOR ATTITUDE WITH LEADERSHIP AND PASSION

Karl Albrecht characterizes the spirit of service as "an attitude based on certain values and beliefs about people, life, and work, that lead a person to willingly serve others and take pride in his or her work" (Albrecht, 1992). Most attitudes are learned through observed behavior. It is important that employees feel valued, respected and appreciated by their peers and their supervisors. Albrecht suggests that many organizations fail in their quest for total quality service, not because their leaders do not understand the technical concept for achieving it, but rather they do not realize that the heart of the service journey is spiritual rather than mechanical. It is this spiritual aspect of service that is a true motivator in the attitudes and values of employees. Core values such as excellence, innovation, joy, teamwork, respect, integrity, generate benefits for all in any organization. Customers, employees and management are not separate entities, but rather integral to the whole value system of a library organization.

To the amazement of some, leadership is not a quality that is confined to positions of authority. Employee leadership is a great asset to any organization. A clear, simple, and honorable code of ethics is a basic tool of leadership, which can influence all employees about service, accountability and loyalty. Does your library have a written statement code of ethics in place? Is it displayed in a location where everyone can review it from time to time?

What kind of service do customers want when they approach an employee in a library? First, they want an answer or solution to their problem. Then, they want to leave the library feeling good about the interaction they have had with the individual who helped them. It is that simple. A higher standard of quality service enhances the perception held by the customer. It is the attitude of the first person the customer meets that will influence his perception about the library and its services. Satisfied customers return for more services. This, in turn, leads to more local support, more funding, and an improved library image in the community.

Helping the customer meet his goals for the use of information or material, along with fulfilling his specific wishes, will increase his expectations that his needs will be met in the future as well. This creates instant customer satisfaction. If these components are the essential attributes of customer satisfaction, does a smile make a difference in customer service? A smile is not irrelevant. A smile is an outward demonstration of an attitude that expresses a perceived desire to help. Staff attitude is integral to the service rendered. The excellence of the augmented product includes by definition the demeanor and degree of helpfulness staff members exhibit. Therefore, the added value of a smile contributes greatly to good quality service, and service could be diminished by its absence (Weingand, 1997).

"M" FOR MOTIVATION STEMMING FROM THE LIBRARY'S MANAGED CULTURE OF SHARED VALUES

Transforming the library into an organization in which members feel responsible for and involved in the library's success is a process that requires constant review and analysis by those in management and supervisory positions. There are many variations of management styles in library operations, ranging from the highly authoritarian to that of full staff participation. Management styles will definitely have a very strong impact on employee participation, behavior, and output.

These varying degrees in management styles can determine the library's culture of shared values. A library manager who tends to operate as an authoritarian will most likely stifle employee involvement, creating poor morale among the staff. This profound effect on staff morale will create an immediate negative environment, and will influence the staff interaction with the customers. In short, managers at this end of the spectrum may be totally uninterested in quality service at all.

On the other hand, a manager who believes in participatory management and who seeks to include employees' ideas and input in the decision-making process will most likely embrace the goal of quality and excellence in customer service. Through the use of teams to review present and potential customer service ideas, this manager is allowing employee involvement. In short, this management style promotes a sense of ownership and fosters increased commitment and spirit among employees. Team interaction can bring fresh ideas to the process of problem solving, as well as provide valuable insights to the planning and implementation of a successful quality service program.

Management's support, enthusiasm, and attitude toward quality service plays a major role in influencing the attitudes that employees may develop toward quality service themselves. Today's information customers are more educated, sophisticated, and demanding than the "patron" was a few years ago. To nurture the vision of quality service, everyone must feel motivated and encouraged to lead the way and meet the goal. Leadership with innovation and style begins in the heart of each individual employee, and is demonstrated by going that extra mile to provide quality customer service with a smile.

SURVEY: CUSTOMER SERVICE PROGRAMS IN FLORIDA PUBLIC LIBRARIES

In an attempt to learn of the existence of any formal or organized customer service programs, a survey was sent to library administrators of all public libraries in the State of Florida. The model was based on the Spec 231, May 1998, *Customer Service Programs in ARL Li-*

braries, published by the Association of Research Libraries. According to the study presented in Spec Flyer 231, organized customer service programs have one or more of the following characteristics: (1) a written statement of customer service philosophy; (2) training for employees in effective service delivery; (3) evaluation and measurement of service quality; (4) use of data to monitor policies, services and operations; (5) established processes for gathering data; (6) service policies that provide latitude for staff to serve customers; or (7) an internal customer service program.

EXTENT OF CUSTOMER SERVICE PROGRAMS IN PUBLIC LIBRARIES IN FLORIDA-ANALYSIS

Seventy-nine libraries were contacted via e-mail or fax, and asked to participate in the survey. Based on one or more of the characteristics listed above, libraries were asked if they currently have a formal customer service program. Seventeen libraries responded to the survey, making the response rate a low 22%, and seven of these have customer service programs in place.

Some libraries that do not currently have a customer service program in place, but are in the process of developing such a program answered "no" to the questionnaire. This analysis will focus on the customer service programs already in place in libraries that answered "yes" to the questionnaire. These libraries are: Brevard County Public Library System, Gulfport Public Library, Indian River County Library System, Largo Public Library, Leon County Public Library System, Niceville Library, and Sanibel Public Library.

It was interesting to note that the impetus to institute their own customer service programs came directly from the libraries. Most of these programs have been in place from one to more than seven years. Even though a written customer service philosophy is used, not all libraries have a written document that defines their customer group. Further analysis shows that, in general, libraries do not distinguish among different levels of service for different segments of their customer group.

Data gathering is an essential tool which most libraries use to monitor their service programs. Even though data gathering techniques vary from "mostly passive" to "evenly divided between active and passive," libraries appear to gather data on a regular basis. Passive data gathering refers to data taken from circulation statistics, ILL transactions, reference and telephone questions, etc. Active data gathering techniques may include surveys given to customers, team and focus group meetings, and other related types of feedback which seek the participation of customers, such as comment cards, suggestion boxes, web page suggestion service, etc. Data gathered is often used to make adjustments in customer service. Several libraries expressed that, even though they are making sufficient use of data, there is always room to do more.

Customer service training includes virtually all staff. However, training session attendance may vary from being mandatory to voluntary. For the most part, libraries leave on-the-job training at the supervisor's discretion. The majority of the training sessions are given by the library's own staff members or a library training officer. Occasionally, the services of an outside trainer, i.e., a local training company, is used. Library cooperatives supplement the library's training with continuing education courses. Generally, all staff undergo the same customer service training.

Libraries that are customer driven are beginning to incorporate customer service performance in their overall appraisal evaluations. Formal written expectations about customer service may include statements such as the following: "employee provides customer driven service which is courteous, prompt and proactive to internal and external customers"; "employee routinely delivers service that exceeds customers' expectation with accuracy and efficiency"; "library management receives no more than one or two valid documented patron complaints about the employee's customer service per year"; "employee has earned praise from a supervisor, co-worker, or customer more than four times during the evaluation period." In addition, levels of performance are being measured by explicitly stating whether an employee meets these expectations of performance at a satisfactory level, exceeds the level of expected performance, or demonstrates outstanding performance by going that extra mile to excel in customer service related matters. For example, outstanding performance is demonstrated when an employee delivers service that exceeds customers' expectation plus always strives for continuous improvement, an employee receives no documented patron complaints about the employee's customer service, plus has trained other staff members in using excellent customer service skills, an employee has earned praise from a supervisor, co-worker, or customer service more than four times during the evaluation period.

A few libraries already have a system of recognition and rewards in place. Some are in the process of developing such a program. Overall, there is an awareness that such a program is essential to the core values of customer service. A customer-driven management wants the employees to know that the system cares. A formal recognition program provides a good opportunity to create a positive spirit within the organization. Examples of non-monetary rewards may include "world of thanks" cards and "outrageous service" star pins. Employee of the quarter recognition and financial awards are already being used at one of the libraries.

Customer service performance and progress require daily monitoring. To measure customer service quality, some libraries are using a variety of methods. For example, staff service transactions are observed and subsequent feedback is given to the staff; materials are periodically sampled for accuracy of reshelving; tracking and feedback on customer complaints are often communicated to the staff.

In most cases, staff at the front line are given considerable authority to bend the rules to satisfy customers. Expressed concern for staff having to put up with behavior on the part of the public that is not acceptable has motivated some libraries to put limitations on this authority. For example, a staff person can become so concerned with customer service and the sense of failure when he cannot resolve every complaint that he puts up with unacceptable behavior. As a rule, customer service has been integrated into the general policies which also include a "help" manual to aid staff in building and public security issues.

Currently, libraries are focusing mostly on establishing organized customer service programs that are concerned with the external customer. Internal customer service programs will mirror the same characteristics that apply to external customer service programs, such as a formal statement of philosophy or guidelines, formal training in internal customer service, effective internal customer service in performance expectations and performance evaluations, and measurement of effectiveness.

Libraries reported the following observations and perceptions about customer service programs in their organizations: (1) most libraries have found that a customer service program has significantly improved service to customers; (2) as a general rule, staff support the program; (3) in general, formal training has been effective in improving customer service; (4) on-the-job training has been effective in customer service; (5) data gathering has contributed to the improvement of service to customers; (6) having a written statement of customer service philosophy or guidelines has improved service to customers; (7) having customer service performance expectations and evaluating customer service performance of staff have improved service to customers; and (8) giving front-line staff the authority to "bend the rules" for customers has improved the services program.

REFERENCES

Albrecht, Karl (1992), *The Only Thing That Matters: Bringing the Power of the Customer into the Center of Your Business*, New York: Harper.

Berry, Leonard L. (1999), *Discovering the Soul of Service: The Nine Drivers of Sustainable Business Success*, New York: The Free Press, a Division of Simon & Schuster Inc.

Czopek, Vanessa (1998), "Using Mystery Shoppers to Evaluate Customer Service in the Public Library," *Public Libraries* (November/December), 370-375.

Davidow, William II (1989), *Total Customer Service: The Ultimate Weapon,* New York: Harper.

Gallagher, Richard S. (1998), *Smile Training Isn't Enough: The Three Secrets of Excellent Customer Service*, Grant Pass, Oregon: The Oasis Press, a Division of PSI Research.

Hendricks, Gay (1996), *The Corporate Mystic: A Guidebook for Visionaries with their Feet on the Ground*, New York: Bantam Books.

LeBoeuf, Michael (1988), *How To Win Customers and Keep Them For Life,* New York: Berkeley Books.

Miller, Glenn (1996), *Customer Service & Innovation in Libraries,* Wisconsin: Highsmith Press LLC.

Paik Sunoo, Brenda (1999), "Praise and Thanks–You Can't Give Enough!," *Workforce* (April, vol. 78), 56-59.

Patton, Fred (1999), "Money Talks When It Comes to Recognition," *Workforce* (May, vol. 78), 101-103.

Selin, George T. (1988), "Achieving and Maintaining Service Excellence," *Transportation & Distribution* (May, vol. 29), 59.

Soete, George J. (1998), *Customer Service Programs in ARL Libraries,* Spec Flyer 231, Washington DC: Association of Research Libraries Office of Leadership and Management Services.

St. Clair, Guy (1993), *Customer Service in the Information Environment,* London: Bowker-Saur.

Theedom, R.C. (1995), "Employee Recognition and a Code of Ethics in the Public Service," *Optimum* (Spring, vol. 25, number 4), 38-40.

Troy, Kathryn (1993), "Recognize Quality Achievement with Non-Cash Awards," *Personnel Journal* (October), 111-116.

Walters, Suzanne (1994), *Customer Service: A How-To-Manual For Librarians,* Number 41, New York and London: Neal-Schuman Publishers, Inc.

Weingand, Darlene E. (1997), *Customer Service Excellence: A Concise Guide for Librarians,* Chicago and London: American Library Association.

Cooperation and Competition at the Reference Desk

Brian Quinn

SUMMARY. A common practice at library reference desks is to have double coverage, in which two librarians work the desk at the same time. Double coverage creates a situation in which two librarians enter into a unique relationship with one another. Competition, criticism, one-upmanship, and other negative behaviors can develop in the relationship. Yet if handled properly, there is also the potential for a wonderfully supportive synergy and collaborative partnership to emerge that is beneficial not only to librarians but to library users as well. This article focuses on practical steps for not only avoiding negative relationships, but also changing unproductive ones, and nurturing optimal relationships that result in a rewarding experience for both librarians and users. *[Article copies available for a fee from The Haworth Document Delivery Service: 1-800-342-9678. E-mail address: <getinfo@haworthpressinc.com> Website: <http://www.HaworthPress.com> © 2001 by The Haworth Press, Inc. All rights reserved.]*

KEYWORDS. Cooperation, competition, reference, behavior, relationships, collaboration, synergy

Many libraries, both academic and public, utilize a practice known as "double coverage" at the reference desk. This means assigning two

---

Brian Quinn is Social Sciences Librarian, Texas Tech University Library, Lubbock, TX 79409-0002 (E-mail: libaq@lib.ttu.edu).

[Haworth co-indexing entry note]: "Cooperation and Competition at the Reference Desk." Quinn, Brian. Co-published simultaneously in *The Reference Librarian* (The Haworth Information Press, an imprint of The Haworth Press, Inc.) No. 72, 2001, pp. 65-82; and: *Doing the Work of Reference: Practical Tips for Excelling as a Reference Librarian* (ed: Celia Hales Mabry) The Haworth Information Press, an imprint of The Haworth Press, Inc., 2001, pp. 65-82. Single or multiple copies of this article are available for a fee from The Haworth Document Delivery Service [1-800-342-9678, 9:00 a.m. - 5:00 p.m. (EST). E-mail address: getinfo@haworthpressinc.com].

librarians to work at the desk together rather than one. The most common rationale for having two librarians working at the same time is improved ability to handle patron traffic during high volume periods. The presence of a second librarian can also be helpful when telephone reference questions need to be answered. In addition to these quantitative considerations, there is an implicit assumption that the two librarians may collaborate at times and assist one another in answering questions, thereby enhancing the quality of reference service. This latter assumption is especially interesting because it brings to light a seldom recognized yet extremely important aspect of reference work. The two librarians who have been assigned to work together have been placed in a unique relationship to one another. Like other dyadic relationships such as friends, teammates, and spouses, there is suddenly the potential for a whole range of behaviors, attitudes, and emotions that librarians manifest toward each other. These can range from simple awareness of the other to more complex interactions that can be potentially negative–such as criticism, competition, or one-upmanship–or positive, such as praise, support and collaboration.

It is the purpose of this study to examine the emotional and behavioral dynamics of cooperation and competition between reference desk partners from a practical standpoint. The emphasis will be not on just describing the nature of cooperative and competitive behavior, but on changing unproductive relationships, and actively developing positive, supportive relationships that make sharing desk work a valued experience that can enrich the development of not only librarians but the users themselves.

Why are cooperative and competitive behaviors so important to reference work? The reason is that a strongly cooperative or competitive relationship between two librarians can have a profound effect both on the quality of librarians' working lives and on the quality of reference service that the user receives. Cooperation and competition play a critical role in reference outcomes because negative competitive interactions between librarians can undercut not only their individual abilities but also the possibility of cognitive and intellectual synergy emerging if their relationship were more cooperative. It is the user who ultimately stands to lose the most when librarians are unable to relate well to one another at the desk.

Given the importance of cooperation and competition in reference work, it seems odd that no one appears to have written about it in the library literature. This may be because in the course of reference work, cooperation and competition may manifest themselves in very subtle, imperceptible ways, rather than overtly. It may also be the case that librarians presume themselves to be good by nature, and thus avoid any aspects of the profession that may draw attention to the fact that librarians are as human as anyone else, with all the imperfections and weaknesses that come with being human. In general, there appears to be a cognitive bias in the reference literature, with most articles focusing on reference work as a largely intellectual process in which emotions have little place.

The library literature on cooperation and competition stands in sharp contrast to the literature in the social sciences. There are hundreds of psychological and sociological studies that have to do with some aspect of cooperation and competition. Most of these, however, are of little practical value. Many of the psychological studies are rigidly controlled lab-based experiments that are not easily generalized to everyday work situations (Good, 1991). The business literature is somewhat better in this regard, but much of it suffers from the problem that it is based on anecdotal case studies or impressionistic accounts that are difficult to generalize to a wide variety of situations. There are, however, a handful of studies from each of these fields that may shed some light on how librarians become cooperative or competitive in their relations and how they can change those relationships when they become unsatisfactory.

SOCIAL AND PSYCHOLOGICAL FACTORS

When two librarians share the desk, they each bring with them a lifetime of social and psychological "baggage" or influences that come to bear on the relationship that develops between them. While it is beyond the scope of this article to attempt to enumerate all of these, it is nonetheless important at least to note some of the more important factors affecting librarians' predispositions toward cooperativeness and competitiveness in shared reference work. To do otherwise would be to suggest that reference work occurs in a vacuum, or that librarians live apart from the larger world.

Librarians, like most other people, live in an intensely competitive society (Argyle, 1991). They have been socialized from an early age to compete with one another. Very young children compete with each other in play, and even siblings engage in rivalry to compete for their parents' approval (Mander, 1991). Our educational system is designed to foster individuality and competition among students. Many of the most popular extracurricular activities, such as sports, reinforce and reward competitive behavior in children and adolescents. By the time a person emerges from the educational system and is ready to enter the world of work, they have internalized many values of the larger competitive society of which they are a part.

There are, of course, variations on the extent to which particular social groups will be more inclined to behave cooperatively or competitively. Gender, class, and ethnicity can all play a role in how individuals will behave. Women, for example, have traditionally been socialized to be more cooperative, supportive, and empathetic than men (Knight, 1989). Yet this traditional socialization process may be changing as women are increasingly being encouraged to pursue the same goals as men in virtually all fields of endeavor, and to compete with them for the same rewards. The women's equality movement has helped enable women to compete both with other men and each other, which may have an overall effect of making our culture even more competitive.

In addition to these social factors, there are many psychological factors that can influence the degree to which an individual is competitive or cooperative. One of the more important ones is locus of control–the degree to which a person believes that she can control her fate and advance her career through her own behavior. The stronger the belief in an internal locus of control, the more competitive a person is likely to act (Lester, 1992). Another important factor is a person's need to achieve. The greater a person's need to achieve, the more likely he is to act competitively (Ward, 1995). A third important factor is a person's orientation toward others. Selfish, uncooperative personalities tend to regard others as objects to be manipulated for one's own self-benefit, while personalities with a more caring, altruistic orientation tend to regard others as persons rather than objects, and try to help them with the idea of genuinely enhancing their welfare rather than for selfish reasons (Cialdini, 1987).

Various instruments have been developed to measure the competitive personality. Individuals that score high on these tests are considered by psychologists to be competitive. One such test is called the Competitiveness Index. It consists of a series of statements that subjects label "true" or "false." To identify the competitive personality, the Competitiveness Index includes statements such as "I get satisfaction from competing with others," "Games that have no clear-cut winners are boring," "I enjoy competing against an opponent," and "When I play a game I like to keep score" (Houston, 1992). In other words, a certain type of personality is predisposed to be competitive.

COMPETITIVE DESK BEHAVIORS

Given these social and psychological factors that predispose individuals to behave competitively, it is not surprising that competition between librarians can emerge at the reference desk. The very nature of the situation lends itself to competition, because it typically involves two librarians who, for all intents and purposes, provide the same kind of service in a fairly similar manner. From the purely instrumental standpoint of the patron, they might as well be the same, and it appears that approaching one librarian for help should make no more difference than choosing one supermarket checker over another.

Yet patrons do sometimes have preferences for a particular kind of librarian, for female over male, young over old, black over white, neat over casual, and so forth. Librarians generally enjoy working with the public and can readily notice if patrons gravitate toward themselves or a partner. Popularity with patrons can easily become a source of rivalry, even though it may have little to do with expertise. It is human nature for librarians who think they are not getting as much "business" as their partner to wonder what exactly it may be that users see in their colleague that they themselves do not possess. These covert comparisons can breed envy and frustration, because popularity with patrons is not something that can be readily controlled by the librarian.

Sometimes a librarian will attempt to compete for patrons by engaging in various kinds of "barkering" behaviors at the desk. Typically, this involves one librarian trying to outdo the other by actively seeking out users in an effort to engage them or draw them in to a reference transaction. It can involve the use of body language, eye contact, verbal entreaties and similar kinds of "in your face" actions that are designed to give them an edge over a more passive colleague who simply waits for a patron to approach. This sort of overt solicitation can, if taken to an extreme, reduce reference service to a kind of popularity contest.

The potentially competitive nature of the reference desk situation is magnified by the public aspect of reference work. Serving at the desk can be thought of as a kind of public performance, in which the two librarians are "onstage" and in full view of not only each other but the users as well (Goffman, 1959). When approached by a user, the librarian is expected to "perform," i.e., to provide assistance to the patron that helps him find the information he needs. Because the reference transaction can be seen as a performance that may be observed by the other librarian as well as users, there is a certain pressure to perform well, to give a complete and accurate answer in as direct a way as possible. Each librarian wants to "look good," to appear knowledgeable and competent in the eyes of her colleague and other patrons as well. Any sort of hesitancy or equivocation on the part of the librarian who responds to a user may be interpreted as a sign of ineptness or ignorance by colleagues or users. This can be embarrassing to a librarian, even though it may be nothing more than a momentary lapse of memory.

The competitive aspect of reference work is fueled not only by the performance nature of the work itself, but also by the inevitable fact that not all reference librarians have equal knowledge of all areas. At some point in the course of working on the desk together, the librarians will encounter a question from a user about which one librarian knows more than the other. Such instances can occur any number of times during a shift on the desk, and these knowledge inequalities can themselves become a source of competition between two desk partners. It is easy to criticize the adequacy of a colleague's answer if one knows more about the subject; and if one believes that one's colleague has provided an insufficient answer, there may be a great temptation to interrupt another's transaction and attempt to interject additional information.

The motive for intervening in another librarian's transaction may be purely altruistic and intended solely for the purpose of helping the user, but that is not always the case. The public nature of the work makes it all too easy to look like an expert and "score points" with users by outdoing a colleague and providing a better or more complete answer. Unfortunately, this usually occurs at the expense of the colleague, who stands to "lose face" in the eyes of the colleague and users who may be present. Colleagues who feel hurt or slighted may be encouraged to regain status and redeem their reputation by engaging in similar one-upmanship behaviors at the next available opportunity. There is the potential for these kinds of competitive behaviors to escalate if allowed to go unchecked, because even cooperative individuals will adjust their level of cooperation to match that of their partners (Kelley and Stahelski, 1970).

Often the librarian who feels slighted cannot tell what the motive of the intervening librarian is. The librarian only knows what it feels like to be bested by a colleague, and may consider it rude and unprofessional. This can lead to further deterioration of the relationship between the two desk partners. In extreme cases, there may be a complete breakdown of communication between the two librarians with no communication occurring at all unless absolutely necessary.

Even in situations in which two librarians have equal knowledge to answer a question there is the potential for competitive behavior to emerge. In these cases, librarians may compete to see who can produce the answer first, or who can get to it quickest. This sort of competition occurs most frequently with easily answered questions with fairly obvious answers. Rapid response then becomes the measure of a librarian's prowess rather than simply finding the answer or giving the most complete answer. Reference service can take on a quiz show air in which speed matters more than thoughtfulness.

Knowledge and responsiveness are just two areas in which reference desk partners may compete. Where a librarian sits may be a source of competition, with two librarians competing for the most prominent spot (Wollman, Kelley, and Bordens, 1994). Reference desk furniture can be a source of contention, such as who gets the most comfortable chair. Patrons can be a source of competition, particularly choice patrons like faculty or graduate students who are likely to ask interesting questions. The type of question asked can also be cause for competition, with the loser likely getting stuck with a "printer is out of paper" level question. Librarians may even compete over the medium by which the question is conveyed, with live questions often being preferred over telephone questions.

With so many ways to compete and things to compete over at the reference desk, it is perhaps surprising that librarians ever cooperate or collaborate. Yet such prosocial behavior can and does occur, and in rare instances two librarians can even achieve an almost ideal synchrony and synergy that would not be possible to obtain from either individual alone (Csikszentmihalyi, 1997). What kind of conditions foster such a duet? Are there ways to change a negative relationship at the desk? The following section will examine some ways of increasing cooperativeness between reference partners.

INTERVENTIONS TO FOSTER COOPERATION

Not surprisingly, much of the research conducted on cooperation and competition between partners comes from the literature on conflict, interpersonal relationships, and couples therapy. Psychologists and sociologists working in these areas have written many books and articles that offer helpful interventions for managing competition and conflict in dyadic relationships. Many of these interventions seem applicable to a wide variety of settings and situations, so it will be worthwhile to take a closer look at some of these and see how they might apply to working at the reference desk.

Most of these interventions fall into two broad categories: cognitive interventions and behavioral interventions. Cognitive interventions can be useful for changing one's thoughts and feelings about one's partner and one's situation. Behavioral interventions are helpful in changing the way one acts toward one's partner. Any attempt aimed at changing a competitive situation to a cooperative one should begin with cognitive interventions. By changing one's cognitions first, it then becomes easier to change one's behavior.

The librarian's initial encounter with a competitive partner at the reference desk may serve as an illustration. Such an encounter will have a tendency to create a strong psychological reaction in the noncompetitive partner. Negative, vulnerable, defensive thoughts arise in the mind and can generate feelings ranging from anxiety and anger to shock and disappointment. These thoughts are immediate and reactive in nature, and cognitive interventions can be an effective way to short-circuit them. The following cognitive interventions may prove particularly useful in contending with a competitive reference partner.

Cognitive Restructuring

In a competitive situation, both partners will tend to resist making any changes in their behavior. There is a tendency for partners to be upset, to blame the other person for the problem, and to adopt a rigid mindset that insists that the other person should change first. Given that each partner's beliefs about the situation may be somewhat irrational and unrealistic, it is first necessary to change those beliefs, or at least the beliefs of one of the two partners. One of the partners has to cognitively grasp that the situation cannot change unless there is a realization that both are actually contributing to maintaining the problem by their inflexible interpretations of the situation (Baucom, 1986). This can only be accomplished by challenging and rethinking one's basic expectations and assumptions about the relationship.

Self-Efficacy

In order for a competitive situation to be changed to a cooperative one, cognitively restructuring one's thoughts to believe that it is one's own responsibility to change the situation is not enough. It is also necessary to believe that one has the ability to effectively change it, which is known as self-efficacy (Magaletta, 1999). Librarians faced with a competitive partner must believe that engineering a cooperative outcome is under their control. Otherwise it becomes too easy to become resigned to the situation or succumb to ineffective and counterproductive behaviors such as arguing, avoidance, or withdrawal, Passivity, futility and defeatism will not lead to any behavioral change and it may at times be necessary for a librarian to muster the will needed to act in the face of an aggressive and inconsiderate partner.

Thought Stopping

Anyone who encounters a competitive partner at the reference desk will likely experience a variety of negative thoughts. Thinking that one's partner is selfish or ruthless will only generate more animosity. Ruminating about one's misfortune in being stuck with such a partner is similarly unconstructive. Yet it is natural to think such thoughts, particularly if one feels under stress, and negative thinking tends to generate additional negative thought and can become automatic and obsessive if not checked immediately. Thought stopping is an intervention that allows the librarian to break a negative thought train by covert interruption of the rumination process (Burk, 1985). Whenever one finds oneself thinking harshly critical thoughts, one can mentally shout "stop" to oneself to refocus one's thinking on one's work. This simple common-sense procedure can prevent one from being overcome by one's own internal "noise" resulting from the stress of being in a competitive situation.

Self-Observation

Entering a competitive situation in which one is in conflict with one's desk partner, it is easy to succumb to one's immediate impulses and emotions. Rather than instantly reacting emotionally with anger, fear, or defensiveness, it is helpful to pause, take a deep breath, and mentally step back from the situation and try to observe one's reaction to it. Watching one's mind and noting one's feelings may seem difficult initially, but with a bit of practice, it can be learned (Guidiano, 1995). Mentally detaching and observing how one talks to the partner, how one feels toward them, and how one talks to oneself about the interaction can give one considerable perspective on the dynamics of the situation and how to control it. Self-monitoring prevents one from being engulfed or overwhelmed by the situation so that one has time to think and reflect.

Reframing

Having a desk partner second-guess one or try to outdo one at the desk is enough to make one view the situation in a very negative way. Yet it is possible to reframe the situation, to alter one's conceptual view or framework of it, in such a way that it appears more manageable and changeable. For example, instead of viewing one's partner as the adversary, one can view him as a potential ally with whom one may possibly achieve mutual success. The competitive desk situation itself may be reframed as a means of promoting contact and involvement, and thus viewed in a most positive light. Another way to reframe the situation would be to view it as a different kind of competition in which each librarian is competing with herself rather than with each other to help instill more of a sense of teamwork and cooperation. Once one has reframed the situation, it is much more difficult to psychologically revert to the old view of things as insidious and insurmountable (Bagwell-Reese, 1997).

Role Reversal

The librarian who must contend with a competitive desk partner is likely to seek the moral high ground and perceive the situation in idealistic terms. The problem with thinking in terms of "what should be" or "what is right" is that it defines the situation in one's own terms rather than those of one's partner. In fact, a better way to effectively influence the other person's behavior may be to empathize rather than moralize. One needs to fully understand the other person's world, and may realize, for example, that the person who seems so cutthroat may actually be acting out of fear of not getting a good performance evaluation. A good way to empathize is to use a technique called role reversal. It involves putting oneself in the role of the other person and experiencing his world and his point of view as fully as possible (Carlson-Sabelli, 1989). Role reversal helps to eliminate misperceptions and misunderstandings that interfere with the process of cooperation. It also helps to quell anger and aggressive reactions that may result from being subjected to competitive forms of aggression by one's partner.

Attributional Style

An important factor in determining the degree of competitive conflict in a relationship is each partner's attributional style. Attributions are the ways in which partners explain each other's behavior. The more one partner attributes the other partner's behavior to internal negative qualities of that partner, the less cooperative and smooth the relationship tends to be. Negative attributions usually call into question a partner's character and portray her behaviors as deliberate, selfish, and aggressive. A partner may develop a negative set of feelings toward the other person that suggests that the other person is responsible for negative events that occur in the relationship. The attributions become a standardized way or "style" of explaining everything negative that occurs in the relationship. The more rigid and predictable the attributional pattern, the more likely it is that the partners will be less open to responding to each other in flexible ways. Instead of genuinely looking at the partner's actual behavior, they are focusing on their own cognitions about the person. One's behavior toward the person cannot change unless one's cognitions change first, and negative cognitions only increase the possibility of negative behavior.

Nonverbal Communication

The most basic way a partner can convey a cooperative approach to reference desk work is through physical gestures. Body language can be used to communicate that one is interested in working closely together with one's partner in a collaborative effort. Standing or sitting close to one's partner, turning toward them, leaning forward, increasing gaze, looking interested, using a friendly tone of voice, and smiling are all cues that signal one is interested in a joint effort (Newton, 1990). Beyond one's basic bodily orientation, one can also use nonverbal communication to compensate for a lack of cooperation on the part of one's partner. A cold, disinterested partner is likely to respond more favorably to friendly nonverbal initiatives than to a partner who behaves neutrally or in an aloof, aversive way.

Modeling

One of the best ways to elicit cooperative behavior in one's desk partner is to model that behavior oneself. Although it might seem like modeling cooperation might open one up to being taken advantage of by a competitive partner, the opposite response is more likely. In one psychology experiment that tested the effects of modeling on cooperation, researchers discovered that subjects would cooperate with a model they had seen behave cooperatively, even if it looked like the person could be exploited (Braver, 1976). Competitive individuals often view all persons as being much like themselves (i.e., competitive) and by demonstrating that there is a good possibility that cooperative initiatives will not be taken advantage of, one's partner may feel secure enough to attempt to make some initial gestures toward cooperation.

Self-Disclosure

With a competitive partner, it is natural to react by becoming defensive and closed and trying to remove oneself from the other person as much as the immediate situation will permit. Unfortunately, this kind of behavior just serves to create further barriers to the possibility of cooperative interaction. What is needed is to move toward the other person rather than away, and not only in an obvious physical sense. A good way to accomplish this symbolically is to let down one's defenses and open up psychologically, by trying to share thoughts, feelings, attitudes, and beliefs as much as possible. This does not, of course, mean that one immediately admits to one's partner that one thinks she is acting obnoxiously and selfishly. It does mean sharing experiences that seem to match those of one's partner, talking about transactions on the desk, patron behavior, "shop talk," or simply what kind of weekend one had. One recent study has shown that self-disclosure is inversely related to competitiveness and that the more self-disclosure in a relationship, the closer its members feel to one another (Busse, 1993).

Paradoxical Reciprocity

Perhaps the most invidious aspect of competitive behavior is that it has a tendency to spiral, to feed on itself. This is because many people will behave competitively when confronted with competitive behavior on the part of their partner. In order to break the spiral, it may be necessary to behave in a paradoxical manner. Every time one's partner acts in a competitive way, instead of retaliating with similar behavior, reciprocate in as cooperative a way as possible (Riordan, 1986). By avoiding negative reciprocity, not only is escalation averted, but the way for new possibilities opens up. Acting in an accommodating and helpful manner makes it easier for one's partner to reciprocate that kind of behavior and has a tendency to create a positive interdependence. One's partner comes to depend on one for one's prosocial behavior which ironically gives one greater control over the behavior of one's partner. Simply acting in a negative way only results in greater conflict or a stalemate. Even the most competitive partners will likely respond to cooperative behavior in order to increase their chances of realizing some degree of civility and decency and avoid the situation deteriorating into open confrontation or a chilly standoff.

Positive Reinforcement

In addition to behaving in as positive and cooperative a manner as possible, it also helps to encourage one's partner to behave cooperatively. An effective way to accomplish this is through positive reinforcement. Every time one's partner acts in a cooperative manner or behaves in any way that approximates cooperation, one should immediately encourage the behavior in whatever way seems most appropriate (Heitler, 1990). Reinforcement can be verbal, such as an enthusiastic "thanks" or "much appreciated," or tactile, as in the case of an affectionate touch, pat, or smile (though one should be cautious about initiating any gesture that could be misinterpreted as a form of sexual harassment), or edible, such as gum, mints, etc. Psychologists recommend that whatever reinforcement one uses should include a description of the behavior one is trying to encourage, for example "I really appreciate you covering the phone while I was trying to help that patron."

Metacommunication

If all the preceding interventions fail, one can try metacommunication. This simply means communicating about communication, about the relationship itself (Fogel, 1997). This is an intervention of last resort because if not used properly, it may elicit a strong negative response. If deemed inappropriate or offensive, it may result in denial, aggression, or withdrawal on the part of one's partner. The timing of the intervention can be critical, as well as the tone and manner that one uses. It helps to prepare mentally by using self-talk to rehearse how one will verbalize one's feelings about the relationship and about one's discomfort with rivalry. One needs to be assertive, without being aggressive. Psychologically, there is a natural fear of making one's partner feel uncomfortable, and of creating a scene. Above all, there is the fear of making matters worse if the partner does not agree with one's assessment of the situation. One has to wait for the optimal time as well. Confronting a partner when there are patrons waiting for help, the phone is ringing, and there are five minutes left to the desk shift is probably not an ideal time. One needs to wait patiently for the right opportunity, though it should be as soon after the offending behavior as possible, while it is still fresh in both partners' minds. It also helps to be able to clearly articulate what the offending behavior is and how one would like it to change.

BEYOND COOPERATION AND COMPETITION: CULTIVATING SYNERGY AND FLOW

In some instances when working at the reference desk two librarians will develop a certain rapport or chemistry with one another. Each librarian seems to possess an intuitive understanding of when and how much support to lend their partner. The suggestions of one partner will often spark ideas or solutions in the other partner that might not have been possible had the person been working alone. This result is synergy, a partnership in which the joint efforts of the two librarians is more effective than either would be by themselves (Covey, 1996).

Is it possible to cultivate synergy at the reference desk? First, developing a synergistic relationship between desk partners begins with an awareness of synergy itself, that it does exist and is a worthwhile goal. Second, while working together, try to become aware of one's partner's strengths as well as his weaknesses. Third, evaluate what one's strongest areas of expertise are, and one's weakest. Fourth, compare one's and one's partner's abilities and look for ways they might complement, enhance, and reinforce each other.

Once one has completed one's analysis, one may then begin to develop a sense of those occasions when it is appropriate to give one's partner professional autonomy, and other instances when one's partner could be helped by one's own expertise. When in doubt, it may be better to give one's partner the benefit of the doubt and not intervene in a reference transaction. If the subsequent course of the transaction ends unsuccessfully, one can try to intervene tactfully in order to prevent a patron from going away dissatisfied. But some librarians who feel strongly about professional autonomy may prefer to wait until afterward to make suggestions.

It is possible for two partners who are in tune with each other to go beyond synergy and enter a state of flow if the conditions are right. Flow is a mental state that occurs when one is totally engaged in what one is doing, and loses self-consciousness and a sense of time (Lefevre, 1988). The flow state may be triggered by one or more complex questions at the desk. This creates a challenge that both partners naturally respond to. These environmental demands challenge the capacity of both partners simultaneously. In order to master the situation there may be a heightened need for interactivity and responsiveness between two partners. Faced with such a situation, cooperative partners will spontaneously snap into action and initiate an interactive mutual effort in which they become totally engaged and focused on answering the question or questions.

In this state they exchange information and skills, bouncing leads and sources off one another, and all the while exhibiting an almost uncanny ability to anticipate each other's needs. This jointly intense pursuit of common goals and activities is called "flow," a psychological state in which two partners become so completely absorbed in their work and so totally in tune with one another that there is an effortless, harmonious rhythm and clockwork to their interaction. It is almost as if there are two minds working as one, a state when challenges and skills are perfectly matched with demands at the desk. Admittedly, this is not something easily achieved, but it illustrates one highly positive outcome that can result when cooperation is taken to its extreme. Unlike cooperation, flow is not something that can be readily cultivated. It is in part a function of the degree of cooperation and rapport enjoyed by two partners as well as the demands of the situation.

CONCLUSION

Cooperation and competition at the reference desk is a topic that has received little attention in the library literature, and this paper represents an initial attempt to outline the nature of cooperation and competition among librarians. An effort has been made to explain the dynamics of cooperative and competitive processes among librarians. The factors that contribute to cooperative and competitive desk behavior were discussed. A series of cognitive and behavioral interventions aimed at reducing competitive behavior was offered as a practical strategy for helping to change a competitive desk situation to a more cooperative one. Two very desirable outcomes of high cooperation, synergy and flow, were also discussed.

These interventions have been presented in as logical a sequence as possible, so that a librarian may attempt to solve the problem in a relatively logical, methodical way. Many of these techniques have proved effective in treating conflict situations that couples experience, and thus may be generalizable to the reference desk environment. However, no one has tested their efficacy in a library setting, and further research is needed to determine how useful such interventions might be. Until then, this paper seeks to offer the reader an initial set of tools for working with a complex and difficult interpersonal situation that many reference librarians are likely to encounter at some point in their careers.

REFERENCES

Argyle, Michael (1991), *Cooperation: The Basis of Sociability.* London: Routledge.

Bagwell-Reese, Mary Kate, and Brack, Gregory (1997), "The Therapeutic Use of Reframing and Worldview in Mental Health Counseling," *Journal of Mental Health Counseling* 19 (January), 78-86.

Baucom, Donald H., and Lester, Gregory W. (1986), "The Usefulness of Cognitive Restructuring as an Adjunct to Behavioral Marital Therapy," *Behavior Therapy* 17 (September), 385-403.

Baucom, Donald H., Sayers, Steven L., and Duke, Autumn (1989), "Attributional Style and Attributional Patterns Among Couples," *Journal of Personality and Social Psychology* 56 (April), 596-607.

Braver, Sanford L., and Barnett, Bruce (1976), "Effects of Modeling on Cooperation in a Prisoner's Dilemma Game," *Journal of Personality and Social Psychology* 33 (February), 161-169.

Burk, Edward, Randolph, Daniel Lee, and Probst, Charles (1985), "Effects of Several Thought Stopping Treatments on Worry Cognitions," *Psychology, A Quarterly Journal of Human Behavior* 22, 31-38.

Busse, Wilfried M., and Birk, Janice M. (1993), "The Effects of Self-Disclosure and Competitiveness on Friendship for Male Graduate Students Over 35," *Journal of College Student Development* 34 (May), 169-174.

Carlson-Sabelli, Linnea (1989), "Role Reversal: A Concept Analysis and Reinterpretation of the Research Literature," *Journal of Group Psychotherapy, Psychodrama and Sociometry* 41 (Winter), 139-152.

Cialdini, R.B., Schaller, M., Houlihan, D., Arps, K., Fultz, J., and Beoman, A.J. (1987), "Empathy Based Helping: Is It Selflessly or Selfishly Motivated?" *Journal of Personality and Social Psychology* 52 (April), 749-58.

Covey, Stephen (1996), "The Spirit of Synergy," *Incentive* 170 (September), 25.

Csikzentmihalyi, Mihaly (1997), *Finding Flow: The Psychology of Engagement with Everyday Life.* New York: Basic Books.

Fogel, Alan, and Branco, Angela Uchoa (1997), "Metacommunication as a Source of Indeterminism in Relationship," in *Dynamics and Indeterminism in Developmental Social Processes,* edited by Alan Fogel, Maria C.D.P. Lyra, and Jaan Valsiner. Mahwah, NJ: Lawrence Erlbaum Associates Publishers, 65-92.

Goffman, Erving (1959), *The Presentation of Self in Everyday Life.* Garden City, NY: Doubleday.

Good, D.A. (1991), "Cooperation in a Microcosm: Lessons from Laboratory Games," in *Cooperation and Prosocial Behavior,* edited by Robert A. Hinde and Jo Groebel. Cambridge: Cambridge University Press, 224-237.

Guidano, Vittorio F. (1995), "Self-Observation in Constructionist Psychotherapy," in *Constructivism in Psychotherapy,* edited by Robert A. Neimeyer and Michael J. Mahoney. Washington, DC: American Psychological Association, 155-168.

Heitler, Susan (1990), *From Conflict to Resolution: Strategies for Diagnosis and Treatment of Distressed Individuals, Couples, and Families.* New York: W.W. Norton.

Houston, John M., Farese, Danielle M., and La Du, Terence J. (1992), "Assessing

Competitiveness: A Validation Study of the Competitiveness Index," *Personality and Individual Differences* 13 (October), 1153-1156.

Kelley, H.H. and Stahelski. A.J. (1970), "Social Interaction Basis of Cooperators' and Competitors' Beliefs About Others," *Journal of Personality and Social Psychology* 16 (September), 66-91.

Knight, George P., and Chao, Chia-Chen (1989), "Gender Differences in the Cooperative, Competitive, and Individualistic Social Values of Children," *Motivation and Emotion* 13 (June), 125-141.

Le Fevre, Judith (1988), "Flow and the Quality of Experience During Work and Leisure," in *Optimal Experience: Psychological Studies of Flow in Consciousness,* edited by Mihaly Csikszentmihalyi and Selega Isabella Csikszentmihalyi. New York, NY: Cambridge University Press, 307-318.

Lester, David (1992), "Cooperative/Competitive Strategies and Locus of Control," *Psychological Reports* 71 (October), 594.

Magaletta, Philip R., and Oliver, J.M. (1999), "The Hope Construct, Will, and Ways: Their Relations with Self-Efficacy, Optimism, and General Well Being," *Journal of Clinical Psychology* 55 (May), 539-551.

Mander, Gertrud (1991), "Some Thoughts on Sibling Rivalry and Competitiveness," *British Journal of Psychotherapy* 7 (Summer), 368-379.

Newton, Deborah A., and Burgoon, Judee (1990), "Nonverbal Conflict Behaviors: Functions, Strategies and Tactics," in *Intimates in Conflict: A Communication Perspective,* edited by Dudley D. Cahn. Hillside, NJ: Lawrence Erlbaum Associates, 77-104.

Riordan, Anthony, Severinsen, Norman, Martin, Don, and Martin, Maggie (1986), "Understanding the Use of Paradox in Counseling," *Family Therapy* 13, 239-248.

Ward, Edward A. (1995), "Correlates of Motivation for Competitive or Cooperative Strategy Among Employed Adults," *Journal of Organizational Behavior* 16 (January), 93-100.

Wollman, Neil, Kelly, Benita M., and Borders, Kenneth S. (1994), "Environmental and Interpersonal Predictors of Reactions to Potential Territorial Intrusions in the Workplace," *Environment and Behavior* 26 (March), 179-194.

On the Fly BI: Reaching and Teaching from the Reference Desk

Susan E. Beck
Nancy B. Turner

SUMMARY. Today's reference librarians are constantly faced with the challenge of orienting users to the complex, ever changing world of the electronic library. A well-structured library instruction program is one important approach to the overall goal of educating users. But library instruction sessions cannot and do not reach all students. Studies indicate that students are most receptive to learning research techniques at the point of need, which most often occurs at the reference desk. Although many reference librarians are committed to "teaching students to fish," they are frequently faced with students whose research needs require in-depth lessons that exceed the time available for most reference desk transactions. This paper offers a way to close the gap by providing a set of techniques and strategies, utilizing behaviors and props, which can be used in those short, one-on-one instruction-based situations. *[Article copies available for a fee from The Haworth Document Delivery Service: 1-800-342-9678. E-mail address: <getinfo@haworthpressinc.com> Website: <http://www.HaworthPress.com> © 2001 by The Haworth Press, Inc. All rights reserved.]*

KEYWORDS. College and university libraries–Reference services, automation, bibliographic instruction

---

Susan E. Beck is Head, Humanities and Social Sciences Services Department, and Nancy B. Turner is Electronic Resources Coordinator, New Mexico State University Library, MSC 4375, New Mexico State University, P.O. Box 30006, Las Cruces, NM 88003-8006 (E-mail: susabeck@lib.nmsu; nturner@lib.nmsu.edu).

[Haworth co-indexing entry note]: "On the Fly BI: Reaching and Teaching from the Reference Desk." Beck, Susan E., and Nancy B. Turner. Co-published simultaneously in *The Reference Librarian* (The Haworth Information Press, an imprint of The Haworth Press, Inc.) No. 72, 2001, pp. 83-96; and: *Doing the Work of Reference: Practical Tips for Excelling as a Reference Librarian* (ed: Celia Hales Mabry) The Haworth Information Press, an imprint of The Haworth Press, Inc., 2001, pp. 83-96. Single or multiple copies of this article are available for a fee from The Haworth Document Delivery Service [1-800-342-9678, 9:00 a.m. - 5:00 p.m. (EST). E-mail address: getinfo@haworthpressinc.com].

Just as college and university faculty are rethinking their roles in the classroom, moving from the traditional teacher-centered, lecture-driven classroom to the student-centered activity-based session, so should reference librarians reinvent themselves. Academic reference librarians need to take heed of this paradigm shift in higher education by seeing themselves not as mere answer machines but as learning facilitators. The typical reference desk scenario of the librarian charging off to the shelves, selecting, finding and then delivering the answer to the often confused but very grateful student is no longer the only viable model of providing reference service. Why? Because our users require instruction in how to choose and use our new electronic resources. They need navigational strategies that go beyond identifying one or two keywords for searching. In the process of conducting reference, we also want to be coaching students in applying problem-solving methods of library research. We need to help students cultivate an awareness of how information of all types is structured and retrieved. As reference librarians begin their role change to teacher/learning facilitator, however, their actions, behaviors and methods must change as well.

Reference librarians do not immediately become teachers just because their tools, audience, and workload demand new focus. This change in methods and behaviors has been a gradual evolution, and one that not all of us have embraced. What are the actions, methods and behaviors of the teaching librarian? What behaviors allow students to learn general rules of research from the particular questions at hand? Can we fit teachable moments into the flow of the reference interaction?

QUESTIONING BEHAVIOR

The reference interaction begins when students first approach the reference desk. As librarian/teachers, we can use our own questions to begin getting students to think through their problem solving. Classroom teachers have long recognized the role of questions in helping students to think critically (Wolf, 1987; Savage, 1998). These techniques can be used at the reference desk as well if we ask questions that encourage students to verbalize their thought processes and thus reveal their problem-solving strategies. Examples of questions that elicit these processes are:

What were you thinking about?
How were you going to go about solving the problem?
Tell me where you've looked already.
What is it you are looking for, exactly?
Can you describe the search strategy you have used so far?

By framing our questions in terms of problem solving, students can begin to think of their own library research as a strategic process. These questions require that students recognize what they already know. They also force students to explain the basis on which they are making their problem-solving decisions. Asking hard questions of students challenges them to clarify their information need before they begin their research process. The reference interview can include other verbal behaviors of the teaching librarian as well. For example, the use of open, neutral questions during the reference interview (Dervin, 1986) encourages students in the verbalization of their information need.

Analogies should also be used as a method for getting students to hook new material onto information that they already know. A popular example of this technique, as reflected in a recent survey of analogy use in reference (Sutherland, 1999) is the telephone directory analogy suggested by Meg Singer. The yellow pages of the telephone book are a familiar example of the use of controlled vocabulary. Librarians can compare the directory headings to the Library of Congress system of subject headings. There are other analogies which can help students grasp unfamiliar library practice: the call number on a book is like a street address; a rental car can be compared to a new database; the turn signals may work differently from one car to another, but all cars have turn signals. So in a new database, the look is different, the location of buttons may be different, but the overall structure and searching functionality of one database is like others one has encountered before.

MODELING PROBLEM-SOLVING BEHAVIOR

The prospect of getting started with research for a student new to an academic library can be daunting. When faced with a sea of computer terminals, how does one identify the library's catalog? The Library of Congress classification scheme, the variety of electronic resources, even the organization of the library, are likely to be unfamiliar. An assignment, like the one described below, is typically given to a first-year college student.

Each semester students approach our reference desk in search of scholarly or professional journals in their academic major or area of career choice. This activity is assigned so students can become familiar with the rhetoric, writing style and issues facing their chosen profession or area of study. Similar to many other university libraries, our periodical collection is cataloged. We also maintain a Current Periodicals reading room where users can browse the most recent issues.

Locating a journal at the library requires a great deal of "procedural knowledge" on the part of the student. This includes informational knowledge and "how-to knowledge" (or skills). How can the librarian/teacher use the reference interview as an opportunity to model a few of these behaviors? First, the steps need to be made explicit.

The basic questions students need to address in order to carry out this assignment are:

1. What types of materials can I access through the online catalog?
2. How do I access the catalog?
3. Is the catalog searchable by title?
4. How do I search the catalog by title?
5. What do I look for in the catalog display? What does it tell me?
6. What information should be evaluated and possibly, recorded from the catalog?
7. Where are the periodicals located in the library?
8. How does the call number relate to the arrangement of periodicals on the shelves?

Thinking about the required knowledge and steps involved for even a simple problem-solving task can help us in making our behaviors explicit, and teaching those behaviors by thinking them aloud. There are several practical ways of doing this. For instance, Ross and Dewdney (1989) describe "inclusion" as the process of explaining to the patron one's actions and thoughts during the activity.

> *I'm checking the library's catalog for this journal by typing "t" for title. I need to find the call number for this journal, so I am going to look at the item record here in the catalog.*

It is important to model our thoughts and decision-making processes for users during the reference interaction primarily for the reason that we cannot assume that our users will make connections between their stated information need and our actions. By explicitly showing the user how we do it, we provide them with a model they can use in future, similar situations.

> *Well, if I were looking for journal articles in a particular field, I would want to find out what the Library of Congress classification letter for that subject was–all the books and journals in that subject field should be shelved under that letter. Let's see now, in journalism, the call number will start with PN . . . Okay.*

Another problem-solving strategy which we may take for granted is the method by which we process information on the computer screen, particularly when using an electronic database. In the context of teaching the reading of books with children, Davey (1963) discusses how the cognitive process of reading can be modeled by teachers. We can apply this modeling behavior to the process of reading a computer screen with a student new to using electronic databases.

What are the clues that we use to de-code information presented on the screen? Our experience has taught us to look at colors, type size, and in specific areas of the screen to find important information. We make decisions about what to pay attention to on that screen. By pointing out the significant text and buttons on the screen as we talk through the screen-reading process, we can help students learn to focus their eyes on the most essential components.

Although librarians are familiar with the format of a bibliographic citation, students may require assistance in making predictions, envisioning the information beyond a citation, verbalizing a confusing point and demonstrating fix-up strategies. All of these are processes that we use when navigating an electronic database. When we make our process explicit by verbalizing our strategy, we can turn the process into a teaching situation.

SELF-VERBALIZATION: THINKING ALOUD

Educators recognize that putting thoughts into words helps students to organize and store information in memory. Kuhlthau (1994) and

Fister (1992) suggest that verbalizing helps students to clarify and focus a search strategy. Self-verbalization is also discussed by Nahl-Jakobovits and Jakobovits (1988) as a useful strategy in library instruction. The example used is one in which call numbers are spoken aloud as the searcher looks for a title on the shelf.

> *Okay, now we have a call number for this journal on communication research. Let's walk over to the current periodicals section and browse those shelves, since you need an article for 1999. Here is the row for P. Let's look down here. Okay, we're at the P's. Now what is the second part of the call number? Hum, no, we've gone too far. Let's see. Ah–here it is, P91 C56.*

PHYSICAL BEHAVIORS: WHY WE NEED TO LEAVE THE REFERENCE DESK

The verbal behaviors of questioning, modeling, thinking aloud and the use of analogies are some teaching techniques that librarians can employ at the reference desk. However, librarians can also use physical behaviors which encourage more active learning on the part of students. First, we need to move out from behind the reference desk and accompany students, whenever possible, to the stacks or to the computer workstation. Helping students *in situ,* in the location they are working, is necessary for modeling many of the behaviors we have discussed. We are accessible and approachable when the barrier of the desk is removed, and we may find that helping one student encourages questions from other students working nearby.

It is important that we keep our hands off the keyboard, although this may increase the time necessary to get a student going. Hands-off coaching forces students to "take the reins" and fosters an independence and responsibility for their work. Students are far more likely to remember how to do something which they have physically done before, than a procedure they have passively watched someone else do. It also teaches the essential lesson that accuracy and spelling are important when searching an electronic database!

By roving through a bank of workstations, librarians can more easily provide assistance at critical points of need (Kuhlthau, 1993). Roving opens up the teaching space, and allows other students in the vicinity the opportunity of listening in on a "lesson." Peer-coaching between students can be engendered in this way as well, with the suitable arrangement of workstations in the reference area.

Question style, verbal modeling, and physical behaviors discussed so far are some of the ways in which librarians can make reference interactions more useful as contexts for teaching library skills. Handouts and other physical materials used during the reference interaction can carry the lesson even further, providing a concrete tool for students to consult and take away with them.

MATERIALS

When teaching a skill or a concept in a short time period, librarians should use materials at hand to their best advantage in communicating the teaching point. Many of these materials can be created ahead of time, designed specifically for a frequently encountered problem, or skill set. However, not every research problem can be managed with a handout. This is especially true in reference desk transactions where all too often a very short, mini-lesson is needed. In these cases the less obvious tools, ranging from well-designed web pages to signage and the physical characteristics of the building, can be presented as teaching materials. Nevertheless, in every reference transaction requiring some type of instruction, reference librarians should always focus on finding the best and most efficient materials to convey the teaching point. Before creating materials for these brief instructional encounters, it is best to examine how to use different teaching aids and what purposes these materials should serve.

Purpose and Use

The first step in designing teaching materials for mini-lessons at the reference desk is to think like a teacher. When developing pathfinders to orient users to library resources on a given topic, librarians often devote more time to including all the pertinent resources available than to thinking about the ways their users might best benefit and make use of the document. By the same token, when creating user guides for specific tools, be they print or electronic, librarians often neglect to highlight the most often used and asked about functions. Stuck in a "just-in-case" mindset, librarians often point out every feature and function found in the database. This barrage of information obscures the initial goal of helping users help themselves. What is often missing in the original design of library guides and pathfinders is the human element. They need not be thought of as a replacement for reference service, but should be considered an equal partner in teaching library use. In other words, when creating learning materials, librarians also need to focus on how they will use the materials to teach the skills and concepts the document addressed. When undertaking material development, Kemp, Morrison and Ross (1998) suggest addressing specific questions, such as the following:

1. What prior knowledge must users have to complete the task?
2. What skills and concepts do students need to acquire to complete specific tasks?
3. When completing the task, what should students be able to do and what must they know?
4. How will librarians use the materials to teach these skills and concepts?

For starters, it is best to choose the one or two most important learning concepts, then design the teaching materials around these. In the previous scenario, where students need to find a professional or scholarly journal in their subject area, the materials created can be a simple Library of Congress Class Outline that both helps students focus rather broadly on their topic (i.e., Nursing instead of Gerontological Nursing) and provides them with the organizational structure for how materials are stored in the library. The main teaching point is to understand that materials are organized generally by subject area within a given system (Library of Congress Classification or Dewey). Other objectives comprise the following:

1. Matching general subject area to the LC class section
2. Locating the selected LC subject area on the shelves
3. Browsing a section by call number to grasp the breadth and depth of the publications available within a discipline.

In this situation, the mini-lesson consists of a quick question-and-answer exchange between reference librarian and student with a one page LC Class Outline serving as the primary teaching material. An important aspect of the lesson is that the librarian guides the student's eye to the important areas by using both questions and gestures. Here, as in all other teaching encounters at the desk, the librarian needs to show restraint by not providing the answer. In this instance the teaching materials are both supplementary and complementary. One of the primary goals is that students recognize that the LC chart is a document to consult in the future when needing to browse the collection by subject. Another important goal is their understanding that information is organized in a coherent fashion and is easily found once they know how the system works.

Topics for teaching materials are usually those that address the myriad of subjects library users find confusing or difficult to grasp. Often engendered by poor signage, inadequacies in library catalogs or regularly given assignments, most teaching topics are comparable in academic libraries. Typical teaching topics could be: differentiating between different types of serial publications, exploring the different facets of a topic as a way to focus one's research, searching for materials by subject compared with searching by keyword. All of these are topics universally taught both in the BI classroom and, we hope, at the reference desk.

Design and Layout

With material design it is important to include commonly recognized signals that define the structure of the text. These graphic or textual signals aid comprehension by providing learners with a known model to incorporate new material. Chambliss and Calfee (1989) found three important design components for printed materials.

1. Structure Signals. Consisting of pointer words or phrases (e.g., first, second, third; step one, step two, step three), these explicitly alert the reader to the overall structure of the material. Typography and printing conventions are other examples of structure signals. For example, using different font sizes or faces as well as making use of paragraph headings, and using bold or italics to emphasize important material are other typically used practices.
2. Text/Content Signals. These are easily recognized and familiar vocabulary and phrases that help to both organize the information and make it easier to recall.

3. Matching Content Delivery to Knowledge Base. Include words, phrases and sentence structures the intended audience will instantly recognize.

Other frequently used text structures that signal important text are bulleted or numbered lists, comparison and contrast structures, temporal sequences (e.g., first, second, third), and definition lists (Armbruster, 1986).

As noted above, it is essential to write in a style that learners recognize and will embrace. Time after time we are told to write in the active voice. Go one step further and use phrases that include learners and that appeal to their needs. Instead of naming your handout something thoroughly descriptive but rather dull such as "Research Methods for Undergraduates: Periodical Indexes," why not use wording that will grab your audience by calling it "Finding Articles on Your Topic: A How-to Guide."

Consider also the impact of illustrations, charts or graphics. It is often said that a picture is worth a thousand words. Vygotsky (1962) called these graphic representations semantic mediators because they help us interpret new material. Not only are pictures and other illustrations easier to remember than lengthy text but they also serve as a mental tool to help the learner focus.

Material Types

Handouts and pathfinders are not the only teaching materials available at the reference desk. In giving a mini-lesson, use any and all materials that will best convey the teaching point. These can range from computer screens, to drawings and flow charts created on the spot, to graphs, signs and charts.

Figure 1 shows a graphic organizer quickly created at the reference desk to help students explore all the different facets of a too-broad topic. In this mini-lesson, the librarian creates the initial drawing by charting out the circles and boxes for main and subtopic and labeling each of the subtopics, but does not fill in all the details. Together the librarian/teacher and student brainstorm examples of possible subtopics, with the librarian/teacher writing these ideas on the chart. As the student becomes more of an equal partner in the brainstorming session, the librarian/teacher can then hand over the pencil or pen, saying "OK, now you take over," but continues to assist with brainstorming

FIGURE 1

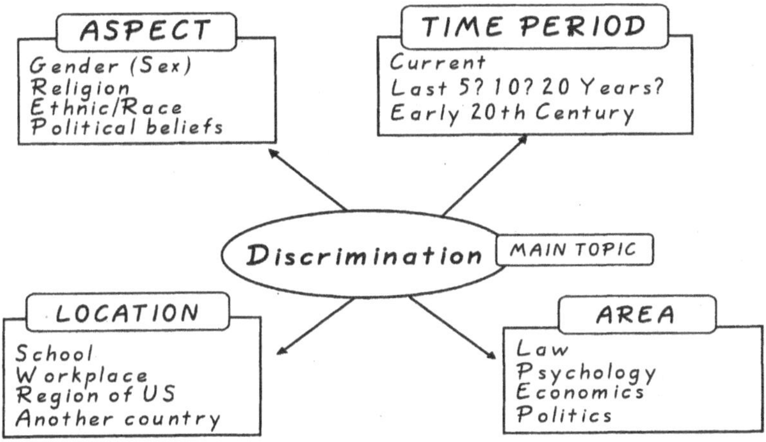

topic ideas. This signals a change in the mini-lesson, where the student is now an active participant in the learning process–a major objective in any library instruction session.

Graphic organizers can be used in other situations as well. The librarian/teacher can quickly map out the steps or procedures students need to follow in finding materials in the library. This type of graphic organizer is a basic, step-by-step guide and can be drawn very quickly. While creating the graphic, the librarian/teacher could elicit the steps from the student, encouraging participation and assessing knowledge at the same time. In fact, creating mental maps or visualizing the problem on paper is a method used by expert problem solvers (Whimbey and Lockhead, 1980). By modeling the process or by getting the student to use this process, librarians are helping to extend students' repertoire of problem-solving methods.

Materials can also be prepared in advance and not rely on the spur-of-the moment creation. Figure 2 shows a worksheet used in formal library instruction sessions that does double duty at the reference desk. This type of worksheet is aimed to get students focused on their topic but is structured in such a way that students are required to take responsibility for most of the decision making about their topic. Unlike the graphic organizer in Figure 1, which was created on the fly

FIGURE 2

Electronic Research Worksheet

TOPIC (describe in a phrase or in a sentence or two)

Terms/Synonyms	AND/OR/NOT	AND/OR/NOT

ELECTRONIC TOOLS TO SEARCH

1. Library Catalog

2. ProQuest

3. WilsonSelect

4. World Wide Web

by the librarian/teacher, the Electronic Research Worksheet is designed so that students use it both as a problem-solving tool and as a research log. On the worksheet students can keep track of their search terms, the databases they have searched, their search methods (Boolean commands, string searches, truncation and wild card searches) and note results. It asks many of the basic questions posed in the graphic organizer but does so in a less dynamic fashion.

CONCLUSION: BEHAVIORS AND METHODS WITHIN THE RESEARCH PROCESS FRAMEWORK

Important models of library research as an active information seeking process have been developed by Kuhlthau (1993), Loomis and Frank (1993) and described by Jacobson and Mark (1995). An example is Kuhlthau's six-step model, which outlines task initiation, topic selection, pre-focus exploration, formulation, information collection, and search closure or presentation. These models help us as librarians and teachers to recognize the complexity of information seeking behavior–as both cognitive and affective processes. In the context of a necessarily brief reference interaction these multi-step models become less helpful. When doing reference in the real world, mini-lessons need to suffice for extended ones. The behaviors and materials presented here are best viewed as techniques that dovetail with these broader schemes. Although our lessons cannot substitute for a thorough bibliographic instruction session, we can reach more students more effectively by applying instructional techniques to behaviors we know to work at the reference desk.

REFERENCES

Armbruster, R. B. 1986. Schema theory and the design of content-area textbooks. *Educational Psychology* 21: 253-267.

Chamblis, M. J. and R. C. Calfee. 1989. Designing science textbooks to enhance student understanding. *Educational Psychologist* 24: 307-322.

Davey, Beth. 1983. Think aloud–Modeling the cognitive processes of reading comprehension. *Journal of Reading* 27: 44-47.

Dervin, Brenda and Patricia Dewdney. 1986. Neutral questioning: A new approach to the reference interview. *RQ* 25: 506-513.

Dewdney, P. and G. Michell. 1997. Asking "why" questions in the reference interview: A theoretical justification. *Library Quarterly* 67: 50-57.

Fister, B. 1992. The research processes of undergraduate students. *Journal of Academic Librarianship* 18: 163-169.

Jacobson, T. E. and B. L. Mark. 1995. Teaching in the information age: Active learning techniques to empower students. In *Library Instruction Revisited.* The Haworth Press, Inc., 105-20.

Kemp, J. E., G. R. Morrison and S. M. Ross. 1998. *Designing Effective Instruction.* Upper Saddle River, NJ: Merrill.

Kuhlthau, C. C. 1997. Learning in digital libraries: An information search process approach. *Library Trends* 45: 708-24.

______. 1993. *Seeking Meaning: A Process Approach to Library and Information Services.* Norword, NJ: Ablex Corporation.

Loomis, A. and D. Fink. 1993. Instruction: Gateway to the virtual library. In *The Virtual Library: Visions and Realities,* ed. L. M. Saunders, 60. Westport, CT: Meckler.

Meyer, B. J. F. 1985. Signaling the structure of text. In *The Technology of Text, vol. 2.* ed. D. J. Jonassen, 64-89. Englewood Cliffs, NJ: Educational Technology Publications.

Nahl-Jakobovits, D. and L. A. Jakobovits. 1998. Problem solving, creative librarianship, and search behavior. *College & Research Libraries* 59: 400-407.

Oberman, C. 1996. Library instruction: Concepts and pedagogy in the electronic environment. *RQ* 35: 315-323.

Ross, C. S. and P. Dewdney. 1998. Negative closure: Strategies and counter-strategies in the reference transaction. *Reference and User Services Quarterly* 38:151-163.

______. 1989. *Communicating Professionally.* New York: Neal Schulman.

Savage, L. B. 1998. Eliciting critical thinking skills through questioning. *The Clearing House* 71: 291-293.

Sutherland, N. <naomis@purduenc.edu>. "Analogy Survey Results Summary," 10 September 1999. In *BI-L.* <bi-l@listserv.byu.edu> Archived at:<http://bubl.ac.uk/mail/bild/>.

Vygotsky, L. S. 1962. *Thought and Language.* Cambridge, MA: MIT Press.

Whimbey, A. and J. Lockhead. 1980. *Problem Solving and Comprehension: A Short Course in Analytical Reasoning*. Philadelphia: Franklin Institute.

Wolf, D. P. "The Art of Questioning." In *Academic Connections.* Winter 1987. Archived at: <http://www.exploratorium.net/IFI/r . . . es/workshops/artofquestioning.html>.

OUR CHALLENGES

Thinking About Reference Service Paradigms and Metaphors

Frederick R. Reenstjerna

SUMMARY. A critical but overlooked aspect of reference service is thinking about paradigms and metaphors. These are subconscious imageries that define how we think about our work–and how our clients think about us. Limitations of the current paradigms affecting reference services are: (1) social-class assumptions about the nature of the library and its clientele; (2) classification systems based on obsolete ideas that subject categories are mutually exclusive; (3) the fortress metaphor implied in physical organization; and (4) failure to capture statistical data that measure contemporary aspects of user service.

New ways of thinking about reference service with new paradigms and metaphors are suggested. Critical elements in a new paradigm are: (1) envisioning the library as portal, both for on-line and in-library service; (2) accepting the fact that knowledge is an open system, not conducive to our closed-system classification systems; (3) breaching

---

Frederick R. Reenstjerna is Cataloging Librarian, Douglas County Library System, 1409 NE Diamond Lake Boulevard, Roseburg, OR 97470 (E-mail: hopefred@rosenet.net).

[Haworth co-indexing entry note]: "Thinking About Reference Service Paradigms and Metaphors." Reenstjerna, Frederick R. Co-published simultaneously in *The Reference Librarian* (The Haworth Information Press, an imprint of The Haworth Press, Inc.) No. 72, 2001, pp. 97-111; and: *Doing the Work of Reference: Practical Tips for Excelling as a Reference Librarian* (ed: Celia Hales Mabry) The Haworth Information Press, an imprint of The Haworth Press, Inc., 2001, pp. 97-111. Single or multiple copies of this article are available for a fee from The Haworth Document Delivery Service [1-800-342-9678, 9:00 a.m. - 5:00 p.m. (EST). E-mail address: getinfo@haworthpressinc.com].

our metaphorical fortress to provide more personal reference service; and (4) updating our statistical measures to match quantitative measures with actual quality of service. *[Article copies available for a fee from The Haworth Document Delivery Service: 1-800-342-9678. E-mail address: <getinfo@haworthpressinc.com> Website: <http://www.HaworthPress.com>*

KEYWORDS. Paradigms, models, metaphors, assumptions, system

The term "paradigm" has recently become over-used to the point of meaninglessness. This is especially unfortunate for those of us who practice reference service in libraries, because the success of our professional activity depends upon our clear and coherent grasp of the multiple paradigms imposed upon us, upon our clients, and upon our service models. Failure to grasp the implications of paradigmatic approaches–especially in situations when paradigms stand opposed to each other–can render our best efforts useless.

The fact that an idea is abused by malpractitioners does not destroy the inherent truth of that idea. For example, the crass manipulation of investors by convicted swindlers posing as evangelists does not disprove whatever fundamental truths about morality might exist in the teachings of Christianity. This world religion transcends its misinterpretation and willful misuse by selfish individuals.

Similarly, the inherent truths of paradigms as bases for any rational planning effort transcend their misuse by misguided individuals whose self-generated organizational agendas long predate whatever current buzzword passes for managerial competence at the moment. It is only by understanding the underlying, elemental, subconscious constructs illustrating both practitioner and customer expectations of system performance that we can begin to design an information delivery system that is both effective and efficient.

Expectations based on paradigms are rarely expressed rationally–i.e., in written or verbal form–because they dwell beneath the conscious sphere of thought processes. Paradigm precedes metaphor, which precedes model, which is perhaps the level of rational discourse at which we begin most of our discussions about problem-solving. Like Assembler language in computer programming, paradigm is at once powerful and elemental. Also like Assembler, paradigm is so powerful precisely because it is so elemental: A shared paradigm allows sender and receiver to transmit information more efficiently, because they do not need to articulate every detail (much less, each nuance) of the matter under discussion.

We will review the ways that paradigms give form to our understanding of the world, and how paradigms drive the formation of subsequent mental constructs such as metaphor, model, and problem iteration. We will consider the impact of paradigmatic presumptions on our organization, on our clients' attitudes or expectations, and ultimately on our own philosophy of professional practice.

PARADIGM AND PARADIGM SHIFT

The first significant statement of the role of paradigm was in reference to scientific research. Thomas Kuhn was one of the creators of the discipline we now call the history of science, through his definitive work, *The Structure of Scientific Revolutions* (1970, 2nd ed.). Kuhn suggested that scientific research was based on a shared fundamental belief system in the structure of the real world, and that individual scientists performed their work in full acceptance of the common paradigm–the shared belief system. The paradigm is the underpinning of scientific understanding in any particular time.

The essential criterion for a scientific paradigm, according to Kuhn, is that it explains things simply. When an existing paradigm requires increasingly more complex processes to achieve its explanation, it will eventually come into question. The result will be that someone will espouse a new paradigm to explain phenomena in a simpler way than the existing paradigm. Widespread adoption of this new basis for thinking creates a paradigm shift (the term originated by Kuhn), and subsequent scientific research is based on the newer, simpler paradigm.

Kuhn used several examples of paradigm shifts in his study of scientific revolutions. The most readily comprehensible might be the debate in medieval and early modern astronomy concerning the place of the earth in the universe. From the time of the early Christian Church, Western astronomers had followed the teachings of Ptolemy of Alexandria, that the earth was at the center of the universe and the sun and stars revolved around it. This Ptolemaic paradigm fit well with Christianity's teaching that human beings were special creations of a God who oversaw the universe: It made sense to have humans and their planet at the center of that universe.

Ptolemy developed a series of mathematical calculations to explain the paths of the planets through the heavens, and these equations were initially fairly simple. Over the centuries, however, observed planetary motions did not fit easily into Ptolemy's system, so the mathematics required to describe and predict such motion became increasingly complex. Finally, in the early 1500s, the Polish astronomer Nicholas Copernicus took the existing data and made a different assumption. Suppose the earth were not at the center of the universe, but rather was one planet of a group orbiting the sun. Suddenly, the mathematics was simplified enormously, and previously unexplained planetary motions were easily incorporated into the model.

Copernicus generated a paradigm shift from the old (Ptolemaic) cosmology to the new (Copernican) one. Although his work was opposed by the Christian church for diminishing the centrality of human beings (even Luther joined the Pope in condemning the new theory), Copernicus created a paradigm that could not be overlooked by serious scientists. The new paradigm became the basis–increasingly unstated, as it was implicitly accepted by all–for all subsequent thinking about how the solar system, the stars, and other astronomical phenomena were arranged.

Kuhn emphasized the rarity of paradigm shift in scientific research. Most experimental science, he asserted, was "mopping up" work, testing and validating implications of the common paradigm in specific applications. A paradigm shift occurred only when the existing paradigm was collapsing under its own complexity, and a new paradigm provided a simpler conceptual structure to comprehend observed events. Hence, few new discoveries are truly paradigm shifts, and fewer still organizational changes reflect any transformation in the fundamental structure of that organization. This is one basis for my assertion that "paradigm shift" has become an overused buzzword in organizational development during this decade.

METAPHORS, MODELS, AND PARADIGMS

One paradigm can generate many different metaphors and even more models, since models are constructed from metaphorical interpretations of the paradigm. Choice of metaphor is critical, because thought processes tend to be limited by the constraints imposed by that metaphor. A metaphor can affect profoundly not only how we do things, but also what happens. For example, viewing world politics as a mathematical zero-sum competition leads to different actions and outcomes than viewing global interactions as a complex ecological system.

Models of any observed behavior–from reference service to economic activity–originate from metaphors, which are supported by paradigms. No model arises from an ideological vacuum: It is based upon certain fundamental assumptions about how people imagine that a particular process operates. These assumptions are a paradigm, which is never a perfectly correct view of reality–hence the need for a paradigm shift when the existing paradigm loses its ability to explain simply and clearly how the observed system operates. Reference librarianship is difficult to practice in the emerging 21st century, because we are all functioning in institutions based largely (sometimes entirely) on 19th-century paradigms of social processes.

PARADIGM PROBLEMS FOR REFERENCE SERVICE

One of our fundamental problems in reference service has nothing to do with emerging technologies or new organizational styles or any of the myriad questions that seem so essential but in reality are so superficial. The fundamental paradigm of the library–both academic and public–in the United States is based on an outdated, century-old idea of "natural order" in society. Libraries were instruments of acculturation–teaching immigrants or other members of lower (i.e., non-monied, non-Protestant, non-governing) social classes how to act in proper (monied, Protestant, governing) society. Free public library service's expansion outside of New England was fueled in significant part by Andrew Carnegie's philanthropy in the later 1800s (Lerner, 1998). This expansion was driven by a desire to give immigrants to the United States opportunities for social advancement (and for productivity improvement). Carnegie's philanthropy was an example from the 19th century of the kind of "business partnership" talked about today, where private-sector businesses get involved in public-policy decisions affecting education and the quality of a future workforce for those businesses. Carnegie envisioned people learning English, accepting the existing social order (instead of radical Central and Eastern

European political theories), and establishing themselves as industrious workers in comfortable communities–all as a result of the drive to better themselves economically through learning.

But public libraries were not the only arbiters of social class. Academic libraries, in a tradition going back probably before the Great Library of Alexandria in Roman times, were part of a rigidly-structured social system acting as gatekeepers to information access for approved classes. This class-structured orientation is maintained today in separate services for faculty, graduate students, and undergraduates (e.g., differential rates for interlibrary loan charges among classes of users–based on presumptions about the information needs of the academic community's various social classes). As college enrollments increased over the last half of the 20th century, student bodies changed to reflect a very different cultural background from the paradigmatic assumptions of academic institutions. Higher-education institutions have added numerous services to address the needs of their students–extension programs, night classes, and on-line instruction–but they have not redesigned library services apace with these service changes. Perhaps this is a result of financial planning–support services for extension programs are costly, lowering profit margins–but I would argue that one motivation is the subconscious paradigmatic view of the academic library by administrators.

The academic library is envisioned as the inner sanctum of the temple on the hill, so that, when the university opens a storefront extension program, the holy-of-holies of the temple is not appropriate to such an enterprise. Thus, the paradigm of the library as a special place is reinforced. The perception of the library as sacred center of the academic temple affects how that library is used by its institution.

The 19th-century paradigm of "natural order, on which library service has been predicated, includes both a social construct and a knowledge construct. Industrial progress and scientific discoveries throughout the 1800s created the impression that everything was knowable. One of the necessary steps in achieving this ultimate knowledge was to classify and arrange known facts. This is why we see the origination of Dewey's classification scheme in 1876, with its precise (and time-specific) organization of knowledge (Reenstjerna, 1999).

From the paradigm of a structured society within a knowable universe flows the need for structured organizations to manage accumulated information in the best, industrial-efficiency style. Hence, the rigid compartmentalization of libraries into Cataloging, Reference, Circulation, and all the other library departments, divisions, and units with which we are all familiar.

So, we are working within the limits imposed by the paradigms of our institution: perceptions of class structure and of ordered, finite structures of knowledge. In 2001, we will be working almost two centuries away from the era when the paradigms defining our libraries, the organization of their collections, and the nature of their clienteles, were defined. We will be living in a different society, one that has very different (in many ways) ideas about how human activity is to be ordered. We must confront the 19th-century paradigmatic limitations placed on us in libraries, and develop action plans to transcend ourselves. Let us confront some of these challenges, and consider appropriate responses.

INHERENT LIMITATIONS IN THE CLASSIFICATION PARADIGM

All of us work with 19th-century classification schemes. Both Dewey and LC schemes are informed with that century's optimistic approach to knowledge acquisition.

Almost a century ago, physicists and mathematicians began to produce discoveries that challenged the know-ability of anything. Beginning with Einstein and followed by the work of such figures as Heisenberg and Gödel, scientists began to accept a greater amount of "undecidability" in their work. Strict categories that separated disciplines such as mathematics and physics began to dissolve in the face of new findings.

Learning and teaching have both become increasingly interdisciplinary, but our collections' classifications fail to address this facet of knowledge in the 21st century. For example, consider the profession of nursing. Within LC, clinical medicine is in class R–a schedule that includes allied health professions and practices. But, contemporary nursing involves far more than clinical procedures. Nursing is a management discipline [within LC class H]; it involves educational skills [LC class L], and a great deal of psychology [LC class B]. Also, unlike clinical medicine, the nursing curriculum can be deeply concerned with social issues [another portion of LC class H]. One university with which I am familiar established a separate medical library to support its school of medicine. They moved all of the books in LC class R to the medical school–and nursing students had to run back and forth between buildings on opposite ends of the campus in order to locate resources for their studies. Increasingly, all sorts of traditionally-unique disciplines like business and law are becoming cross-disciplinary as the knowledge base both expands and diffuses across the artificial barriers we have erected to organize knowledge.

If we as professional librarians desire genuinely to live our professed ideals of customer service, we will plan around the inhibitions that our classification tools place on knowledge acquisition. We now have such tools as discipline-specific Internet web pages, providing specialized access to information for a particular clientele. Since multiple links are possible to the same resource, specialized Internet pages do not have to be unique in all of their contents. In planning for effective reference service, we must anticipate the limitations that our own discipline places on access to information, and design "workarounds" (to borrow from the lingo of software developers) that heighten access to our materials.

I am in no way advocating the sort of "every client an end user" mantra that so many on-line services seem to believe. I do not think that every library client is capable of being an end user of sophisticated information services, any more than they are all equally capable of being their own auto mechanic or their own brain surgeon. We do have a body of knowledge within our profession of librarianship that makes us skilled specialized practitioners. Realizing our professional creed of universal information access is not the same thing as turning everyone loose on web pages of our own design. We must maintain contact with our clientele, something that was called "the reference interview" in days gone by and is even more relevant in these days of information overload than it was in the old days of relative information scarcity.

INHERENT LIMITATIONS IN THE ORGANIZATIONAL PARADIGM

Just as our customers' knowledge acquisition is increasingly interdisciplinary, so the internal distinction between Cataloging and Reference is dissolving within the nature of contemporary professional practice and available technology. With the advent of the Anglo-American Cataloging Rules (AACR and AACR2), cataloging began to focus on access points as the critical decision points. In a real way, cataloging has transformed philosophically from descriptio (iterating the chief physical characteristics of a work) to access (identifying ways that users can locate the information content of a work).

Increased interaction between the formerly separate Reference and Technical Services departments is driven by the need for any library to provide a seamless access system for its clients. As we move on even further, from OPACs (Online Public Access Catalogs) to WEBPACs (world-wide-WEB-based Public Access Catalogs), and catalog online sites just as if they were monographs or videocassettes, our traditional structural paradigm becomes less relevant. Who is more significant: the cataloger who codes the web site so that it displays in the Webpac, or the reference librarian who searches out relevant web sites to support known information needs for the academic community? Which one does more analysis of information content–increasingly, the key role for librarians? Some institutions' organizational charts, fresh from the time-and-motion studies of the 19th century, need to be discarded and replaced with flow charts that integrate the shared functions of librarians working in the 21st century.

A fundamental area needing a paradigm shift is the collection and interpretation of library usage statistics. We might have the brightest reference desk in the latest organizational fashions, equipped with PCs running the most advanced software, but our statistical compilations show an institution little changed from the mid-1950s–at the latest. Library statistics are, to apply a metaphor, the Achilles heel of library modernization. As practitioners, we may imagine that we are functioning in a technologically-rich environment more akin to the movie, *The Matrix,* a futuristic adventure. Looking at our statistical record of service, however, we appear to be in *Pleasantville,* a flashback to the 1950s. One author has called this anomaly the "Rule of 1965": Any service that existed before 1965 in libraries is essential, and any service implemented since that date is a frill (Hyman, 1999). Library statistics are a major way that we enforce the Rule of 1965 at best, if not the Rule of 1955.

While Internet vendors in the "real world" are developing all sorts of valuable usage measures–number of site visits, length of stay per visitor, number of transactions, next and previous sites visited, etc.–we sit at the Reference Desk and make our little Roman-numeral tick marks that get cumulated into some endless page of numbers that gets sent off to non-library administrators who never even ask questions about the pile of numbers (other than occasionally to check the statistics against a colleague's institution to see who has "bragging rights" for that year/quarter/month). Recent articles have indicated the need for addressing such "soft" indicators as Internet use (Hennen, 1999), but the conclusion is that such measures cannot be taken at present because they are not being recorded by the national center from which quantitative measures are derived.

A numerical model of an institution–whether it is a budget or a statistical report–is a means to reconstruct a narrative description of that institution. What do our library statistics say about us? How can some manual tabulation of reference-desk tick marks reflect the usage of our Webpac, or the value of courses taught, or any of the myriad things we do that (1) define us as professional librarians and (2) enhance the health of the communities we serve? Many of us–from the front desk to the Director's Office to administrative halls–have grabbed at what is measurable, not what is significant, to quantify our existence. If an activity is difficult to measure, we usually have not measured it.

This is a bizarre twist on our standards of professional practice. As reference librarians or developers of collections, we don't provide our clients with information that is easiest to obtain. We analyze their information needs, and do whatever we can to provide them the information *they need.* And, after completing our professional task, we put a little tick mark on a sheet of paper and turn quality into quantity. But because quality is difficult to quantify, we go along with an acceptance of available statistical measures in a manner that would shame a newly-minted MLS if he were to approach his client's information needs that way. Because State and Federal agencies are not collecting certain data, we cannot include them in our measures of library quality (Hennen, 1999). Why don't we militate to *have* such measures as Internet access into and out of our libraries included, using established standard measures that search engines and Internet portals find both meaningful and commercially successful? Why do we accept the status quo as the only way to measure the quality of our work, instead of demanding that these huge, bureaucratic, number-filing agencies modernize? The Consumer Price Index (CPI) has been revised, and the

Dow Jones Industrial Average (DJIA) has been modified many times as stocks have been added or removed to reflect economic realities. What is so difficult about library statistics that they cannot be modified, while the CPI and DJIA can? Are we saying that MBAs are smarter than MLSs? I for one do not accept that judgment of my profession.

Awareness and definition of a problem are the first two steps to effective solution. I call on professional librarians to assess their use of quantitative service measures, in light of proven models in the private sector and in light of the complexity of our professional practice as reference librarians. We must create a quantitative image of our library that matches the rhetoric and reality of our daily work in the new paradigm of information organization. We must make sure that the quantitative image describing our library matches both our professional image and the reality of our service to our clienteles.

PHYSICAL/STRUCTURAL LIMITATIONS ON REFERENCE SERVICE

To borrow Brulé and Blunt's (1989) idea of the importance of metaphor in defining activity, let us consider the metaphorical message that our physical setting in Reference conveys to library clients. The operative metaphor for public service seems to me to be a fortress–not unlike the besieged fort in *Beau Geste* or "B" Westerns. We, the experienced troops, wait inside our fortress for people to come to us for assistance. We are separated from them by a desk, often some kind of wraparound structure, but almost always a semi-sealed unit like a castle or log fort. We have the expertise, and we are defending it against all comers.

Naturally, this does not describe the attitudes of many reference librarians with whom I have worked, but I am not talking about the metaphorical message being transmitted to us. I am talking about the metaphorical message to our clientele. People have to approach us (and we are often strangers to them), admitting that they don't know how to find some bit of information and that they need our help.

Think for a moment about the tremendous psychological pressures caused by such an action. It might be called a secular confession. At the very least, it is an admission that, regardless of the level of learning the person has attained (undergraduate, graduate, or faculty), they lack not only some specialized bit of information but the ability to locate that information on their own. We are asking a lot from people, when we expect them to surrender some part of their sense of self-value and admit to strangers that they need help. While such an admission is fundamental to 12-step recovery programs, experts in such programs will tell you that it is an incredibly difficult step for people to take. And we reference librarians expect people to take that step as a matter of course.

Another result of the "Fortress Reference" metaphor is that it is inherently passive. People go into forts or castles to protect themselves from outside invaders. While some sorties might be made out of forts, the essential purpose of the fort is to provide a safe haven that protects essential resources. When we are ensconced in "Fortress Reference," we keep with us the items deemed most valuable for our continued professional practice. Whether we call this the "Ready Reference" collection or something else, items kept within our fort are items that we want most to protect.

I am not saying that we should abolish the Reference Desk as a library institution. Rather, I am encouraging everyone to think deeply about the psychosocial implications of our metaphorical fortress. We can try to sally forth more frequently from "Fortress Reference," walking the ranges and tables and computer banks, asking people open-ended questions about their work and suggesting resources they might know exist. At the very least, we should be sufficiently aware of our area that we can spot someone who is repeatedly leaving and returning to a catalog terminal or to an index–an obvious sign of an inability to locate needed information in our library using the indicators available in the catalog or index available. This is the value of Nardi and O'Day's (1999) concept of information ecosystems. Envisioning our communities as ecosystems, with reference librarians observing and enhancing the interrelationships unique to particular ecosystems, gives us a different perspective on our relationships with individuals than viewing our tasks as defenders of "Fortress Reference."

SUGGESTION FOR A NEW PARADIGM

Even if problem identification is important, suggesting solutions should be at least expected of me in this article. Now that I have identified limitations on our professional practice stemming from our resources' paradigm of the finite nature of knowledge, and our organizational paradigm of division and segregation of labor into discrete units, what suggestions can I make for a new paradigm? What will embrace the reality of knowledge flow in the 21st century, and known (even unknown) information-management technologies that will be applied?

First and most importantly, I believe that we should adopt the paradigm and attendant model of Reference Service as Portal, analogous to the leading search engines currently active on the Internet. While there is some debate that the concept of "portal" sites might be peaking with the growth of the Internet, the portal is still the most valuable paradigm for us to evaluate our professional practice as reference librarians facing the 21st century.

Portal sites on the Internet range from search engines such as Yahoo! and AltaVista to enhanced ISPs (Internet Service Providers), the most conspicuous of which might be America OnLine (AOL). A portal is the place at which someone begins their Internet search, based often on past successful experience with the site. The portal might be structured to allow the individual to preselect broad search categories for their information (e.g., AOL, Yahoo!), or it might be just a search engine to begin a natural-language query (e.g., Google), or it might be a combination (e.g., AltaVista). At any rate, the characteristic of the Internet portal is that it mediates a searcher's query with available information resources, identifying the most likely sites to answer the searcher's information needs. A portal is an individual's choice as the preferred place to begin an informational inquiry. The portal is chosen because its resources are accessible, they are coherently arranged from the perspective of the client, and the portal has been shown from experience to have a high probability of success in delivering information. Conversely, portals are rejected that are too cumbersome, incoherently organized (again, from a client-need perspective), and have a low probability of success.

Second, we must recognize that our informational environment is an open system, not at all like the closed system imagined by our classification systems. We must work within some of the limits imposed by our closed-system tools, but we must strive to make connections in our resources that help our clients locate information in the ways that they themselves organize their information. The cross-disciplinary nature of all subject areas–nursing being the conspicuous example outlined previously–mandates rethinking how we organize our service to our various communities.

Third, and most importantly from a managerial perspective, we must redefine how we measure our service, checking to see that our quantitative measures accurately reflect our inner philosophy of librarianship. Creating a 1955-era statistical picture of reference service at the dawn of the 21st century is not only meaningless, it gives decision makers a dangerously-outdated vision of what we do and how we do it. We must study the ways that ISPs and Internet portals evaluate their clienteles, and adapt to the library environment those measures of on-line use that make sense to us as librarians and to our non-library managers. We must keep in mind that, however positive our ultimate decision makers sound (who wants to come out against libraries?), we are in the end communicating with people who do not share our professional education or even vision. Whether it be an academic library that reports to a Vice-President or Provost, a special library that reports to a corporate officer, or a public library that reports to elected officials or appointed administrators, the person making critical decisions about our library's financial needs is most likely someone who lacks our vision of our profession and who is dealing with competing demands for scarce resources from other agencies with their own political/financial demands on the decision maker. If our statistics make us resemble the library from *The Music Man,* we stand little chance to defend our valid demands for funding to support 21st-century information resources.

Finally, and most importantly, we must strive to see that our practice reflects our philosophy of reference service. If we say we are client-centered, then we must abandon the "Fortress Reference" metaphor and think about ways to live our professional commitment. We must go out into the midst of our clientele, asking open-ended questions that elicit the real nature of our clients' information needs, studying the information ecologies of our community. Those of us at the Reference Desk have a special responsibility to transcend the metaphorical–and very real psychological–barriers between us and our clients. We must assess not only our clients' information needs, but also the psychosocial implications of our setting and the limitations of the closed-system paradigm in which many of our basic tools evolved. If we believe that we librarians are essential mediators in an information-overloaded society, we must design systems–both electronic and human–to help people in our service communities.

It is much easier to learn new computer commands, or new reference-interview techniques, than to rearrange our fundamental system of thinking about our professional practice. Nevertheless, confronting the issues raised by paradigms and metaphors about reference service can lead us into a new way of thinking about ways to provide the highest-quality information services in an era of rapidly-changing technology, client needs, and institutional structures. Once again, the simplest or easiest thing to do is not the most important thing to do. An old management slogan is that efficiency is doing things right, while effectiveness is doing the right things. We must transcend efficiency, becoming ever more effective through our exploration and understanding of those elemental, nonverbal, thought processes of metaphor and paradigm.

REFERENCES

Brulé, James F., and Alexander Blunt (1989). *Knowledge Acquisition*. New York: McGraw-Hill.

Hennen, Thomas J., Jr. (1999). "Great American Public Libraries: HAPLR Ratings, Round Two," *American Libraries* 30 (September): 64-69.

Hyman, Karen (1999). "Reference Service and the Rule of 1965," *American Libraries* (November): 54-58.

Kuhn, Thomas (1970). *The Structure of Scientific Revolutions*. Chicago: University of Chicago Press.

Lerner, Frederick (1998). *The Story of Libraries: From the Invention of Writing to the Computer Age*. New York: Continuum.

Nardi, Bonnie A., and Vicki L. O'Day (1999). *Information Ecologies*. Cambridge, MA: MIT Press.

Reenstjerna, Frederick (1999). "19th-Century Ideas." Available at http://sites.netscape.net/reenstjerna/libraries.

Taking Control: A Reference Approach to the Internet

Patricia J. M. Rodkewich
JoAnn DeVries

SUMMARY. Libraries are at a crossroad. Down one road are the traditions long accepted by libraries as the proper way to run a library. The other way leads the libraries into the challenges and chaos of the Internet. There are innovative attempts to use the potential of the Internet to redirect traditional patterns of access to information and services. *[Article copies available for a fee from The Haworth Document Delivery Service: 1-800-342-9678. E-mail address: <getinfo@haworthpressinc.com> Website: <http://www.HaworthPress.com> © 2001 by The Haworth Press, Inc. All rights reserved.]*

KEYWORDS. Internet, World Wide Web, WWW, digital resources

Librarians are generally organized people. Such a person when presented with a problem works through it in a systematic, methodical, and thorough manner. And while it is true that many librarians are this kind of person, there are also librarians who are not well organized and systematic; however, both kinds of librarians are successful in their work. The reason this is true is that it is not as important to have

---

Patricia J. M. Rodkewich and JoAnn DeVries are Reference Librarians/Bibliographers, Magrath Library, University of Minnesota, St. Paul, MN 55108 (E-mail: p-rodk@tc.umn.edu; j-devr@tc.umnedu).

[Haworth co-indexing entry note]: "Taking Control: A Reference Approach to the Internet." Rodkewich, Patricia J. M., and JoAnn DeVries. Co-published simultaneously in *The Reference Librarian* (The Haworth Information Press, an imprint of The Haworth Press, Inc.) No. 72, 2001, pp. 113-122; and: *Doing the Work of Reference: Practical Tips for Excelling as a Reference Librarian* (ed: Celia Hales Mabry) The Haworth Information Press, an imprint of The Haworth Press, Inc., 2001, pp. 113-122. Single or multiple copies of this article are available for a fee from The Haworth Document Delivery Service [1-800-342-9678, 9:00 a.m. - 5:00 p.m. (EST). E-mail address: getinfo@haworthpressinc.com].

an organized librarian working in a library as it is to have an organized library for the librarian to work in. Success depends in large measure on the organization of the library, not the librarian.

Reference librarians get questions about any subject ever studied or written, every adventure taken, every word spoken. A patron looks for hours and cannot find what he needs. He turns the problem over to the reference librarian and ten minutes later there is an answer. To the patron it seems a miracle, but we know there is nothing supernatural about it. It has to do with organization. We are able to answer a botanical question because long ago a bibliographer traced the first listing of a newly discovered plant. We have a copy of his work in our library. Or, maybe the scholars in a discipline decided they could no longer easily find what they needed in a 50-year run of their journal and they prepared an index of the articles. We have that index in our collections as well as those that followed it, and we are able to find something when it is needed by our patron 50 years later.

Traditionally, librarians have not been the producers of information; that has been the work of the scholar. The job of the librarian is to sift through the mountains of published resources and choose the best research produced to be gathered into a collection. We then organize the collection so that it is usable. And finally, we protect and preserve this collection for future generations. Selecting, collecting, organizing, preserving, and sharing are the principles upon which a library is built.

THE GOLDEN YEARS

The library world was stable for hundreds of years and librarians were content doing their job–building collections and assisting people in using them. Along came the 1960s and things began to change in our society and in the library world as well. By the early 1970s the computer had become the main tool used to organize collections. We could "borrow" catalog records prepared at other institutions and use them for our own records. Card catalogs were converted to on-line catalogs. OCLC and RLIN provided a way to see what other libraries owned. We could quickly identify a book or document even if it were not in our own collection.

On-line databases replaced paper indexes, and they were wonderful. A search in a paper index took a very long time–slowly going through index volumes by hand, moving to the citations and, finally, writing down the bibliographic information. Now an electronic search in the same index takes only a few minutes and, in addition, the ability to combine words from anywhere in the record brings us a much refined subject approach to the literature.

The years from 1960 to 1990 were surely the golden age for libraries. We had better tools for organizing and using our libraries. Patrons came to us for services and assistance. We were in control of our world. We had no warning that the next ten years would be the most unsettling time in library history, and that the changes we had seen in the previous 30 years would be mild compared to what was to come.

WINDS OF CHANGE

The Internet seemed to burst forth. Librarians did not have a great deal of interest in the Internet at first. The library was doing quite nicely, thank you; we had our computers and our databases and everything was pretty perfect as it stood. Well, we did have escalating journal subscription prices that were a worry, so it was not quite perfect. But what exactly was this Internet and who were these people putting stuff on it and sending it all over the world? We librarians did not let just anyone put anything into our libraries. We have standards for our collections and one of the basic requirements is that authors have some level of knowledge/expertise in the subject they are writing about. This Internet had no standards at all and even worse, it did not want any. Anyone could create a site and put anything they want on it for the entire world to see and use.

More changes were coming: PDF full-text files–a small advance for the Internet, but one that has untold effects on libraries. At first, a few and then hundreds and now thousands of organizations put at least some of their publications in full text on their Internet sites. It is a cost-effective way for these organizations to get their information out to everyone–much less expensive to put their publications up electronically than to print and mail paper copies. Librarians are used to collecting and cataloging publications in print format. But now, in electronic format, we are not quite sure what to do with them. We have a number of choices. We can print them out, bind them in some fashion, catalog and classify them and put them into our paper collections. Or, we can prepare a catalog record and attach a hot link to the electronic version. Or, we can just ignore them.

While librarians have been slow to determine the best approach to the Internet, our patrons have not been. Those who use the Internet love the Internet. When they have a question, they turn to their computers. The Internet quickly become their "Library of Choice," and it is not hard to understand why this is so. Users do find answers to many questions so why should they travel to or even call the library and ask the reference librarian for assistance. As librarians well know, it is personally rewarding to find answers without assistance. The Internet is not only easy to use, it is fun, and beyond that, there is an element of surprise that unexpected discovery brings. Look for one thing and something else pops up and surprises you. The Internet is an adventure that you do not need to climb a mountain to experience. Staid libraries can not compete with commercial web sites in promotion, glitter, and sheer aggressiveness in attracting clientele.

Librarians are divided on how we should adapt to this beast at our door. Will the Internet replace the librarian and library? Will search engines become the new reference librarians of the digital world? Will we eventually become redundant or is the need for human reference interviews and services greater than ever before? Will our traditional values of fairness, quality, and unbiased assessment be more important then ever before? Some articles even contained thought-provoking and imaginative scenarios (Heckart, 1998).

THE CHALLENGES

In light of these developments there are pressures to think of the Internet as the "New Library." The librarian in response poses the question, "What would be gained and what would be lost, if indeed, the Internet became the library?" You and I know that librarians have worked long and hard to build collections and make them usable, and we also know that libraries have served the world very well for hundreds of years. But we recognize that the Internet has so much potential that it cannot be ignored. What does each offer?

In order to compare a library and the Internet we must begin with a discussion of what each embodies. What are the principles upon which a library is built? What are the values of the librarian? A library is a collection of information resources. The first and most important task of the librarian is to build this collection–the source for answers to all questions asked, all information sought. To properly answer these questions the information must be accurate. Selection of materials for the collection calls for a judgment of the quality and accuracy of new resources available. The librarian judges the quality and accuracy of the materials to be added to the collection.

But it is not enough to gather a qualified collection. Users need to be able to locate what they are seeking. Librarians have created a very effective indexing, cataloging and classifying system in order to assure that whatever is needed can be found. This carefully selected and arranged collection is made available to users and stored for future users. Collections play an important role in the research and discovery process used to further knowledge. Advances in knowledge are made based on what has been learned before. What has been learned is reported in great detail in research reports and journal articles. If reports of previously completed research were not available to current researchers, the research would have to be repeated before the next level of knowledge could be achieved. Libraries maintain the storehouse of previous research reports for those working presently to build upon. This carefully selected and organized collection of information forms the basis for whatever new is to be learned in the future.

Now, in comparison, is the Internet a usable source of information? There is no doubt that there is a lot of information on the Internet. If you want the latest phone number or address for a company, the Internet is the best place to look. If you want weather information or travel tips, the Internet is the best source. If you want the history of a topic or a critical review, the library is a better source. It all depends on what you are looking for. The array of information available on the Internet is astounding and it is hard to put limits on the possibilities it offers. It is a mish-mash of information; no selection process applied to the Internet collection, no weeding out of poor, false, or extraneous information. If you were able to inspect all the printed materials that are actually produced in a year's time you would find the expected books, journals, newspapers and documents. In addition, you would see handbills, signs, advertisements, comic books, tickets, pornographic materials, pictures, research reports, speeches, letters, play scripts, music scores, etc.–an endless array of things produced by an endless number of authors. The reason you do not find all of this material in the library is that a librarian has sorted and selected only the most suitable or the best for a library. If a library collected everything printed in a year, the library would begin to look like the Internet. The difference is the library has a knowledgeable, discerning librarian. The Internet does not have a librarian–at least, not yet.

The Internet is not systematically organized. There are massive search engines that retrieve huge numbers of hits. These search engines have divided the Internet into broad subject categories so searches can be limited somewhat. Librarians have made attempts to organize chosen sites on the Web by preparing guides to useful sites. They have also begun cataloging Internet sites, and enhancing the records with Metadata to improve the search engines retrieval (Ahronheim, 1998; Chepesiuk, 1999). However, none of these attempts to bring order to the Internet have resulted in the same level of control that indexes and catalogs have done for libraries.

One troubling aspect of the Internet is that there is no assurance that what you are finding on the Internet today, will be there tomorrow. The Internet delivers fast dissemination of information, but it does not offer any guarantee for the future. We have all had the experience of trying to return to a site only to find that it has disappeared. Often Web sites are the work of a single individual. After a period of time the upkeep becomes too much or the individual's interests/job change and he no longer wishes to continue. The site might remain as it was the last time it was updated, or it might just disappear. Organizations have more of a commitment to their sites. More of a commitment, but not necessarily commitment to preservation of research as libraries do. Will all of their publications be kept on their Web sites, or will the old ones be removed when space becomes an issue or when the first rush of use is over? These are unanswered questions.

There are areas in which the Internet is far superior to the library. It outshines the library in its ability to share information. Although libraries have for many years shared collections through interlibrary loans, that kind of sharing cannot begin to equal the ability of the Internet to serve the world. There needs to be only one copy of a research paper available full-text on the Internet to provide access to anyone who needs that information. Cost saving and ease of access gives the Internet a major advantage over a collection rooted to one place and serving only one person at a time.

The "Internet Library" at this time does not match the value of the traditional library as a selector, collector, cataloger/indexer, and preserver of information. While librarians do not see the need to discard the traditional library, we see that there are better ways to do some things. We must take advantage of the ease and cost effectiveness of electronic distribution of information. There are libraries making fundamental changes.

TAKING CONTROL

Librarians realize the Internet can not be ignored, and have begun to think of it as an extension of their library. We have eagerly put our on-line catalogs on the Internet. This increases awareness of what is available, but does not increase access because the collections are mostly in paper format and cannot be accessed remotely. In-library electronic indexes are now Web-based versions and these can be accessed remotely from the offices and home computers. The use of these indexes is controlled by contracts with the producers of the indexes and is limited to each library's own patrons. The advantage of Web access for our patrons is that they have access from their offices and homes–a convenience but not an additional service.

Librarians recognize the amount and worth of portions of the information on the Internet and are beginning to exert control of this information by creating guides to Internet resources. This is a small but real attempt to apply a traditional function of the library (selection) to Internet resources. There are also attempts to place some bibliographic control on these Web sites by creating enhanced cataloging records with metadata embedded in the records. These enhanced records make searching resources on the Internet more precise. A second traditional library function (cataloging/indexing) has been added.

There are two ways in which librarians can utilize the resources of the Internet. One is to identify and use what someone else has put on the Internet–making it to some extent an extended part of the library's collection. This use is described in the paragraphs above. A second way is to create a new Internet site with new information that is designed to be shared by all. Mann Library at Cornell University provided this sort of Internet resource when it mounted USDA ERS and NASS agricultural statistics on a library server (collected), created a search engine (controlled) for these statistical tables, and made them freely available (sharing) to users (*http://usda.mannlib.cornell.edu*). These statistical resources have become part of Mann Library's collection (retaining). No other library needs to duplicate this database as it is available on the Internet and can be used by all. This is a major advance in libraries using the powers of the Internet in a manner that reflects traditional library values.

Another example of libraries sharing resources and workload is the National Agricultural Library (NAL) sponsored project Agriculture Network Information Center (AgNIC). AgNIC is a discipline-based distributed network that is a focal point for agriculture-related information on the Internet *(http://www.agnic.org)*. NAL provides a home and organizational base and partner with land-grant universities and other organizations to offer subject-specific "centers of excellence" with access to quality resources so that users can find answers to most questions. AgNIC is one of the first discipline-specific distributed networks on the Internet and a model that can be applied to almost all other disciplines. The Internet used in this way can and does alter what constitutes a collection and for whom it is collected.

AgNIC sites do more than point to other Internet sites. Librarians offer reference services to all users. This results in requests from users located all over the world. The request might come from a farm in North Dakota, somewhere in Latin America, or in central Africa. This is helpful to those who need information, but have no library resources in their area.

AgNIC sites focus on selected subject areas and design pages and content that are most appropriate to that subject. Each AgNIC site has unique features. Randeland Management (University of Arizona) has current and back issues of the *Journal of Rangeland Management* as well as other full-text reports *(http://ag.arizona.edu/OALS/agnic)*. Water Quality (University of Nebraska–Lincoln) includes a K-12 section designed to assist teachers to prepare lessons on water and water quality issues *(http://deal.un.edu/agnic)*. Two other AgNIC sites are particularly well-known because they are produced at the University of Minnesota. Agricultural and applied Economics (University of Minnesota) is produced by author, Patricia Rodkewich *(http://agecon.lib.umn.edu/AgNIC)*. The forestry librarian publishes the Forestry (University of Minnesota) site at *(http://www.lib.umn.edu/for/agnic)*.

The forestry librarian has compiled and edited four bibliographies/indexes for many years. The indexes are: *Social Sciences in Forestry, Urban Forestry, Trail Planning, Construction and Maintenance,* and *Tropical Forestry Conservation and Development.* Because of the interdisciplinary nature of the subjects covered by these indexes, many papers published in these subjects appear in journals in disciplines other than forestry. The papers could be found in geography, economics, landscape architecture, anthropology, sociology and other journals. The two main forestry/agricultural indexes, AGRICOLA and CAB, do not index these journals. In 1992 the *Social Sciences in Forestry* was transferred from a paper-based publication to an Internet publication. All four indexes were mounted on the Internet over a period of years. When the Forestry AgNIC was created the four indexes were linked to it and became the centerpiece of the site. This shows how the Internet has allowed the librarian to expand her role from collector of information to producer of information.

The Agricultural and Applied Economics AgNIC, in addition to being a guide to Internet sites, is linked to the University of Minnesota, Magrath Library site, "AgEcon Search: Research in Agricultural and Applied Economics" (*http://agecon.lib.umn.edu*). AgEcon Search is a full text electronic library dedicated to collecting, indexing, preserving and sharing full text copies of agricultural and applied economics research papers. The papers are publications of university agricultural economics departments and other organizations related to agricultural and applied economics. The full text papers mounted on this site are the beginning of a true Internet library, built by librarians, and based on the values and traditions of the library; traditional in its approach to the literature it includes, but modern in that it takes full advantage of the capabilities of the Internet. No other library needs to collect the research papers in the AgEcon Search collection, but the users of many libraries may access them whenever they wish and they can depend on them being there when needed. AgEcon Search is a reality because the University of Minnesota Library entered into an agreement with the American Agricultural Economics Association, the University of Minnesota Department of Applied Economics and other university departments to collect, mount, index, preserve and share these publications.

OUR FUTURE WITH THE INTERNET

We do not have a crystal ball to see exactly what the future holds for libraries, but we can speculate based on changes we have seen so far. The Internet is expanding so rapidly and becoming more important in almost every facet of daily life. We have only to look at our personal use of the Internet to know that this is so. We get more information from e-mail than we do over the phone. This was not true three years ago. We visit our bank via the Web. This past year we bought billions of dollars worth of Christmas presents without leaving our houses. When we want an address of a company we look for their Web site. We plan our vacations and book our plane tickets on-line. It is reasonable to believe that the library can be a full participant in this movement to the Internet.

We predict libraries will position themselves to use the full capabilities of the Internet to cooperate, collaborate, and share resources. The idea that a book or journal has to reside on a shelf in a library in order to be part of a collection is no longer valid. We also predict collaboration between the traditional producers of information–researchers and scholarly societies–and libraries. We see an expanded role for librarians as producers of information and publishers of information, as well as providers of information.

The library is a collector of and a storehouse for information. If we do not collect we can not store and if we do not store, chances are likely no one else will do it. Paper copies disappear, but not as quickly or completely as electronic publications do. An organization might think at the moment that it will keep its own publications forever, but it does not always happen. The best archive for electronic literature is in a library collection. Libraries must make this happen. We have some beginnings, but much more has to be done. We have made tentative steps, but there is so much more taking control yet to do.

BIBLIOGRAPHY

Ahronheim, Judith R. (1998), "Descriptive Metadata: Emerging Standards," *Journal of Academic Librarianship* 24 (5), 395-403.

Chepesiuk, Ronald (1999), "Organizing the Internet: The 'Core' of the Challenge," *American Libraries* 30 (1), 60-63.

Ferguson, Chris and Charles Bunge (1997), "The Shape of Services to Come: Value-based Reference of the Largely Digital Library," *College and Research Libraries* 58 (5), 252-265.

Hechart, Ronald J. (1998), "Machine Help and Human Help in the Emerging Digital Library," *College and Research Libraries* 59 (3), 250-259.

Humanities Reference Librarians in the Electronic Age: Strategies for Integrating Traditional and On-Line Resources in an Academic Library

Peggy Keeran

SUMMARY. Humanists build new ideas and arguments based upon studies done in the past. Although research requires these scholars to pick through the literature that has come before, much has been lost because of the lack of adequate comprehensive reference tools. In the age of technology, new projects are available which enhance and enlarge the body of work upon which future scholars can build. For reference librarians helping with research questions in the humanities, the marriage of traditional reference tools and new on-line resources means a richer cumulation of past scholarship. In this paper, I will discuss strategies for academic humanities reference librarians to integrate traditional and electronic reference resources, and the need to continue learning the skills to use both. Humanities reference librarians must continue the great humanist tradition of building new ideas upon older foundations by successfully acquiring and using both new and old reference resources.

Peggy Keeran is Arts and Humanities Reference Librarian and Associate Professor, Penrose Library, University of Denver, 2150 East Evans Avenue, Denver, CO 80208 (E-mail: pkeeran@du.edu).

[Haworth co-indexing entry note]: "Humanities Reference Librarians in the Electronic Age: Strategies for Integrating Traditional and On-Line Resources in an Academic Library." Keeran, Peggy. Co-published simultaneously in *The Reference Librarian* (The Haworth Information Press, an imprint of The Haworth Press, Inc.) No. 72, 2001, pp. 123-136; and: *Doing the Work of Reference: Practical Tips for Excelling as a Reference Librarian* (ed: Celia Hales Mabry) The Haworth Information Press, an imprint of The Haworth Press, Inc., 2001, pp. 123-136. Single or multiple copies of this article are available for a fee from The Haworth Document Delivery Service [1-800-342-9678, 9:00 a.m. - 5:00 p.m. (EST). E-mail address: getinfo@haworthpressinc.com].

KEYWORDS. Reference librarians, research skills, humanities, humanists, scholarly research, academic libraries

A new on-line index to 19th century art periodicals is developed and made available through RLIN. Digitization projects are being developed and launched which include the full-text of 19th century African-American women writers and pre-20th century British periodicals. A CD-ROM is published which provides subject access to 19th century British periodicals. All of these initiatives are examples of how technology can be beneficial to humanist researchers and librarians. Since humanists' scholarship is cumulative and much has been lost because of the lack of adequate comprehensive reference tools, these projects provide greater access to materials that may not have been widely distributed or may not have been adequately indexed in print resources. How do these new resources fit into the larger research picture? On-line resources provide new and exciting possibilities for research, but they do not exist in isolation; they must be situated in the larger context of reference tools for the humanities in order that their true value be evaluated and understood. It is the role of humanities reference librarians in academic settings to determine this context, and to explain it to members of their communities.

TRADITIONAL RESEARCH METHODS OF THE HUMANIST

In order to provide satisfactory reference service for humanists, one needs to understand how these scholars conduct research. Much has been written in library literature about the traditional characteristics of the humanist researcher (Watson-Boone, 1994; Fabian, 1998; University of Illinois, 1989). The humanist starts with a question, which is explored using a wide variety of primary and secondary texts, and in which "her or his personal interpretation of material is central to the conclusions reached" (Watson-Boone, 1994). The interaction between the humanist, and the question and its text is very personal, and the resources needed by one scholar to answer a question may be completely different from those needed by another to answer what is seemingly a similar question.

> With the author at the center, humanities research is text, drawing on text, drawing on text–all dependent on individually created

> connections, responsivity to multiple voices and multiple messages which are nonetheless grounded in text and produce a textual product. (Plum and Smalley, 1994)

Although most studies which report research patterns of humanists were done before the Internet and web became widely available, the basic characteristics and needs appear to be unchanged (Fabian, 1998). Humanists tend to work on their own; they do not make regular use of librarians as resources except in specialized collections where the librarian's grasp of the collection makes her invaluable; they seldom consult indexes or abstracts but, instead, depend upon bibliographies, journals, and colleagues to keep them abreast of new theories and texts; they depend more upon books than journal articles; and they are inclined to seek out only what they need. Since they are aware of the scholarship and scholars in their particular areas, they most often search by title or author, not by subject. Browsing and serendipitous discoveries are also important avenues for discovering relevant materials. And, finally, they are not interested in being overwhelmed by vast amounts of information, but do need to have a firm grasp on the relevant material. Throughout this process, the scholar "accumulates, selects, and interprets information in a way that transforms it into knowledge" (Watson-Boone, 1994).

EVERYTHING OLD IS NEW AGAIN

For on-line resources to be valuable to humanists, they must either provide better control over the material than print sources do, provide better access, or provide unique research possibilities. Indexes, bibliographies, and library catalogs are standard tools for researchers to use. Over the past decade or so, these have been repackaged in electronic format. Librarians may point out to the humanist researchers that these exist in electronic format, as well as print, but this does not reveal to the humanist how the electronic version can cast new light on the past. For example, *MLA International Bibliography* and *ABELL* are essential for literary research. *WorldCat* and *RLIN*, as well as individual web/Internet library catalogs from around the world allow remote searching of the most traditional library research tool of all: the library catalog. Scholars can search these as they always have: to identify works by specific authors or titles, or to find locations for materials needed. However, these can also be searched in more sophisticated ways to serve as more than verification tools. Multiple years of bibliographic reference tools, many cumbersome to use in print, can be searched. Thanks to keyword and descriptor searching and Boolean operators, scholars can be creative researchers. Titles, subtitles, and descriptors of records can be mined and different concepts combined within a single search, thus focusing on precisely the information needed. For example, instead of using *Art Index* in print to find everything written since 1929 on the images of music to locate those specifically depicted in 19th century American paintings, the researcher using the on-line index can combine Boolean logic and keyword searching to discover if anything has been written on the precise question. Interdisciplinary research becomes a reality when multiple databases can be searched at one time. Instead of basing scholarly arguments on works by the same scholars or canonical figures, searches become much more democratic and searchers can find forgotten literary works or scholarship not deemed important at some point in the past, never cited in bibliographies of books or articles, and thus overlooked by subsequent generations. The electronic world allows traditional resources to look fresh and stimulating.

REDISCOVERING THE PAST IN THE ELECTRONIC AGE

In addition to these electronic versions of print resources, new web-based projects, which allow scholars to explore primary and secondary sources, are being developed which provide a fresh look at publications from bygone eras. Two types of projects, bibliographic and digital, bring back to light lost voices and images. For example, *Index to 19th Century American Art Periodicals,* a web-based index to 42 titles, allows searching of American art magazines from the latter part of the 19th century. In 1961, Helene Emylou Roberts identified, in her library master's thesis, the titles and scope of the journals published in 19th century America. In her introduction she laments:

> Back rooms and basements of libraries often contain shelf upon shelf of forgotten volumes, little used and seldom dusted. Many of these are periodicals, a century ago eagerly awaited and avidly read, but now overlooked and threatened with discard. The sheer bulk of these periodicals and the lack of guide books and indexes

> to their contents have intimidated scholars and librarians alike; yet a wealth of material representative of American life is concealed there. (Roberts, 1961)

Nearly 40 years later, an electronic finding tool was created. Librarians with these titles can promote them anew by publicizing the new index. Those who do not own these journals can acquire them through out-of-print periodical vendors or on microfilm. And, of course, patrons can request via interlibrary loan. The index itself provides scholars with the opportunity to explore and reinterpret forgotten and neglected aspects of our cultural past.

The Wellesley Index to Victorian Periodicals, 1824-1900 is another small, specialized database which provides electronic access to 43 19th century British magazines. The project, begun in 1967, provided the tables of contents and publishing history for each title, plus the identification of the author of each title. The long-awaited subject index was published, not in print, but on CD-ROM. What could have been cumbersome and enormous became flexible and compact.

The *Internet Library of Early Journals* (*ILEJ*) (http://www.bodley.ox.ac.uk/ilej/), at present available for free over the Internet, is an experimental project, intended to evaluate the possibility of digitizing non-copyrighted 18th and 19th century British magazines. The creators of this project digitized partial runs of three 18th century and three 19th century British journals, to explore the feasibility of making available, over the Internet, non-copyrighted journals on a large scale. *Gentleman's Magazine* (1731-1750) and *Blackwood's Edinburgh Magazine* (1843-1863) were chosen because these are highly representative titles from their eras and would most likely attract scholars to such a pilot project. The scanned text of journals is full-text searchable, and existing print or electronic indexes are keyed in or linked to provide subject access. The system cannot be searched across titles, but could be used as an alternative to microfilm or paper. This project allows scholars to push beyond the static page and to explore the text using the technology, a technology which allows the scholar to print out and read the scanned image of the text as it originally appeared in print and to use the software to scan for words and themes within the publications.

The Digital Schomberg (http://www.nypl.org/research/sc/sc.html) is another digitizing project which includes *African American Women*

Writers of the 19th Century and *Images of African Americans in the 19th Century.* Such special collections, made available over the web, allow scholars to delve into materials which have not, in the past, received concentrated scholarly inquiry and which may not be included in standard print bibliographies found in reference collections. The collections in this special library make widely available literature and images which extend the traditional literary and historical canon, and help us recover part of our past history.

None of these projects provide comprehensive coverage to any discipline or even part of a discipline, but each does have the potential to broaden the base of scholarly research. Periodicals included in *ILEJ* have long been part of the traditional canon, while the art periodicals have languished on back shelves. Technology allows scholars to look afresh at established texts and to reclaim those which have been lost. Projects such as those described above rescue from obscurity voices upon which, consciously or not, humanists have built their own interpretive scholarship.

INTEGRATING PRINT AND ELECTRONIC RESOURCES

On-line bibliographic databases cannot yet completely replace print resources; for example, at present *MLA Bibliography* on-line covers the years 1963-present, while the paper index covers the years 1920-present. And, with all the might of technology, if the citations are not keyed into the database in the first place, the record cannot be found. Until all libraries convert their card catalogs into on-line databases, neither *WorldCat* nor *RLIN* can replace Mansell's *The National Union Catalog, pre-1956 Imprints.* The reference librarian needs to assess the question the humanist asks, and determine what will constitute a thorough search of the literature.

A humanist starts with a question which interests him, and explores the issues surrounding the question in search of an answer. The humanist does not know initially everything she will need during the research journey, so the library needs to have the resources available or accessible, allowing the scholar to advance. In other words, the humanist needs to have and librarians must make available vast amounts of materials. The humanists' research is cumulative: They need more than the most current articles or research findings. The very nature of the humanist research process demands that the librarian integrate a wide variety of research tools into the library collection. Since the question drives the research, and the scholar does not know which direction the research will take, he needs tools that will both expand the boundaries of the question and push the research forward. This basic understanding of the humanist researcher allows the reference librarian to think beyond the format of reference tools and to think of the coverage and scope of the reference tool and how its use will help explore the question.

If a scholar is exploring a topic concerning images of music in American paintings from the latter part of the 19th century, both print and electronic sources will expand the boundaries of the research. *WorldCat, RLIN,* and web/Internet-based library catalogs will allow the scholar to go beyond the walls of her own library and to seek out materials which may not be available on-site but which can be located and perhaps borrowed. The *Archives of American Art* database can be searched through Smithsonian Institution Research Information System for papers of artists who used such imagery, and the microfilm of these papers borrowed through interlibrary loan. The *Index to 19th Century American Art Periodicals* can be used in conjunction with *Poole's Index to Periodical Literature* to explore how issues of music and art were discussed in both popular and art magazines in 19th century America. Museum catalog sets such as those from the Metropolitan Museum of Art, Harvard University of Fine Arts, and the Winterthur Museum provide indexing to art journals and analyze contents of monographs for late 19th to early 20th century topics in art. The scholar can search on-line databases such as *America: History and Life, Art Index, Art Index Retrospective, Bibliography of the History of Art, Humanities Index,* and others to discover scholarly writings on similar or supportive topics. In sum, there are almost as many resources to help answer the scholar's question as there are avenues to explore. Each tool, whether print or electronic, will allow the question to be observed from a different perspective, which helps the scholars advance their own understanding and interpretations of the texts and images.

Neither the format of the reference tools nor the materials needed guide humanist research. "If by some means most of the secondary literature consulted by humanists were to be available only in electronic form then of course humanists would make use of it in that form just as sources available only in microfiche or microfilm are used by them now" (Jones, 1995). The electronic world will be integrated into the research process as long as it contributes. As it is, the humanist cannot avoid integrating different formats or avenues of retrieval. An on-line web-based research tool may lead to a microform collection only available through interlibrary loan. Humanists and librarians need to take advantage of the strengths of each format, and to be flexible about accepting the material in whatever form it exists.

PRACTICAL TIPS FOR THE HUMANITIES REFERENCE LIBRARIAN IN THE DIGITAL AGE

Technology has not changed the basic skills necessary for academic humanities librarians to serve effectively their institutions. Instead of concentrating on the techniques of on-line searching, the librarian needs more than ever to develop and hone the core skills which make reference librarianship so important: communication, teaching, and building collections.

Communication

Knowledge of the community served is vital for effective reference service, and communication is key. If the librarian does not know who constitutes the community, collections cannot be built effectively or appropriate reference tools selected. If the librarian and faculty do not converse, then the fabulous resources the library holds or has made available on-line mean nothing. Who are the members of the community and what are their current and future needs?

In order to assess the teaching and research needs, academic humanities librarians must build liaison relationships. Once the faculty's requirements are identified, the librarian can more effectively respond through collection development, including selection of appropriate reference tools. If the library has formal liaison relationships, the librarian is more likely to get a larger picture of departmental needs because faculty members in the department know all their colleagues whereas the librarian may know only a few who are heavy library users. If the library, however, does not support formal liaison relationships, librarians need to establish these themselves. As liaisons, librarians must be honest about what the library can and cannot offer due to budget and space considerations, but should communicate the concerns of faculty to their administration for strategic planning, budget, technology, and space planning purposes.

Librarians need to send faculty updates about new library resources on a regular basis, and to distribute such publicity selectively and strategically so that it is not ignored. The publicity should be accompanied by short evaluations of the products which place the reference tool in the context of other reference sources. Librarians providing reference services for humanists must remember that humanists do not use what they do not need, so the need to understand why a particular resource may be valuable is critical.

As librarians can appreciate, change is constant within the library, and anyone who has not visited it in a while may feel alienated. Communication helps alleviate this stress. When librarians speak knowledgeably about their collections to the faculty, the faculty come to realize that this is the librarians' area of expertise. The faculty then feel more comfortable asking questions.

Librarians must master the research process and its tools as much as they can, but they also need to be aware of what it is that they do not know. To broaden their knowledge about faculty research habits, the librarians can ask faculty for resources that they find most useful and why. Specialized annotated research guides, such as the annotated guides to literature, James L. Harner's *Literary Research Guide* and Michael J. Marcuse's *A Reference Guide for English Studies,* provide in-depth descriptions of, evaluations of, and comparative information about reference resources. Library colleagues are another good source of information. For example, art librarians have an excellent electronic distribution list with very helpful colleagues, *ARLIS-L.* If librarians are afraid to ask for help, how can faculty be expected to feel any differently?

Teaching

The mission of the academic institution in which the academic humanities librarian works will provide guidance for teaching goals. Within the framework of the academic mission, librarians can discuss, with faculty, methods for integrating library research into course work. Because of the overwhelming importance of electronic research, it is important for faculty and librarians to cooperate and to develop strategies for teaching students to become effective researchers. The allure of the electronic can seduce students into believing that everything they need is on-line. If students are provided with the skills to create effective search strategies, to begin to think critically, and to evaluate materials during the research process, they can become comfortable within and less awed by the on-line environment. To build effective researchers, the librarians and faculty can establish a graduated bibliographic instruction program and identify certain goals for teaching research skills at each class level. As students progress through their upper-division coursework, the on-line and print resources needed to conduct effective research can then be integrated through specialized bibliographic instruction and pathfinders. Using such a format, librarians can begin to teach research skills–including creating search strategies and critical evaluation of materials–in the electronic environment that at the moment may seem so overwhelming. Librarians can also open up the research process for more advanced students by integrating print and on-line resources.

At the University of Denver, we have traditional library instruction programs, including first-year English library research projects, individual classes covering specific topics, and a for-credit quarter-long research methods class. Students develop research skills during their freshman composition classes, in which they learn to use the on-line catalog and a full-text database to write a research paper. The goals of this class are to teach students to conduct research, to evaluate their resources, and to write a persuasive argument based upon authoritative materials. At the other end of the spectrum, graduate students and senior honors students enrolled in the English department are required to take a quarter-long class entitled "Bibliography and Research Methods," co-taught by an English faculty member and the humanities reference librarian. These students use and evaluate a wide variety of resources, including standard indexes, web pages devoted to literary movements or authors, and a vast array of print resources which provide unique access to both primary and secondary resources.

Bibliographic instruction and annotated web-based pathfinders are ideal opportunities to create an overview of resources and how these fit together. Research guides do exist which exhaustively cover every type of reference tool within a discipline, but a clear, concise guide to the holdings in the library, the electronic resources available, and even collections in nearby research libraries will provide a starting point for your community. The humanities reference librarian needs to clarify the path, to be the guide.

By offering hands-on workshops for the faculty in which new resources can be discussed and various search strategies explored, reference librarians can share their expertise and start dialogues about library instruction strategies. These partnerships with the faculty can be invaluable. During workshops, for example, librarians can discuss with faculty the quality of student research expected. This knowledge will help librarians develop more meaningful library instruction classes and will provide students with more explicit direction during reference desk interactions because the goals of both the faculty and librarians are in sync.

Building Collections

Susan Szasz Palmer encourages reference librarians to reassert their mastery over their collections. She writes, "We need to encourage librarians not simply to learn new skills (which is really a euphemism for becoming more computer literate), but to learn more content, to attempt to have some specialization, some knowledge base" (Palmer, 1999). This knowledge base includes more than understanding the scope of reference tools; it includes knowledge of the library's collections as well.

Librarians need to build collections that support the mission and teaching/research needs of their communities. Although the future predicted indicates a wealth of information will be available on-line, librarians have to build collections for the present, be realistic about what will be made available electronically, determine the stability of electronic access to the site, and decide if it is affordable. For example, the *Index to 19th Century American Art Periodicals,* which has no print equivalent, provides access to cultural information that has not been widely used because of the lack of access. This unique resource may be valuable to any academic discipline which concerns American studies. However, the periodicals themselves are not available electronically and may never be available electronically. If the library does not hold any of the titles indexed, the librarian as builder of collections can purchase the periodicals. If lucky enough to have space for the hard copies, there are vendors who specialize in selling runs of periodicals. If not, there are several vendors who have filmed microform sets which cover these titles. Thus, the librarian invests in a new web-based database but, in order to support access to the articles found using it, may end up investing in a more archaic form of technology, microform. This should not be viewed as a problem, but as an opportunity to provide scholars with neglected texts by coordinating the purchase of an index and the titles it covers.

Libraries have been called the humanist's laboratory, since libraries are the facilities which provide the materials, or access to the materials, that the humanist needs to conduct research. Since none but the most extensive research librarians can provide extensive collections, librarians in smaller libraries can contribute to the research needs of their academic communities by knowing their own collections, and, if possible, the special collections, including on-line resources and microform collections, of the libraries in the geographic area. Knowledge of the library collections inspires confidence in skills of librarians. One scholar suggests that reference librarians in academic libraries learn from those who work in small special collections:

> . . . there is something else that is special about such libraries that can perhaps be instructive in our thinking about bibliographic and reference personnel. The people who man these libraries are very often the same people who are responsible for acquisitions, for receiving, and for running the cataloging and shelving operation. . . . The intimate knowledge librarians and staff members have of the collections they manage is available to the researcher as he works side-by-side, often in the same room, with them, and casual conversations (including introductions to other investigators working there) are part of the normal order of things. The "casual" conversation is often a highly instructive exchange. (Freeman, 1989)

In larger libraries, where responsibilities are distributed amongst bibliographers, library instructors, and reference librarians, this commitment to building collections and knowledge of collection can still be accomplished through communication and cooperation with library colleagues as well as with faculty.

In addition to knowing and understanding one's own collections, it is worthwhile to become familiar with special types of collections in other area libraries or which are available on-line or in major microform collections. For example, although individual records from major microform collections may be searchable on-line using *English*

Short Title Catalogue (*ESTC*) or *WorldCat,* not all libraries include records for individual parts of major microform collections in their databases. If a member of the community needs one of the periodicals found using *Index to 19th Century American Art Periodicals* which is not owned by the home institution, it may be included in a larger collection of periodicals such as the *American Periodicals Series,* which provides access to serials published in the United States between 1741-1900. These types of materials are not always catalogued and humanities librarians must know how to go beyond searching union catalogs to find individual titles; they must also know if possibilities exist to find needed materials in alternative formats such as web-based electronic journals or in microform.

CONCLUSION

Traditional skills of the reference librarian are the key to integrating electronic and print resources. Communication, teaching, and knowledge of collections are core skills. Just as humanist research is cumulative, humanities reference librarians' knowledge of reference tools and library collections is cumulative. The format of the resources is not the deciding factor about an item's usefulness; the content is the key. The publishers of the web-based resources discussed above, intended for scholars, are being developed to allow the content of old favorites and forgotten voices to emerge. These publishers understand the needs of the humanist researcher, and are using technology to push the traditional boundaries of research. This allows scholars to look more easily beyond tracing bibliographies in monographs or journal articles and to discover new texts or new ways of looking at old texts. The librarian understands the research practices and needs of the humanist and can and should play a central part in bringing electronic resources into the research fold.

REFERENCES

Burnette, Michaelyn, Christina M. Gillis, and Myrtis Cochran (1994). "The Humanist and the Library: Promoting New Scholarship Through Collaborative Interaction between Humanists and Librarians," *The Reference Librarian,* no. 47, 181-191.

Crawford, Walt and Michael Gorman (1995). *Future Libraries: Dreams, Madness, and Reality.* Chicago, IL: American Library Association.

Fabian, Bernhard and John J. Boll (1998). *In Close Association: The Humanities, Research, and the Library.* Urbana-Champaign, IL: University of Illinois.

Freeman, Susan Tax (1989). "An Anthropologist in Europe: Resources and Problems of Study," in *Humanists at Work: Disciplinary Perspectives and Personal Reflections*. Chicago, IL: The University of Illinois, 1-22.

Himmelfarb, Gertrude (1997). "Revolution in the Library," *American Scholar,* 66 (Spring), 197- 204.

Jones, William Goodrich (1995). "The Disappearance of the Library: Issues in the Adoption of Information Technology by Humanists," *New Directions for Higher Education*, no. 90 (Summer), 33-41.

Manoff, Marlene (1997). "Cyberhope or Cyberhype? Computers and Scholarly Research," *Canadian Journal of Communication,* 22, 197-212.

Palmer, Susan Szasz (1999). "Creating Our Roles as Reference Librarians of the Future: Choice or Fate?" in *Racing Toward Tomorrow.* Chicago: Association of College and Research Libraries, 140-153.

Plum, Terry and Topsy N. Smalley (1994). "Research as Repatriation," *The Reference Librarian,* no. 47, 147-165.

Reynolds, Judy (1995). "A Brave New World: User Studies in the Humanities Enter the Electronic Age," *The Reference Librarian,* no. 49/50, 61-81.

Roberts, Helene Emylou (1961). American Art Periodicals of the Nineteenth Century. Master's thesis, University of Washington.

University of Illinois (1989). *Humanists at Work: Disciplinary Perspectives and Personal Reflections*. Chicago, IL: The University of Illinois.

Unsworth, John (1997). "Some Effects of Advanced Technology of Research in the Humanities," in *Gateways to Knowledge: The Role of Academic Libraries in Teaching, Learning, and Research*, edited by Lawrence Dowler. Cambridge, MA: The MIT Press, 81-92.

Watson-Boone, Rebecca (1994). "The Information Needs and Habits of Humanities Scholars," *RQ,* Winter, 203-216.

A CAUTIONARY NOTE

Readin', Writtin' [sic], 'Rithmetic: Reference Desk Redux

Mark Y. Herring

SUMMARY. Much has been written about the education of reference librarians. Lamentations have been long, frequent and loud regarding library school education, and on-the-job training. Little, however, has been written about the education of librarians *before* they reach library school. If predictions regarding education are only half true, the future pool of reference librarians will be shallow indeed. Moreover, it is not entirely out of the question that those remaining in the pool may be so poorly educated as to require not on-the-job training, but a remedial education so extensive as to foreclose real on-the-job training for several years. Definition of the problem coupled with focused follow-up may help current reference librarians prepare now for the not-so-rosy future we may inherit. *[Article copies available for a fee from The Haworth Document Delivery Service: 1-800-342-9678. E-mail address: <getinfo@haworthpressinc.com> Website: <http://www.HaworthPress.com> © 2001 by The Haworth Press, Inc. All rights reserved.]*

Mark Y. Herring is Dean of Library Services, Dacus Library, Winthrop University, Rock Hill, SC 29733 (E-mail: herringm@winthrop.edu).

[Haworth co-indexing entry note]: "Readin', Writtin' [sic], 'Rithmetic: Reference Desk Redux." Herring, Mark Y. Co-published simultaneously in *The Reference Librarian* (The Haworth Information Press, an imprint of The Haworth Press, Inc.) No. 72, 2001, pp. 137-154; and: *Doing the Work of Reference: Practical Tips for Excelling as a Reference Librarian* (ed: Celia Hales Mabry) The Haworth Information Press, an imprint of The Haworth Press, Inc., 2001, pp. 137-154. Single or multiple copies of this article are available for a fee from The Haworth Document Delivery Service [1-800-342-9678, 9:00 a.m. - 5:00 p.m. (EST). E-mail address: getinfo@haworthpressinc.com].

KEYWORDS. Reference librarians, education of librarians, remedial education, library reference

DOCTORS GRATIFIED ONE OUT OF TWO PATIENTS SURVIVE

ATTORNEYS HAPPY TO WIN ALMOST HALF OF ALL CASES

Headlines such as these would give almost anyone pause. "Has the world gone mad!" we'd all say, "How can 50% performance rating be anything close to good?" And yet a positive reaction to such headlines is nearly exactly the reaction some librarians had when greeted with a report that proved the 55% rule, i.e., that only 55% of all reference questions answered were answered correctly, and that was a pretty good track record (Hermon & McClure, 1986). Of course, if as a patron you ended up in the 55%, it no doubt did seem good. For the remaining 45% it must seem abysmal. Numerous reasons (i.e., excuses?) followed for this egregious performance of reference librarians. Chief among the object of finger-pointing proved to be inadequate library education, and much of the blame fell upon our hapless library schools. Presented here is another possible reason, and it is one that has far more internecine outcomes if true.

No, this isn't *another* article about weak library school education for reference librarians. That horn has been tooted for so long and for so loud that we've almost become accustomed to the ringing in our ears (Avenick, 1993; Blenkinsopp, 1992; Cromer & Testi, 1994; D'Aniello, 1989; Katz, 1990; Nofsinger & Lee, 1994; Rothstein, 1985, 1989; Sherrer, 1996; Spang, 1996; Stabler, 1987; Stam, 1992; Weingand, 1994; Wogaman, 1992; Woodward, 1991). What I fear more are headlines within the next five to ten years that read like these:

LIBRARIANS DEMAND CIVIL WAR BE MOVED TO LATER CENTURY

"CARLIST WARS A NEEDLE IN A HAYSTACK," SAYS LIBRARY HEAD

Laugh all you want, but these may not seem so outrageous if present trends continue. Recall but a little more than a decade ago when real headlines screamed to us about a nation in intellectual mediocrity, a nation we were told that was at risk and rapidly awash in a "rising tide of mediocrity" that threatened to undo us (United States, 1983; Dougherty, 1984). While the concern for the education of reference librarians is real, even palpable, and should not go unnoticed, yet another graver concern faces us: the quality of future reference librarians *before* they make it to library school. Library schools must be updated, must experience their tsunami of change from time to time. About that there can be no argument. But changing library school education is, after all, something within our control. What we are less able to control (though we can still influence), is the backwash we face if this rising tide of mediocrity reaches high tide in the pool of potential library school students, and especially in future reference librarians. Furthermore, it underscores the importance that the new reference librarian understand that her education has, as the old song says, only just begun.

That the general education of reference librarians, or anyone for that matter, is cause for grave alarm has been sounded throughout academy (Bennett, 1992; Chubb & Moe, 1990; D'Souza, 1991; Finney, 1992; Frazier, 1996; Hirsch, 1996; Kilpatrick, 1992; Kimball, 1990; Kramer, 1991; McGuinness, 1997; Marsden, 1994; Roche, 1994; Schlesinger, 1992; Sizer, 1996; Sowell, 1993; Stotsky, 1999; Sykes, 1995; Wirt, 1989). Indeed, the complaints have been sounded early and often. Universities are racked by competing political ideologies that have recently begun to interfere, or at the very least impede, education (Sokal & Bricmont, 1998).[1] Meanwhile, learning takes a backseat as more and more survey courses are taught by fewer and fewer PhDs in favor of their teaching assistants. Furthermore, we do know of at least one profession where this poor training is beginning to show up: teacher preparation. Over the last decade more than two dozen books (see above) have been written chronicling the sad saga of teacher education schools and the inherent lack of intellectual rigor. This is neither the time nor the forum to hash out the merits and defects of these arguments. One thing is certain: There is a problem in education and nearly everyone recognizes it.

This brings us to the subject, *ad rem*, so to speak: What happens when college graduates who have endured high school but learned very little, have managed to struggle through four years of colleges and emerged with what at best can be described as dubious skills, land in library school where, as nearly everyone in the profession has said (even in print) that their intellectual sojourn may be less than desired?

The concern about librarians being miseducated, or poorly educated expressed itself before, nearly a century ago:

> It is the peculiar vice of librarians–even more characteristic than their propensity to talk shop–that as they know intimately the backs of so many books, they are likely to persuade themselves that they know its contents as well. The temptation is subtle and powerful, and its operations are not confined to the custodian of books. Let no one deceive himself into thinking that because he knows the royal road to learning, its guide posts, its directories, its ins and outs, the various vehicles that carry men on it, he is necessary [sic] travelling [sic] thereon himself. There is no virtue and no praise in this knowledge, if it is not applied to help either oneself or another to actual progress. (Bishop, 1912)

To have such warning so long ago does little to assuage the threat we face today. One hundred years ago it was possible for a young person to be subjected to Greek and Latin *in high school.* (Now before anyone charges forth with protestations that knowing either language is a mark of an educated person, let me hasten to add that while one may not have to be, in fact, very smart to know one or both languages, the discipline of mind required to learn either, not to mention the world of learning opened by virtue of knowing the languages, cannot be gainsaid by anyone.) What libraries face today is a monumental threat, not only in the guise of a lack of education, but in the transmogrification to a banality of mind.

This charge has been laid down again as a warning: "No man is really trained in books who has not made himself the master of at least a few . . . " (Bishop, 1912). Not only does this fly in the face of modern education, but it also defies even the acme of library school education (Henry, 1994). Clearly, when both a high school education and four years (or, as is increasingly common, five or six) of college have become less than meaningful in the context of learning, the Lake Wobegon effect notwithstanding, library school at its best will be hard-pressed to do more than provide what it has often been criticized for most: rote memorization of a handful of "factoids."

While it is admirable that there are those among us who call for "more stress on enthusiastic intellectualism . . . to improve the deplorable amount of misinformation, or no information, given by at least some reference librarians," it also appears vain in light of the spectre that awaits us (D'Aniello, 1989). Take high school education, for example. Here is but a partial list of what young people do not know, as variously reported in *this* decade alone:

- A *decade* following *A Nation at Risk,* the reading proficiency of nine- to thirteen-year olds continued to decline.
- Only 2% of all high school juniors can write well enough to meet national goals.
- Some mid-western states accept Agriculture courses as fulfilment for traditional Physics and Biology requirements.
- Only one in eight thirteen-year-olds can understand and apply intermediate scientific knowledge and principles.
- According to the National Assessment of Educational Progress, only 3% of American fourth, eighth and twelfth graders can write above a "minimal" or "adequate" level.
- Only 15% of college faculty say their incoming freshmen are adequately prepared in mathematics.
- Out of 22,000 students tested, 60% of high school seniors could not define the Monroe Doctrine, did not understand the political concept of containment, or knew what the term "Camp David Accords" referred to.
- Only one in five nine-year-olds can perform even basic mathematical operations (Sykes, 1995; Bennett, 1992; Schlesinger, 1992; Ravitch & Finn, 1988).

And this is only the tip of the iceberg. The director of the National Right to Read Foundation argues that, "In practice, what the child believe[s] and [feels has become] more important than what he [knows], and schooling [has become] a process of 'changing students' fixed beliefs . . . instead of imparting substantive knowledge" (Woods, 1996).

Without entering the stramash of argument about why these problems persist (and even granting that some of these charges may be overstated), all critics agree that the problems in high school education are real, and that their long-term solutions are critical to the future success of this country. Suddenly, that headline of librarians calling to move the Civil War to a century they are more likely to pick, isn't as ludicrous as, perhaps, at first.

SURMOUNTING THE INSURMOUNTABLE

Is it possible to overcome these potential deleterious effects? One hopes so. But consider the long-term effects of such a problem, however small. If incoming high school graduates are, indeed, poorly prepared, where will they gain this education? In college? If they complete college and go to graduate school, is it reasonable to expect them to "catch up" in library school? We've already established that prospect is not possible. Library school education, for all the bad that has been written about it, really is neither intended for such a purpose, nor constructed in such a way as to be capable of delivering it, even if required (Rothstein, 1985). Moreover, the very nature of library schools these days is more likely to turn out "machine tickling aphids" (Butler, 1955). This is not meant to be a term of contempt, though it may sound like one. Many library schools *intend* to produce technologically astute graduates. Additionally, many library employers *purposely* search for graduates who can hit the technological ground running. Nothing, of course, is wrong with this approach. But it will do libraries precious little good if reference librarians can master zip drives with ease, FTP files while blindfolded, string together the most complicated of search statements while ghosting dumb terminals, if they search for limpid proteins in *America: History and Life*.

ELEMENTARY MY DEAR WATSON!

Some might rebut in this manner: "A weak high school background, while regretable, can be overcome with a good four years in college. Many young people mature appropriately in college and end better than they began." This is a compelling argument, but is it true? If a good portion of the reference librarian's library education comes after she is on the job, where is she to learn all that should have come before if not in high school and college (Stabler, 1987; Woodward, 1995; Cromer & Testi, 1994; Rothstein, 1989; Avenick, 1993)? If the high school education proves weak, and college not much better, what future is there for reference librarians? Will we not be driving people to the Internet in spite of ourselves? How will it is be possible for the newly minted reference librarian to learn everything about reference work when her general education is at best spotty, at worse, abject?

Are the college years a good proving ground to make up for the inadequacies of a weak high school background, or are those years, too, intellectually undemanding?

Consider a handful of some important facts. In 1914, required or mandatory courses numbered about 10; today's average is barely more than three. In 1914, the number of universities that did not have any required prerequisites numbered on 23. Today that number exceeds 600. Today only 12% of the very best institutions require a thesis or comprehensive examination for a Bachelor's. Just 30 years ago, more than half did. So also has the academic year been shortened, from a high of just over 200 days in 1914, to barely over 150 today (National Association of Scholars, 1996). Gallup reported that one in seven adults cannot find the United States on a blank map of the world. Only 21% of college graduates knew that Plato wrote *The Republic,* while 71% could not identify Martin Luther as the founder of Protestantism. In fact, so bad has it become, that at least one well-known intellectual has called for parents to consider keeping their college-aged children at home (Kirk, 1993).

Advising the college-aged to stay at home is, perhaps, a bit extreme. But the caution is well-taken, for over the last decade we have seen education dollars surpass the trillion mark. Yet we are at the crossroads of a rising American generation, the first such, by the way, who will know less intellectually than their parents.

The point is belabored to underscore not only how very important continuing education is and will become for the newly minted reference librarian, but also how grim the education situation is becoming, and how ominous the cloud that darkens the reference desk's horizon. Cromer and Testi say it well: "Cultivating an atmosphere of life-long learning, continuing education, and self-evaluation for reference personnel is essential in responding to and anticipating challenges" (Cromer & Testi, 1994). Of course, this may prove difficult when the first 15 or 16 years of formative education are generally unexceptional. Woodward seconds Cromer and Testi by arguing convincingly that "reference librarians are made, not born" (Woodward, 1995). But to newly minted reference librarians, this does not come as news. Already many of you, on the job for the first month or two, are finding out the hard way how little you learned in library school. Indeed, in survey after survey, you have complained that your library education was poor and that its depth was shallow (Stabler, 1987). What may be more difficult to admit, however, is that the general education you received may not have been as rigorous as you'll soon discover you'll need to be successful at the reference desk. Practical library education–even down to the training in the myriad of reference sources–will come with time on the job. What will be harder to master, however, will be placing the Carlist Wars under Queen Isabella when one doesn't even know what the Carlist wars were, who fought them when, or in what century they occurred.

Certainly one complaint that will be made is that no reference librarian can know everything. This is both unquestionably true and irrefutably banal. The fact of the matter is this: Good reference librarians are polymaths, are jacks-of-all-trades and may even master one or two. But the best are know-it-alls in the literal sense of that phrase. With a continuing attenuation of general education requirements ongoing in both high school and college, the need for additional education beyond the library science degree will not only become necessary, but may become so critical as to crowd out all else.

NOW HE TELLS ME!

No, not really. Much of the fallout of the decline–however great or small in general education–is likely to show up in the *next* generation of reference librarians, or so say a few dozen library experts. The issue does raise an important point, however: Continuing education may be required on *two* fronts in order to equip the reference librarian of tomorrow with the proper intellectual panache to handle the job at the reference desk. While it is possible that both the newly minted reference librarian and the undergraduate she serves will be in the same boat intellectually, it does not need to become, nor can we ever allow it to become, a case where the blind are leading the blind. For now, the important thing to remember is that it is likely your undergraduate education (not to mention your high school education) left you with some blind spots, perhaps many, perhaps only a few. The need to embrace lifelong learning becomes, now, more essential, even *sine qua non,* than ever before.

The good news is that many of your employers and future employers not only feel you are well-educated, but that you come to libraries or to library school ready to hit the ground running. While one would not want to dismiss entirely a "Lake Wobegon" effect here (i.e., *our* reference librarians are fine; others, however, need a stronger background), the fact remains that newly minted reference librarians–those educated in the last five years–are adequately prepared.

For this article, more than two dozen reference heads, directors, deans of library services and heads of library schools were surveyed in an effort to find out where we now stand with respect to this potential problem: "Are incoming reference librarians weaker academically than their predecessors?" Granted, this survey amounts to little more than anecdotal information, but it should serve as a guide or benchmark for the future. There is much good news to report. For example, when asked, "In your opinion, is the general, non-library education of your (students or recent hirees) very good, generally good, spotty, not very good, or poor?" most said it was good. While two deans of library service indicated a growing concern over general education requirements, others were more optimistic.

One reference head wrote, "The general non-library education of our students and our recent hirees that work for us at the reference desk is very good. This is probably thanks to the admission standards . . . and the fact that we would not hire someone to work professionally in reference who did not have an excellent general education background." Another reference head was more guarded: "I think the general education of recent hirees is generally good." Yet another correspondent answered in this wise: "I find that as a rough breakdown the non-library education is very important, especially from those people with liberal arts backgrounds. The level of resourcefulness seems to be the critical issue there. It's a characteristic that will make a decent reference librarian great once they get the chance to apply it." A provost at a major institution reported that recent hirees were, "generally good and sometimes very good." Others expressed the hope that the non-library education would improve and that library school students would realize early on the critical importance of that education to both their success and longevity in the profession. One library dean wrote ruefully that the "non-library education . . . was spotty. They seem to be technically proficient and quick to learn but I worry about their ability to spell correctly, write coherent sentences, think critically, etc."

Another question sought to gather opinions on whether the explosion of technology in this profession had left reference librarians for the 21st century masters of both machine and intellect, or merely machine efficient. Again, respondents were by and large positive. One reference head said, "21st century librarians must understand when to use print and when to use electronic resources. What many people outside reference fail to grasp is that this is not an either/or. Most of our questions involve using print and electronic sources together to come to the best answers." Another wrote, "21st century librarians will have to be masters of both machine and intellect." A library dean replied, "[Reference librarians] are more [technology efficient]. Too often [the machine monomania] sidetracks the best of us. We apply technology because 'we can' sometimes before we think it out. . . . The technology is in our face so we use that tool first just because it's the one we have in our hand at the time." Finally, another library head remarked that, "We see in some candidates a strong technical orientation to the exclusion of other content and values. We tend not to hire these people because there are always more balanced candidates in our pools. I would not use the phrase 'masters' of both machine and intellect, however, but they are generally well-educated, curious, well-informed and intellectually vibrant people." Another added, "While public service librarians . . . may not be towering intellects I do think that most of them read, take additional graduate courses, and are trying to be intellectual as well as technological."

In an effort to get at what may be perceived as a dichotomy between the reference librarian as polymath, and the reference librarian as "tekkie," respondents were asked if modern librarianship had "matured" beyond the need for reference librarians on the order of reference *extraordinaire* Francis Neel Cheney, or if technology had made such reference librarians not only less possible, but also less practicable. The answers were as varied as the respondents.

One wrote, "It is not technology that has made the need for master reference librarians less possible, it is the explosion of information and the specialization that has accompanied growth. Even the increase of multinational enterprise has meant that no one can be expert on all of it. In small libraries and especially in public libraries, a single knowledgeable reference librarian is still a great resource, but collaboration is essential in meeting the reference demands of an academic library." Another correspondent added, "Technology is enlarging and improving librarianship's basic philosophical base, but in the meantime we are operating on a more mechanical philosophical base." Another wrote, "Most recent library school graduates have very little understanding of librarianship's intellectual issues. They certainly do not know what is expected of them as tenure-track library faculty. A long-standing complaint of mine is that library schools do such a poor job of immersing their students in the field of literature. Recent librarians, and their more experienced colleagues, for that matter, do not know their own literature."

Finally, in an effort to get at what, in the long run, great technological advances might mean at the expense of intellectual acquisition, correspondents were asked if technology would make reference librarians more important than ever, or if increasingly user-friendly technology would slowly make obsolete the reference librarian. While many answered that technology will only make the reference librarian more needed than ever, two provided more thoughtful, if ominous answers. One wrote, "We will evolve into educators, teaching our users how to choose and evaluate resources, and how to navigate through free and proprietary information. Over time we will lose many of our customers who are happy with a quick answer, any answer, when they have a question." Another added, "[W]e have revived the for-credit library instruction course with nearly 20 sections offered last year. If we had more instructors we could offer even more sections and still not meet the demand." Perhaps the most thoughtful respondent wrote, "I am beginning to wonder more and more about the future of the traditional reference librarian. I believe we as a profession could lose our role unless we take control of the new information environment and continue to be the experts on finding information regardless of the medium. I don't think we will be totally replaced because it is very obvious at the reference desk that people still need someone to explain the use of whatever holds the information they want." Indeed. If the first part of this article–the discussion about the future intellectual equipment of not only future reference librarians but all college graduates is true, the competent reference librarian may indeed prove to be worth her weight in gold.

The matter, however, should give all of us involved intimately in reference service, or indeed in any part of librarianship, pause. Although *Hotbot, Yahoo!, AltaVista, Excite, Inference Find, Profusion, DogPile, Starting Point* and the like may be awkward to use, search in very unsystematic ways as far as librarians are concerned, and are filled with glitches and risible indexing mistakes no first-month library school student would ever make, they are also cheap, not given to moody outbursts, not forever complaining about their low pay or endless hours, and not subject to emotional outbursts for any reason. It may serve the newly minted reference librarian well to remember this when the 500th patron walks up and asks where he might find the *Encyclopedia Britannica*.

QUO VADIS?

So, where do we go from here? If we grant that future reference librarians may indeed enter the profession a step or two behind their modern-day counterparts, what is the possible solution? Offered below are just a few things that reference librarians can do to stay both current and aware. And in the unlikely event that any current reference librarians just entering the profession find their own education to be lacking, consider this a prescription for remediation. Some will no doubt seem too facile to mention. But as a wiser man than I said, "What is known is not always obvious, and what is obvious is not always present" (McAdam & Milne, 1963).

Read

It seems so simple as to be simple-minded (as no doubt some will call it) and yet there is hardly *anything* more important. Reading as used here isn't pleasure reading but what will help the budding reference librarian do her job better. Of course, news weeklies obtain. But more contemplative materials are also important. For example, magazines like *Commentary* or *The New Criterion* are both difficult to read and assume a general knowledge of world events. But they offer far more in-depth reading than almost anything else around. *Newsweek* and *Time* are important, but the morning newspaper will serve just as well, and perhaps better. The more difficult reading will provide connections where there weren't any before.

Reading also refers to monographs, not novels. Of course, many like to read the latest fiction best-seller, but its intellectual advantages are, by and large, marginal.[2] Even the most popular of fiction writers may not enlarge one's mind beyond one's ken. For that, the reader will have to move to more advanced reading. For example, if one finds one's education lacking in American history, Paul Johnson's

Modern Times is hard to beat. If it's European history, Norman Davies's *Europe* is not only entertaining but also comprehensive (Davies, 1996).[3] Of course, many librarians are already familiar with Daniel Boorstin's books and know these make great reading for the subjects treated.

One cannot overlook E. D. Hirsch's *Cultural Literacy: What Every American Needs to Know* (Hirsch, 1987). Of course there is controversy surrounding this book, not the least of which is whether its contents really constitute what an educated person should know. But the book is perfect for catching up on those things we know, those things we think we know, and the many we thought we knew. Biographies, especially those now being written, are more than useful, not only for the subject being treated, but for the subject matter that surrounds the figure or figures central to the volume's contents (Strouse, 1998; Chernow, 1998; Gibson, 1998; Eisler, 1999; Kennedy, 1999). Such tomes are generally quite expansive and range much beyond the narrow subject of the book's title.

Enroll in Graduate Level Courses

Graduate education appears, for now anyway, less susceptible to the virus infecting high school and undergraduate education. Of course, this is not exclusively true. Education programs throughout the country are notorious for their weak content and intellectually unrigorous demands. For now, most graduate programs at accredited colleges and universities still offer students a chance to learn, and learn a lot. The best way to take these courses is *not* to audit them where the full academic rigor may be by-passed or omitted altogether, but to sign up for credit and work as hard as one can. Many reference librarians who have worked for me have found great advantages to this fact and have come away better reference librarians for it.

Applied science courses in the undergraduate program may also prove useful, but even here there is a cautionary tale (Sokal & Bricmont).[4] Courses in computer science, for example, may prove useful for some, but only if they extend beyond the newly minted reference librarian's knowledge. Likely she is already well-versed in these areas and will not need any more training.

Continuing Education Courses

Courses available in the community might also provide the newly minted reference librarian some help in updating or completing his education. These courses must be chosen carefully, however. Courses that do not also offer continuing education units should be avoided. Again, there are bound to be computer-related courses offered in surfeit but the newly minted reference librarian is likely to have had her fill of them. Older reference librarians could probably do with a refresher, and some even with the basics. The fare of continuing education courses offered at nearby universities may prove the best bet. Community colleges are likely to be offering courses geared to a different clientele.

Collaborate Often with Colleagues

Readers will note this rubric says nothing about meetings (for that, see below). Collaboration here means working together with other reference librarians, especially those who have been at it for a few years. The returns one reaps will enrich the newly minted reference librarian's experience and knowledge base. If the reference tyro can arrange to work on an article with a veteran reference librarian, so much the better. If this sounds a lot like mentoring that is only because it is. But it is mentoring in a little bit different fashion, with strict goals and palpable outcomes. Mentoring just to be meeting with another more seasoned reference librarian will have *some* rewards. In the long run, however, those rewards will seem few and far between when charged against one's time and energy. It's better to structure the mentoring arrangement and specify goals and measurable outcomes to make certain success follows. Of course, such an arrangement does not guarantee success, but it at least establishes the conditions for success and more often than not, as night follows day, success will follow good planning and hard work.

Go to Professional Meetings Sparingly

Having served in this profession for nearly two decades now, I can say with some assurance that after having attended scores of professional meetings, everything from local groups, to national conferences, I have rarely gotten out of them what I invested in them in time, cost and preparation. I wish this were merely anecdotal but scores of others have expressed to me the same sentiment. And yet, we continue to go. Hope does spring eternal. Nothing will discourage the newly minted reference librarian more than to hear that attendance at such conferences yields less than desired, unless of course she actually attends one and finds out for herself. There are exceptions to every rule, and the carefully chosen conference, the carefully chosen professional meeting, may equal the perfect outcome for the new reference librarian. The key here is the adverb: Choose *carefully.*

While these five areas will certainly improve one's education, they cannot replace a general education that has yielded a less than optimum result. The good news is that so far, anyway, newly minted reference librarians continue to enter the profession with reasonably strong backgrounds, backgrounds capable enough of making their first year in service to the profession a real and important contribution. But evidences of a weakening high school and undergraduate education, however small now, should at least sound the alarm for those in library service everywhere. Librarians, and not just reference librarians, need to pay more attention to this matter, and, whenever they can, particularly those serving academic institutions, should do all that is in their power to help improve undergraduate education. It is, after all, what librarianship has been about for centuries: providing a service that enhances and augments the education of others.

NOTES

1. The authors have spleen to vent against just about everyone in the academy from the right, to the moderate, to the left. Their point is a sobering one: When ideologies interfere, education ceases. They show that in their speciality, Physics, the problem is reaching critical mass, so to speak.

2. One well-known example is Umberto Eco's *Name of the Rose,* a book that is an education in itself!

3. One caveat must be added here, however. Davies did make a few factual mistakes, more than he ought to have in this book. But given its scope (more than 1,300 pages) these *lapsus linqua* should be overlooked.

4. Sokal and Bricmont's book, for example, offers a stunning display of the slipshod thinking and outrageous statement now being made with respect to the mathematical science by *soi-disant* academicians. When educated people can get by with saying that gravity is merely a verbal construct–and not have their hands called, or be laughed out of the academic square–you know the orchard is in trouble in the groves of academe.

BIBLIOGRAPHY

Avenick, Karen (1993), "Orientation to the Reference Desk," *New Jersey Libraries,* 26 (1), 26-28.

Bennett, William J. (1992), *The De-Valuing of America: The Fight for Our Culture and Our Children,* Summit Books.

Bishop, William (1912), "Training in the Use of Books," *Sewanee Review* 20 (July): 280.

Blenkinsopp, Heather (1992), "How's the Water? The Training of Reference Librarians," *The Reference Librarian* 38, 175-181.

Butler, Samuel (1955), *Erewhon and Erewhon Revisited,* New York: Modern Library.

Chernow, Ron (1998), *Titan: The Life of John D. Rockefeller, Sr.,* New York: Random House.

Chubb, John and Moe, Terry (1990), *Politics, Markets and America's Schools,* Washington: Brookings.

Cromer, Donna E. and Testi, Andrea R. (1994), "Integrated Continuing Education for Reference Librarians," *Reference Services Review* 22 (4), 51-58, 80.

D'Aniello, Charles A. (Spring 1989), "Cultural Literacy and Reference Service," *RQ* 28, 370-380.

D'Souza, Dinesh (1991), *Illiberal Education: The Politics of Race and Sex on Campus,* New York: Free Press.

Davies, Norman (1996), *Europe: A History,* Oxford: Oxford University Press.

Dougherty, Richard M. [et al.] (1984), *Libraries and the Learning Society: Papers in Response to A Nation at Risk,* Chicago: American Library Association.

Eisler, Benita (1999), *Byron–Child of Passion, Fool of Fame,* New York: Alfred A. Knopf.

Finney, Joni (1992), *At the Crossroads: Linking Teacher Education to School Reform,* Denver: Education Commission of the States.

Frazier, Calvin (1993), *A Shared Vision: Policy Recommendations for Linking Teacher Education to School Reform,* Denver: Education Commission of the States.

Gibson, Ian (1998), *The Shameful Life of Salvador Dali,* New York: W. W. Norton.

Henry, William A. (1994), *In Defense of Elitism,* New York: Doubleday.

Hermon, Peter and McClure, Charles (1986), "Unobtrusive Reference Testing: The 55 Percent Rule," *Library Journal* 111 (April 15), 37-41.

Hirsch, E. D. (1996), *The Schools We Need and Why We Don't Have Them,* New York: Doubleday.

Katz, William A. (1990), *Continuing Education of Reference Librarians*, The Haworth Press, Inc.

Kennedy, Michael (1999), *Richard Strauss: Man, Musician, Enigma,* Cambridge: Cambridge University Press.

Kilpatrick, William (1992), *Why Johnny Can't Tell Right From Wrong,* New York: Simon & Schuster.

Kimball, Roger (1990), *Tenured Radicals,* New York: Harper & Row.

Kirk, Russell (1993), "The Lunatic American Campus," *St. Croix Review* 26 (5), 43-49.

Kramer, Rita (1991), *Ed School Follies: The Miseducation of America's Teachers,* New York: Free Press.

McAdam, E. L. Jr. and Milne, George (1963), *Johnson's Dictionary: A Modern Selection,* New York: Pantheon Books.

McGuinness, Diane (1997), *Why Our Children Can't Read: And What We Can Do About It,* New York: Free Press.

Marsden, George (1994), *The Soul of the American University: From Protestant Establishment to Established Nonbelief,* New York: Oxford University Press.

National Association of Scholars (1996), *The Dissolution of General Education: 1914-1993,* Princeton, NJ: National Association of Scholars.

Nofsinger, Mary M. and Lee, Angela S. W. (March 1994), "Beyond Orientation: The Roles of Senior Librarians in Training Entry-Level Reference Colleagues," *College & Research Libraries, 55,* 161-170.

Ravitch, Diane and Finn, Chester (1988), *What Do Seventeen Year Olds Know? A Report on the First National Assessment of History and Literature,* New York: Harper & Row.

Roche, George (1994), *The Fall of the Ivory Tower: Government Funding, Corruption, and the Bankrupting of American Higher Education,* Washington: Regnery Press.

Rothstein, Samuel (1989), "The Making of a Reference Librarian," *The Reference Librarian* (Nos. 25-26): 321-350.

______. (1985), "Why People Really Hate Library Schools," *Library Journal* 110 (April 1), 41-48.

Schlesinger, Arthur (1992), *The Disuniting of America,* New York: Norton.

Sherrer, Johannah (1996), "Thriving in Changing Times: Competencies for Today's Reference Librarians," *The Reference Librarian* 54, 11-20.

Sizer, Theodore (1996), *Horace's Hope: What Works for the American High School,* New York: Houghton Mifflin.

Sokal, Alan and Bricmont, Jean (1998), *Fashionable Nonsense: Postmodern Intellectuals' Abuse of Science,* New York: Picador.

Sowell, Thomas (1993), *Inside American Education: The Decline, The Deception, The Dogmas,* New York: Macmillan.

Spang, Lothar (1996), "A Staff-Generated Cross-Training Plan for Academic Reference Librarians: The TQM Approach at Wayne State University Libraries," *Reference Services Review* 24 (2), 77-85.

Stabler, Karen C. (Spring 1987), "Introductory Training of Academic Reference Librarians: A Survey," *RQ* 26, 363-369.

Stam, Deirdre C. (Winter 1992), "What Reference Librarians Need to know," *The Bookmark* 50, 173-179.

Stotsky, Sandra (1999), *Losing Our Language: How Multicultural Classroom Instruction Is Undermining Our Children's Ability to Read, Write, and Reason,* New York: Free Press.

Strouse, Jean (1999), *Morgan: An American Financier,* New York: Random House.

Sykes, Charles (1995), *Dumbing Down Our Kids: Why America's Children Feel Good About Themselves But Can't Read, Write, or Add,* New York: St. Martin's Press.

United States. National Commission on Excellence in Education (1983), *A Nation at Risk: The Imperative for Educational Reform: A Report to the Nation and the*

Secretary of Education, United States Department of Education, Washington, DC: The Commission.

Weingand, Darlene E. (1994), "Competence and the New Paradigm: Continuing Education of the Reference Staff," *The Reference Librarian* 43, 173-182.

Wirt, Frederick (1989), *Schools in Conflict: The Politics of Education,* Berkeley, CA: McCutchan.

Wogaman, Mariol R. (January 1992), "Training Newly Appointed Reference Librarians," *College & Research Libraries News,* 8-9.

Woods, Regina (1996), "Open Letter," *National Review* (September 30), 49.

Woodward, Beth S. (1991), *Training, Development, and Continuing Education for the Reference Staff,* Littleton, CO: Libraries Unlimited.

______. (1995), "Reference Staff Training and Development," In *Reference and Information Services: An Introduction,* edited by Richard E. Bopp and Linda C. Smith. Littleton, CO: Libraries Unlimited.

Phyllostachys Aurea– Didn't He Work with Socrates? Reference Work in Science Libraries by Librarians Who Are Not Scientists

James Morris-Knower

SUMMARY. Over half of all science librarians do not have science degrees. The author–one of these non-science science librarians–offers some stories and some advice about how a humanities major navigates the complex world of reference work in a science library. *[Article copies available for a fee from The Haworth Document Delivery Service: 1-800-342-9678. E-mail address: <getinfo@haworthpressinc.com> Website: <http://www.HaworthPress.com> © 2001 by The Haworth Press, Inc. All rights reserved.]*

KEYWORDS. Science libraries, science librarians, humanities

James Morris-Knower is Reference/Public Services Librarian, Albert R. Mann Library, Cornell University, Ithaca, NY 14853 (E-mail: jpk15@cornell.edu).

[Haworth co-indexing entry note]: "Phyllostachys Aurea–Didn't He Work with Socrates? Reference Work in Science Libraries by Librarians Who Are Not Scientists." Morris-Knower, James. Co-published simultaneously in *The Reference Librarian* (The Haworth Information Press, an imprint of The Haworth Press, Inc.) No. 72, 2001, pp. 155-169; and: *Doing the Work of Reference: Practical Tips for Excelling as a Reference Librarian* (ed: Celia Hales Mabry) The Haworth Information Press, an imprint of The Haworth Press, Inc., 2001, pp. 155-169. Single or multiple copies of this article are available for a fee from The Haworth Document Delivery Service [1-800-342-9678, 9:00 a.m. - 5:00 p.m. (EST). E-mail address: getinfo@haworthpressinc.com].

> *Reference departments (of science libraries) are filled with librarians with social science and humanities degrees who provide adequate library services to sci-tech and engineering students. However, this basic service is not meeting the needs of faculty and research staff whose time and energy are valuable assets.*
>
> –Crit. Stuart and Miriam Drake, 1992

After a somewhat contentious public services meeting recently, a colleague of mine let out an exasperated sigh and said, "I think the group has really changed a lot in the past few years." Not sure what he was referring to, I responded good-naturedly, "What, have we become more right wing?" "No," he said, "It's just that in the past I think we were more analytical. Now we're more touchy feel-ey. I think it's the English major effect." He turned to me. "No offense."

THE ENGLISH MAJOR EFFECT

Yes, I'm one of those–a fuzzy-headed humanities guy with course work in 17th century religious poetry and the western films of John Ford and Howard Hawks. Before receiving my MILS from the University of Michigan in 1997, I got a PhD in American Culture from Michigan and a BA in English from Hobart College.

My current position is as a public services/reference librarian at Cornell University's Albert R. Mann Library. Mann serves the College of Agriculture and Life Sciences (CALS), the College of Human Ecology, and the Division of Nutritional Sciences. Of the 20 departments and programs we serve, eight are more or less social science fields–ranging from human development to communication–and 12 are "hard" sciences–like plant pathology and animal science. In general the ag and life sciences departments are bigger than those in the social sciences, and the library's collections and reference questions "feel" about 70% science vs. 30% social science.

And yet here I am, a dyed-in-the-wool film and literature guy working with patrons asking questions about tomato blight and chicken sexing. And I'm not alone–the English major effect at Mann is clear when you look at the background of the library's reference staff. Of the 14 or so regular reference staff members, only six–or about 40%–have either degrees or substantial coursework in science (my exasperated colleague being one of them). The rest of us are a mixed bag of non-science majors, including English lit, anthropology, and psychology.

These numbers are pretty much in line with national statistics for the past 10 to 15 years. In 1983 Ellis Mount published his oft-quoted study of 16 sci/tech college libraries which showed that only 46% of the librarians had degrees in scientific or technical subjects (Mount, 1985). A 1993 report presented at the annual SLA conference documented that at California public university libraries, about two-thirds of the librarians did not have a science background (Liu and Wei, 1993). And a 1995 survey of SLA members working in engineering environments found that less than one-third had any kind of science degree (Mosley, 1995).

Which is all to say there are more people like me working in science libraries than not. Is this a problem? Is this a crisis we in the library community should be addressing by recruiting more science types? Is there anything that can be done to help folks like me do a better job serving a community with whom we don't share much of an intellectual background?

These are good questions, but I'm not going to address all of them here. What I will do is show how I serve a particular community of scientists by offering some anecdotes from the trenches and specific tips I've learned along the way. It's all meant to reassure librarians, especially new and prospective science librarians without science backgrounds, that you can do a fine job without that degree. It just takes a little practice.

Very little has been written about how librarians like myself actually do reference work in science libraries and how we might do it even better. While in the past 15 years there have been about a dozen articles in library journals addressing the fact that most science librarians do not have science degrees, almost all focus on the crisis and problem angles. They are usually either calls to action about the lack of science majors in library schools (one provocative proposal is to drop the library science requirement for science librarians and recruit science majors straight out of college) or debates about the worthiness of librarians without science degrees working in science libraries (many conclude we are not worthy).

Articles about the "crisis" are the most numerous. An entire 1998 issue of *Science & Technology Libraries* (where most of these debates go on) was devoted to how to better prepare librarians for science library careers *before* they become librarians. These articles, which avoid the hand-wringing tone of some of the earlier writing on this topic, focus on new directions in formal educational programs (subject-oriented coursework, concentrations, and certificate programs) to educate library students thinking of careers in health sciences, geoscience, chemistry, and engineering. Earlier articles which also look at the education and recruitment of science librarians include Susan Vazakas and Camille Wallin's 1992 article "Where Are All the Science Librarians?" and Donald Frank's 1989 article "Education for Librarians in a Major Science-Engineering Library: Expectations and Reality."

Where the literature gets more heated and contentious is when the question isn't simply "What can we do?" but rather "What can we do about this *problem*?" The problem here is the English major effect: The majority of science librarians, while being perfectly fine librarians, are not really qualified to be *science* librarians. The epigraph which opens this article, which comes from Crit. Stuart and Miriam Drake's 1992 *Science & Technology Libraries* article "Education and Recruitment of Science and Engineering Librarians," is a succinct summary of this position. They argue that non-science librarians are not serving scientists well enough because the latter group avoids such librarians as "unproven sources." Thus we need to recruit more librarians with science backgrounds; ways to do this include dropping the MLS requirement and increasing the pay for science librarians.

A similar tone is found in one of the earliest articles I found on this topic, Robert Krupp's 1984 article "What Education is Best?" The question asked is what education is best for science librarians, and the answer has something to do with face: Namely, non-science librarians need to ask patrons to clarify questions that a scientist would never have to ask. This can cause the patron to lose confidence and respect for the librarian.

To show what he means, Krupp offers as an introduction a series of factual questions like *"Where are fast breeder reactors used in Asia?"* and *"Which university is doing current research on MHD?"* Krupp says of such questions:

> The task of helping the inquirer is not impossible for a librarian with a very minimal science training, but, since there is a good possibility that readers who may ask such a question will also

> have a science background, any questions asked by the librarian to clarify the query may cause the reader to lose a certain amount of confidence.

The implication is simple: A good science librarian will have the background to know off the top of her head that "mhd" refers to magnets (magnetohydronamics to be precise) and fast breeder reactors are in the realm of nuclear science. When a science patron walks to the reference desk and asks me such a question, however, I will . . . panic. And lose face with the patron. And down the slope we go.

I know I sound a little defensive here. When confronted with such arguments, I find myself pressed to counter with a resounding affirmation of my ability to do a good job. While the focus of this article is not to debate whether current science librarian demographics are a problem, the defensive tone creeps in almost unconsciously. It's as if I feel the need to respond to some underlying "No you can't" with an extended, almost childlike "Yes I can. Really."

This defense of the "unproven sources" is also found in those few articles which actually offer specific advice and tips to the non-science science librarian. In their 1994 article "Issues Related to the Education and Recruitment of Science/Technology Librarians," Paula Storm and Wei Wei argue that the importance of a science degree is less important for science librarians today than it once was. This is mainly because the rise of networked digital information means that most scientists can now get answers to specific factual questions themselves through their computers. Storm and Wei offer some general tips for non-science librarians such as working with an experienced science librarian, reading science journals and attending science lectures. Their argument is summarized in this sentence: "A degree in one of the sciences may be beneficial, but the skills crucial to the success of the sci/tech librarian in the near future will have little relation to knowing how to dissect a frog or design a car engine" (Storm and Wei). Amen.

Donald Frank and Christine Kollen also defend the role of humanities and social science librarians in sci/tech libraries in their 1989 article "Humanities and Social Sciences Librarians in the Science-Engineering Library: Utilization and Implications for Effective Collection Development and Reference Services." The keys to effective service by non-science librarians, they argue, are rapport with patrons, a willingness to refer difficult questions, and knowledge of how to successfully place reference questions in appropriate scientific fields or disciplines.

And in her 1984 article "The Making of a Science Librarian," Kathleen Haselbauer offers some of the most extensive advice for making good science librarians out of non-scientists (a group, she admits, that includes herself). Her list, like those of Storm and Wei, and Frank and Kollen, is right on target while somewhat short on details: You must understand what science is and what scientists do, know the structure of a science discipline from its earliest discoveries, acquaint yourself with basic references, do citation analysis to trace developments in research areas, and produce annotated research guides for students. In a direct rebuttal to the sort of argument offered by Stuart and Drake, and Krupp, Haselbauer asserts that in terms of rapport, "the better scientists I have known have never been averse to requesting the service of skilled and intuitive librarians, regardless of degree" (Haselbauer, 115).

This is all excellent advice, and here I'd like to add some of my own. None of this is exactly revolutionary–just some (hopefully good) advice from one struggling to be an effective science librarian. It's one more voice in the choir of "Yes we can," which shouldn't need a revolution anyway.

Let me start with fear. It is fear which is generated by a list of factual scientific questions like the one offered by Krupp as the sort of "typical" thing you'll run into at the reference desk. I'll admit it's been my nightmare since I starting working at Mann Library that a bearded grad student in Birkenstocks and a frayed Fisherman's sweater will come to the reference desk and say, "Hi. Can you tell me what the refractive index increments of proteins like thyroglobulin and ovalbumin are?" These kinds of questions–about thyroglobulin or mhd–generate fear because I honestly don't know what they refer to or if they're even in English.

But here's lesson #1, which is pretty much the heart of what I'm getting at here: Factual questions like these don't get asked as often as you might think, and when they do you can effectively answer them without knowing right away what they mean. With most of the reference work in a science library, you don't really need to be a forester or environmental scientist; you need to be a *good reference librarian*. (What you are far more likely to get at the reference desk is a patron asking you, "Can you find this?" with *this* being a book or article for which he or she has an incomplete citation or the citation is complete but it's some obscure government publication which they can't seem to find, like an article from the *Technical Note* of the Forest Department of Zambia or a 1974 EPA report on Cayuga Lake from the National Environmental Research Center in Las Vegas.)

I'd like to share a tough-reference-question-at-the-desk tale of my own, a true story, warts and all. This is dedicated to anyone whose dreams occasionally entail visits by shadowy figures asking for a good reverse-phase high-performance liquid chromatographic method for analyzing complex mixtures of triglycerides in aged cheese, followed by an almost primordial desire on your part to run.

Scene: It's April, near the end of the term and final exams at Cornell. A young woman comes up to me at the reference desk, looking like either she's got the flu or she's pretty frustrated with her final Bio 204 research project, or both. She tells me, quickly, that she needs specific applications of immunology, like protein purification. "I don't need just a book on immunology. I need a specific application."

This is where the humanities librarian is supposed to panic. And I really don't know what protein purification or immunology are. Instead of panicking (o.k., I panic just a bit), I do this: I try a little active listening, hoping that this will elicit further clarification of what she's after. I say something like, "Sounds like you're looking for specific applications of immunology," to which she replies "Yes." That's all. "What specifically about immunology are you looking for?" "Specific applications, like protein purification."

My mind is spinning her, thinking about what immunology means. I know the suffix *ology* suggests the study of something–in this case an immuno or immunos. Could this be related to immunization, the study of protection from viruses like polio and hepatitis b which my 9-month-old daughter just got at the pediatrician? I have a feeling not, though I'm not going to ask her this; she has given me this deadpan, slightly annoyed expression throughout our exchange.

It's after the second interaction, however, that I pick up on the words "protein purification." A clue! I turn to the on-line catalog and do a key word search for immunology and protein purification. I luck out and get one record for a book on "immunoadsorbents in protein purification" which is part of a series from *The Scandinavian Journal of Immunology.* I disregard the Greek and Latin parts and focus on the subject heading: proteins–purification. I do a subject search for this and get 20 records. I show this to the patron and explain to her how I got them. She hesitates, as if waiting for me to volunteer to go fetch these references for her, but then thanks me and walks off.

While knowing nothing of protein purification, I am able to help this patron by using solid (and basic) information retrieval skills. Skills like conducting a reference interview, just as you learned in library school (it really does help), and using the on-line catalog as a tool for more than just finding call numbers. I wonder why so many skeptics worry about the loss of face when I ask a question, when one of the foundations of good reference work is the belief that what your patron really wants often lies hidden underneath the fat blanket which is his first question. You use active listening (rephrasing the question) and open-ended questions (which encourage the patron to reply with something other than yes or no) to help you pick that heavy thing off and find out what's really underneath. Usually the reference interview allows me to get the patron to supply me with the additional information I need without having to confess to them that I haven't a clue about what they're talking about.

Another very basic tool I used here was the on-line catalog, which we sometimes forget is an excellent way to dig up clues about the plain English meaning of subjects like protein purification or fast breeder reactors. The clues you get–abstracts, publishers, L.C. subject headings, library location–can be used to determine where to turn next for the answer. A keyword search in the catalog for fast breeder reactors, for example, tells me that the subject heading is "Liquid metal fast breeder reactors" and that several titles are published by the International Atomic Energy Agency. *Nuclear science.* A search on MHD brings up 68 records with subject headings like "Fluid dynamics" and "Magnetohydrodynamics." *Magnets.* It's enough to get started.

I think it's important to note here that this sort of searching in an electronic database was all but impossible for librarians in 1984 when Krupp wrote "What Education is Best?" Digital technology is making our patrons more self-sufficient and at the same time giving librarians the ability to instantaneously find the sort of information that would remain hidden in the card catalog if we didn't know the exact Dewey or L.C. subject headings (try looking up MHD in a card catalog).

So here comes my graduate student with his hydroglobulin and ovalbumin. In real life, this guy would not tell me that these were proteins; that would be too easy. So I would ask him an open-ended question ("How are you going to use this information?") or come straight out and ask what they are or what field they are part of. Or I could do a quick keyword search and find out that they are in fact proteins and their L.C. subject heading is Proteins–Synthesis. As far as asking my patron a question, I certainly don't want to sound like an unqualified idiot but neither do I worry about losing face by asking for more information.

Of course, knowing these are proteins isn't enough to get the patron what he's after. Once I feel that I know what we're talking about, I can turn to another tool in the proverbial chest of knowledge: some good friends in the reference collection.

I can safely and authoritatively tell you that the answer to my graduate student's question is "It depends." I also know that more details than this can be found in the tables on pages 372-382 of *The Handbook of Biochemistry and Molecular Biology.* I know this because *The Handbook* is one of my friends in the reference collection.

That's right, I'm talking about old acquaintances like encyclopedias, handouts, and dictionaries. I have found it helpful to get to know a few reference resources well enough that I can instinctively turn to them for a favor when I start my search for the answer to any kind of factual question. For statistical questions I start with *Statistical Abstracts.* For general science factual questions, I often turn to the *McGraw Hill Encyclopedia of Science and Technology.* Also handy are FAQ science resources like The Carnegie Library of Pittsburgh's *Science and Technology Desk Reference* or *The NY Public Library Science Desk Reference*, which list frequently asked science questions and their answers. They lend themselves nicely to the sort of questions my 7-year-old is fond of asking (How deep is the Atlantic Ocean? What's a precious metal?). And there's a very good chance that if you're asked this sort of question, it's been asked before by someone else and will show up in one of these books.

All these well-trusted general reference resources provide the sort of straightforward answers which are enough for most patrons. I've found in most of these cases that the library user doesn't want the sort of applied research found in indexes of scholarly literature; they want an authoritative but clearly written overview. Or they just want one specific fact like a refractive index (whatever that is).

Beyond specific reference resources I am familiar with, each subject area or discipline covered in our reference collection usually has some sort of encyclopedia or general information source. There's *Grzimek's Encyclopedia of Mammals* in the QL's (zoology) and Springer-Verlag's *Encyclopedia of Plant Physiology* in the QK's (botany). If I can determine the subject area, I always have some place to head.

So if I can get my grad student to tell me that he's after proteins, I can steer him to the *Handbook of Biochemistry and Molecular Biology*, which is in the physiology section (QP's) and deals with, well, really small living things. I know this multi-volume set has all sorts of information on this sort of topic because I've used it before. If the question is about something alive and bigger, like a cow ("What's the arterial blood pressure of bos taurus?"), I turn to the QH's–Biology and Natural History–and to the multi-volume *Biology Databook*. The *Databook*, like the *Handbook*, is full of all sorts of tables and figures and statistics on subjects most of which I know nothing about. But because I've been introduced to them and know their areas of expertise, I can automatically call on them when these sorts of questions come up. They may not always have the answer, but they are good places to start.

One clever thing the head of our reference services did before the summer 1997 general orientation for new reference staff (which included me) was to hand out round yellow stickers to all the other reference staff (the old timers). They were then given free reign to place these stickers on any number of resources in the reference collection which they had found in the course of their reference work to be particularly helpful. When it came time for our tour of the collection, these stickers served to highlight especially valuable resources that we wouldn't have otherwise known about, and it was immediately apparent that volumes with multiple stickers were the collection's all-stars. It was through these stickers that I learned about the *McGraw-Hill Encyclopedia* and the science desk reference volumes, as well as valuable social science resources like *The City and County Databook* and *The Commodity Price Index*.

In addition to getting well acquainted with key reference resources, it helps to have an instinctive spatial mapping of your reference collection. The other day a patron came to the desk wanting to find information on the average annual snowfall in eastern Maryland. I knew our climatology reference collection was in the stacks behind the public access computers, so I marched him over there. There in the *Climates of the States* series (another volume with a yellow sticker) he was able to find exactly what he was looking for. The ease with which I was able to direct him to the answer was based not only on knowing about the *Climates* series, but also because I had developed through practice a spatial mapping of the reference collection that allowed me just to walk over to the OC's (meteorology) and pull out a resource without having to think of where to go. I can also do this by using the on-line catalog to get a subject heading, but it is usually much easier and faster if I can just know where in the reference stacks to steer myself. I know, for example, that the education material is on the far wall behind the study tables while the agricultural stuff is on the other side of the second short bookcase near the reference desk.

This whole process, of course, involves getting to know the basics of the L.C. subject classifications: geography in the G's and medicine in the R's, for example. One of the really handy resources we have in reference for learning all this is a reference collection map and subject guide which is posted at the end of the stacks facing the room's entrance. This guide includes a map of the reference collection showing where call numbers are as well as a list of L.C. subject classes. The list includes all subject categories, but has detailed lists of the subclasses of areas in Mann's particular subject foci (G's, H's and L's for the social sciences in the College of Human Ecology and Q's, R's and S's for the ag and life sciences departments). While this is principally designed to help patrons find the call number of a resource they are after, it also helps me learn, for example, where the natural resources collection lies (it's split between the GE's–environmental sciences–and the QH's–biology and ecology). I find it useful both at the time I'm helping a patron and other "down" times when I'm just passing through the collection ("Oh, that's right; human anatomy is in the QH's").

Now it just so happens that sometimes your patrons are going to want more than a definition of, say, a tsunami (a giant wave set in motion by a large earthquake; *Science & Technology Desk Reference*, p. 487). They're going to come to the desk and ask about something you don't know anything about and they *are* going to want to get their hands on all the latest research and scholarship. In this case you have to turn to other friends–like electronic databases.

But the same basic rules apply to this relationship: Get to know a handful of the best electronic resources and turn to these first. And here's another example where the humanities-to-science cross-over isn't really that big a deal. While I worked on my PhD, I became familiar with the Modern Language Association's periodical index (then in print) as the best source for articles in both literature and film. I always turned to it first. In science, I've learned, the same rule applies and I've gradually developed the same sort of familiarity with resources like Biosis (biology) and CAB (agriculture) as I've worked at Mann Library.

How did I get hooked up with these new databases? Like any friendship, this was sometimes through an introduction by an experienced reference librarian we knew in common and sometimes by just stumbling across each other. Of course, this whole process is a lot less complicated than any blind date because of something called the Library Gateway.

The Gateway (http://www.library.cornell.edu/) is a web-based single point of entry to all of Cornell's networked electronic resources. One of its features is a shortcuts page listing the databases most frequently used by our patrons. By referring to this page, I quickly learned the associations between subjects and databases–psychology topics are indexed in Psycinfo, medicine in Medline, etc.

Almost all subject areas have one major database which indexes the major and minor journals in that field, and it's just a matter of getting to know them. The Gateway is also handy for this, as it organizes databases by subject areas (chemistry, music, geology, etc.) and then by resource type in each area (I can limit my search to just periodical indexes in natural resources, for example). Once I started learning the major player(s) in each subject area, it was easy to direct patrons to them.

Scene: A grad student (goatee, no Birkenstocks) comes to the desk looking for information on point-source pollution by manufacturers in the Gulf of Mexico. Now this topic, while not as incomprehensible to me as magnetohydronamics or protein purification, is still about something I really don't know much about. I've heard of non-point source pollution, and can assume that point-source is the opposite of it, but actual definitions are beyond me. Note this is not a factual question–the student wants information for a research project and not a specific answer found in a reference book.

What do I do here? The most important thing, besides not panicking, is to remember that it's less important that you know at the time particular definitions (What is point source pollution?) than knowing what broader subject area the question falls in. Here it is obviously pollution. As I've mentioned, I have become familiar enough with the various electronic resources to know that Biosis is the go-to database of choice for all biological topics, including pollution. I mention this, but he says he's already searched Biosis and found nothing. At this point, because I know that the topic has to do with pollution, I can search the Gateway for other appropriate periodical indexes I'm not as familiar with. I find *Pollution Abstracts* and *Toxline*, and he finds lots of good stuff and is happy.

While the patron knows far more about this topic than I do, as a librarian I usually know more about how to find information on this topic. This is always good to keep in mind while working the reference desk. So while he's searching these other databases, I decide to do a search of my own in Biosis. I find several excellent sources on point source pollution in the Gulf of Mexico; the reason the patron found nothing is because "of" is a stop word in the databases, and you need to type "gulf and mexico."

Later I can look in *McGraw Hill* under water pollution and find succinct definitions of both point source pollution (discrete discharge from a single place, like a plastics plant dumping into a river) and non-point (diffuse discharge such as runoff from an irrigated cabbage field or range land). This information could very well prove useful in some way in the future, but not knowing it at the time did not impede my ability to help the patron find what he was looking for on the topic. This is the essence of being a reference librarian in any type of library: Most often it is not a matter of knowing the answer, but knowing where to find it.

Here's my last anecdote. While working at the reference desk, I get this question from a patron: "How do I find dairy bull sire summaries?" My first response is: What the hell is a sire summary? But instead of panicking I head over to the ag section of the reference collection and consult several agriculture dictionaries before finding a definition of a sire evaluation as "the best measure of a bull's true transmitting ability." This gives me a general idea of what I'm looking for, so I forge ahead with a keyword search on "sire summary" in the on-line catalog. I find a USDA publication *Sire Summary*, with the subject heading of Cattle–Pedigrees. Unfortunately it ceased publication in 1975. I find an article on INTERBULL (an international bull pedigree standard setting association of some kind) on the Agriculture Research Service's website (ARS, a USDA agency, is listed as publisher of *Sire Summary*), which links to the Animal Improvement Programs Laboratory's website, which informs me "most of INTERBULL's information is available in a user-friendly form on the World Wide Web at http://www.aipl.arsusda.gov/" and bingo, there are all the sire summaries in pdf format. Whew, take a breath.

You may be asking yourself at this point what the patron was doing while I did all this research. And here's the answer: I have no idea. My patron, Iris, e-mailed her question to me from Missouri, where she lives. E-mail reference questions like this allow me to take my time finding the answers without having to wonder whether the "What the hell is a sire summary?" look in my eye is leading Iris to lose confidence in and respect for me.

And this is increasing (e-mail reference, not the lack of respect). Statistics for Mann Library's reference desk show a dramatic increase in the past few years in e-mail reference coupled with a simultaneous decrease in questions asked in-person at the actual reference desk. From 1996/97 to 1998/99, reference questions asked at the reference desk were down 14%, about 250 fewer, while reference e-mail questions were up 75%, from 817/year to 1430/year. Which is all to say that the sort of fear-inducing reference interactions with polysyllabic Latinate questions that skeptics like Krupp throw out as proof that non-scientists don't make good science librarians are becoming increasingly moot, both because patrons are increasingly finding these answers themselves via the Internet and because they are using the Internet to ask us their questions. If no one knows you're a dog on the Internet, certainly no one knows you're a humanities major either.

Oh, and by the way: *Phyllostachys Aurea* is fish pole bamboo, native of Japan and China and growing up to 20 feet. It forms a good hedge and blooms every 15-30 years. I know this from looking it up in the New York Botanical Garden's *Encyclopedia of Horticulture*. It's in the SB's (plant culture). It's on the far end of the third free standing bookcase near the entrance. You can't miss it.

BIBLIOGRAPHY

Frank, Donald G. and Christine Kollen (1989), "Humanities and Social Sciences Librarians in the Science-Engineering Library: Utilization and Implications for Effective Collection Development and Reference Services," *Science & Technology Libraries* 9 (Spring), 63-71.

Hallmark, Julie (1998), "Education for the Successful Geoscience Information Specialist," *Science & Technology Libraries* 17(2), 81-91.

Haselbauer, Kathleen (1998), "The Making of a Science Librarian," *Science & Technology Libraries* 4 (Spring/Summer), 111-116.

Holland, Maurita Peterson (1998), "Modeling the Engineering Information Professional," *Science & Technology Libraries* 17(2), 31-43.

Krupp, Robert G. (1984), "What Education is Best?" *Science & Technology Libraries* 4 (Spring/Summer), 105-109.

Liu, Meng Xiong and Wei Wei (1993), "Science/Technology Librarians in California: Their Background, Performance and Expectations," Special Libraries Association Annual Conference, Cincinnati.

Lucker, Jay K. (1998), "The Changing Nature of Scientific and Technical Librarianship: A Personal Perspective over 40 Years," *Science & Technology Libraries* 17(2), 3-10.

Mosley, Pixey Anne (1995), "Engineering and Librarians: How Do They Interact?" *Science and Technology Libraries* 15 (1), 51-61.

Mount, Ellis (1985), *University Science and Engineering Libraries*, 2nd ed. Westport, CT: Greenwood Press.

Penniman, W. David (1998), "Educating the Scientific/Technical Information Specialist: Description of the Program at the University of Tennessee (at Knoxville)," *Science & Technology Libraries* 17(2), 11-21.

Smith, Linda C. (1987), "Education for Sci-Tech Librarianship: Retrospect and Prospect," *Science & Technology Libraries* 8 (Fall), 75-88.

Smith, Linda C. (1998), "Education for Health Sciences Librarianship." *Science & Technology Libraries* 17(2), 59-80.

Storm, Paula and Wei Wei (1994), "Issues Related to the Education and Recruitment of Science/Technology Librarians," *Science & Technology Libraries* 14 (Spring), 35-42.

Stuart, Crit. and Miriam A. Drake (1992), "Education and Recruitment of Science and Engineering Librarians," *Science & Technology Libraries* 12 (Summer), 79-89.

Vazakas, Susan M. and Camille Clark Wallin (1992), "Where Are All the Science Librarians?" *College & Research Libraries News* 3 (March), 166-171.

Wiggins, Gary (1998), "New Directions in the Education of Chemistry Librarians and Information Specialists (at Indiana University, Bloomington)," *Science & Technology Libraries* 17(2), 45-58.

GETTING SOME ASSISTANCE FOR OURSELVES

"Do You Have Any Information on the Goth Lifestyle?" Or How Does a Reference Librarian Keep Up-to-Date?

Elaine Coppola

SUMMARY. One of the biggest challenges of a Reference Librarian is trying to respond to an information request on an unfamiliar topic. This article will cover techniques to use when confronted with a request on a subject with which the librarian is completely unfamiliar. It will explore techniques that librarians can use to keep up-to-date with current events, styles, music, and trends. It will also deal with staying informed about relevant terminology, print resources, and electronic sources of information. *[Article copies available for a fee from The Haworth Document Delivery Service: 1-800-342-9678. E-mail address: <getinfo@haworthpressinc.com> Website: <http://www.HaworthPress.com> © 2001 by The Haworth Press, Inc. All rights reserved.]*

Elaine Coppola is Head, Reference Department, Syracuse University Library, Syracuse, NY 13244-2010 (E-mail: emcoppol@library.syr.edu).

[Haworth co-indexing entry note]: "'Do You Have Any Information on the Goth Lifestyle?' Or How Does a Reference Librarian Keep Up-to-Date?" Coppola, Elaine. Co-published simultaneously in *The Reference Librarian* (The Haworth Information Press, an imprint of The Haworth Press, Inc.) No. 72, 2001, pp. 171-177; and: *Doing the Work of Reference: Practical Tips for Excelling as a Reference Librarian* (ed: Celia Hales Mabry) The Haworth Information Press, an imprint of The Haworth Press, Inc., 2001, pp. 171-177. Single or multiple copies of this article are available for a fee from The Haworth Document Delivery Service [1-800-342-9678, 9:00 a.m. - 5:00 p.m. (EST). E-mail address: getinfo@haworthpressinc.com].

KEYWORDS. Reference services, reference librarians, in-service education, continuing education, professional development, reference materials, reference skills, tips and techniques

New reference librarian or seasoned veteran, we have all had it happen. A library user eagerly approaches you and asks a question that elicits a "What on earth is he talking about?" thought in your mind. While a brief survey of the literature finds a number of articles on the desired characteristics of reference librarians and recommendations for professional development and training (e.g., Duckett, 1989 and Weingand, 1994), few articles offer specific tips and techniques.

"A good old fashioned liberal education" (Duckett, 1989) might indeed be the best preparation for reference work. Lacking one, you could take courses or read widely (Stieg, 1980), both to increase your all around knowledge as well as to develop specialized knowledge in a particular subject. D'Aniello, in referring to cultural literacy on the part of the librarian as a major factor in the success of a reference transaction, suggests that librarians regularly read newspapers and news magazines (D'Aniello, 1989). But for most of us, the problem is not our general educational background nor is it our basic cultural literacy. The real problem is how do we keep that education and literacy up-to-date given both the rapid change in and the exponential increase in growth of information.

In 1981, Charles Bunge conducted an informal survey of reference librarians at an institute for managers of reference services sponsored by the Reference and Adult Services Division (RASD, now RUSA) of the American Library Association (ALA). He asked them to "describe strategies they use to keep up-to-date on reference materials and information sources and techniques" (Bunge, 1982). The most commonly named practices included professional reading, staff meetings, staff sharing, and conferences/workshops (Bunge, 1982).

Paul Frantz discusses "self-study" as a way of developing a "repertoire of reference" (Frantz, 1991). He lists browsing the reference collection, making use of bibliographic aids, collegiality, and professional reading and study as components of an effective self-development program (Frantz, 1991).

I recommend the Bunge and the Frantz articles to both new and more experienced librarians. In addition, drawing on some of their comments as well as the experiences of my colleagues and myself, I offer the following suggestions on how we can keep ourselves up-to-date, keep up with new sources, and, given that no one can know everything, how we can cope with an unfamiliar topic.

TECHNIQUES FOR KEEPING UP-TO-DATE

Newspapers

Long recognized as a great source of current information on a wide variety of topics (D'Aniello, 1989), newspapers are very often the source of your user's question. The user may have read an article that raises a question and generates a trip to the library. If you, too, have read that article, you will at least have some background information and be somewhat familiar with the terminology used. While none of us has time to read completely all available newspapers, I suggest a scanning technique. Skip over articles on topics already well-known to you unless they offer new information. Peruse areas of marginal interest weekly instead of daily.

What newspapers are most helpful? You might consider the following:

- Your local daily newspaper.
- A national newspaper. If you don't have time to read it on a daily basis (and most of us don't), try the Sunday edition. I find the Sunday *New York Times* with its weekly summaries and special sections especially valuable and interesting.
- Your local alternative newspaper (usually a weekly). These newspapers are often essential in keeping up with trends in music and lifestyles.
- Your campus newspapers. If you are an academic reference librarian, you want to know what's happening on your campus. Read not only the "official" campus newspaper but any student produced newspapers including student-oriented inserts.

Magazines

While taking a bit more of your time, you can also use a scanning technique with magazines. Take special care to read magazines of interest to your clientele. Here are some possibilities:

- News magazines (e.g., *Time* and *Newsweek)*
- General interest magazines (e.g., *The New Yorker* and *Readers' Digest*)
- Specific subject magazines (e.g., *Smithsonian* and *Scientific American*). Personally, as a non-science person, I find that scanning *Scientific American* gives me a fighting chance at least to recognize scientific terms and trends.
- Magazines aimed at a particular audience (e.g., *Modern Maturity, Rolling Stone*)

Radio, Television, Film

Do you commute several miles to work? If so, use that time. While listening to books on tape is great, listening to the radio is an alternative if your commute is too short to really get into a book. Listen to a variety of radio programs. Try different types of music to acquaint yourself not only with the music but the major performers. Try talk radio to find out who the major hosts are and what topics they cover. Remember, your library users are a varied group so take a minute to listen even to the hosts whose views and topics you don't find comfortable. For information of all types, listen to your local National Public Radio station.

Even without turning yourself into a couch potato, watching television can help you keep up-to-date. In addition to your local news, the national news, and news programs like *60 Minutes,* television offers programs on all subject areas. View ones in areas in which you'd like to increase your knowledge (e.g., history). I've found that a number of questions, especially from students, relate to programs they regularly watch. You might find it helpful to acquaint yourself with the "hot" programs of the year, perhaps by watching just one or two episodes to get a flavor of the program.

Films, too, have a role in cultural literacy. If you're not a movie buff or seldom have time to see a movie, at least read reviews of the current movies.

Talk to Your Clientele

In order to be most helpful to your clientele, not only do you need to read, listen and view what they do, you need to talk to them.

For example, if you serve mostly senior citizens, involve yourself with them:

- Attend a function at a senior center
- Visit a retirement home
- Take an older relative to lunch

If you're in a college library, you might:

- Have informal chats with your work-study students
- Attend a faculty lecture
- Lunch with students or faculty

If you're serving a younger clientele and don't have children yourself:

- Spend time with nieces and nephews
- Give your friends a break and spend some time caring for their children
- Wander the nearest mall with a teenager

Staff Meetings/Staff Development

A common way to update your knowledge and skills is through regular reference departmental meetings and training sessions (Bunge, 1982). This is an excellent opportunity to share challenging reference questions and how answers were found. Staff can share information on new reference tools and techniques. Experts can hold in-depth training sessions on particular products or subject areas.

Conferences/Workshops

Reference librarians will want to take advantage of formal conferences and workshops on the local, regional, state, and national level. While time and cost may prevent everyone from attending every useful program, those who do attend can come back to the home institution and share the knowledge they acquired.

TECHNIQUES FOR KEEPING UP WITH SOURCES

Another challenge for reference librarians is to stay informed about relevant terminology, print resources, and electronic sources of information in both interdisciplinary and specialized subject fields.

Reading relevant library journals is essential. Start with *American Libraries* and *Library Journal* and then expand to those targeted to your area of librarianship. All reference librarians will want to look at *Reference & User Services Quarterly* and *RSR: Reference Services Review.* Academic reference librarians may also want to look at *College & Research Libraries* and *College & Research Libraries News.*

Read relevant journals in your subject area. Academic librarians will want to read the *Chronicle of Higher Education* in addition to journals covering the subject areas in which they regularly have questions.

Additional sources of information on reference sources are varied. Among the most helpful are:

- *Choice* magazine
- *American Reference Books Annual* (ARBA)
- Scout Report (http://scout.cs.wisc.edu/report/sr/current/index.html)

Another very important source of information is listservs. You may wish to join both library listservs like LIBREF-L (to subscribe, contact listserv@listserv.kent.edu) and subject oriented listservs.

TECHNIQUES FOR DEALING WITH UNFAMILIAR SUBJECTS

What if, despite all your efforts to keep up-to-date, you encounter a question on an unfamiliar topic? Do not despair, there are several solutions.

First, you will want to conduct a really good reference interview. Since there already are many good articles in the library literature on this topic (e.g., RASD, 1996), I will just briefly list some questions I might ask:

- What else can you tell me about the topic?
- What information do you already have?
- What is the source of that information?
- Is this a current topic or an historical one?

Once you feel confident that you really understand the question, you will want to check relevant sources. If you are unclear as to what source might be appropriate for the topic, consult guides like the *Guide to Reference Books.* Often your best source may be a colleague. Always remember that reference is a great teamwork activity. You could ask a colleague working right in reference with you, a colleague in another department of the library, or a colleague in another library.

If this approach is unsuccessful, you can post your question to a listserv. LIBREF-L (LIBREF-L@listserv.kent.edu), STUMPERS-L (STUMPERS-L@listserv.cuis.edu), and subject specific listservs are all good sources.

You may also wish to consult experts in the field. Academic librarians often find that professors can clarify terminology, provide information, and/or suggest appropriate sources. Often a professional in the specific field can provide assistance. When local sources are unavailable, a good source for finding professional expertise is the *Encyclopedia of Associations.*

Sometimes just a quick web search proves successful. This is especially true when you are looking for a topic that includes unique words or phrases.

CONCLUSION

Reference librarians are often expected to "know it all" or at least be able to find information on everything. While no one person can possibly be familiar with all topics, I believe that these tips and techniques will give you the knowledge and tools you need to handle that next "stumper."

BIBLIOGRAPHY

Bunge, Charles A. (1984), "Strategies for Updating Knowledge of Reference Resources and Techniques," *Journal of Academic Librarianship* 10 (July), 128-132.

D'Aniello, Charles A. (1989), "Cultural Literacy and Reference Service," *RQ* 28 (Spring), 370-380.

Duckett, Bob (1989), "Reference Work, Staff Selection and General Knowledge," *Library Review* 38 (5), 14-21.

Frantz, Paul (1991), "Expanding the Repertoire of Reference," *Reference Services Review* 19 (Winter), 85-90.

RASD Ad Hoc Committee on Behavioral Guidelines for Reference and Information Services (1996), "Guidelines for Behavioral Performance of Reference and Information Service Professionals," n. pag. Online. Internet. 4 Sept. 1999. Available: http://www.ala.org/rusa/behavior.html.

Weingand, Darlene E. (1994), "Competence and the New Paradigm: Continuing Education of the Reference Staff," *The Reference Librarian* 43, 173-182.

The Librarian's Library: Fugitive Reference Files

Susan Gangl

SUMMARY. The breadth and depth of subjects and the size of user population of a major university library demand a well-organized reference service. To manage such diverse disciplines and clientele, librarians rely on each other for shortcuts recorded and saved in a staff-access vertical file. A team approach of sharing useful reference sources helps all reference librarians improve their service to library users. If reference staff can efficiently store and organize fugitive material that can be shared by all staff members, they can use that material to meet immediate ready reference needs, and later develop sophisticated information-access tools such as pathfinders and knowledge bases. *[Article copies available for a fee from The Haworth Document Delivery Service: 1-800-342-9678. E-mail address: <getinfo@haworthpressinc.com> Website: <http://www.HaworthPress.com> © 2001 by The Haworth Press, Inc. All rights reserved.]*

KEYWORDS. Fugitive, ephemeral materials, vertical files, reference services, team/teams

INTRODUCTION

Recorded information is fugitive when it is elusive, capable of moving from place to place, or likely to change, fade or evaporate.

Susan Gangl is Reference Librarian, General Reference Service, 180 Wilson Library, University of Minnesota Libraries–Twin Cities, Minneapolis, MN 55455 (E-mail: s-gang@tc.umn.edu).

[Haworth co-indexing entry note]: "The Librarian's Library: Fugitive Reference Files." Gangl, Susan. Co-published simultaneously in *The Reference Librarian* (The Haworth Information Press, an imprint of The Haworth Press, Inc.) No. 72, 2001, pp. 179-194; and: *Doing the Work of Reference: Practical Tips for Excelling as a Reference Librarian* (ed: Celia Hales Mabry) The Haworth Information Press, an imprint of The Haworth Press, Inc., 2001, pp. 179-194. Single or multiple copies of this article are available for a fee from The Haworth Document Delivery Service [1-800-342-9678, 9:00 a.m. - 5:00 p.m. (EST). E-mail address: getinfo@haworthpressinc.com].

Another definition of fugitive is "difficult to grasp or retain" (WWWebsters, 1999). When needed information is difficult to remember or access easily using standard search techniques, librarians find creative ways to capture it and make it accessible. Fugitive material is traditionally stored in a vertical file. In an on-line environment, is there good reason to support the maintenance of such a tradition? The advantages include speed and convenience. Over time, more valuable or constantly accessed information should be converted to a more widely accessible resource such as a knowledge base. But the importance of having an immediately accessible place to store items should not be ignored. Storing information in on-line formats takes time. Reference professionals need resources *before* they are formally recorded and made accessible via standard print or on-line formats. A fugitive *reference* file can be the crucial intermediate step between the librarian's memory and a polished and published pathfinder. Saved and filed until the librarian can formalize access to it, fugitive reference items form raw material for finding aids from simple bibliographies to pathfinders and knowledge databases. Characteristics that distinguish a vertical file of fugitive reference materials from the standard vertical file are the content and the primary audience. Library users need and want substantive information. What librarians need is bibliographic information or a combination of bibliographic and brief descriptive information that will help them refer library users to substantive content (McInnis, 1978). The file's audience is comprised of reference librarians who want fast, convenient access to a bank of shared information compiled by their colleagues in order to serve library users. This article stresses the importance of organizing reference/referral information at the service desk, and follows with methods to accomplish this task in a way that facilitates the later development of sophisticated tools such as print and on-line pathfinders and knowledge databases.

LITERATURE REVIEW RESULTS

Most of the literature on vertical files addresses single-format collections of published ephemera, particularly pamphlets, exhibition catalogs or reports. Although a few authors describe the process and the value of organizing this genre of materials, no one addresses the organization, storage and access to fugitive reference materials for staff use. The recent trend in providing reference information is toward on-line storage and retrieval of such information, with good reason. However, there still exists an intermediate "limbo" stage between the initial encounter of valuable information, and the re-recording of it into an on-line system. Further, such on-line systems tend to focus on high-demand information (FAQ's) rather than esoteric bits and pieces.

The overlap of the terms "reference services," "academic libraries" and "vertical files" brought up only two articles in a *Library Literature* search executed November 11, 1999; both were published nearly a decade ago. Total results from search words "ephemeral materials," "vertical files" and "fugitive literature" resulted in a few hundred titles. Of these, even the most promising titles focus on pamphlet files for library user direct access, including a highly respected survey and follow-up study by Hodgson and Garoogian (1981). "Information systems" led to articles treating the cataloging of pamphlets, exhibition catalogs and the like for library user access.

When information systems such as knowledge bases are created to provide storage of and access to reference questions, the tendency is to store only the frequently asked questions, which are the tip of the iceberg of all potential content. Similarly the term "automation" when linked to "vertical files" pulls up records about the creation of on-line catalog records for quasi-published substantive documents intended for end-user access.

There is a need for staff to save and organize disparate and fugitive materials in order to facilitate direct reference desk service. The author proposes to explore the ways in which reference staff can organize their own in-house reference and referral information that comes to them in true ephemeral form: printouts, internally produced pathfinders, handwritten notes, e-mail messages, internal announcements and the like, all of which will be needed repeatedly *by the reference staff* as they assist library users. These ephemeral materials in many cases are not intended to be used directly by the public, either because of their temporary nature, their fragile or semi-legible state, and/or the need for staff interpretation of the contents. The materials are often in a sense "shorthand" notes to prompt librarians to recall more detailed strategies that they can then pursue with the library user.

THE HISTORY AND DEVELOPMENT OF A FUGITIVE FILE

The General Reference staff at the University of Minnesota Libraries–Twin Cities work with a large and growing reference collection: 48,000 volumes occupying 5,460 linear feet of shelf space. They also provide basic reference to library users in 20 humanities and social sciences disciplines. Detailed and/or advanced questions are referred to other staff or handled during off-desk hours. The librarians must be generalists in addition to their subject expertise. To handle such variety, they work as a team, using any shortcuts colleagues develop. One form of such sharing occurs in daily logbooks, but valuable information can be difficult to retrieve. Staff must attempt to index entries while on duty at a public service desk, and the format of the logbook limits the entries to a chronological arrangement.

In the early 1980s, a logical and orderly system of storing master copies of in-house printed guides was developed. The system was initially limited to staff-produced guides arranged alphabetically by discipline in 3-ring binders. This collection of guides became known as *Everybody's Library Guides,* hereafter referred to as *ELG*. When created, *ELG* filled five binders. By 1999 it had grown to 36 hanging binders, even after six were weeded out as obsolete.

Currently there are approximately 100 general and 100 subject-specific library guides stored at various display racks throughout the humanities and social sciences reference area. Formats include print and on-line bibliographies, pathfinders and printed point-of-use guides. In addition, there are another 30 forms of printed internal publications–maps, brochures, etc.–from other parts of the library or university system. With this many guides, not all can be displayed on racks near the reference desk.

ELG has grown from five ring binders on a shelf to 36 hanging file binders suspended on frames in two lateral file drawers–a vertical file. However, there is a dramatic difference in the contents of *ELG* from those of most vertical files. Although it began as a repository for uniformly produced 8.5″ × 11″ printed guides, *ELG* now has many items that are more accurately described as fugitive material. This material has migrated from many sources to *ELG*, its growth due to the on-line environment. And in return, this fugitive material has allowed staff to create pathfinders more easily.

Throughout the many years of reference service prior to the era of e-mail, a staff-only logbook was the primary tool for recording and sharing reference service information about strategies, problems, etc. It remains in use today. The logbook is a simple lined notebook with numbered pages, and was originally intended for the recording of handwritten notes by staff. It was and is a front-line communication tool. Anyone who adds an entry is expected to enter a keyword heading and page reference at the front part of the notebook. At one time the format was entirely limited to handwriting. With the advent of the Internet, the staff began to replace or supplement handwritten entries with taped-in printouts of e-mail messages and catalog or index records. Taping entries is faster and more legible than handwriting. The introduction of printouts into the logbook inspired the logical progression of saving certain information in the *ELG* in addition to the logbook.

Since the printouts are more convenient to compose and more legible than handwritten entries, and because printouts are standard 8.5″ × 11″, the logical progression has been to file duplicate copies of valuable items into *ELG*. Two advantages are that *ELG* is kept in ring binders, which permit easy inter-filing, and have an alphabetical arrangement by subject that makes the items immediately accessible. In addition to guides, items added now include catalog entries for hard-to-remember reference titles, search history and results of complex keyword searches, web pages, and e-mail memos.

The logbook remains the first receptacle for recently recorded reference information, and serves to alert librarians to new items. Most of the logbook entries become quickly obsolete. However, when an entry has continued value, it is filed in *ELG* in a manner sometimes as informal as photocopying a handwritten logbook entry, using a three-hole-punch tool, and inserting the page into the notebooks. If a topic has sufficient library user interest or need, any accumulated material in the *ELG* helps the librarian create or revise a more formal guide, in print and/or on-line form. For esoteric topics, an informal guide may be retained without any public display or distribution. In the unlikely event that a guide may need to be updated before it has been used very often, staff could limit its publication to a web format, and thus avoid the problem of having to print and store more paper copies than are needed.

A more democratic system would be hard to find. Any staff member can contribute to it; the only requirements are a reference to some hard-to-find information, a piece of paper, and a three-hole-punch.

Minnesota's development of a fugitive collection is not an isolated experience. Le Roy Barnett describes the "fruits of my investigatory labors in the Quick Reference File . . . Now and then, a folder of these randomly-acquired, thematic facts will grow to such size that a compilation of the data can be prepared for the benefit of clients. Drawing in part up on the resources present in the Quick Ref files my unit has produced 53 circulars on a wide array of topics" (Barnett, 1997). Recently a visiting librarian from Indiana noted that she had seen a similar system in use at a university in Australia. Although such in-house systems exist, librarians have not regularly documented their practice or their value.

Physical Organization of Materials

Some humble tools are too useful to discard in the face of higher technology. The three-hole-punch and the three-ring binder are good examples. The amassed collection of guides-plus-clippings has grown from five notebooks to more than 30 in a decade. The contents for art and art history alone fill three notebooks now. The collection is actively used. Its major advantage remains the immediacy of time and place. Just as Tyckoson (1997) reaffirms traditional founding principles of reference services, we can reaffirm use of simple tools that continue to support reference services and complement on-line technology.

History of a Ubiquitous Tool

> *The Wilson Jones Company was formed in 1893 when a jewelry repairman in Chicago invented and started manufacturing the first aluminum sheet holder. Six years later, this company, then called The Chicago Shipping and Receipt Book Company, came under the control of Ralph B. Wilson. What followed . . . dramatically changed the way we keep records–the invention of the ring binder in 1904. This event, coupled with a merger with the Jones Improved Loose Leaf Specialty Company, owned by W. Gifford Jones and his two brothers, catapulted the company into a leadership role in the office products industry. These were the humble beginnings of the Wilson Jones Company.*
>
> –ACCO Brands, retrieved 1999

Despite the rise in ownership of personal computers in homes, people want to save and organize information on paper. Witness the proliferation of popular titles on organizational systems for paper files such as *File–Don't Pile* (Dorff, 1994) and *Kiplinger's Taming the Paper Tiger at Work* (Hemphill, 1998). Positive customer feedback concerning paper files is archived on a business website. Customer feedback and on-line discussions confirm the convenience and speed of 3-ring binder (*123SORT IT!*, 1999).

Organizing the Contents of ELG

ELG is more efficient and effective due to improved office products:

- The hanging file binder–permitting files to be easily organized and maintained in a cabinet
- Clear, sturdy plastic pocket inserts for storage of thick, heavy or small items
- Numbered tab dividers and table of contents indexing system.

The dividers and indexing allow easy flexibility: one can easily change the contents while the tab labels remain the same. Leaving some tabs unassigned at first allows later insertion of new topics. Refiling is needed only occasionally.

Each notebook spine is labeled with a letter of the alphabet. Any content that could directly answer a reference question is included. The "I" file, for example, includes Inflation, Interlibrary Loan, and International Studies, among other headings. Classification is generally avoided, applied occasionally within subdivisions of a broad entry: for example, the L sequence has three notebooks covering "Libraries on Campus," "Libraries in Minnesota," and "Libraries Outside of Minnesota," each organized alphabetically by library name. All remaining "L" topics are stored in a fourth notebook. Patrons are allowed to borrow a volume for photocopying purposes. No volume has ever disappeared for more than a few days.

Document Types in the Fugitive Files

- Pathfinders and bibliographies–56%
- Web page printouts–10%

- Fliers, maps and guides from other libraries and institutions–5%
- Photocopies of title and other useful pages from reference books–4%
- On-line public access catalog printouts for hard-to-find titles–6%
- Clippings about collections, libraries, etc.–3%
- Point-of-use guides to software–3%
- Pamphlets, brochures, maps–5%
- Handwritten notes by staff–3%
- E-mail messages among librarians, Stumpers listserv responses, etc.–3%
- Local call number/location annotations for titles listed in reference sources (e.g., list of foreign language encyclopedias; periodicals listed in Alternative Press Index, etc.)–2%
- Staff contact information for public use (selectors, instruction librarians, etc.)–1%

Who Is the Audience?

Reference librarians are the primary intended audience. The *ELG* fugitive file serves as a behind-the-scenes, uncatalogued support system for library staff at a multidisciplinary academic reference desk. Although few library users see the file, staff will either photocopy the applicable contents, or briefly allow the patron to browse a lengthy entry, take notes and/or photocopy pertinent pages. As demand on a topic increases, the contents facilitate the creation of a guide suitable for public distribution, ultimately benefiting many library users.

Information restricted to staff access is stored in a different location. These include the "LIPPs" notebook (Library In-house People, Policy and Procedures) and the "SOS" notebook (a collection of staff-only help contacts primarily for computer crashes, building emergencies, problem patrons, etc.).

Advantages of a Physical File

Immediacy

A physical file is not dependent on access to electricity, hardware or software. Being the original "PDF" (portable document format) file, paper is immediately available for input and output. Staff with little time or predisposition toward data entry can contribute to the collection. Staff can quickly tag, remove, correct or replace outdated or erroneous items.

Machine Independent

While the need and importance of automation in libraries is unquestioned, there are still occasions where the paper format offers access that is free from machine-dependence, and actually offers a flexibility, comfort level, and speed that is inexpensive.

Familiarity

Because the file is created in-house and is relatively small, staff can become familiar with the location of contents without having to memorize the information within. The headings are created by the reference staff members as they add the contents. Cross-references can be written in as needed. New additions and their headings are registered in the logbook. Use of the file over time increases familiarity. The file serves as one of several training tools for new staff.

Compatibility and Flexibility

A physical file can include published brochures, maps, and other documents that could not be added or converted to an on-line file due to legal or technical issues. Mixed formats are not a problem: on-line printouts, class assignments, handwritten notes, printed guides from other libraries, pamphlets, post-it notes, fliers, internal forms: all can be interfiled. Plastic pockets can hold thicker items.

Visual Cues

The recognition factors of signals of size, shape, color, condition of paper, thickness, and relative location in drawer, are all advantages of a physical collection of resources. In fact, because a guide or map is filed there, the person seeing it knows exactly what to look for on a rack of published guides, to get a copy to give to the library patron. In the case of new staff–or new guides–this speeds up access to printed guides. For further discussion of the virtue of physical resources, see Doty (1997).

Natural Language

Librarians using the files have regularly indicated their preference for natural language headings. A typical notebook table of contents page for *ELG* appears in Appendix A.

AUTOMATION AS PARTNER

The physical file is ideal for a single local setting, but that also is its major limitation, if staff outside the service point wish to use the contents. The portions of the file that have a broader application must eventually be reformatted. In the meantime, the fugitive file serves as a form of information storage for later evaluation and reformatting. The reformatting allows content to be added to pathfinders, catalogs and/or a knowledge base.

Subsections of *ELG* file contents can be used to create formal print and on-line products such as pathfinders and point-of-use guides, online library instruction products such as Research QuickStart (Research QuickStart, 1999) and OCLC's CORC pathfinders (CORC, 1999).

Another partnering of electronic resources with *ELG* occurs with the addition of the *ELG* file's table-of-contents entries to an html file that can be updated by the editor, and accessed by staff members. The full list of headings is available at http://wilson.lib.umn.edu/reference/elghead.html. A portion of the list appears in Appendix B.

Pathfinders

Printed pathfinders have become easier to develop when they draw on contents filed in *ELG*. *ELG* was created as a repository of printed pathfinders, and retains that role today. Those pathfinders, now created on word processors, can easily be reformatted into html and added to various locations on the library's website. *ELG* is a good resource to check when one is revising and updating a pathfinder, since loose entries such as printouts, handwritten notes and corrections may have been added to a filed copy of a pathfinder. However, *ELG* not only serves as a resource for one's own pet topics; it is a shared set of materials. New staff or interns looking for projects can learn about research topics early in their employment period by browsing the *ELG*.

On-line pathfinder databases such as *Research QuickStart* drew heavily from printed guides and notes, particularly during the early months of development. Live links enhance the convenience to library users. The contents of *ELG* have been used to some extent in the development of certain *Research QuickStart* subject pages. Another knowledge base, *Ask Us!* and a related *Question and Answer Database,* could tap into *ELG* to find additional resources for their own files.

On-Line Catalogs

The contents of *ELG* should not be listed in an on-line catalog, since the file serves primarily as a staff support tool. However, there are ways in which *ELG* might be mined for resources to add to an on-line catalog. OCLC's experimental Cooperative Online Resource Cataloging Project (CORC, 1999) is the most recent example. CORC is an attempt to provide quality access to web sites by involving librarians to voluntarily "catalog the web." Contents cover all disciplines, topics and interests but initially were–and may remain–limited to web resources. Contributions to the database draw on a wide range of resources maintained by contributing librarians, including bookmarks, print and on-line pathfinders, memory and on-line exploration.

How can a reference support file like *ELG* be used for CORC? It is because *ELG* serves as a tool in that intermediate stage of saving information for later use. One volume of *ELG* is simply called Web Sites and contains printouts of recently identified web sites useful to reference service. This notebook allows staff to save the URL, the site title, date printed, and the visual look of the page that often contains further clues for returning to the site if the URL changes. Ironically, printing these out is easier than bookmarking sites because there are multiple workstations at the desk. Staff would have to either merge saved bookmarks from multiple machines, only save them at a single workstation and/or continuously update bookmarks on each of the workstations. The notebook is being used as a source for new titles to add to CORC.

The concept of adding on-line resources to an on-line catalog is a controversial one being discussed at the local and national level. The library makes a sea change decision when it adds to the OPAC URLs for sites that are not locally produced and maintained. The planning team for CORC has discussed this issue. As librarians debate how to provide access to the web, local staff must find easy ways to quickly locate useful sites. There are a range of appropriate ways to do so–from the formal, national level of CORC right down to the most recently identified site that is filed in a fugitive file. The forms of retrieval should complement one another.

Knowledge Bases

A knowledge base can be used to answer FAQ's, thereby meeting library user needs and saving staff from constantly repeating the same basic information. At the University of Minnesota–Twin Cities, the *Question and Answer Database* (*Q & A*) is under development as an additional on-line service of Ask Us! (AskUs!, 1999). Coordinated by a University Libraries system-wide team–the Distance Learning Development Project–Ask Us! is being developed with two levels of access: patrons and staff.

The *Question-and-Answer Database (Q & A)* has a different scope and audience than the *ELG* files. *ELG* was designed for use by staff in humanities and social sciences. *Q & A* spans all disciplines and functions, designed for access from service points that include multiple circulation, information, and general reference desks as well as specialized service points and staff offices. The format will be on-line, requiring staff to input the brief entries. Both *ELG* and *Q & A* include general navigational and procedural information about such topics as photocopy machines, campus maps, etc. Informational content in *Q & A* responds to FAQ's and other reference and orientation queries of a general nature. *ELG* is limited to humanities and social sciences, and includes more esoteric content, in addition to the disciplinary and topical guides for which it is named. There is no direct relationship between the *ELG* and *Q & A,* but if *ELG* can be used to assist staff in compiling contents for *Q & A,* that is an indication that the maintenance of a paper file can support new reference services that can reach a wider audience.

CONCLUSIONS

A staff-only vertical file can and should be maintained if it efficiently and effectively can support reference services to patrons, directly or indirectly. The advantages of a physical file include immediacy, familiarity, compatibility, flexibility, visual cues and natural language. Whenever possible, staff should expand the access to information by uploading responses to a frequently asked questions database. The fugitive file is a reliable warehouse readily available to staff under any conditions. It can be added to and maintained with minimal effort. The file serves as an information resource for the development and updating of more polished and sophisticated tools including pathfinders, catalogs and knowledge bases, which can serve a broader audience of staff and library users.

BIBLIOGRAPHY

"123SORT IT! Business Bulletin Board," 1999. *123SORT IT! Organizing Solutions, Innovating Tools* ©copyright, 1996-1999. Retrieved November 4, 1999 from the World Wide Web: *http://www.123sortit.com/bboards/*

ACCO Brands, "A Walk Through ACCO Brands History." Copyright 1999 ACCO® Brands, Inc. Retrieved November 4, 1999 from the World Wide Web: *http://www.acco.com/world/html/history.html*

Ask Us! [Reference question online submission form.] University Libraries–LUMINA. ©1999 by the Regents of the University of Minnesota, Twin Cities. University Libraries. All rights reserved. Retrieved from the World Wide Web December 2, 1999: *http://askinfo.lib.umn.edu/*

Barnett, Le Roy. "Sitting in the Hot Seat," *The Reference Librarian* no. 56, 1997, p. 40.

CORC–Cooperative Online Resource Catalog. Dublin, OH: OCLC, 1999. Retrieved from the World Wide Web December 2, 1999: *http://www.oclc.org/oclc/research/projects/corc/*

Dorff, Pat. *File–Don't Pile: For People Who Write: Handling the Paper Flow in the Workplace or Home Office.* New York: St. Martin's, 1994.

Doty, Paul. "Tears Live in an Onion," *The Reference Librarian,* no. 59, 1997, p. 113-119.

Everybody's Library Guides Subject Headings. Compiled by Susan Gangl. Retrieved from the World Wide Web December 3, 1999: *http://www.wilson.lib.umn.edu/reference/elghead.html*

Hemphill, Barbara. *Kiplinger's Taming the Paper Tiger at Work.* Kiplinger Books & Tapes, 1998.

Hodgson, Tom; Garoogian, Andrew. *The Vertical File in the Libraries of the City University of New York: A Survey.* 1981 ERIC document ED221216.

Makepeace, Chris. *Ephemera: A Book on its Collection, Preservation and Use.* Aldershot, Hants, England; Brookfield, VT, USA: Gower, 1985.

McInnis, Raymond G. "The Substantive-Bibliographic Continuum and the Functions of Intermediary Sources," Chapter 15, pp. 135-144, *New Perspectives for Reference Service in Academic Libraries.* Westport, CT and London: Greenwood Press, 1978.

Research QuickStart. Retrieved November 30, 1999 from the World Wide Web: *http://research.lib.umn.edu/*

Sitter, Clara. *The Vertical File and Its Alternatives: A Handbook.* Englewood, CO: Libraries Unlimited, 1992.

Spencer, Michael. *Readings on the Vertical File.* Englewood, CO: Libraries Unlimited, 1993.

Tyckoson, David. "What We Do: Reaffirming the Founding Principles of Reference Services," *The Reference Librarian,* no. 59, 1997 (pp. 3-13).

WWWebster Dictionary copyright © 1999 by Merriam-Webster, Incorporated. Retrieved from the World Wide Web on December 2, 1999: *http://www.m-w.com/netdict.htm*

APPENDIX A

Table of Contents Page as Used in Actual Notebook

Everybody's Library Guides
AG–AR

15	Alphabet Transliteration Chart
16	Alternative Viewpoints
	Alumni Access to Internet
17	American Archives
	American Indian Studies see INDIANS of North America
18	American Studies
19	Ancient and Classical Studies
20	Animals encyclopedia
21	ANTHROPOLOGY
	-- Anthropology, general info
	-- Anthropologists (Autobiographies, Biographies and FestSchriften)
22	-- HRAF (Human Relations Area Files)
23	-- Serials relating to Anthropology
24	Approval Plan publishers–url for staff web page
25	Arabic Studies/Middle East collections for
26	Archeology guides/overview
27	Archaeology, Classical Archaeology, Roman
28	Archaeology, Prehistoric
	Architecture see Art & Architecture notebook
	Archives, American see American Archives, above
29	Area Codes
30	[*unassigned space holder for new topic*]
31	Austrian Microform Collections

APPENDIX B

Portion of Table of Contents Page (A-Art) in HTML File at Reference Staff Workstation

Everybody's Library Guides Subject Headings

A

African American Studies
Afro-American Studies
Afro-American Writers
--Black Women Oral History Project (Schlesinger Lib)
--Martin Luther King: Great Minds . . .
--Genealogy
African Studies
African Area Studies
African History
--Black African Literature
--Middle Eastern, African and Asian History
--Senegal, Africa and The Third World
--Using Wilson Library for Research on Africa
Alphabet Transliteration Chart
Alternative Viewpoints
Alumni Access To Internet
American Archives
American Indian Studies See Indians of North America
American Studies
Ancient And Classical Studies
Animals Encyclopedia
Anthropology
--Anthropology, General Info
--Anthropologists (Autobiographies, Biographies and Festschriften)
--HRAF (Human Relations Area Files)
--Serials Relating To Anthropology
Approval Plan Publishers-URL for Staff Web Page
Arabic Studies/Middle East Collections For
Archeology Guides/Overview
Archaeology, Classical
Archaeology, Roman
Archaeology, Prehistoric
Architecture
--Gargoyles in Architecture
--Minnesota Architecture Bibliography
--Weisman Gallery Article
Archives, American See American Archives, Above
Area Codes

Art (see ELG notebooks labeled ART 1-ART 3)
--Alternative Art Journals
--American Art 19th-20th Centuries
--Artists/Biography-Researching An Artist; Interview An Artist; Visit Studio

Training, Supervising, and Evaluating Student Information Assistants

Jacqueline Borin

SUMMARY. Training, supervision, and evaluation of student assistants is not a topic covered in most library school curricula; it is a skill that it is assumed one will have or acquire through on-the-job experience. This article focuses on the hiring, supervision, training, and evaluation of student information assistants in the reference/electronic resource setting. Student Information Assistants are known by many names–reference assistants, peer counselors, research assistants, and database assistants, to name a few–but within this article I will use the name Student Information Assistants (SIAs). *[Article copies available for a fee from The Haworth Document Delivery Service: 1-800-342-9678. E-mail address: <getinfo@haworthpressinc.com> Website: <http://www.HaworthPress.com> © 2001 by The Haworth Press, Inc. All rights reserved.]*

KEYWORDS. Student library assistants–training of, reference services (libraries), academic libraries, library personnel management

The Student Information Assistant program at the California State University, San Marcos Library started as a grant proposal to hire and train students or "peer counselors" to work with the electronic information resources in the library. The original grant proposal stated in part:

Jacqueline Borin is Coordinator, Reference & Electronic Resources, Library and Information Services, California State University-San Marcos, San Marcos, CA 92096-0001 (E-mail: jborin@csusm.edu).

[Haworth co-indexing entry note]: "Training, Supervising, and Evaluating Student Information Assistants." Borin, Jacqueline. Co-published simultaneously in *The Reference Librarian* (The Haworth Information Press, an imprint of The Haworth Press, Inc.) No. 72, 2001, pp. 195-206; and: *Doing the Work of Reference: Practical Tips for Excelling as a Reference Librarian* (ed: Celia Hales Mabry) The Haworth Information Press, an imprint of The Haworth Press, Inc., 2001, pp. 195-206. Single or multiple copies of this article are available for a fee from The Haworth Document Delivery Service [1-800-342-9678, 9:00 a.m. - 5:00 p.m. (EST). E-mail address: getinfo@haworthpressinc.com].

> It has been well-documented that students are at best uncomfortable with libraries and many either hate or fear them. This is true of our students also; especially the re-entry women and under-represented students who are usually less likely to have extensive library experience. Moreover the State of California is ranked 50th of all the states in terms of its support of libraries in schools. The lack of K-12 school libraries exacerbates the uneasiness that undergraduates generally feel towards using a library or doing research. As libraries become more automated the problem is compounded with the fear of, or lack of familiarity with computers.
>
> It has been shown that students are more likely to discuss their problems with, and feel less intimidated by other students. To help them overcome their negative feelings and to get started on basic research a peer counselors program would be established in the library . . .
>
> The Library sees this as a first step in developing a program not unlike that at the University of Michigan's undergraduate library. This program hires students of color as information peer counselors who also go to student dorms and do outreach in an attempt to help undergraduates develop research skills. An added benefit to the counselors is their improved understanding of career possibilities in a world where technology and information are keys to empowerment. (Sonntag, 1993)

Special attention was paid to hiring students of color with the hope of mentoring and interesting them in a career as a librarian/information specialist, similar to the University of Michigan program where undergraduate minority students were hired to assist at the reference desk, provide term paper assistance and produce instructional materials (MacAdam & Nichols, 1988). Another similar program at SUNY-Oswego had goals to increase the communication between library staff and non-traditional or minority students, to improve basic library skills in these groups and to encourage students of color to pursue a career in library science (Judd et al., 1994). Earlier research had shown that students prefer initially to consult with other students when they have questions, and therefore we reasoned that the Student Information Assistant would help build bridges between students and library faculty. The initial grant provided funding for two students, and a second year of funding allowed us to expand the program. Although the program is no longer grant-funded (it relies on the library's student assistant budget), a strong effort is still made to hire a diverse group of students who will interact easily with our diverse student population. Currently we have a group of five students who are scheduled, individually, to be on duty in the reference area all open hours.

HIRING

The selection of student assistants for a reference/electronic resource area is a difficult one because of the need for more specialized skills. These include the following:

- Someone who is computer literate and has a general understanding of how computers and programs operate;
- A mature stable individual who can work under pressure on the "front lines" and deal with difficult patrons when necessary;
- Someone who can understand the organization of knowledge and the varying database structures;
- A people-oriented person, one who is outgoing and friendly with a desire to help and who has a high degree of patience;
- A person with the ability to differentiate between those questions they can answer and those that should be referred (Bowser, 1996).

Hiring can be accomplished in a number of ways: (1) through advertisements in the career center and on the library bulletin board; (2) through word of mouth; (3) through existing student assistants advertising to their friends, and (4) through internal hiring of student assistants from other library departments who wish to move into a position seen as higher level and more interesting (in our library it also pays accordingly). Each method has its advantages and disadvantages. Hiring through the career center can target freshmen and sophomores who may remain in the position for some time but who may take more training. Hiring through word of mouth often works well but can result in a too homogenous group of assistants. Hiring from within brings students who already have knowledge of and training within the library but can lead to resentment from other departments who have put the work into training that student (Winston & Downing, 1998).

An important part of the hiring process is the development of an accurate job description for the position. A job description for a Student Information Assistant should include the department, job title and supervisor as well as a list of expected duties and responsibilities. The qualifications for the positions should be included and may be categorized under such headings as "Knowledge of . . . " "Ability to . . . " and "Experience." In addition, it is advisable to develop a list of competencies that Student Information Assistants will be expected to have achieved by a defined date. This list of competencies can then be used as a source for SIA evaluations.

TRAINING

The training of Student Information Assistants is a high priority especially with the continually changing electronic resources we have available. Initial training will vary depending on the library, but a minimal list is outlined below:

- Orientation to the library and introductions to staff members;
- Locations within the library–evacuation procedures;
- Personnel issues–timesheets, working hours, evaluations (when, what will be evaluated, expectations);
- Training on the "floor"–extensive time to practice on the databases using real life questions;
- Training on printing and downloading;
- Training on the on-line catalog (including subject headings and classification);
- Training on simple problems with the machines/printers.

Additional training will depend on the tasks assigned to student information assistants within your library. In our library their main task is to assist students in using the computers and the single networked printer on the floor. This responsibility includes directing students to an appropriate database for their topic and helping them in retrieving and printing documents. Librarians do "reference roving" during their shifts but reference roving is also an important component of the information assistants' duties. Through their reference roving, they encourage hesitant users to ask for help and they let the user know that it is OK not to know. In addition, their offering of point-of-use database help often leads to a reference referral (Ramirez, 1994). Additional tasks include loading paper in all printers, copiers, and microform machines regularly; fixing minor problems as necessary; and notifying their supervisor and Systems when problems arise with the machines or printers on the floor. During break times, which are slower, additional tasks may be added, which include such items as aiding in the production of reference flyers, updating signage, the entering of statistics into spreadsheets, etc.

The supervisor should not be the only staff member involved in the training. In my own setting, staff from Cataloging provide training on the on-line catalog; Systems provides training on the reference machines and the printing system; Public Services provides training on copiers and microform machines, and reference librarians provide ongoing training on specific subject areas and resources (both print and electronic). In some cases, experienced Information Assistants who have been employed for at least a year can also assist in providing a portion of the training.

One of the major parts of a Student Information Assistant's job is usually answering general questions about the databases and directing students to an appropriate resource. There are several concerns here regarding training. One concern is that the student will not know how to recognize when a more complicated question is concealed within a general or directional question. The second, related, concern is that a student may not refer a question or ask for help when necessary. These concerns can be answered through a training process that focuses on providing training in reference interviewing techniques. In addition, all staff (including librarians) need to refer questions when appropriate to the subject specialist in that area (McCarthy, 1984). Praise and encouragement when questions are referred correctly is essential. In our library we also have SIAs keep statistics on how many questions they refer each month. In this way it is possible to see who may not be referring enough and, conversely, who is referring a lot and may need additional training in some areas.

In order to help students correctly identify a patron's needs, as well as the need for referral, we teach reference interviewing skills. These skills include the following:

- Teaching the skills of acknowledgement and restatement;
- Showing how to ask open-ended questions;

- Asking that SIAs spend time clarifying what the user needs;
- Determining how the patron might be using the information (term paper, presentation, debate, etc.);
- Most importantly, following up with the patron to see if the direction or information provided has been helpful.

The second part of the training consists of having the students take questions from reference appointments and annotate them as to which database or reference source the student should use and why. We have also constructed a Student Information Assistant workbook where they go through a series of questions, ranging from the simple, "Where are the encyclopedias located?" to the more difficult, focusing on particular topics and the resources needed. The students work on the workbook individually after the initial training, although their supervisor is available for questions. The workbooks are turned in to the supervisor within six weeks of the start of the semester so that any problem areas can be identified.

In addition to more formal training methods, observation and practice of reference skills are extremely important. One way to assist students with the dilemma of when to refer is through the use of role-play and active learning. This provides them the opportunity to work through some actual situations and questions. Doing this in a group meeting allows for all to participate and all to join in on evaluating each student's response to his question: Was his answer good enough; should the question have been referred? The role-playing stimulates discussion, allows for human relations skills training, and provides for more effective problem solving (Sheets, 1998). These role-play situations provide students with new knowledge and ways to integrate that knowledge into their interactions on the floor. Sessions may be divided into three parts: icebreaker, role-play, closure. Use the icebreaker to make everyone feel comfortable and ready for the session. Let the students know that it is OK to make mistakes and that there is always more than one answer to a question; encourage risk-taking. In the closure phase, reinforce the learning that has taken place and talk about how that learning can be transformed into on-the-job behaviors (Swink, 1993).

In training students to refer to a subject specialist when there is any question of their ability to answer fully a question, one also has to make sure that the subject specialist is then available. In a study conducted by Halldorsen and Murfin (1977), they found that of six questions referred to subject specialists, only two were referred successfully because of the unavailability of the subject specialist. One way we try to avoid this is by having students make reference appointments. If the Student Information Assistant (or librarian) cannot assist the patron in enough depth or locate the information needed, she is encouraged to fill out an appointment form for a reference appointment with a librarian.

A problem is that students do not easily recognize the difference between reference librarians and SIAs, and so expect SIAs to be able to answer all their questions. Conversely, SIAs may feel they are giving students good answers, but are often not aware of additional resources that could help. Surveys conducted at my own library over the past few years have shown that students do not know or recognize the difference between Student Information Assistants and librarians. The latest survey, conducted in Spring 1999, showed that of those responding, 61.2% said they did not know the difference between SIAs and reference librarians, while 38.8% said they did (Biggs & Borin, 1999). The difference often becomes the most blurred when the student is a graduate student and can legitimately answer many specialized questions within the discipline. There are few easy answers to this dilemma; possibilities include adding the word "student" to identification badges and referring to the individuals as students. Most important, however, is training so that the students accept the idea that they should not attempt to answer every question they receive and so they are willing to actively ask for help at any stage of the reference process. This same survey also showed (as have other surveys on perceptions of reference student assistants) that students used the SIAs extensively and were appreciative of the amount of help they received as well as the willingness of the assistants on the floor to provide requested help (Dawkins & Jackson, 1986).

Other training issues might best be dealt with in regular meetings or in a small workshop. This might include such issues as student use of the Internet, dealing with difficult patrons, and student use of e-mail on research computers. Ongoing training on new databases or changes in existing ones should be provided to both reference librarians and SIAs on a regular basis. One important aspect of our ongoing training has been to have different subject librarians provide training on the resources within their discipline, for example, science and business.

This provides SIAs with a greater awareness of the wide variety of material available and encourages them to refer in-depth questions in that area to the subject librarian. Maintaining a training manual for the Student Information Assistants can be a real help in the training process. There is so much information to cover in this type of training that a student cannot be expected to remember it without assistance. Providing individual manuals for each SIA provides the SIA with a constant source to refer back to, as well as giving him the opportunity to annotate it with his own additional notes.

SUPERVISION

Once the student assistants are trained, the daily supervision can still be time consuming. Providing daily feedback throughout the semester is important in order to give immediate praise or correction and to prepare the student for the end-of-semester evaluation by providing time for improvements in weak areas. Regular meetings are essential if a student is working in a reference/electronic resource area because of the constantly changing environment. Databases are constantly updating search and help screens, new databases are added, classes come in with specific assignments, and all these require communication. In addition to regular meetings, a mailbox for each student is essential as is access to an e-mail account that can be checked as a part of his daily duties.

Retention of students is a priority because of the extensive training required for this position. Retention can be encouraged in a number of ways. As we have required more technical knowledge of our students, for example, we have increased the minimum starting salary level that these assistants start at to compensate. On a smaller level we hold potlucks at the end of each semester for the students where staff provide the food and students are encouraged to attend. At these potlucks we highlight student achievements, impending graduations, etc.

On an ongoing basis we work to mentor students and to develop their interest in graduate study in library and information science and other related careers. This was a goal of the original program and one we are trying to continue. We have had some small success in this area with one former SIA having gone on to achieve her MLS, while another is working as a library paraprofessional and two current members of our SIAs are now applying to library school.

EVALUATION

Evaluations for Student Information Assistants often need to be tailored differently from the generic evaluation forms provided by the Human Resources department. In the early years of our program we used both the generic form and an additional form, which looked at the competencies we expected the students to have mastered. In more recent years we have moved to having them evaluated not only by their supervisor, but also by the librarians with whom they work. At the end of every semester each reference librarian is asked to fill out an evaluation form on the Student Information Assistants with whom she has worked. The form (see Figure 1), which was adapted from one used at Leavey Library, University of Southern California, provides input, both to the students and the supervisor, on the strengths, weaknesses, and areas where extra training might be needed. The students are given the forms with the ratings only, comments are typed and annotated separately and names and identifying notes are removed so that librarians feel free to be candid in their ratings. Work qualities that are especially important in this area and that should be included either in a generic or specific evaluation include the following: cooperation with fellow workers; customer service philosophy; ability to accept and respond to constructive criticism; communication skills; and approachability (Kenney & Painter, 1995).

Effective hiring and training provide a solid basis for the retention of student employees throughout their degree program. Including higher-level as well as routine tasks keeps them motivated. This has proved true for our library in that the higher level of tasks (and pay) involved in the Student Information Assistant positions attracts students from within the library as well as outside and provides motivation to stay in the position, while in school. As students become more experienced in the position additional duties may be added based on the students' abilities, experience and interests. These might include acting as librarian assistants in instruction sessions, leading informational tours of the library, updating library information guides, and creating new point-of-use guides for the databases (Stephenson & St. Clair, 1996). Additionally, it is possible to develop student supervisory

FIGURE 1

CSU San Marcos
Librarian Review
Information Assistants

Information Assistant_______________ Date__________

Librarian_________________ Signature______________

On the average how often have you worked with this student?

_____2-3 times week _____once a week _____occasionally

Please rate your response to the following statements, where one is strongly agree and four is strongly disagree. If you feel unable to evaluate the student in a particular area, skip to the next statement.

	SA			SD
1. The student is aware of patrons and appears approachable.	1	2	3	4
2. The student is courteous, helpful and professional to all patrons.	1	2	3	4
3. The student communicates well with patrons.	1	2	3	4
4. The student circulates the floor regularly without being reminded.	1	2	3	4
5. The student conducts a reference interview to ascertain a patron's need, asks questions to clarify if necessary.	1	2	3	4
6. The student makes referrals to a librarian or equipment technician when appropriate.	1	2	3	4
7. The student is able to choose an appropriate database to answer a patron's question.	1	2	3	4
8. The student is eager to learn and listens to suggestions from the librarian.	1	2	3	4

Comments:

positions such as Lead SIA to provide additional training opportunities, a career ladder, and the possibility of a higher pay scale.

These supervisory positions can be responsible for any number of designated tasks. As an example, the Lead Information Assistant position at CSU San Marcos Library is responsible for the following:

- Statistics entering and maintenance in Excel (including SIA, reference and database statistics);
- Timesheet collection and submission to Reference Coordinator;
- Updating of flyers and signs on floor as necessary or as requested by Reference Coordinator;

- Keeping the SIA schedule up-to-date and making changes;
- Filing of reference newsletters, updates, etc., in the Reference Office;
- Upkeep of the printed serials list.

CONCLUSION

Paraprofessional staff supervise most student assistants who work in libraries. Reference librarians, however, more generally supervise Student Information Assistants. The hiring, supervision, training, and evaluation of these assistants is time-consuming and offers many challenges but it also provides a way for libraries to enhance the academic success of students, and to target the program particularly to assist minority and disadvantaged students. While there is not universal agreement on the role of student assistants in the reference area, I would suggest that university students at-large profit through their interaction with role models in the reference area (Chu, 1997). Student Information Assistants in our library have proved to be a worthwhile and valued investment, certainly in terms of helping students to succeed with their immediate research needs but more importantly in assisting us as a library to build the lifelong information literacy skills toward which we aim.

REFERENCES

Biggs, Bonnie and Jacqueline Borin (1999), "Library Survey," CSU San Marcos, Library & Information Services.

Bowser, Eugene O. (1996), "Database Assistants: The Student Workers of the New Era of Automation," *Colorado Libraries* (Winter): 13-16.

Chu, Felix (1997), "Another Look at Staffing the Reference Desk," *College & Research Libraries News* (November): 713.

Dawkins, Willie Mae and Jeffrey Jackson (1986), "Enhancing Reference Services: Students as Assistants," *Technicalities* 6 (August): 4-7.

Halldorsson, Egill A. and Marjorie E. Murfin (1977), "The Performance of Professionals and Non-Professionals in the Reference Interview," *College and Research Libraries* 38 (September 1977): 385-95.

Judd, Blanche E., Michael J. McLane and Nancy Seale Osborne (1994), "Valuing Diversity: Students Helping Students," *The Reference Librarian:* 93-110.

Kenney, Donald J. and Frances O. Painter (1995), "Recruiting, Hiring and Assessing Student Workers in Academic Libraries," *Journal of Library Administration* 21: 29-45.

MacAdam, Barbara and Darlene P. Nichols (1988), "Peer Information Counseling at the University of Michigan Undergraduate Library," *Journal of Academic Librarianship* 14: 80-81.

McCarthy, Constance (1984), "Paraprofessionals, Student Assistants and the Reference Clan: An Application of Contemporary Management Theory," *Proceedings of the ACRL Third National Conference, Seattle (*April 4-7, 1984): 382-386.

Ramirez, Jennii L. (1994), "Reference Rover: The Hesitant Patron's Best Friend," *College & Research Libraries News* (June): 354-357.

Sheets, Janet (1998), "Role-Playing as a Training Tool for Reference Student Assistants," *Reference Services Review* (Spring): 37-41.

Sonntag, Gabriela (1993), "Information Technology Peer Counselors: A Proposal," Lottery grant proposal. CSU San Marcos.

Stephenson, Nina K. and Linda St. Clair (1996), "Extending the Clan: Graduate Assistantships in the Reference Department," *Reference Services Review* 24 (Fall): 29-36, 66.

Swink, David F. (1993), "Role-Play Your Way to Learning," *Training and Development* (May): 91-97.

Winston, Mark and Karen Dowling (1998), "Helping Students of Color Succeed: Implementing and Managing a Peer Information Counseling Program," *Leading Ideas* (Winter). *http://www.arl.org/diversity/leading/issue3/pic.html*

Integrating Informal Professional Development into the Work of Reference

Karla J. Block
Julia A. Kelly

SUMMARY. The dynamic environment of reference work demands that reference staff engage in ongoing professional development opportunities. The Bio-Medical Library at the University of Minnesota offers an informal, flexible, and highly interactive professional development program for those who staff the Reference Desk. The program, suitable for librarians and paraprofessionals at all levels of experience, combines a variety of opportunities, among them e-sessions on new tools, a review of basic Reference Desk competencies, a summer search camp, and a Library Staff Resources web site.

KEYWORDS. Professional development, reference work, interactive training

---

Karla J. Block is Head of Access Services, Bio-Medical Library, University of Minnesota, 505 Essex Street SE, Minneapolis, MN 55455 (E-mail: block006@tc.umn.edu). Julia A. Kelly is Reference Librarian/Bibliographer, Magrath Library, University of Minnesota, 1984 Buford Avenue, St. Paul, MN 55108 (E-mail: jkelly@tc.umn.edu).

The authors would like to acknowledge the contributions that all members of the Reference staff at the Bio-Medical Library, in particular Kathy Robbins, Sunny Worel, and Del Reed, have made to the Library's professional development program.

[Haworth co-indexing entry note]: "Integrating Informal Professional Development into the Work of Reference." Block, Karla J., and Julia A. Kelly. Co-published simultaneously in *The Reference Librarian* (The Haworth Information Press, an imprint of The Haworth Press, Inc.) No. 72, 2001, pp. 207-217; and: *Doing the Work of Reference: Practical Tips for Excelling as a Reference Librarian* (ed: Celia Hales Mabry) The Haworth Information Press, an imprint of The Haworth Press, Inc., 2001, pp. 207-217. Single or multiple copies of this article are available for a fee from The Haworth Document Delivery Service [1-800-342-9678, 9:00 a.m. - 5:00 p.m. (EST). E-mail address: getinfo@haworthpressinc.com].

In today's dynamic library world, reference librarians routinely play a multitude of roles. "No longer are basic desk reference and on-line searching the parameters of the job. Currently, web pages, networked campuses, community outreach, and distance education are all falling under the purview" of reference librarians (Robles and Wyatt, 1996). In addition to these expanding roles, "libraries are experiencing unprecedented changes in technology, clientele, services, and organization" (Painter, 1992). This change has been "so dramatic and so rapid that many librarians and support staff are truly suffering from future shock" (Shaughnessy, 1992). In addition to these rapid and dramatic changes, many new graduates are entering the field as reference librarians (Robles and Wyatt, 1996). Today's dynamic environment of reference work demands that reference staff–whether newly-hired or seasoned, professional or paraprofessional–engage in ongoing professional development opportunities. We must remember that "as information providers, we need to focus on and provide training for those functions that are uniquely ours, and we need to do this *well.* Good reference service is one of the most basic services libraries provide" (Kalvee, 1996).

The Bio-Medical Library at the University of Minnesota, just like so many other libraries, has encountered expanding professional roles for Reference librarians, a growing staff, and profound changes in technology, resources, library services, and clientele. The Bio-Medical Library serves five professional schools (Medicine, Nursing, Pharmacy, Dentistry, and Public Health) and several additional programs in the health sciences. The Library's collection contains over 437,000 volumes, including 4,800 current journal subscriptions and 1,000 curriculum-related media and computer programs. The Library has one hundred public workstations with wired Ethernet access and supports BioMedSearch, the library's database search system, which is available remotely to all members of the University of Minnesota's community. The Library employs fifty-nine full-time-equivalent (FTE) staff, including fifteen professional librarians.

The Bio-Medical Library's Reference Desk is headed by a professional librarian, with the assistance of two paraprofessionals who are employed to work primarily in the Reference area. Additionally, most of the Bio-Medical Library's professional librarians and many of its paraprofessionals work several hours per week at the Reference Desk. A few student employees also staff the Reference Desk, primarily during weekend and evening hours. The Reference collection includes almost 1200 books along with thirty active subscriptions to print indexes and fifteen active subscriptions to electronic indexes.

Staff new to the Reference Desk receive an orientation to the services and resources available there, and spend their first few months working closely with more experienced staff members. Faced with the desire to provide ongoing Reference-related professional development opportunities, several librarians recognized that not only must learning be a continuing process for *all* Reference staff, from the director to entry-level librarians (Painter, 1992), but training should be structured to include both formal and informal activities (Creth, 1986). As a supplement to the more formal training provided to all new Reference staff, a voluntary, informal, flexible, and highly interactive professional development program evolved. The program, suitable for librarians, paraprofessionals, and student employees at all levels of experience, combines a variety of opportunities, many of which will be highlighted below. The program combines opportunities and resources in three areas: interactive activities, informational activities, and professional development tools.

INTERACTIVE ACTIVITIES

Including active learning activities in the Bio-Medical Library's professional development program has been a consistent priority. "Adults learn best with active involvement, by solving realistic problems. If adults work training questions out for themselves, they are more likely to be able to work out a similar problem on the job. Active learning promotes the use of ingenuity and imagination rather than performance of a task in a set manner" (Woodard, 1995). Based on this idea, many of the Bio-Medical Library's informal sessions are interactive in nature, including either audience participation or voluntary exercises completed before or after the scheduled meeting.

In the early 1990s, with Gopher just on the horizon, the librarians would gather in one another's offices for weekly self-help sessions, pooling the tidbits of knowledge they had gained and experimenting with the rudimentary search capabilities of the Internet. These meetings continued for several years, growing somewhat more formal in nature, with topics announced in advance and an occasional visit from one of the Library's computing staff.

As the collection of Reference tools, both print and electronic, became larger and more varied, there was a need for a more structured method of training new staff. The idea of refreshing the skills of veteran staff also seemed important. A small group of librarians developed a list of "Reference Competencies," or the basic skills that were needed by any person working at the Reference Desk. These competencies include knowledge of the major tools in the print Reference collection, searching proficiency in the databases in the health sciences field, exposure to specialized tools, and background on customer service principles. The identified competencies are listed in Appendix A and are also available at http://www.biomed.lib.umn.edu/staff/ RefComp_main_page.html.

The Reference Competencies have been used in several ways. One or two staff members have taken responsibility for each area, and thus build special expertise. They develop an outline for the topic, which is mounted on the Staff Resources web site (http://www.biomed.lib.umn.edu/staff). Many of the topics include exercises and suggested answers in addition to an outline. When new staff begin work at the Reference Desk, part of their Reference training includes a one-on-one session with those responsible for a topic. To enhance the skills of experienced staff, presentations on individual subjects are given regularly at staff meetings. When appropriate, voluntary exercises are distributed, and those who complete them are recognized at future meetings. To enhance motivation and an element of fun, small prizes are often awarded to those staff who complete multiple competencies successfully.

Although library users now do most of their own literature searching, library staff are still expected to be expert searchers. Maintaining these skills without doing a large number of mediated searches can be a challenge. To address this issue, a summer "Search Camp" was organized. A different database was the focus each week, and organizers sent out sample searches for participants to try. One Medline search was included each week to build expertise in the primary database in the field. Participants then gathered to discuss their search strategies and results. In all, fifteen databases were explored during Search Camp this year, among them CINAHL, CancerLit, Popline, PsycInfo, PubMed, International Pharmaceutical Abstracts, Health and Psychosocial Instruments, Current Contents, and others. Commemorative t-shirts were awarded to all Search Camp participants, and plans were made to conduct future Search Camps during the summer months.

Another activity used to enhance searching skills was a hands-on search contest, which was used to introduce the staff to PubMed, a new version of Medline available free-of-charge to the general public. The leader of the project sent out background information and sample searches in advance, and staff in attendance were given searches of increasing difficulty. To encourage friendly competition, those who successfully completed the searches most quickly were recognized.

An interactive component was also apparent in exchanges with other libraries. These exchanges often served as a catalyst for growth among library staff. Six staff members from different units traveled to the University of Wisconsin-Madison Health Sciences Libraries for a two-day visit, spending the majority of time with the unit that most closely corresponded to their own. A similar exchange was organized with the University of Minnesota Law Library, and in this case, whole units such as Access Services and Reference made a visit to the other library. In the same vein, individual staff members have taken advantage of cross-training, spending one day a week for several weeks working in related units such as government documents or the history of medicine.

The interactive aspects of training also have carried over into training programs for student employees who staff the Reference Desk during evening and weekend hours. In order to enrich their training experience, their supervisor developed weekly exercises focused on answering specific types of Reference questions or utilizing various print or electronic resources. Many of the questions are real-life examples contributed by seasoned Reference staff. They include the intricacies of the on-line catalog, gems found in the appendices of Reference books, and special challenges in verifying citations. After these exercises had been developed for student employees, it seemed logical to encourage voluntary participation as well by the librarians and paraprofessionals who staff the Reference Desk. Staff–whether professional, paraprofessional, or student–new to the Reference Desk stand to gain the most from these exercises, though seasoned Reference staff may find the exercises valuable as well. Some sample questions include:

- Who is the director of nursing at Norwalk Hospital (Norwalk, CT)?
- How many colleges in the United States offer graduate degrees in international health? Are any of them in Minnesota? If so, where?
- Does any library on campus own "Improvement of Blood Compatibility of Membranes by Discharge Polymerization," H.K. Yasuda, M.O. Bumgarner, R.G. Mason: ACS ORPL Prepar. 34(1) 5740577 (1974)?
- A patron brings in a copy of the chapter of a book. It is chapter 19 and is titled "Martha Rogers' Unitary Person Model." The authors are Stephanie I. Muth Quillin and Judith Aumente Runk. The chapter begins on page 285 and the most recent citation in the bibliography is 1986. What is the title of the book? Does the Bio-Medical Library own the book?
- How many Minnesotans were diagnosed with cancer in 1998?

INFORMATIONAL ACTIVITIES

Informational activities, while more traditional than participatory activities, also play an important role in the Bio-Medical Library's professional development program. To introduce new electronic tools or provide background on resources that are outside the main subject area of the health sciences, a traditional lecture and demonstration format is sometimes used. Known within the Library as "e-sessions," these gatherings grew out of the weekly self-help meetings held in librarians' offices in the early 1990s, and emphasize practical examples and may serve as a springboard for individual practice. With new databases or full-text resources, one of the staff prepares an informal presentation which may take place in the Reference area or a small classroom. The scope of the tool and its strengths and weaknesses are covered, with an emphasis on search capabilities and features that may be of interest to particular users. Recent e-sessions have included:

- WebCT and demonstration of a real class offered on First Class
- Books in Print vs. Amazon.com for locating books
- Using web phone books efficiently
- Inference Find (a meta search engine)
- Substance abuse resources

- Statistical sources on the Internet
- Using the Internet to find the "best doctors" and "best hospitals"
- Minnesota Health Profiles (an on-line database)
- Eudora (e-mail) filters
- Endnote and other bibliographic formatting software

For subject areas where there may not be an in-house expert or specialist, librarians from across campus are invited to share their knowledge. For the health sciences, these related topics have included chemical structure searching, patents, and government documents. Presenters often provide background reading material and exercises for library staff to complete at their own pace after the presentation. An added benefit of these sessions is the fact that the staff get to know the local expert and feel more comfortable calling that person for help in the future.

Other informational activities include weekly staff meetings of Public Services and Reference staff. The meetings typically consist of announcements and discussion of library services and resources, along with frequent demonstrations of new resources and tools. Notes from the meetings are distributed via e-mail messages, as is reference-related information about policies, resources, and services. Professional staff who have attended conferences or meetings are also encouraged to share what they learned via an e-mail message.

PROFESSIONAL DEVELOPMENT TOOLS

As the variety and number of Reference resources and services continue to grow and change, librarians have turned to various professional development tools designed to help them stay current. Notes from e-sessions and reference-related e-mail messages are kept on file at the Reference Desk, while a bulletin board is used to display information about services, resources, or particularly important news items. A traditional rolodex of important phone numbers and database passwords is heavily used, and an electronic version of the rolodex has just been developed through the use of FileMaker Pro.

Another important tool is AskRef, a database of unusual, common, or difficult reference questions that have been asked by Bio-Medical Library patrons, along with sources that provide the answers to these questions. The database was created by staff using inexpensive software (askSam) that supports free-text searching. AskRef previously resided on a stand-alone workstation at the Reference Desk, but was converted to a web page in 1998 (http://www.biomed.lib.umn.edu/staff/ask.html). Over two hundred questions are included in the database, and while most of them are not asked frequently, they typically were difficult questions that involved extra time and effort to answer. AskRef enables staff to avoid duplication of work if the same question is asked again. Questions are added at the suggestion of those who work at the Reference Desk, and the database is updated about once a month. Sample questions from the database include:

- What is the GPEP report?
- Who discovered the association between ulcers and the helicobacter pylori?
- What causes knuckles to crack?
- What is the Rainbow series?
- Where can you find a human anatomy atlas that uses photographs of cadavers?
- Where is a database on post-traumatic stress syndrome located?
- Where can you find lists of companies that contract to do clinical trials?

Several of the librarians who work at the Reference Desk, attempting to manage the abundance of electronic Reference resources, created a Bio-Medical Library Staff Resources web site for training and professional development purposes. The site (http://www.biomed.lib.umn.edu/staff.html) includes links to several important professional development resources, several of which are highlighted here. The Bio-Medical Library Reference Desk page, which serves as the homepage for the staff workstations at the Reference Desk, includes links to important and frequently used resources organized into three areas: (1) Health Reference (medical indexes and databases, science indexes and data bases, chemical and drug information, classification/taxonomy, government resources, and statistics); (2) Organization and Administration (campus referral, company information, employment, grants and funding, health education, hospital and clinic resources, and meetings and events); and (3) General Reference (general indexes and catalogs, general reference sources, biographical directories and information, electronic publications, news, and subject lists and search engines). The page was developed by one of the librarians as a training tool and a centralized alternative to maintaining ever-changing Netscape bookmarks on individual Reference workstations.

The Reference Competencies, an important interactive professional development tool discussed previously, are supported by a web page on the Staff Resources web site. Outlines and exercises for each of the competencies are included, along with links to additional web resources when appropriate.

Another web page provides links to a variety of professional development and training opportunities offered by the University of Minnesota for its professional and paraprofessional staff. The training opportunities listed cover a range of topics, including general computer skills, specialized software and web development skills, supervisory and managerial skills, career enrichment, and teaching skills. The training opportunities also include a variety of methods, including user groups, computer training aids, videos, workshops and seminars, short courses, and for-credit courses. Bio-Medical Library staff are encouraged to browse the offerings periodically and discuss professional development offerings with their supervisors.

Bio-Medical Library staff bring together an extensive array of work experience, educational background, foreign language skills, and software and database experience. In order to capitalize on this fact, staff were surveyed for their educational degrees and experience in work, foreign languages, software, and databases. A web page based on the survey results was created, allowing staff to search for individuals with expertise or experience in a specific area, from foreign languages to FileMaker Pro to the Library's circulation system software.

CONCLUSION

Most libraries probably already follow a fairly formal method of training new Reference staff. But recognizing that there is a constant need for updated professional knowledge, Reference librarians may wish to focus more attention on the need for a supplement to these more formalized programs. It must be stressed that "reference librarians are truly in the knowledge business, both on behalf of their users and for themselves. Librarians cannot help the users fulfill their information needs if they themselves are ignorant of the sources, lack the ability to acess the information they know exists, or are unwilling to go that extra step to gain that knowledge and skills. A well-planned training and continuing education program will at least give the reference staff the tools they need to tackle the tasks at hand and strategies for approaching new problems as they arise" (Woodard, 1995). An informal, flexible, and interactive professional development program need not be overwhelming or burdensome. Starting with small steps and building on professional development opportunities already in place, libraries can build flexible and informal professional development programs that evolve to fit continually changing needs.

REFERENCES

Association of College and Research Libraries (1996), *Clip Note: No. 24. Reference Training in Academic Libraries*, compiled by Kimberly Robles and Neal Wyatt. Chicago: American Library Association.

Creth, Sheila A. (1986), *Effective On-the-job Training: Developing Library Human Resources*. Chicago: American Library Association.

Kalvee, Debbie (1996), "Successful Reference Training on a Shoestring," *Library Administration & Management* 10, no. 4 (Fall), 210-13.

Painter, Frances O. (1992), "Definitions of Staff Development: A Sampling," in *Staff Development: A Practical Guide*, edited by Anne Grodzins Lipow and Deborah A. Carver. Chicago: American Library Association, 89-94.

Shaughnessy, Thomas W. (1992), "Approaches to Developing Competencies in Research Libraries," *Library Trends* 41, no. 2 (Fall), 282-98.

Woodard, Beth S. (1995), "Reference Staff Training and Development," in *Reference and Information Services: An Introduction*, edited by Richard E. Bopp and Linda C. Smith. Englewood, CO: Libraries Unlimited, Inc., 185-206.

APPENDIX A. Reference Competencies at the Bio-Medical Library

Basic Skills	**Specialized Skills**	**General Methods**
Ready reference	Clinical practice guidelines	Reference interview
Citation Clarification	History of Medicine & HistLine	Working with patients & families
Database Searching	Consumer health resources	Confidentiality
Dictionaries	Tests, surveys & questionnaires	Problem patrons
History of Medicine	Genetics databases	Phone guidelines
Quotations, biological facts, and syndromes	Bibliographic formatting software	Referring clients to BIS (fee-based service) & other sources
Remote access to & output from electronic databases	Standards (health-related and science/technology)	Disability Resources
Locating & using electronic journals	Chemical structure searching	Reference consultation & research service
Use of the Internet for Reference questions	Patent basics	
LUMINA (online catalog)		
Taking in requests		
Access details (alphabetizing, problem titles, etc.)		

These competencies are available online at http://www.biomed.lib.umn.edu/ RefComp_main_page.html

Acquiring Subject Knowledge to Provide Quality Reference Service

Kierstin C. Hill

SUMMARY. A reference librarian frequently provides assistance in disciplines with which he is not well acquainted as to terminology or fundamental principles. Whether an advanced subject degree has been obtained or not, reference librarians have an obligation to themselves and the community they serve to broaden and expand their subject knowledge continually. This article outlines the justifications for gaining subject knowledge and the kinds of subject knowledge that reference librarians should possess, as well as offering practical suggestions for its acquisition. *[Article copies available for a fee from The Haworth Document Delivery Service: 1-800-342-9678. E-mail address: <getinfo@haworthpressinc.com> Website: <http://www.HaworthPress.com> © 2001 by The Haworth Press, Inc. All rights reserved.]*

KEYWORDS. Subject knowledge, reference service, reference librarian education

INTRODUCTION

"The reference librarian is one of the few professionals who is being paid not only for doing, but also for knowing" (Donovan,

---

Kierstin C. Hill is Chemical Sciences Subject Specialist, Brigham Young University, 2320 Harold B. Lee Library, Provo, UT 84602 (E-mail: kierstin_hill@byu.edu).

[Haworth co-indexing entry note]: "Acquiring Subject Knowledge to Provide Quality Reference Service." Hill, Kierstin C. Co-published simultaneously in *The Reference Librarian* (The Haworth Information Press, an imprint of The Haworth Press, Inc.) No. 72, 2001, pp. 219-228; and: *Doing the Work of Reference: Practical Tips for Excelling as a Reference Librarian* (ed: Celia Hales Mabry) The Haworth Information Press, an imprint of The Haworth Press, Inc., 2001, pp. 219-228. Single or multiple copies of this article are available for a fee from The Haworth Document Delivery Service [1-800-342-9678, 9:00 a.m. - 5:00 p.m. (EST). E-mail address: getinfo@haworthpressinc.com].

1969). If such a statement is true, then what kinds of things is a reference librarian responsible for knowing? Surely, knowledge of reference sources, a wide variety of search engines, and steps of the research process are all critical. General bibliographic knowledge and structure of information is also mandatory, along with others. There is another piece of knowledge underlying every reference transaction that is oftentimes never noticed until it is not present. That knowledge sometimes taken for granted is subject knowledge. Every reference librarian has experienced at one time or another the insecurity felt when a patron asks a question that concerns a subject completely unheard of or at least unfamiliar. Without some relevant subject knowledge, a reference librarian is unable to understand the patron's question, let alone identify a reference work that might contain the answer. In short, all other knowledge and training that the reference librarian possesses will not solve the problem unless the librarian first understands what information is needed (D'Aniello, 1989).

There are many proponents in the literature for advanced subject degrees for librarians. Often these voices call for advanced subject degrees so that librarians will gain respect, equality, credibility, and intellectual parity with teaching and research faculty, overlooking the effect it might have on the quality of reference service (Herubel, 1990, 1991; Jones, 1991). While the subject knowledge acquired through attainment of an advanced subject degree may enhance the quality of reference service, it is also recognized that obtaining an advanced subject degree can be challenging while continuing to work as a librarian and may not be possible in all instances.

The focus of this article lies not in arguing for or against advanced subject degrees for librarians, but rather in the value of obtaining relevant and pertinent background subject knowledge for use in the reference setting through less formal avenues. Whether an advanced subject degree has been obtained or not, reference librarians have an obligation to themselves and the community they serve to broaden and expand their subject knowledge continually.

WHY?

A review of the literature on the value of subject knowledge in reference work identifies several justifications for acquiring such knowledge. First, background subject knowledge at the reference desk is often necessary just to understand the question being asked and to conduct an effective reference interview (Stieg, 1980). Schiller (1965) states, "It is apparent that some common recognition of the subject must exist between the inquirer and the librarian before an answer can be supplied." For instance, if a patron is looking for a heat of combustion, the librarian must first recognize that this is a thermochemical property before identifying an appropriate reference source for the answer. In addition, background subject knowledge is necessary for an understanding of the context of the inquiry, the related issues involved, and any hurdles in locating an answer that may not be readily apparent to one without the appropriate background. Simply stated, the more the librarian knows about a topic, the more capable she is of supplying information about it (Swan, 1990).

Similarly, the effectiveness of the reference interview increases as subject knowledge increases. Determining the subject field of the inquiry is usually the first obstacle in conducting a search (Stych, 1972). The reference interview provides the information needed to make such a determination. The more extensive the librarian's background knowledge, the easier this first step is made. D'Aniello (1989) writes of the reference interview:

> . . . however, sometimes it is the interpretative ability of the librarian, a major determinant of which is the level of general or particular knowledge he or she possesses, that is the major factor in either the success or failure of a transaction. Further, human nature being what it is, patrons are far more open with a librarian who appears to know something of their topic than with one who is essentially ignorant of it.

Patrons who feel that the librarian understands their topic talk more freely about their information need; the reference interview proceeds with greater ease, and the librarian and patron reach an understanding more readily.

Second, background subject knowledge assists the librarian in providing accurate and useful information confidently. A study by Halldorsson and Murfin (1977) found that the reference desk staff's personal subject knowledge aided them in recognizing "faulty information," defined as misspellings or other inaccurate details, given during the reference interview. In these instances, where no personal subject knowledge was present, reference transaction success rates dropped to zero. Personal subject knowledge further assisted reference staff by helping to suggest possible solutions and to select the best sources. It also deterred the librarian from pursuing an erroneous path to finding the desired information.

Consequently, subject knowledge reduces uncertainty and discomfort in reference work and increases librarian confidence. Mendelsohn (1997) writes, "Knowledge is very often referred to in the discomfort felt at not knowing, and this is particularly true of subject knowledge." Without background subject knowledge, it is difficult for the librarian to determine whether the requested information simply does not exist or is just available in an unknown source (Whitlatch, 1990). This hampers the reference librarian's ability to provide effective service and to instill patron confidence in the answer. Reference librarians with subject knowledge are able to assist researchers with added self-assurance (McInnis, 1978).

Third, and perhaps most encompassing, is the patron's perception that the librarian is providing quality reference service. In a qualitative study conducted by Mendelsohn (1997) using both librarians and library patrons, knowledge and willingness to provide assistance are both identified as prerequisites to quality reference service. It was noted that willingness and knowledge are interrelated attributes because increased willingness is often due to greater librarian knowledge. As the librarian exhibits more willingness to provide help, the patron perceives that he is receiving quality reference assistance.

In addition, patrons prefer a librarian who demonstrates an understanding of their inquiries. As with other interpersonal relationships, the greater the common interests between people the stronger the relationship. In a patron-librarian relationship the common interest is the research question at hand. When the librarian exhibits an understanding of that problem, patrons realize there is a common interest and will return again for assistance. In such cases, the reference librarian is more likely to be perceived as giving good service (Stieg, 1980).

A study by Whitlatch (1990) found that high librarian expertise is associated with shorter service times that in turn may be associated with quality reference service. A brief example illustrates this point. Consider giving directions to a city museum to a passer-by who is obviously a local to the area. The instructions given will be much briefer than those given to a tourist who needs the same directions; the reason for this being that assumptions about what the local passer-by already knows about the area can be made. Directions given to the tourist must of necessity be more detailed because it must be assumed that the stranger knows very little about the city (Hirsch, 1987). Similarly, patrons asking for assistance at the reference desk can be more succinct if they know that the librarian understands the context of the research problem. It seems likely that increased librarian subject expertise would enable more efficient reference service, and, therefore, positively affect patron perceptions of the reference service received.

WHAT?

It might be concluded, then, that the most successful reference librarians are those who have a very broad base of subject knowledge. This subject knowledge is made up not only of the specialized knowledge of a given discipline, but also knowledge of the world at large.

Duckett (1989) outlines a checklist of qualities necessary in a person who provides reference service and includes "a good level of all-round knowledge" and "a good awareness of current events." Such all-round knowledge might include recognition of major literary figures and authors, consciousness of world history and geography, or cognizance of the most popular music groups. An awareness of current events enables the reference librarian to place into context a variety of inquiries resulting from news reports concerning politics, medicine, technology, or the environment.

D'Aniello (1989) explores the idea of general knowledge and reference service under the concept of "cultural literacy." Cultural literacy "lies above the everyday levels of knowledge that everyone possesses and below the expert level known only to specialists" (Hirsch, 1987). Culturally literate librarians do not necessarily have detailed subject knowledge, but possess an understanding of the common cultural vocabulary used by patrons. A library community has a right to expect that the reference librarian will have a frame of general knowledge in which to contextually place their queries. A reference librarian who is not culturally literate is unable to use her technical expertise to its fullest because the information need is not understood in the first place. Thus, the reference librarian has an obligation to have a broad understanding that includes a variety of interests and topics. This understanding does not necessarily have to be in depth, although specialties are also desirable, but it should be expansive.

Obviously, the kinds of subject knowledge a given reference librarian needs will vary depending upon the type of library and the community the collection serves. A librarian in a special library needs to be familiar with language and concepts of a specialized field while a librarian in a public library must be aware of concerns for which that community is likely to require information (Watson, 1992). A given level of specialization is certainly advantageous in any reference setting. Librarians who provide reference in specialized settings, however, have a particular obligation to know something of the subjects pertaining to that specialty. This includes a familiarity with the technical vocabulary used by the patrons as well as a broad understanding of the main theories, concepts, and developments in the discipline.

HOW?

While there is some, if not much, discussion in the literature on the value of subject knowledge in the reference setting, there is virtually no mention of how one is to acquire such knowledge. Stieg (1980) offers a very simple answer–read, read, read. Granted, this suggestion will build subject knowledge, but it is impossible to read widely in all fields. Watson (1992) states:

> This is at the crux of the problem created by the information explosion: no one can be widely read enough to have the knowledge needed to respond to every information request. It is not just difficult. It is impossible. Yet the librarian is somehow expected to have the necessary knowledge needed to help every individual who asks for assistance.

Aside from formal training programs or obtaining additional subject degrees, the following suggestions are offered as a way to broaden both general and subject knowledge for use at the reference desk.

Know Your Current Events

Frequently reference questions arise from items that have recently been in the news. Reading newspapers and magazines like *Time* or

Newsweek, watching the evening news, or listening to the radio provide you with general knowledge for use at the reference desk.

Watch Educational Television Programs and Visit Museums

Look for television documentaries that concern topics of possible relevance to research questions presented at your library. Museums can also be a useful place to pick up background knowledge to assist you in providing quality reference service to your patrons.

Browse Core Research Journals and Trade Journals

Browsing journals keeps you up-to-date on new developments in a given subject area. Even glancing at the Tables of Contents of key journals used by your patrons increases your knowledge. Trade journals and popular literature, such as *Popular Science*, provide understandable articles on current research or developments in a given field.

Browse Book Prefaces

Scan the prefaces, forewords, or introductions of books as they are added to the collection. Sometimes the books themselves may be too technical for complete understanding, but the prefaces often summarize the background research or the basis for the new book. This provides a frame of reference and a familiarity with some of the vocabulary patrons might use as they describe their research problem.

Browse the Reference Collection

Learning the sources in the reference collection and what kinds of information they contain is a useful way to pick up on the vocabulary and fundamental concepts of a given subject area. Due to the nature of reference sources, these items can provide basic introductions or comprehensive overviews that can assist you in establishing a foundation of knowledge. Plan to spend some time going through major reference works from the standpoint of familiarizing yourself with the information presented, not simply how the indexes work or what kind of ready reference tables they might contain. Specialized encyclopedias are especially useful. The *Magill's Survey* series provides concise, readable summaries on a variety of topics. Also, scan the contents of new reference books as they arrive in your library. These can alert you to recent advances and developments in a given discipline.

Meet with Teaching Faculty

Arrange one-on-one meetings with faculty teaching or conducting research in areas with which you would like to become familiar. The author's experience has been that professors enjoy talking about their research projects to someone who is interested. Such one-on-one meetings not only build public relations for the library, but also help to acquaint you with research topics that may later show up at the reference desk.

Attend Classes

If you work in an academic library, take advantage of all the courses being offered on campus. Make arrangements with the professor ahead of time to visit the class and listen to lectures. This is an easy, and often fun, way to pick up on major concepts or theories of a given discipline. It is not essential to understand every item of discussion, but the exposure to the subject is valuable and will provide a frame of reference the next time a student asks you for assistance.

Attend Seminars

Similarly, take advantage of seminars that may be offered at your institution or in your community. Seminars given by individuals in your community alert you to local research interests while seminars given by guest lecturers broaden your understanding of the world at large.

CONCLUSION

Reference librarians have an obligation to themselves and the community they serve to broaden and expand their subject knowledge continually. With such background knowledge the librarian is better able to provide quality reference service. Acquiring such knowledge for use in the reference setting can be challenging. McInnis (1978) summarizes:

> The task of informing oneself to this extent is a long process, requiring considerable individual capability and capacity. To those who consciously and deliberately seek to perform at a high level of achievement, progress does, however, occur with regularity. . . . Of course, acquiring this level of expertise requires that the individual have an inherent interest in the subject matter involved. Given such an interest, achieving an increasing level of expertise has its own momentum and is more or less self-sustaining.

As stated, informing oneself will take time and effort, and an interest in the subject involved does make the task easier. However, the suggestions offered above can be implemented on an individual basis without formal programming or schooling and as time permits. The rewards of subject knowledge at the reference desk will make the process well worth it.

REFERENCES

D'Aniello, Charles A. (1989), "Cultural Literacy and Reference Service," *RQ* (Spring), 370-380.

Donovan, William (1969), "The Reference Librarian and the Whole Truth," *RQ* 8 (Spring), 196-199.

Duckett, Bob (1989), "Reference Work, Staff Selection and General Knowledge," *Library Review* 38 (5), 14-21.

Halldorsson, Egill A., & Murfin, Marjorie E. (1977), "The Performance of Professionals and Nonprofessionals in the Reference Interview," *College & Research Libraries* 38 (September), 385-395.

Herubel, Jean-Pierre V.M. (1990), "The Ph.D. Librarian: A Personal Perspective," *College & Research Libraries News* 7 (July/August), 626-628.

_______. (1991), "To 'Degree' or Not to 'Degree': Academic Librarians and Subject Expertise," *College & Research Libraries News* 7 (July/August), 437.

Hirsch, E.D., Jr. (1987), *Cultural Literacy: What Every American Needs to Know.* Boston: Houghton Mifflin.

Jones, William G. (1991), "The Education of Academic Librarians: How Many Degrees Are Enough," *College & Research Libraries News* 9 (October), 584-586.

McInnis, Raymond G. (1978), *New Perspectives for Reference Service in Academic Libraries*. Westport, CT: Greenwood Press.

Mendelsohn, Jennifer (1997), "Perspectives on Quality of Reference Service in an Academic Library: A Qualitative Study," *RQ* 36 (Summer), 544-557.

Schiller, Anita R. (1965), "Reference Service: Instruction or Information," *Library Quarterly* 35 (January), 52-60.

Stieg, Margaret F. (1980), "Continuing Education and the Reference Librarian in the Academic and Research Library," *Library Journal* 105 (15 December), 2,547-2,551.

Stych, F.S. (1972), "Decision Factors in Search Strategy," *RQ* 12 (Winter), 143-147.

Swan, John C. (1990), "Rehumanizing Information: An Alternative Future," *Library Journal* 115 (September 1), 178-182.

Watson, Bob (1992), "Reference Services in an Information Age: A Public Library Perspective," *RQ* 31 (Summer), 499-506.

Whitlatch, Jo Bell (1990), *The Role of the Academic Reference Librarian*. New York: Greenwood Press.

LOOKING AT OUR USERS

Undergraduate Perceptions of the Reference Collection and the Reference Librarian in an Academic Library

Sandra Jenkins

SUMMARY. Many undergraduate students have no clear idea of the purpose and function of the reference collection and the services offered by the reference librarian. Uncertainty about these resources may cause students to overlook their usefulness, unsatisfactorily complete assignments, and develop a negative attitude concerning libraries. Through a survey, students related their perceptions of the reference collection and reference librarian. The results are intended to give the reference team insight into the students' conceptions and perhaps improve and enhance reference services to undergraduates. *[Article copies available for a fee from The Haworth Document Delivery Service: 1-800-342-9678. E-mail address: <getinfo@haworthpressinc.com> Website: <http://www.HaworthPress.com> © 2001 by The Haworth Press, Inc. All rights reserved.]*

Sandra Jenkins is Instructor, James C. Kirkpatrick Library, Central Missouri State University, JCKL 1458, Warrensburg, MO 64093 (E-mail: jenkins@libserv.cmsu.edu).

[Haworth co-indexing entry note]: "Undergraduate Perceptions of the Reference Collection and the Reference Librarian in an Academic Library." Jenkins, Sandra. Co-published simultaneously in *The Reference Librarian* (The Haworth Information Press, an imprint of The Haworth Press, Inc.) No. 73, 2001, pp. 229-241; and: *Doing the Work of Reference: Practical Tips for Excelling as a Reference Librarian* (ed: Celia Hales Mabry) The Haworth Information Press, an imprint of The Haworth Press, Inc., 2001, pp. 229-241. Single or multiple copies of this article are available for a fee from The Haworth Document Delivery Service [1-800-342-9678, 9:00 a.m. - 5:00 p.m. (EST). E-mail address: getinfo@haworthpressinc.com].

KEYWORDS. Undergraduate, student, reference collection, librarian, perception, attitude

As an instructor of LIS1600–Information Resources, an undergraduate course that addresses library resources and research skills, I have become aware that many students have little or no concept of the purpose of the reference collection and the reference librarian. As these are both vital resources in any library, it is important for students to utilize each to its full potential.

The reference collection incorporates many print resources, including encyclopedias, atlases, dictionaries, gazetteers, bibliographies, biographies, and directories. Electronic resources such as the on-line catalog, the Internet, and CD-ROM periodical indexes are considered a part of the reference collection as well. These materials are designed to be used quickly and easily. The reference librarian is an integral part of the reference department. Many students do not even notice the reference desk, let alone realize that the librarians are there to assist in a number of ways. The reference librarian can direct library users to other areas of the library, assist with locating appropriate information, instruct users in the use of electronic and print resources, and answer specific research questions. Most importantly, perhaps, the reference librarian often serves as a public relations representative for the entire library organization. How the students perceive the reference collection and the reference librarian, plus their utilization of these essential resources, can have a significant impact on their entire academic experience.

REVIEW OF THE LITERATURE

Geffert and Christensen (1998) note that there has been little in the library literature concerning students' attitudes toward the library. They make the point, "For bibliographic instruction and reference services to be truly effective it is essential to know more about the attitudes and skills that incoming students bring with them as they first encounter our libraries." For their study, 521 incoming freshmen were asked to answer the questions on the survey.

The finding of the study reinforced many of the preconceived ideas that Geffert and Christensen held. It also contradicted a few of their previous ideas. In regard to the reference collection, two interesting items surfaced. In answer to the question, "Which of the following tools have you used?" 49.9 percent had used the World Wide Web and 36.2 percent had used e-mail, the most used component of the Internet. Conversely, 89.4 percent had used *Encyclopedia Britannica* in print, and 73.7 percent had used *Readers' Guide to Periodical Literature* or other print periodical indexes. Is this a commentary on electronic versus print resources, or simply an indication of which resources are available in most high school libraries?

Radford (1998) conducted a study to measure the role of nonverbal communication in the student's interaction with a reference librarian. She spent a total of 37 hours observing 155 library users who interacted with 34 librarians at the reference desk. After the students had spoken with a reference librarian, Radford asked if she could interview them. All agreed. She wanted to discover what caused a student to approach a particular librarian over another, or to avoid the encounter altogether.

Five categories were developed to show why students chose one librarian over another; answer: (1) initiation–"the librarian initiates the encounter through multiple signals that include eye contact, body orientation, movement toward the user, and/or verbal enforcement"; (2) availability–basically the same as initiation, but does not involve any verbal enforcement; (3) proximity–this category addresses the physical location of one librarian as opposed to the other in relation to the student; (4) familiarity–the student indicated a previous encounter with the librarian; (5) gender–some students approached a particular librarian simply on the basis of this person being a man or a woman. Radford followed each of these categories with applicable comments from the students involved in the study.

Massey-Burzio (1998) used a focus group to gain insight into the viewpoint of people on the other side of the reference desk. Seeing things from the library user's or student's point of view can be very useful when evaluating effectiveness of services offered. "The goal of this study was to gather information from library users about their experiences in the library in order to see if the library was providing the kinds of services library users really wanted . . . and how helpful they felt reference staff were to them."

Thirty-eight people participated in the study. The main themes that came from her discussions with the focus groups were as follows:

Many people are uncomfortable asking questions. Most feel they know how to find information reasonably well and can manage the library well enough. In spite of their self-confidence with their library skills, most have difficulty utilizing resources, and most are not aware of the services and resources available in an academic library.

Eckwright, Hoskisson, and Pollastro (1998) maintain that observing proper etiquette at the reference desk is the ideal way to show patrons that reference librarians are approachable. They compare the work at the reference desk to any other job that requires close contact with the public. "The reference desk is the nerve center of the library. . . . Reference desk staffers fulfill a vital function for the public, and–for better or worse–are public relations representatives for the library." Appropriate behavior by the reference librarian goes a long way in alleviating anxiety and allowing for a positive library experience.

ANALYSIS OF THE DATA

In March 1999, the James C. Kirkpatrick Library (JCKL) was opened on the campus of Central Missouri State University in Warrensburg. Of course, this caused many changes in the way the library collection and services are viewed by the students. Many were very apprehensive about using the new facility. As the survey used in this study was administered within two weeks of transferring operations to the new building, questions regarding the location of resources may be skewed. Instructions were given on the survey asking the students to check all appropriate answers for each question.

Table 1 and Table 2 reflect a bit of this confusion. In the former building the reference librarian and collection were located on the first floor. In JCKL, both have been moved to the second floor. Additionally, an information desk has been added to the first floor. Some students may have confused this service point with the reference desk. A 65.1 percentage, or 131 of the 201 respondents, correctly indicated that the reference desk is on the second floor of JCKL. Fifty-nine students, or 29.3 percent, said that the reference desk is located on the first floor. Four students, or 1.9 percent, tried to cover both areas and answered both first and second floor.

The other question regarding location asked where the reference collection is located. One hundred fifty-four, or 76.6 percent, of the students marked second floor.

TABLE 1. Desk Location

Locations	Responses
First floor	59
Second floor	131
Third floor	5
All three floors	1
First & second	4
No answer	1

TABLE 2. Collection Location

Locations	Responses
First floor	27
Second floor	154
Third floor	9
All three floors	1
First & second	1
Second & third	6
No answer	3

Twenty-seven, or 13.4 percent, respondents checked first floor. Older reference resources are housed on the third floor in the Reference Annex. This could account for the nine students, or 4.4 percent, who marked third floor, and six, or 2.9 percent, that marked second and third floor. While knowing where to find the reference librarian and the reference collection are important aspects of utilizing them, it is more important to know the function and purpose of each. At the very least, being willing to ask questions when necessary is vital to successful use of the library.

When asked to select choices regarding the function (Table 3) of the reference librarian, 104, or 51.7 percent, of the students indicated that the only correct answer was direct patrons to resources. An additional 66, 32.8 percent, selected all of the options which included directing patrons to resources. The five students who marked "other" offered specific information. One wrote, "all that have to do with resources and references." Another wrote, "everything." Does this simply mean all of the choices given on the survey, or does this student believe the reference librarian can do everything in regard to libraries and research? A third student wrote, "to help patrons with questions as pertaining to the reference tools/sources." This seems to be merely a rewording of the given choice of assistance with using electronic and print resources. The fourth student wrote, "suggest where in references to find topic (keywords, etc.)." The significance of this comment lies in the use of the word "suggest." Obviously, this student expects to do his own work with only assistance from the reference librarian unlike the fifth student who wrote, "to get me the reference book or books I need." This student may be expecting the librarian to know exactly which resource(s) would be appropriate and then retrieve them for the student. There is a thin line between offering assistance to the student and blatantly doing the work for the student.

Since the reference collection is housed separately from the circulating collection, students can be confused about the purpose of the reference collection. Table 4 shows that 47, or 23.3 percent, of the students surveyed believe reference materials are meant to give quick

TABLE 3. Librarian's Function

Functions	Responses
Direct patrons to resources	104
Answer research questions	43
Direct patrons to other areas	39
Assist with using resources	71
Other	5
All	66
No answer	1

TABLE 4. Purpose of the Collection

Primary purpose	Responses
Quick answers	47
Leads to answer	105
All	47
No answer	2

answers to questions and lead the user to the answer. The same number of students perceive the primary purpose of the reference collection as giving quick answers to questions. More than half of the respondents, 105, or 52.2 percent, answered that reference materials only lead the user to the answer.

When items are selected for inclusion (Table 5) into the library collection, a decision is made regarding whether it should be put into the circulating or the reference collection. A few things are taken into consideration including the expense of the item, the necessity of the item being available at all times and that reference books are not meant to be read from cover-to-cover. Instead, one looks up a specific piece of information such as a statistic, a definition, or a telephone number and puts the item back on the shelf. Forty-nine, or 24.3 percent, checked all three answers as appropriate reasons for an item to be non-circulating. Over half of the respondents, 111, or 55.2 percent, only checked "always available." This makes one wonder if the students are thinking of items housed at the Reserves Desk. It is mentioned in class lectures that items that instructors want to be made available at all times are pulled from the collection and put on reserve.

In this era of technology, reference materials are available in a wide variety of formats (Table 6). Eighty-five, or 42.2 percent, of the respondents found that all of the suggested formats are represented in the reference collection. Interestingly, print resources received the second largest number of check marks. Seventy-eight, or 38.8 percent, of the students perceived the reference collection as only being available in print format. With all of the attention being placed on the Internet and all it has to offer, it is a bit surprising that only 42, or 20.8 percent, of the students found that this format applied to reference materials.

TABLE 5. Inclusion Considerations

Reasons for non-circulating	Responses
Expensive	27
Always available	111
Not read cover to cover	44
All	49
No answer	2

TABLE 6. Resources Formats

Formats	Responses
Print	78
On-line catalog	65
Internet	42
CD-ROM	53
Microform	55
All	85
No answer	2

Many different types of resources make up the reference collection (Table 7). Again, the print materials received more check marks than the electronic resources. Only 47, or 23.3 percent, of the students selected all of the choices available on the survey. Indicating the most commonly used reference source, 124, or 61.6 percent, of the students checked "encyclopedias." Dictionaries and almanacs received the same number of checks with 111, or 55.2 percent, each. Another popular choice was "atlases" with 106, or 52.7 percent, of the students selecting this choice. Print periodical indexes were selected by 105, or 52.2 percent, of the students. Gazetteers, 63, or 31.3 percent; biographies, 64, or 31.8 percent; and quotation books, 67, or 33.3 percent, received the least number of individual checks. Is this an indication of unfamiliarity with terminology such as gazetteer? Perhaps students thought of full-length biographies rather than the overview type of biographical resources available in most reference collections. Quotation books may not be something with which students are familiar. Other low marks may have occurred for similar reasons.

Asking for assistance is sometimes necessary when using a new resource or new library for the first time. Table 8 shows an overwhelming number of students, 142, or 70.6 percent, have asked for assistance at one time or another. The next question on the survey asked the students to elaborate on the type of assistance they had required. The most often marked response was "locating another area of the library." Sixty-three, or 44.3 percent of the 142 students who indicated they had asked for assistance, said that they needed help finding another area of the library (see Table 9). This could be due to the recent move to JCKL. Or is it an indication of how students

TABLE 7. Types of Resources

Reference resources	Responses
Print periodical indexes	105
Internet	75
LUIS	74
CD-ROM periodical indexes	95
Almanacs	111
Atlases	106
Book review indexes	91
Biographies	64
Bibliographies	70
Encyclopedias	124
Gazetteers	63
Manuals	86
Handbooks	72
Quotation books	67
Dictionaries	111
Directories	91
All	47
No answer	2

TABLE 8. Assistance from Librarian

Asked for assistance	Responses
Yes	142
No	53
No answer	6

perceive the role of the reference librarian? Fifty, or 35.2 percent of the 142 students who indicated they had asked for assistance, said that they wanted to know where to find the answer to a specific research question. Thirty-two, or 22.5 percent, needed help with an assignment. Only 10, or 7 percent, admitted that they simply wanted the librarian to answer a research question for them without the student needing to look for the answer.

Six, or 4.2 percent, of the respondents marked "other." One stu-

TABLE 9. Assistance Required

Types of assistance	Responses
Locating other areas	63
Using LUIS	55
Using CD-ROM index	39
Using Internet	16
Using print resource	49
Where to find answer to question	50
How to do assignment	32
Answer to research question	10
Other	6

dent wrote in "*Readers' Guide* help," while another also needed help "using [a] paper index." A third student wrote he needed "to get a sample test for econ." This item was probably located at the reserve desk and probably the student was instructed to go there. The other three students who marked "other" needed help finding the location of resources. This may have been due to the move to JCKL. However, the last of these three indicated a need for assistance locating a book at another library. Perhaps the student was informed of JCKL's interlibrary loan service. Or it could be that the student inquired, if a book has a call number at JCKL, would it have the same call number elsewhere.

The final question of the survey asked for reasons why the student had not asked for assistance (Table 10). Interesting information can be gleaned from the answers to this question. Thirty-four, or 64.1 percent, of the 53 students who said they had never asked for help claimed never to have needed assistance. Six, or 1.1 percent, of the 53 said no one was at the reference desk when they required assistance. This could be due to the busy nature of the reference desk at certain times. It can, and often does, happen that three or four librarians are on duty at the desk at one time. Depending on the number of students requiring assistance, however, all could be on the floor at the same time. This could briefly cause the reference desk to appear to be unattended. Two of the students who marked "other" did not specify the reason. Two others said they had not used the reference collection yet. The fifth student wrote, "not sure they will take the time to help." This student had also checked "uncertain how to ask for help." There is probably a

TABLE 10. No Assistance Required

Reasons	Responses
Never needed assistance	34
No one at Reference Desk	6
Uncomfortable	8
Uncertain	9
Didn't know they were there to help	7
Other	5

connection between these two responses. Uncertainty or apprehension by the student could cause him to perceive the librarian as intimidating and perhaps unwilling to help.

Nine, or 16.9 percent, said they were uncertain how to ask for help. It is interesting to note that an additional three students marked "uncertain how to ask for help" even though they had asked for assistance at some point. Eight students, or 15 percent, who have never asked the reference librarian for assistance, marked "uncomfortable asking the librarian, asked another student instead." The problems with this approach should be obvious. Sadly, seven, or 13.2 percent, of the respondents checked "didn't know they were there to help." There is a dangerous lack of communication at work there. Another noteworthy point is that two students marked that they had never needed assistance, but they had marked "yes" to the question "have you ever asked the reference librarian for assistance?" and checked an area or two to indicate what had caused them to require assistance.

CONCLUSION

The results of the survey suggest that many students do not have a clear perception of the purpose of the reference collection or the reference librarian. Some of the students, however, may have a firm enough grasp on the concepts to make at least rudimentary use of resources available in an academic library. The most important findings of the study suggest a tendency toward a more familiar understanding of print materials than electronic, and the view of a very basic function of the reference librarian.

REFERENCES

Eckwright, Gail Z., Hoskisson, Tam, & Pollastro, Mike (1998). Reference etiquette: A guide to excruciatingly correct behavior. *American Libraries, 29*(5), 42-45.

Geffert, Bryn, & Christensen, Beth (1998). Things they carry: Attitudes toward, opinions about, and knowledge of libraries and research among incoming college students. *Reference & User Services Quarterly, 37*(3), 279-289.

Massey-Burzio, Virginia (1998). From the other side of the reference desk: A focus group study. *Journal of Academic Librarianship* [Online] *24*(3), Available: EB-SCOHost/805686 [1999, June 6].

Radford, Marie. L. (1998). Approach or avoidance? The role of nonverbal communication in the academic library user's decision to initiate a reference encounter. *Library Trends* [Online] *46*(4), Available: EBSCOHost/948108 [1999, June 6].

APPENDIX

Undergraduate Perceptions of Reference Materials
and Services in an Academic Library Survey

Check ALL answers that apply for each question

1. Where is the Reference Librarian located?
___ first floor ___ second floor ___ third floor

2. What is the function of the Reference Librarian?
___ direct patrons to resources ___ answer research questions
___ direct patrons to other areas within the library
___ assist with using electronic and print resources ___ other (please specify)

3. Where is the reference collection located?
___ first floor ___ second floor ___ third floor

4. Which formats does the reference collection include?
___ print ___ online catalog ___ Internet ___ CD-ROM ___ microform

5. What is the primary purpose of reference materials in regard to research?
___ materials give quick answers to questions ___ leads user to the answer

6. Why are reference materials usually non-circulating?
___ expensive ___ always available to patrons
___ not read from cover-to-cover

7. Which of the following are considered reference resources?
___ print periodical indexes ___ Internet ___ LUIS
___ CD-ROM periodical indexes ___ almanacs ___ atlases
___ book review indexes ___ biographies ___ bibliographies
___ encyclopedias ___ gazetteers ___ manuals ___ handbooks
___ quotation books ___ dictionaries ___ directories

8. Have you ever asked the reference librarian for assistance?
___ yes ___ no

9. If yes, what type of assistance did you require?
___ locating another area of the library ___ using LUIS
___ using a CD-ROM index ___ using the Internet
___ using a print resource
___ where to find an answer to a specific research question
___ how to do an assignment
___ wanting an answer to a research question without looking for the answer yourself
___ other (please specify)

10. If not, why have you not asked the reference librarian for assistance?
___ never needed assistance
___ no one at reference desk when I needed help
___ uncomfortable asking the librarian, asked another student instead
___ uncertain how to ask for help
___ didn't know they were there to help
___ other (please specify)

Reference Assistance to Remote Users

Deborah Stanley
Natasha Lyandres

SUMMARY. This article identifies and discusses the particular information needs of the growing community of remote users of academic libraries. In addressing the practical considerations of providing reference assistance to this group, the authors concentrate on telephone and e-mail reference, the use of video technology and the World Wide Web. The article also discusses the importance of having a dedicated distance education librarian to ensure that the needs of remote library users are given high priority. *[Article copies available for a fee from The Haworth Document Delivery Service: 1-800-342-9678. E-mail address: <getinfo@haworthpressinc.com> Website: <http://www.HaworthPress.com> © 2001 by The Haworth Press, Inc. All rights reserved.]*

KEYWORDS. Reference, remote reference, virtual reference, distance education, academic libraries

THE COMMUNITY OF REMOTE USERS

Advances in telecommunications technology increasingly afford academic libraries the possibility of connecting their internal networks

---

Deborah Stanley is Reference Librarian, University Libraries, University of Georgia, Athens, GA 30602 (E-mail: dstanley@arches.uga.edu). Natasha Lyandres is Reference Librarian, Joyner Library, East Carolina University, Greenville, NC 27858 (E-mail: lyandresn@mail.ecu.edu).

[Haworth co-indexing entry note]: "Reference Assistance to Remote Users." Stanley, Deborah, and Natasha Lyandres. Co-published simultaneously in *The Reference Librarian* (The Haworth Information Press, an imprint of The Haworth Press, Inc.) No. 73, 2001, pp. 243-252; and: *Doing the Work of Reference: Practical Tips for Excelling as a Reference Librarian* (ed: Celia Hales Mabry) The Haworth Information Press, an imprint of The Haworth Press, Inc., 2001, pp. 243-252. Single or multiple copies of this article are available for a fee from The Haworth Document Delivery Service [1-800-342-9678, 9:00 a.m. - 5:00 p.m. (EST). E-mail address: getinfo@haworthpressinc.com].

to the Internet and thereby offering university faculty, students and staff remote access to electronic resources and services. In addition, academic libraries serve remote users who are members of the community and may not be students at all. As the amount of information that the library can provide remotely increases, librarians can no longer make assumptions about who their remote users are. It is important to get to know the different groupings among the remote user community in order to meet their information needs effectively. "Remote users cannot be neatly packaged. They come from a wide variety of backgrounds, skills, and expertise. Remote users, in particular, are challenging libraries in new ways to rethink their mission and their services" (Haricombe, 1998).

Cooper defines a remote user as "any individual accessing electronic library resources from any site outside a library without regard to physical distance or enrollment in a formal curriculum" (Cooper, 1998). Thus, remote library users are not only distance education students, who might be located hundreds or thousands of miles from the library, but also regular on-campus students, faculty, and staff who might be only a few buildings away.

Distance education and full-time, on-campus students can have very different educational backgrounds, technical skills, and needs. On-campus remote users are usually members of the Net Generation, young and sophisticated people, who grew up with computers and who feel comfortable using technology and accessing information independently and remotely. Often, however, they lack information literacy–the ability to find the best information and evaluate it effectively.

The statistics show a significant increase in the number of older students returning to school. "Between 1985 and 1995, the enrollment of students under age 25 increased by 13 percent. During the same period, enrollment of persons 25 and over rose by 22 percent" (Digest of Education Statistics, 1997). A growing number of adult learners are able to return to school, taking advantage of distance education programs. Distance education is becoming an integral and increasingly important part of the higher education curriculum. In addition, more and more universities are experimenting with on-line classes. In 1998 the National Center for Education Statistics published a survey on distance education courses offered by higher education institutions, which found that in fall 1995 a third of institutions offered distance education courses (Greene, 1998). During the academic year 1994-95 more than 750,000 students were enrolled in distance education courses; an estimated 25,730 courses with different catalog numbers were offered. These numbers continue to increase. For example, at East Carolina University the number of on-line classes offered to regular and distance education students doubled between 1999 and 2000.

Adult learners differ from younger students in many ways. Niemi indicated that adult learners usually return to school after a period of time spent in other pursuits (Niemi, 1998). They have a rich background of life and work experience. Thus, more often than not, adult learners are more motivated than younger students and their educational goals more clearly defined. At the same time, adult learners may fear change and often lack the necessary technical skills to conduct library research and use electronic resources effectively.

MEETING THE INFORMATION NEEDS OF REMOTE USERS

It is important to recognize that on-site and remote library users have the same information and research needs and therefore, according to the ACRL guidelines, "members of the distance learning community are entitled to library services and resources equivalent to those provided for students and faculty in traditional campus settings" (ACRL Guidelines for Extended Academic Campus Library Services, 1997). However, most traditional services offered by academic libraries are incompatible with educating at a distance. Distance learners cannot browse stacks, access non-networked databases, go to the reserve room, or check out a book (Wolpert, 1998). Therefore, in serving them we need to be clear about what the library can and cannot do to fulfil their needs: "It is important that a user's expectations of the service be based on reality and that this reality be clearly stated" (Hahn, 1997). Along with making remote users aware of our services and their possible limitations, we also need to work to offset those physical limitations by using creative means to provide reference service via electronic means.

At the same time, the types of assistance and support needed by remote users located just a few buildings away from the library may differ from those of distance education students accessing library resources thousands of miles away from campus. We must, therefore, bear in mind these different needs, modes of access, and ways in which people like to be helped: "An appropriate service would include print handouts, electronic help pages, perhaps search demos in video or via satellite, or individual consultation via e-mail, telephone, telefax or mail" (Cooper, 1998).

Both on-campus remote users and distance education students need unrestricted and reliable access to library resources 24 hours a day, 7 days a week. A 1997 study of Internet users (Banaghan, 1997) indicates that having 24-hour help desk support is extremely important for on-line customers. In a remote context, access to electronic services becomes critical. Remote library users frequently need "just in time" assistance while they are working on a project. "It may be that remote customers actually define service in terms of accessibility" (Cooper, 1998). For the library staff these findings may mean extending library hours, allocating a dedicated telephone line for answering questions from remote users, checking and responding to e-mail reference questions regularly during the day, and, finally, sharing reference responsibilities with technical support staff from the systems department. It should be noted, however, that most libraries do not have the budget and staffing to provide these services around the clock. Therefore, in addition to telephone and e-mail assistance the library also needs to provide for users to help themselves through creative Web services and instruction.

TELEPHONE ASSISTANCE

Telephone reference has been offered for many years by academic libraries and is a standard service. The value of phone reference is that it is synchronous, immediate, and personal. The disadvantage is that the librarian cannot see the user's screen or use non-verbal indicators to assess the person's understanding, satisfaction, or skill and comfort level with the technology. Therefore, when assisting remote users by telephone, one may need to ask more questions than one would in a face-to-face transaction at the reference desk. If the reference librarian has the choice between multiple databases, it is necessary to bear in mind how intuitive the interfaces are and to balance the need for specialized sources against the desire for full text. The librarian should use his or her experience of past interactions with patrons to discern likely pitfalls for the patron.

E-MAIL ASSISTANCE

While librarians have been experimenting for some time with a variety of electronic media for the provision of remote reference service, electronic mail remains the most prevalent. The benefits to the patron include being able to ask a question at any time, the convenience of e-mail access and being able to keep the information received from the librarian in written form. For the library, it allows the question to be forwarded to the most appropriate librarian for a response at a convenient time and enables the library to provide access to reference service without the significant cost of extending opening hours. Negatives for the library include receiving questions from all over the world that would be better directed to patrons' local libraries, "lost time between messages, loss of message richness, and system vulnerability" (Hahn, 1997).

In a study of e-mail reference interviews conducted in 1993-94 (Abels, 1996), Eileen Abels concluded that for the sake of clarity and to reduce the number of e-mail exchanges needed between librarian and client, it is advisable to use some kind of form to elicit information about the client's needs, any constraints they may face, and where they have already looked for information. We found that e-mail reference forms currently being used by many libraries vary from the very simple to the much more comprehensive, such as those used by Babson College (Babson College, 1998) and the Internet Public Library (Internet Public Library, 2000).

The libraries at the State University of New York at Buffalo studied transaction logs of their e-mail reference service and distributed questionnaires to those who had used the service between January 1993 and June 1994 (Bushallow-Wilbur, 1996). It was found that 90% of the questions were submitted during hours that the reference desk was open, suggesting that these patrons were either unable to come to the library or preferred the anonymity and convenience of e-mail service. Indeed, 58% of respondents said e-mail was their favorite format, followed by face-to-face (37%) and telephone (5%). This shows the potential demand for remote service, not just to distance education students for whom a trip to the library is impractical, but for many university and community patrons who would be less comfortable approaching a person at a reference desk. Electronic mail also lends itself to other, innovative forms of interaction with patrons. For example, a librarian offering instruction to a class through cooperation with the instructor may wish to set up a listserv or chatroom for the class (Niemi, 1998).

VIDEO ASSISTANCE

Increasingly, the immediacy and "greater media richness" (Sloan, 1998) of interactive video may be attractive to both librarians and patrons, and various experiments have already taken place in the use of video in reference service. For example, in the 1995-96 academic year, the University of Michigan Shapiro Undergraduate Library (Westwood, 1997) used CU-SeeMe desktop videoconferencing software and video cameras to establish a link with students' residence halls. Generally, such projects have thus far had low take-up because of inconsistent technical quality and support and the self-consciousness of patrons, but their popularity may increase in the future as these problems are reduced.

A more successful project, the Interactive Reference Service, was initiated at the University of California, Irvine (Sloan, 1998) using the Apple VideoPhone Kit, which has audio, video, a chat window, and a whiteboard that can display Web pages. The IRS service linked librarians at the science library with students in a computer lab at the College of Medicine. The chat and whiteboard facilities seemed to greatly enhance the experience in comparison with services that use only video or only interactive software with no video connection.

It seems clear that different technologies suit different patrons, either in terms of their access to such services or their level of comfort in using them. For people who prefer to talk to a person, video technology, as it becomes cheaper and more reliable, offers many possibilities. For others, who prefer to access services out of hours or to help themselves and seek information in anonymity, the many Web-based services provided by libraries to "add value" and organize and educate users about resources are particularly important.

WEB ASSISTANCE

The library home page is now the first point of access to library services for many patrons. As such it should be a major focus for librarians aiming to improve access to services for remote users. Libraries must organize resources on the Web in as clear, effective and intuitive a manner as possible in order to allow these patrons to help themselves. In order to compensate for the lack of immediate reference assistance, libraries must also provide assistance at the point of use. "With access to information just keystrokes away, reference professionals must play an aggressive and active role in designing and developing front-ends, user guides, instruction programs and guides/directories to this growing mountain of information" (Rockman, 1998).

One example of a library's effort to help patrons navigate the myriad of electronic databases and find the most appropriate sources is that of Pennsylvania State University library. From the library's instruction page, the patron can select "Tell Me Where" and specify the type of information required (journal articles, government publications, full text, etc.) and select one or more subject fields. The system then produces a listing of databases, with descriptions further down the screen, plus the option to connect straight from the listing http://www.lias.psu.edu:80/alallrem.html.

As well as Web resources for remote users in general, it is especially crucial to have a clearly organized Web page for distance education students. Distance education students "might need different delivery mechanisms or emphasize different services" than regular on-campus remote users (Cooper, 1998). The Distance Education Librarian at East Carolina University shared with us an on-line discussion she had with some distance education students regarding library services. It was surprising to see how little distance education students actually knew about what the university library had to offer them. On their wish list were services that were already available through the library homepage such as the ability to e-mail a question to a reference librarian, search the library catalog and electronic databases, fill out an electronic interlibrary loan form, or ask for assistance with literature searches.

One of the ways in which library staff can help distance education students with their information needs is to create a distance education homepage which would incorporate all library services that might be of help to distance education students. This page should be clearly constructed and include reference handouts, descriptions and on-line tutorials for reference databases, guides to searching for particular types of information or in specific disciplines, information on how to obtain full text materials if they are not available on-line, advice on how to cite sources, explanations of how information is organized and can be retrieved, and advice on the many technical aspects of accessing information on-line. Finally, it should also include a contact person. One example of the university library that currently provides such a page is the University of Indiana, Bloomington (Indiana University Bloomington Libraries, 2000).

Although technology has expanded access to information it has also depersonalized some library services. A remote patron often needs a person to contact and with whom to identify. Gloria Lebowitz studied different approaches taken by university libraries in the past few years in regard to helping distance education students. She concluded that the most effective was "the model that offers the dedicated unit, with a specific librarian to work with off-campus students to ensure that they receive all services, including user education, reference and referral assistance, document delivery, and assistance with documentation of papers" (Lebowitz, 1997). Such a person has to have excellent computer and communication skills. He also has to be an advocate of distance education and be proactive by anticipating the various needs of remote users and identifying ways to help them. "Working with distance-based students means that librarians cannot afford to be reactive since distance learners cannot physically approach them with questions" (Kirk, 1999).

A survey of the curricula of *US News & World Report's* ten top-ranked library schools in the United States found that although some universities, like Illinois–Urbana-Campaign, offer library science degrees through distance education, most do not teach specialized classes in distance education librarianship. There does, however, seem to be an emerging market in library jobs that involve working with remote users. A review of the job advertisements in the 1999 issues of *College and Research Libraries News* shows that different libraries are taking quite varied approaches to this in terms of the combination of responsibilities and the job titles used. Some libraries concentrate on the delivery of electronic information to both remote and on-campus users, while others have a dedicated distance education librarian. Examples of jobs advertised include "academic technologies center librarian," "educational technology librarian," "digital library coordinator," "director of off-campus library services" and "outreach services librarian." Although the situation is still developing, it seems that library schools need to consider this growing area when revising their curricula.

Librarians who already find themselves in the position of providing remote services need to prepare themselves in a number of ways. For example, it is helpful to maintain ready reference Web pages and collections of useful bookmarks, to use alerting services such as the Scout Report (Internet Scout Project, 2000) to keep abreast of new resources, and to share ideas and experiences with colleagues through listservs, attendance at meetings, and other professional development activities. For librarians serving distance education students, it is also vital to build strong links with teaching faculty in order to learn as much as possible about the students and their needs.

CONCLUSION

Just as the needs of remote users are perhaps more varied than ever before, so are the possibilities for assisting them, as communication technologies continue to evolve. Academic libraries should make a commitment to providing equivalent access to information for both on-campus and remote library users. Librarians directly involved in helping remote patrons should have excellent communication and technical skills, be advocates for the needs of remote clients, and be creative in service development and delivery.

REFERENCES

Abels, Eileen G. (1996), "The E-mail Reference Interview," *RQ* 35 (Spring), 345-358.

"ACRL Guidelines for Extended Academic Campus Library Services" (1997), *College & Research Libraries News* 58 (February), 98-102.

Babson College (1998), *Ask a Library Reference Question*. Wellesley, MA: Babson College. Retrieved February 18, 2000 from the World Wide Web: http://domino.babson.edu/WEBforms.nsf/Library_Reference_Question?OpenForm

Banaghan, Margaret (1997), "Internet Users Shop for the Best Service Provider," *Business Review Weekly* 19, 63-64.

Bushallow-Wilbur, Lara, Gemma S. DeVinney and Fritz Whitcomb (1996), "Electronic Mail Reference Service: A Study," *RQ* 35 (Spring), 359-363.

Cooper, Rosemarie et al. (1998), "Remote Library Users: Needs and Expectations," *Library Trends* 47 (Summer), 42-64.

Digest of Education Statistics (1997), Washington, DC: U.S. Department of Education. National Center for Education Statistics.

Greene, Bernard and Anne Meek (1998), *Distance Education in Higher Education Institutions: Incidence, Audiences, and Plans to Expand.* Issue Brief. National Center for Education Statistics, February 1, 1998.

Hahn, Karla (1997), "An Investigation of an E-mail-Based Help Service," *CLIS Technical Report* No. 97-03 (January). College Park, MD: College of Library and Information Services, University of Maryland. Retrieved December 1, 1999 from the World Wide Web: http://www.clis.umd.edu/research/reports/tr97/03/9703.html

Haricombe, Lorraine J. (1998), "Introduction," *Library Trends* 47 (Summer), 1-6.

Indiana University Bloomington Libraries (2000), *IUB Libraries Distributed Education Services Homepage.* Bloomington, IN: Indiana University Bloomington Libraries. Retrieved February 18, 2000 from the World Wide Web: http://www.indiana.edu/~libdist/

Internet Public Library (2000), *IPL Ask a Question Form.* Ann Arbor, MI: University of Michigan School of Information. Retrieved February 18, 2000 from the World Wide Web: http://www.ipl.org/ref/QUE/RefFormQRC.html

Internet Scout Project (2000), *The Scout Report.* Madison, WI: University of Wisconsin, Madison. Retrieved February 18, 2000 from the World Wide Web: http://scout.cs.wisc.edu/report/sr/current/

Kirk, Elizabeth E. and Andrea M. Bartelstein (1999), "Libraries Close in on Distance Education," *Library Journal* 124 (April 1), 40-42.

Lebowitz, Gloria (1997), "Library Services to Distant Students: An Equity Issue," *Journal of Academic Librarianship* 23 (July), 303-308.

Niemi, John A., Barbara J. Ehrhard and Lynn Neeley (1998), "Off-Campus Library Support for Distance Adult Learners," *Library Trends* 47 (Summer), 65-74.

Rockman, Ilene F. (1998), "Challenges and Opportunities in Reaching the Remote User," in *Recreating the Academic Library,* edited by Cheryl LaGuardia. New York: Neal-Schuman, 241-255.

Sloan, Bernie (1998), "Service Perspectives for the Digital Library: Remote Reference Services," *Library Trends* 47 (Summer), 117-143.

Westwood, Karen (1997), "Lights! Camera! Action!" *American Libraries* 28 (January), 43-45.

Wolpert, Ann (1998), "Services to Remote Users: Marketing the Library's Role," *Library Trends* 47 (Summer), 21-41.

REACHING OUT

Faculty: An Essential Resource for Reference Librarians

Catherine Cardwell

SUMMARY. Teaching faculty are a key resource for reference librarians. This paper includes a discussion of major forces affecting reference service as well as suggestions on ways for librarians to become better acquainted with teaching faculty. One benefit of making these connections is that when faculty know and have confidence in librarians, they are more likely to urge their students to get help at the desk, to schedule course-related instruction sessions, and to let librarians know if they have a particularly difficult or complex assignment. Another benefit is that such connections often lead to increased opportunities,

Catherine Cardwell is Assistant Professor and Library User Education Coordinator, Bowling Green State University's Jerome Library, Bowling Green, OH 43403 (E-mail: cardcat@bgnet.bgsu.edu). In her previous position, she was Assistant Reference Librarian at Youngstown State University (YSU).

The author thanks Lee-Ann McAllister, Assistant Reference Librarian at YSU, for her contributions on ways to collaborate with faculty.

[Haworth co-indexing entry note]: "Faculty: An Essential Resource for Reference Librarians." Cardwell, Catherine. Co-published simultaneously in *The Reference Librarian* (The Haworth Information Press, an imprint of The Haworth Press, Inc.) No. 73, 2001, pp. 253-263; and: *Doing the Work of Reference: Practical Tips for Excelling as a Reference Librarian* (ed: Celia Hales Mabry) The Haworth Information Press, an imprint of The Haworth Press, Inc., 2001, pp. 253-263. Single or multiple copies of this article are available for a fee from The Haworth Document Delivery Service [1-800-342-9678, 9:00 a.m. - 5:00 p.m. (EST). E-mail address: getinfo@haworthpressinc.com].

from participation in campus-wide initiatives to the development of collaborative projects and other scholarly work. As a librarian relatively new to the profession, I know that such connections with teaching faculty have enriched my own career.

KEYWORDS. Faculty relations, teaching faculty, professional development

Reference librarians face many challenges. Not only do they need to know an institution's print and electronic resources, but they also need to understand the idiosyncrasies of their department, library, and campus. Beyond serving at the reference desk, reference librarians work in many other capacities. Their training, as a result, can be particularly complex. Looking back over my own library experience, first as an assistant reference librarian participating in instruction and now as an instruction librarian with reference responsibilities, I have realized that library school prepared me for reference service in most ways. I was introduced to print and on-line resources, effective search strategies, and the importance of a good reference interview. Throughout this instruction, however, a key resource for reference librarians was overlooked: the teaching faculty. While it is necessary to know an institution's collection, resources, and procedures, it is also important to remember the function of the library on campus. Librarians, whether they have faculty or administrative status, support students in their learning and support faculty in their teaching and research. As a result, communicating and cooperating with teaching faculty members are as essential as understanding on-line resources or any other often-consulted reference tool. Throughout my own career, building good working relationships with faculty members has helped me to fulfill my daily job responsibilities, participate more effectively in campus-wide initiatives, and collaborate on extensive long-term projects, which, in turn, led to increased opportunities for professional development.

SERVING DUAL BUT RELATED FUNCTIONS: REFERENCE AND INSTRUCTION

Along with providing service at the reference desk, most reference librarians also participate in instruction programs. A 1995 survey conducted by the LOEX Clearinghouse for Library Instruction indicated that reference departments or other public service departments oversee instruction at most of the reporting libraries, which included all types of institutions, from two-year community colleges to special libraries. Only a small percentage of the respondents, however, a little more than one-tenth, indicated that their libraries have separate departments for instruction. The same survey also found that only a very small percentage of schools require a library course for credit while a more substantial number of schools offers such courses as electives. Most notably, however, course-related instruction increased significantly, specifically in terms of modules created by librarians for subject-specific credit courses offered outside of the library (Shirato and Badics, 1997).

That instruction and reference are closely related is essential for new public service librarians to understand, especially as they go on the market looking for their first jobs. According to Lizabeth A. Wilson, instruction is just another reference service: "Reference and instruction are intrinsically linked, complementary, and intertwined. To separate instruction from reference is to do a disservice to users." Instruction at the reference desk, though perhaps a highly effective and "intimate" form of teaching, does not always meet the needs of all users. To do so, libraries must also offer other types of instruction, including computer-assisted instruction, course-related instruction, workshops introducing specific research tools, print and on-line guides and handouts, tours, and signage (Wilson, 1995).

ADDITIONAL CIRCUMSTANCES AFFECTING REFERENCE

Aside from the close relationship between reference and instruction, other factors strongly affect reference service.

Nature of Contact with Students

Though librarians do a great deal of instruction, the environment in which they work is highly different from the one in which teaching faculty operate. Typically, teaching faculty, who have the same group of students for an extended period of time, offer sustained, discipline-specific, credit-bearing instruction for which they have very defined objectives. They are generally able to develop their own assignments. Librarians, however, must meet objectives defined by an outside source, work with assignments created by someone else, and work with all types of students, often from one moment to the next. Sustained contact is rare and is considered a luxury.

Diverse Responsibilities

Complicating matters further, reference librarians often have several competing demands on their time. Typically, they have diverse responsibilities, such as working on the reference desk, participating in course-related instruction, creating print and on-line instructional material, and contributing to web site development. Perhaps the most difficult responsibility facing librarians is that they need to stay current, not just with overall trends in libraries but with new and changing services and resources in their own libraries. Change occurs rapidly. Typical examples of change include a familiar database adopting a different interface, the addition of new on-line resources, and migration of CD-ROM and telnet-based applications to the web. Most libraries are also experiencing dramatic changes in document-delivery services with full-text materials becoming increasingly accessible on individual workstations.

Campus-Wide Initiatives

At many colleges and universities, two notable campus-wide initiatives, information literacy and assessment, require library involvement, especially from public service librarians.

All types of institutions have come to realize the increasing significance of information literacy. However, faculty members are often reluctant to incorporate skills in information literacy into their own courses since they do not feel qualified to address such concerns. Along with faculty, campus administrators turn to librarians for guidance in this area. Because of the nature of their expertise and skills, librarians are often the best people on campus to be given this responsibility: "To be information literate, a person must be able to recognize when information is needed and have the ability to locate, evaluate, and use effectively the needed information. . . . Ultimately, information literate people are those who have learned how to learn. They know how to learn because they know how information is organized, how to find information, and how to use information in such a way that others can learn from them" (American Library Association Presidential Committee, 1989).

Another campus initiative facing reference librarians is assessment. Traditionally libraries measured effectiveness by the number of books acquired, the number of course-related classes taught, or the number of reference questions answered. Also known as "inputs," these measures are no longer accepted as proof of effectiveness. Because of the current requirements for accreditation and state boards, institutions of higher education are asked to be more accountable for what they are teaching. They are asked to prove that students are learning what they are supposed to learn. Libraries, as a result, must participate in campus-wide assessment efforts (Association of College and Research Libraries, 1998).

SERVICE-RELATED BENEFITS OF WORKING CLOSELY WITH FACULTY

Together, all of these factors, from the close connection of reference and instruction to participation in campus-wide initiatives, create a complex, formidable environment for reference librarians. An effective way to meet the challenges of such an environment is to work closely with faculty who, as individuals, are often overlooked as a resource for reference librarians.

Excellent reference desk service goes beyond interaction between the librarian and user at the desk. The quality of service improves when faculty have confidence in librarians' abilities and expertise, when faculty create effective library assignments, when librarians are able to provide course-related instruction, and when librarians are able to implement assessment procedures and act on the results. All of these situations require good working relationships, cooperation, and communication among librarians and teaching faculty. In fact, effective reference service requires cooperation from teaching faculty, especially as librarians must find ways to act as advocates for the library.

In my own experience, having a good working relationship with faculty members has helped students at the reference desk. Sometimes faculty members tell me that their students are afraid to go to the desk and interrupt a librarian, but a course instructor familiar with the librarians and confident in their abilities and willingness to help are more likely to encourage students to ask for help at the desk. In fact, they often tell students to ask for a particular librarian by name.

Most librarians who have worked any time on the reference desk can recall at least one afternoon lost on a problematic assignment, one perhaps taken from a textbook that did not take the institution's resources into consideration. Another different but related problem occurs when faculty members are not aware of changes in library resources. Perhaps a new on-line database has been added, or perhaps a resource has been eliminated, both of which can lead to problems for faculty who tend to teach the same course semester after semester and who rely on previously developed assignments. Nothing can be more frustrating for students and librarians than working through inaccurate assignments. Such a situation places librarians in a delicate position since they must tactfully find a way to tell students that their assignment is problematic, without appearing to criticize the course instructor. To prevent this situation as much as possible, instruction librarians at Bowling Green State University (BGSU) have a handout called "Elements of an Effective Assignment," which we make available on the web, to new teaching assistants during their orientation, and in our print handouts accessible to all users. The handout alerts instructors to the common pitfalls of research assignments and perhaps helps them develop, plan, and test their assignments before distributing them. Some institutions go even further to help instructors. Pixey Anne Mosley (1998) describes a workshop on creating library assignments that her library offers several times a year.

Charged with taking a leadership role in implementing information literacy instruction and participating in assessment efforts, librarians can face even greater obstacles. Librarians are often required to participate in information literacy and assessment initiatives, but faculty members are not required to cooperate with librarians. Course-related information literacy modules and the implementation of assessment tools are effective only when course instructors are supportive.

In an attempt to respond to the need for information literacy instruction, some libraries are moving toward offering required, credit-bearing courses as part of their general education curriculum, but this solution is not always feasible for at least two reasons. First, there are often not enough librarians to teach general classes on information literacy. At BGSU, my own institution, for example, we have only seven general instruction librarians, and approximately 5500 students in the first-year class. Our English department, which has a composition requirement of all students, employs about 100 instructors and graduate assistants to handle the load. The other problem is that though it is possible to teach retrieval strategies in general information literacy classes, information needs vary greatly from discipline to discipline. Journalism students, for instance, have highly different needs than chemistry students. At BGSU, our strategy to counter these two problems, then, is not to create our own general credit-bearing course and offer it on a widespread basis; rather, our strategy is to work closely with the teaching faculty in general education and discipline-specific courses. We are attempting to develop curriculum, create web pages, or develop modules to support their information needs.

Like all areas of the campus community, librarians are under the same pressure to participate in assessment efforts and to be accountable for their efforts. Unlike teaching faculty, however, librarians do not have the same advantage of having the same class over an extended period of time. Often, librarians meet with students for one-on-one help at the reference desk or give a 50-minute instructional session for a class. Librarians then must figure out ways to integrate their assessment efforts into the teaching faculty's arena, where there is a more captive audience. At BGSU, we have found it nearly impossible to do any meaningful assessment on a volunteer basis. When we first started administering assessment tools, we asked for volunteers to complete the survey in the library. So few surveys were completed that the results were meaningless. To solve this problem, we attempt to take advantage of the teaching faculty's captive audience. After asking program directors and certain course instructors to distribute our assessment materials to their classes, we have been able to collect data and have begun to act on the results.

PROFESSIONAL DEVELOPMENT OPPORTUNITIES

Effective reference librarians must also look for professional development opportunities in addition to fulfilling their daily job responsibilities. Once again, teaching faculty can serve as a valuable resource for librarians, who will have increased opportunities for collaborative projects and other scholarly efforts. In my first position as an assistant reference librarian, I was able to collaborate on two instructional web sites funded by small grants from OhioLINK, Ohio's statewide library consortium. The first, *Research and Argument: Tools for Instructors and Students* <http://karn.wright.edu/~sg-ysu/> was used in English composition courses, and the second, *CORE: Chemistry Online Research Explorer* <http://iws.ohiolink.edu/chemistry/> was used as support material in sophomore-level organic chemistry and biochemistry courses. Both projects involved writing grants and developing instructional material with faculty members and other librarians. Perhaps the element that was most eye-opening to me at that point was working with top-level administrators in the university system–the university's grant officer as well as a dean of the participating college and the library director. Collaborating on both web sites gave me the chance to understand the place of the library in the university community and increased my awareness of working with people outside of my area.

The benefits of such projects did not end with the completion of the web sites; in many ways, the completion was just another step in a more extensive process. Turning projects into research and writing opportunities is important for librarians, especially for those in tenure-track positions. Many librarians new to the profession are overwhelmed, often believing that conference presentations and publishing opportunities are best left to those who have been in the field for a long time. However, any librarian interested in contributing to the field can do so.

The first web project, for instance, led to two national conference experiences. Initially, I developed and created a poster session for a conference of the American Association of Higher Education (AAHE), presenting the site and ways we were using it on campus. The second opportunity resulting from the same project came in the form of a truly collaborative opportunity. The English Department at Youngstown State University, my previous institution, was rapidly moving towards computer-assisted instruction in its research-based composition course, and a substantial amount of collaboration was taking place among the English Department, Maag Library, and the Computer Science Department. As such, along with three members of the English Department and a member of the Computer Science Department, I participated in a roundtable presentation at the Conference on College Composition and Communication (CCCC). Developing group presentations is a natural result of collaborative projects.

The second instructional grant project also led to another national conference opportunity, this time at the Association of College and

Research Libraries' national conference. In a collaborative effort with the librarian who worked on developing the web site, we presented a poster session on aspects of developing instructional sites with departments outside the library. Without working on these projects, I would not have had the opportunities to participate in national conferences as I was just beginning my career.

Instructional web sites are just one possible way to collaborate with faculty members. To explore additional collaborative projects which have also resulted in continued research opportunities, consult Cohen (1995); Burnette, Gillis, and Cochran (1994); Isbell with Broaddus (1995); McKinzie (1997); Stein and Lamb (1998); and Roddy (1997).

STRATEGIES FOR GETTING TO KNOW FACULTY

Expectations and opportunities for working with faculty may vary from institution to institution. If you are looking for ways to expand or initiate a better working relationship with faculty, use some or all of these strategies:

- Create a faculty guide detailing the types of instructional services you offer as well as contact information. The guide should be available both in print and on-line.
- Get to know the departments for whom you are a liaison, and ask to be invited to departmental meetings, especially at the beginning of the year. This will give you the opportunity to tell them about changes and let them know that you are available to help. Include information about services your library offers.
- When you talk to faculty at the reference desk, let them know the library is available to assist them and their students with research questions or projects, especially if they talk to you about the assignments they are constructing.
- Advertise new and changing resources and services. Check on your campus to see if a faculty listserv or newsletter is available. Update faculty in a timely way.
- Ask to be invited to new faculty orientation. It is a good opportunity to meet faculty just as they are starting. A different library is sometimes an obstacle to new faculty members, even though they are undoubtedly expert researchers.

- Try to get on a campus-wide committee. This will introduce you to more people. In fact, you may be able to get some non-library users to start using the library.
- Surf faculty web pages in your assigned subject area to discover their research interests. Try to make contact with those faculty teaching research courses or those faculty whose research interests relate to your own.
- On a lighter note, attend events on campus, such as lectures, lunches, or discussion groups, for example. Again, this will familiarize you with people outside of the library.
- Subscribe to BI-L, or search its archives available at BUBL-L <http://www.bubl.ac.uk/mail/bild/>. An active listserv, BI-L hosts informative discussions on all types of instruction issues. You will learn about programs, successful and unsuccessful, that have been implemented at other institutions. It is also a place for posting questions and joining in on current discussions.

CONCLUSION

Effective reference librarians understand their institution's print and on-line resources, keep abreast of changes in technology, and follow trends in librarianship. They are, however, even more effective when they rely on faculty members since excellent reference service goes beyond interaction at the reference desk. Faculty may be more likely to ask for help when developing an assignment if they know librarians, and librarians may also be able to approach an instructor in a friendly and productive way about a problem with an assignment if they already are familiar with her. In addition to providing better reference service, librarians will also have increased opportunities to pursue collaborative projects, participate in campus-wide initiatives, and find ways to pursue professional development (e.g., presenting at national conferences)–all of which contribute to creating a better, more well-rounded library professional.

REFERENCES

American Library Association (1989), *ALA Presidential Committee on Information Literacy: Final Report*. Chicago: American Library Association.

Association of College and Research Libraries (June 1998), "Task Force on Library Outcomes Assessment Report." Online. Internet. 20 July 1999. Available: http://www.ala.org/acrl/outcome.html

Burnette, Michaelyn, Christina M. Gillis, and Myrtis Cochran (1994), "The Humanist and the Library: Promoting New Scholarship Through Collaborative Interaction Between Humanists and Librarians," *The Reference Librarian* 47, 181-91.

Cohen, Charlotte (1995), "Faculty Liaison: A Cooperative Venture in Bibliographic Instruction," *The Reference Librarian* 51/52, 161-69.

Isbell, Dennis, with assistance from Dorothy Broaddus (1995), "Teaching Writing and Research as Inseparable: A Faculty-Librarian Teaching Team," *Reference Services Review* 23 (Winter), 51-62.

McKinzie, Steve (1997), "Librarians and Faculty in Tandem: Taking Our Cue from the Evening News," *Reference & User Services Quarterly* 37 (Fall), 19-21.

Mosley, Pixey Anne (1998), "Creating a Library Assignment Workshop for University Faculty," *Journal of Academic Librarianship* 24 (January), 33-41.

Roddy, Kevin M. (1997), "How to Build Librarian/Instructional Faculty Collaborative Partnerships." Online. Internet. 6 Aug. 1999. Available: http://www2.hawaii.edu/~kroddy/poster/

Shirato, Linda, and Joseph Badics (1997), "Library Instruction in the 1990s: A Comparison with Trends in Two Earlier LOEX Surveys," *Research Strategies* 15 (Fall), 223-37.

Stein, Linda L., and Jane M. Lamb (1998), "Not Just Another BI: Faculty-Librarian Collaboration to Guide Students Through the Research Process," *Research Strategies* 16 (Winter), 29-39.

Wilson, Lizabeth A. (1995), "Instruction as a Reference Service," *Reference and Information Services*, edited by Richard E. Bopp and Linda C. Smith (2nd ed). Englewood, CO: Libraries Unlimited, 152-84.

Marketing Reference Resources and Services Through a University Outreach Program

John Cruickshank
David G. Nowak

SUMMARY. In many respects the Outreach Program at Mississippi State University Libraries provides an excellent framework for the marketing of reference services and resources. It is often the close, long-term collaboration between academic faculty and reference librarians, however, that makes the discovery of crucial information needs possible. In-depth interviews with strategically selected faculty and continuous feedback provide the basis of effective planning for reference services and a wise marketing strategy. *[Article copies available for a fee from The Haworth Document Delivery Service: 1-800-342-9678. E-mail address: <getinfo@haworthpressinc.com> Website: <http://www.HaworthPress.com> © 2001 by The Haworth Press, Inc. All rights reserved.]*

KEYWORDS. Outreach programs, academic libraries, distance education

Traditionally, outreach has been associated with public library extension services to patrons who are in need of special attention. The

---

John Cruickshank is Interim Head Librarian, College of Veterinary Medicine, Mississippi State University, P.O. Box 9825, Mississippi State, MS 39762-9825 (E-mail: jcruickshank@library.msstate.edu). David G. Nowak is Reference Librarian, Mitchell Memorial Library, Mississippi State University Libraries, P.O. Box 5408, Mississippi State, MS 39762-5408 (E-mail: dnowak@library.msstate.edu).

[Haworth co-indexing entry note]: "Marketing Reference Resources and Services Through a University Outreach Program." Cruickshank, John, and David G. Nowak. Co-published simultaneously in *The Reference Librarian* (The Haworth Information Press, an imprint of The Haworth Press, Inc.) No. 73, 2001, pp. 265-280; and: *Doing the Work of Reference: Practical Tips for Excelling as a Reference Librarian* (ed: Celia Hales Mabry) The Haworth Information Press, an imprint of The Haworth Press, Inc., 2001, pp. 265-280. Single or multiple copies of this article are available for a fee from The Haworth Document Delivery Service [1-800-342-9678, 9:00 a.m. - 5:00 p.m. (EST). E-mail address: getinfo@haworthpressinc.com].

ALA Office for Literacy and Outreach Services stipulates that the mission of their organization is to provide training, resources, and technical assistance to librarians developing programs for neglected user populations like the rural and urban poor, new and non-readers, people with disabilities and people generally discriminated against based on race, ethnic background, social class, or age (ALA Office for Literacy and Outreach Services, 1999). In contrast, academic outreach is a relatively new phenomenon and may have a variety of functions. For example, the Academic Outreach Library at the University of Illinois at Urbana-Champaign provides reference and research assistance to students registered in off-campus courses offered through the Division of Academic Outreach. Students enrolled in the distance education program can obtain advice through e-mail in selecting and searching research tools from the library's digital information resources (Academic Outreach Library, 1999). On the other hand, library outreach at the University of Oregon concentrates on creating new relationships with particular campus user groups, targeting students of color, international students, and community college students making the transition to a four-year university (University of Oregon Library Outreach, 1997). At the University of Michigan, Ann Arbor, outreach is characterized as the design of services to reach patrons outside of the library whether undergraduates in their dorms or faculty in their departmental offices. In fact, the success of the Ann Arbor outreach initiative has been credited to the one-to-one personal contact made with patrons at the time of need (Westbrook, 1993). Academic outreach has also been employed specifically as a public relations tool for gaining support for new electronic resources from university faculty and administrators. At George Washington University, the position of Faculty Outreach Librarian was created to develop programs to keep faculty informed on the increasingly important role of information technologies provided by the library to research and instruction. Through a series of brown bag lunches, house calls to key administrators and computer slide presentations, outreach librarians demonstrated how, for example, the Internet will change traditional patterns of scholarly communication and publishing (Stebelman, 1999). At Mississippi State University the reference department has been gaining new insights into patron needs and expectations from the outreach program. Feedback obtained from the close, long-term collaboration of academic faculty and librarians provides a sound basis for the planning of innovative reference service.

THE OUTREACH PROGRAM AT MISSISSIPPI STATE UNIVERSITY LIBRARIES

Originally established as a land grant institution for Agricultural and Mechanical Studies, Mississippi State University is currently a comprehensive doctoral degree granting university. MSU Libraries serves a user community of more than fifteen thousand students and eight hundred faculty with a collection of more than eight hundred thousand books and seven thousand serial titles accessible at Mitchell Memorial Library and at branch libraries that support The College of Veterinary Medicine and the School of Architecture.

The Outreach Program at MSU was initially conceived as a public relations initiative to encourage direct communication with patrons by linking librarians with faculty, administrators, staff and students. As a new program, the MSU Outreach program was originally administered by an Outreach Coordinating Committee whose members were chosen by the Dean of Libraries. The planning and organization phase of outreach took place during the summer of 1998. The implementation phase encompassed the entire 1998-99 academic year. Evaluation of outreach, which is ongoing, culminated in the appointment of a permanent Coordinator of Outreach for the 1999-2000 academic year. The coordinator is supported by an Outreach Advisory Committee which will organize future outreach activities.

During the planning and organization phase, the coordinating committee decided that the initial target audience for outreach would be academic deans, departmental chairs, and faculty, with particular attention to new faculty. All professional librarians were invited to participate in the outreach program. Each librarian in the reference department volunteered as a participant. Librarians were organized into teams of three to four members and assigned to represent an academic department within a specified college or school. Each team elected a team leader who acted as liaison between the team members and the Outreach Coordinating Committee. The Dean of Libraries personally contacted academic deans to inform them of the goals of the outreach program. The Dean of Libraries also requested that academic deans communicate their support of the outreach initiative to departmental chairs.

At the beginning of the implementation phase, team leaders met with departmental chairs to introduce the outreach program and to request a time slot during the first departmental meeting at the beginning of the academic year in order that all outreach team members could make personal contact with the faculty. At these initial departmental faculty meetings, outreach reference librarians chose to present an overview of the resources and services available from the reference department. Special emphasis was placed on the on-line resources accessible through the Mississippi State University Libraries Reference Department web page (http://nt.library.msstate.edu/reference). Reference Librarians pointed out that our reference home page was designed to facilitate the research process for off-site users. The reference home page contained on-line tutorials to popular databases as well as downloadable handouts providing tips on searching the more scholarly and technical databases. The reference home page also functioned as a gateway to web resources that have been critically evaluated by the reference staff and judged to contain information equivalent in value and authority to the print resources. Finally, the course-integrated library instruction program was emphasized as the most important reference service that allows the teaching faculty to take advantage of the professional expertise of reference librarians as intermediaries between students' needs and the complexities of the print and electronic information environment at MSU Libraries.

OUTREACH AS A MARKETING TOOL

Academic outreach activities have been too often identified with the promotion of an established program of library resources and services. The MSU Libraries Outreach Program proved no exception in its initial focus. Communication with patrons about the library program may be motivated by the desire to upgrade the image of the library as a showplace of electronic resources or to enhance the perception of librarians in the eyes of patrons by emphasizing their technological expertise. Although promotion and public relations are important aspects of marketing, these activities do not, in and by themselves, define the breadth and depth of the marketing function in nonprofit institutions. According to Darlene E. Weingand, in *Future Driven*

Library Marketing, "marketing is a process of exchange: the exchange of elements of value between producer and consumer. In many ways, marketing can be regarded as a partnership that is established based upon the premise of mutual benefit" (Weingand, 1998). The establishment of this mutually beneficial partnership is accomplished by a marketing plan that should be utilized by the library as an institution but may be adapted by departments within the library. At Mississippi State University, the library administration came to realize the value of conceptualizing outreach within the framework of a strategic marketing plan. For Weingand, a well-conceived marketing plan follows a logical sequence of events or steps. Foremost is the marketing audit which analyses the external environment (patron needs and expectations) and compares it to the library's internal environment (collection, services, personnel). Before considering a new product or service, an environmental scan is necessary to project the impact on the library of trends in scholarly communication influenced by the information industry. The proposed new product or service must be congruent with the library's organizational mission and must support operational goals and objectives for a particular time period. Other factors that determine the choice of a new product or service are the direct or indirect cost to the library as well as the mode of distribution (means through which patrons will access the product or avail themselves of the service). Once a decision is made, the new product or service needs to be promoted through officially recognized communication channels. Finally, an ongoing evaluation determines the effectiveness of the new product or service with respect to the target audience. Working within the administrative framework of the MSU Outreach Program, reference librarians at MSU made a deliberate attempt to develop their own marketing plan following the process outlined by Weingand. By adapting a marketing plan that was focused on analyzing patron satisfaction with reference resources and services, the reference department obtained enough information to justify a shift toward a more client-centered model of reference service.

MARKETING REFERENCE: THE EXTERNAL AUDIT

As follow-up to the initial outreach contact with faculty at departmental meetings, the external audit to obtain information on faculty information needs and library service expectations was conducted as in-depth personal interviews targeting a selection of faculty in each department, with special attention to the department head, senior research faculty, undergraduate teaching faculty and new faculty. Outreach reference librarians, representing academic departments in the sciences, social sciences and humanities, shared the results of their interviews during reference department meetings. It was apparent that the development of the MSU digital library of web-based on-line indexes and abstracts had changed the information-seeking behavior of the faculty. Faculty now expected to be able to access a wide range of databases supported by full text or full image at any time, day or night, from their home or offices. The user interface for the databases needed to be intuitive, allowing searching at the novice as well as the expert level. For those databases not supported by full text, the faculty relied upon our subsidized document delivery service which guaranteed that hard copy of articles from publications not held in the library were faxed to them within two business days.

Not surprisingly, reference librarians reported that faculty were reluctant to come to the library in person unless it was absolutely necessary. This trend was substantiated by reference desk statistics collected over the past two years which recorded not only a considerable drop in the quantity of encounters at the reference desk, but also a change in the quality of reference questions. Most transactions at the reference desk focused on the use of the Galaxy on-line catalog to verify holdings for journal titles in the collection. For journal articles that were in the library's collection, the faculty sent graduate assistants to photocopy the articles. Most faculty used electronic current contents services and no longer came to the MSU Libraries Current Journals Department to browse the shelves to scan recent issues of publications in their field. Moreover, the in-depth interviews with faculty confirmed the fact that the Internet has irrevocably changed the pattern of scholarly communication in many disciplines. At present, faculty depend upon listservs in their field to gain input from peers on their research in progress. A growing trend, especially among science faculty, is to consult electronic journals accessible through the web to keep abreast of the latest research in their field. In certain cases, these electronic journals have no print equivalent. Paradoxically, given the faculty's sophistication with MSU Libraries' digital library and the Internet, outreach reference librarians reported that there were instances where reference expertise would prove invaluable to facilitate faculty research and teaching.

In general, faculty seemed to prefer searching a small selection of specialized databases directly related to their academic discipline while completely neglecting comprehensive or interdisciplinary databases. Moreover, observing faculty in their offices as they interacted with our electronic resources, outreach reference librarians noted that faculty would habitually execute the same keyword search across different databases without taking advantage of controlled language searching through thesauri. In addition, faculty seemed to be unaware of the advantage of using proximity operators in searching full text databases. On another level, the teaching faculty who required undergraduates to use the library's resources to complete class assignments often did so without adequate knowledge of relevant resources in the electronic collection–not to mention the print reference collection. On the other hand, some faculty were training their graduate students in electronic resources to which they had private access through departmental subscriptions and that were not available on the MSU Libraries Reference Department web page. More often than not, new faculty were most apt to assume that the resources available at their former university library would, of course, be available at MSU Libraries.

The initial outreach program implemented in 1998 involved every department on the MSU campus. Teams of librarians met with the faculty of each department. While it was clear that faculty were becoming more aware of the information resources and services available to them, the extent to which many of their information needs were being met was unclear. More intense interaction with faculty on an ongoing basis would be necessary to identify many information needs and to determine how well they were being addressed. As a next step in the development of the outreach program the faculty and students of the College of Veterinary Medicine (CVM) were targeted as a test case. The CVM Library is a branch of Mississippi State University Libraries. It is situated in the Learning Resources Center of the Wise Center which also contains a teaching hospital, a diagnostic laboratory, research laboratories, and administrative and faculty offices. The proximity of the library to CVM students and to faculty offices permitted a high degree of interaction between librarian and patron. The information needs of faculty and students could be monitored closely by the librarian not only through formal meetings with faculty and students in offices and in the library, but also through casual conversation with patrons in such informal settings as building corridors and the cafeteria.

The external audit at the CVM formed the basis for an intensive library marketing project. Interviews at CVM held during the follow-up phase of the outreach program were generally more involved than those held in departments across campus during the initial phase of the program. Faculty and students at CVM were interviewed on an individual basis and interviews typically lasted for forty-five minutes to an hour. Patrons were encouraged to share their opinions regarding the quality of library service and to communicate any difficulties encountered in using library services and resources. The nature of difficulties experienced by patrons was often found to vary considerably between individuals working within the same specialization. Two faculty members specializing in clinical small animal medicine, for example, had substantially different needs from the standpoint of information currency. One veterinarian relied on access to the most current information possible and required documents to be delivered within well under a week, while the other specialist, working on essentially the same topics, was content to have database searches performed and documents delivered within several weeks and often months. The discrepancy resulted from the difference in the types of publications being produced by the two faculty members: One was making contributions to weekly newsletters while the other was publishing in quarterly journals.

It was revealed through in-depth interviews with these patrons that accessing and receiving current literature was a problem. This problem originated in part from the fact that a number of patrons were unaware of the possibility of ordering documents electronically through their own computers. It was clear that the outreach efforts of librarians in the previous year had failed to inform certain faculty members of these possibilities for information retrieval. This problem was exacerbated by confusion among the faculty at CVM regarding details on the use of the table of contents current awareness service. The problem was identified through interviews and immediately rectified. The problem was created by misunderstandings among librarians working in different library departments concerning details of the document delivery service. Interviews with patrons showed that negative public relations can result from a lack of communication among librarians concerning the implementation of an important service. For a brief time, until the situation was rectified, patrons at CVM expressed not only concern regarding limitations to the service, but discontent with the discrepancy between the quality of current awareness services provided to CVM and the other departments across campus. The problem was quickly rectified and patron confidence was restored. The communication circuit of librarians and administrators at both the CVM Library and Mitchell Memorial Library was studied and monitored very closely in the weeks and months that followed the incident. The need for closer working relationships between librarians at the branch and main libraries became evident. Librarians at CVM worked closely with Document Delivery Services at the main library to develop a more integrated approach to providing documents to patrons. Many patrons are contacted on a regular basis to monitor patron satisfaction with library services. Reporting procedures between the two libraries were altered to facilitate communication between the patrons at CVM and librarians involved in the outreach program, as well as administrators at the two libraries.

Interviews with faculty members revealed a significant potential for the occurrence of problems in the use of library services and resources. For example, some of the faculty were receiving tables of contents for journals which had little or no relevance to their information needs. This occasionally resulted from the cooperative efforts of faculty members attempting to help one another. A faculty member working in one field would sometimes select inappropriate journal titles for a faculty member working in another field. Faculty members were often slow to inform librarians of significant problems in meeting their information needs. Some individuals were simply too busy to bother seeking assistance in rectifying problems.

The quality of database searching by faculty members was also investigated at CVM. Searches on specific topics were performed by faculty members using the resources of their choice. Librarians ran searches on the same topics using all of the electronic databases at their disposal, including any of the databases accessible through Dialog. The results were compared. Deficiencies in the faculty's results were identified. There was a very wide range in the levels of competence in on-line searching among the faculty. Some faculty members do not have computers and have assistants or librarians perform all their searches. Others claim to be very uncomfortable in performing database searches and are aware that they overlook important information which becomes evident when they attend conferences and observe the work of their counterparts at other institutions. Some faculty members claim to be fully confident in their searching capabilities and do not trust others to perform searches for them. Interviews with a number of patrons indicated difficulties in receiving documents through the interlibrary loans service at the CVM Library. The process was carefully examined and changes to the internal procedures of the CVM Library were instituted in cooperation with the Coordinator of Document Delivery at the main library on campus. Requests were closely monitored and patrons were informed on a regular basis of the progress of the library in meeting their requests. Patrons are now contacted on a regular basis so the library can monitor their levels of satisfaction with the service.

It was found to be crucially important to base the marketing of library resources and services on feedback from library patrons. Faculty members' knowledge of the appropriateness of various information resources, particularly in interdisciplinary fields, however, may be rather limited. Faculty members at CVM tended to have different opinions about the usefulness of various databases in the field of veterinary medicine. Site visits at veterinary libraries in various states provided valuable information on the information resources that should be promoted. There was a clear consensus on this matter among veterinary librarians. When faculty at CVM were encouraged to perform searches using a collection of trial databases, opinions changed and a much clearer consensus emerged.

The promotion of end-user information resources presupposes a relatively high degree of competence on the part of faculty and students in the use of these resources. The external audit at CVM, however, revealed a wide range of abilities among faculty in the use of these resources. In many cases, the inability of faculty members to use appropriate information resources hindered their work and productivity. Overall, a high degree of reliance on outreach librarians was necessary to enable many faculty members to meet their information needs. In the absence of a strong outreach initiative on the part of librarians, important information needs of faculty often go unfulfilled.

MARKETING REFERENCE: THE INTERNAL AUDIT

In light of what the outreach reference librarians learned through in-depth interviews with our segmented faculty target market, the

MSU Reference Department decided to review the present state of the reference program and the service model upon which it is based. Stuart A. Sutton has supplied a typology of libraries with appropriate reference service models that can be adapted to best describe the reference program at MSU Libraries. Sutton defines the traditional library as a "specific place with a finite collection of tangible information bearing primary entities like books and journals" (Sutton, 1996). The service model appropriate for this type of library is one of "resource-dispensing" whose goal is to "provide the user with a subset of information bearing objects from the collection which have the highest probability of satisfying the user's information need" (Sutton, 1996).

A typical transaction at the ready reference desk at Mitchell Memorial Library illustrates this service model. A patron approaches the ready reference desk and undergoes a reference interview to determine the nature of the information needed. Depending upon the complexity of the information required, the librarian retrieves data from a volume in the ready reference collection or searches either the on-line catalog or a periodical index to retrieve the call number of a book or the citation to a journal article that is relevant. The patron is then directed to the physical location of the desired item in the collection. Sutton also recognizes the existence of the more contemporary and prevalent "hybrid library" within which there is a coexistence of both primary digital and non-digital information as a result of the steady migration from print resources to a technology that depends upon the electronic storage and retrieval of information.

To help patrons cope with this new environment, Sutton posits a shift toward a consultative model. This model of reference service is most effectively employed at the Mitchell Memorial Library electronic reference desk, which is separated from the ready reference desk and positioned in close proximity to the thirty computer workstations available in the reference room. Typically, the reference librarian works on a one-on-one basis with the patron. Depending on the scope and breadth of the research project, the librarian suggests appropriate databases, and helps the patron choose keywords or controlled vocabulary particular to the database. The reference librarian collaborates with the patron in the formulation of a search statement using Boolean or proximity operators. For those databases that are comprehensive and inclusive in scope, the librarian teaches the patron to analyze the results for relevancy and authority. Finally, the librarian must instruct the patron on the correct procedure to e-mail, download, or print the results of the search.

It is obvious that the consultative service model demands a high degree of personal involvement between librarian and patron at each stage of the research process in a digital library environment. Although it may appear that there is a natural evolution away from the resource-dispensing model adequate for a print collection toward the consultative service model necessary in a digital library, nothing could be further from the actual situation in the daily operation of reference service. For example, the bibliographic instruction program at MSU Libraries is typically limited to one session in the electronic classroom. It is arranged at the request of the course instructor and focuses only on those resources and research strategies necessary to complete a given class assignment. Typically, the instructional objective of the session determines the level of service offered to students. The resource-dispensing service model is useful to highlight categories of reference tools like encyclopedias, atlases, directories, almanacs, and statistical compendia. At the same time the consultative service model is indispensable in suggesting criteria for students who must choose an appropriate electronic research tool and critically evaluate the results of their search.

MARKETING REFERENCE: NEW SERVICE PROGRAM

The internal audit and analysis of the current program convinced reference librarians at Mitchell Memorial Library of the necessity to emphasize the consultative reference service model based upon a firm knowledge of patrons' needs and expectations. The reference librarians were fortunate to be able to take advantage of the MSU Outreach Program to refashion themselves in a new role as that of "information partner." Reference librarians were now available to establish research partnerships with the faculty through personal consultation, to identify electronic information resources relevant to their research project, to develop effective database search strategies, to evaluate results, and to obtain materials through interlibrary loan or document delivery services.

At CVM librarians placed a strong emphasis on gaining name recognition. Documents were frequently hand-delivered to faculty offices. Faculty members were contacted by librarians and offered individualized assistance and instruction in the use of information resources. In faculty and other group meetings, individuals who raised concerns regarding information resources and services were referred by their colleagues to librarians by name.

At the same time, reference librarians were anxious to establish instructional partnerships with the teaching faculty to develop a library-based research assignment that would support the learning objectives of a particular course, and introduce students to information literacy skills appropriate to their intellectual level. In fact, an ongoing team teaching partnership was established between the reference librarian who serves as subject bibliographer in Biological Sciences/Chemistry and the faculty chair of the Biology Department who is responsible for teaching the Biochemical Research Methods course for advanced graduate students beginning their doctoral dissertation. Instruction in the classroom was divided such that the librarian was responsible for teaching the effective use of print and electronic reference tools. The faculty was involved in developing the critical thinking skills necessary for graduate students who must analyze the results of their literature search for scholarly credibility and relevancy to their research topic. The classroom sessions were supplemented by an office consultation with each graduate student. This consultation allowed the librarian to individualize instruction to bring the student to a level of comfort in interacting successfully with the electronic information environment at MSU Libraries.

For collection development, the partnership between reference librarian and faculty member served as the basis for establishing a reference core collection of print and electronic resources responsive to departmental research and curriculum. Academic faculty were frequently invited to participate in the evaluation of information resources. This process allowed faculty to alert librarians to important information needs. Scientists who sought information through the use of a heavily promoted database by MSU Libraries were disappointed in the quantity and quality of information relevant to their needs. Librarians, being alerted to the problem, were then able to identify and provide access to other more appropriate resources. In-depth discussions of how, when, and for what purpose specific information resources were used by faculty in particular fields, and what alternatives were used in their place, enriched librarians' understanding of how various resources should be promoted. Trial searches of interdisciplinary databases were run by scholars, for example, and often gave librarians an accurate indication of the true content value of these databases in specific subject areas. One database was recently evaluated by faculty members for content in key subject areas. Coverage in some fields was excellent, while the coverage in other areas was hardly worth mentioning. Although a database and its producer may have an excellent reputation, weak topic or subject-specific content areas of the database may fail to deliver basic information needs. Faculty can be of assistance in identifying alternative resources.

Thus, the MSU Outreach Program provided the reference department with an administratively supported and sanctioned communication structure whereby reference librarians were given an invaluable opportunity to initiate innovative reference services and to personalize and customize these services based on direct knowledge of patron needs and expectations.

MARKETING REFERENCE: NEW SERVICE PHILOSOPHY

No matter how committed a reference department may be to moving from a "resource dispensing" to a "consultative" model of reference service, success in this enterprise depends, to a large extent, on the degree to which the library as an institution changes its corporate culture from an operationally focused entity to a client-centered enterprise. In formalizing contact with faculty through the MSU Libraries Outreach Program, the library administrators came to realize that certain organizational changes needed to be made to reflect not so much the impact of automation on library operations, but the impact of automation on scholarly communication, research, publication and teaching. To facilitate a more direct response to the specialized needs of faculty, MSU Libraries administration has adapted an organizational model more reflective of the image of a user-centered library. Increased professional staffing has permitted the reorganization of user services through the appointment of separate coordinators of reference, library instruction and outreach. Compared to the conventional hierarchical library management system wherein the reference staff reports to head of reference who reports to the head of public services who reports to the dean of libraries, this new reorganization calls for multiple reporting relationships to be established between reference librarians and their professional colleagues no matter what their position, rank or department. The new relationship between librarians engaged in cooperative reference services has been identified by Chris Ferguson as the matrix model of management (Ferguson, 1994). Given the flattening of the hierarchical management model and the sharing of decision-making authority and accountability, the matrix model creates an organizational environment that encourages collegiality, and rewards librarians who develop the team building skills of negotiation and compromise necessary to focus energies on meeting client needs.

An indisputable result of the outreach program has been a renewed commitment to a client based philosophy of user services that now forms the essence of the mission statement of Mississippi State University Libraries. The expression of this philosophy in the reference department has been an emphasis on consultation services based upon sustained contact with the individual client. The impact of this service model on the role of the reference librarian is important to consider. Although there will be continuous need to perform as information access provider, the reference librarian will find it necessary to develop information management skills in order to meet the demands of clients. Stuart A. Sutton has eloquently expressed the possible consequences of intense involvement of reference librarians with their clients:

> This level of human intermediation represents a fundamental shift away from the simpler resource sharing dispensing model of service . . . toward a consultative, value added model where the librarians are actively engaged in the process of direct information access and assessment. And, in many special and some academic libraries, the consultative process goes beyond access and assessment to include synthesis and the preparation of information products designed to meet the specific information needs of the client. (Sutton, 1996)

If academic librarians will be expected to assume the information management responsibilities associated with librarians in special libraries even to the extent of preparing information products, it may be inescapable that a requirement for success as an academic reference librarian will include a graduate degree in an academic discipline to supplement the professional credential. In any event, Mary M. Nofsinger has noted with pertinence that the essential core competency for reference professionals in the 21st century will be a personal commitment to users, especially by "serving as essential conduits for information . . . between library managers and customers" (Nofsinger, 1999). Thus, the advocacy role of reference librarians, within a marketing context and facilitated by outreach, will enhance the library's ability to adjust its products to accommodate changes in user expectations. It is only through this activity that the academic library can justify its existence in the years to come.

REFERENCES

Academic Outreach Library–University of Illinois at Urbana-Champaign (1999), Home Page. Online. Internet. 22 February 1999. Available: http://talon.extramural.uiuc.edu/~xlibrary/homepage.htm

ALA Office for Literacy and Outreach Services (1999), Home Page. Online. Internet. 23 June, 1999. Available: http://www.ala.org/olos/

Ferguson, Chris (1994), "Reshaping Academic Library Reference Service: A Review of Issues, Trends and Possibilities," in *Advances in Librarianship,* 18. San Diego: Academic Press, 73-109.

Mississippi State University Libraries: Reference Department (1999), Home Page. Online. Internet. 9 August 1999. Available: http://nt.library.msstate.edu/reference/index.htm

Nofsinger, Mary M. (1999), "Training and Retraining: Reference Professionals: Core Competencies for the 21st Century," in *Coming of Age in Reference Services: A Case History of the Washington State University Libraries.* New York: The Haworth Press, Inc., 9-19.

Stebelman, Scott, Jack Siggins, David Nutty, and Caroline Long (1999), "Improving Library Relations with the Faculty and University Administrators: The Role of the Faculty Outreach Librarian," *College and Research Libraries* 60(2), 121-130.

Sutton, Stuart, A. (1996), "Future Service Models and the Convergence of Functions: The Reference Librarian as Technician, Author and Consultant," in *The Roles of Reference Librarians: Today and Tomorrow,* edited by Kathleen Low. New York: The Haworth Press, Inc., 125-143.

University of Oregon Library Outreach (1997), Home Page. Online. Internet. 2 March 1997. Available: http://www.uoregon.edu/~jcawthor/Outreach/home.html

Weingand, Darlene, E. (1998), *Future-Driven Library Marketing.* Chicago: American Library Association.

Westbrook, Lynn and Robert Waldman (1993), "Outreach in Academic Libraries: Principle into Practice," *Research Strategies* 11(2), 60-65.

Selling the Library from the Reference Desk: Service Points as Advertisements

Sarah Reneker Andeen

SUMMARY. Many library directors and administrators spend a significant portion of their time attempting to market the library and its services. Getting patrons into the library and keeping their business is an integral part of the day-to-day management of the library. This mission, however, is not always effectively passed on to the front lines to the one group of people who face the patrons on a daily basis–the reference librarians.

This article will show how the library's service points can be used as marketing tools; outline what librarians and public service staff should know about their library; and discuss ways in which reference service librarians can help further the library's marketing and public relations goals. *[Article copies available for a fee from The Haworth Document Delivery Service: 1-800-342-9678. E-mail address: <getinfo@haworthpressinc.com> Website: <http://www.HaworthPress.com> © 2001 by The Haworth Press, Inc. All rights reserved.]*

KEYWORDS. Reference services, reference desk, marketing, advertising, public relations

In this day and age when everyone is convinced that everything is available on the Internet and that libraries and librarians are a dying

---

Sarah Reneker Andeen is Reference Librarian, law firm of Greenberg Traurig, One East Camelback Road, Suite 1100, Phoenix, AZ 85012-1656 (E-mail: Andeens@gtlaw.com).

[Haworth co-indexing entry note]: "Selling the Library from the Reference Desk: Service Points as Advertisements." Andeen, Sarah Reneker. Co-published simultaneously in *The Reference Librarian* (The Haworth Information Press, an imprint of The Haworth Press, Inc.) No. 73, 2001, pp. 281-292; and: *Doing the Work of Reference: Practical Tips for Excelling as a Reference Librarian* (ed: Celia Hales Mabry) The Haworth Information Press, an imprint of The Haworth Press, Inc., 2001, pp. 281-292. Single or multiple copies of this article are available for a fee from The Haworth Document Delivery Service [1-800-342-9678, 9:00 a.m.-5:00 p.m. (EST). E-mail address: getinfo@haworthpressinc.com].

breed, it is more important than ever that everyone in your library be committed to and effective at promoting the library. This does not mean that the entire staff should spend all their time coming up with catchy slogans or writing promotional literature for the library, but rather that there is an overall commitment to selling the library to everyone–both within the library walls and to the outside world. Promoting the library effectively can be a difficult balancing act; you need to make sure that you are informing people of the services you offer while making sure that staff are not skimping on those services in order to find time to promote the library.

With all the competition libraries are facing these days, from bookstores like Borders and Barnes and Noble to the Internet and Amazon, it is more important than ever that libraries have strong marketing strategies. With the ease of access to the Internet, it is becoming easier for people to access information without ever leaving their homes. In academic communities, there is a push to wire all the dorms and offices to provide access to library databases and services to the students and faculty–without them ever having to visit the library. As librarians know, however, having access to information and being able find what you need are two entirely different matters. Librarians still have a key role to play in the information "food chain" and it is important that we learn how to promote these services to our patrons.

A review of the literature on marketing the library shows the importance of getting out of the physical library to sell our services. In an article for *Library Administration and Management,* Arant and Clark state that: "In essence, it is necessary for librarians to follow information out of the library, making themselves known to the customer, an evangelical approach" (Arant and Clark, 1999).

Many times, especially in large public and academic libraries, a committee will be formed to develop a marketing strategy and public relation plan for the library. Upper management will be the ones making the decisions on how to go about selling the library to its customers. The library literature shows that the development of a clear marketing strategy is critical to the long-term success of your library, and management should develop this plan as they oversee the budget and are aware of the big picture. Once this strategy is put into place, however, it is critical that the overall plan and service goals be disseminated to the entire staff.

It is important to note the difference between developing a marketing strategy and promoting the library. Management will be the ones to develop the marketing strategy for the library. True marketing involves assessing the user base for the library, determining what services will be effective, obtaining funding, and evaluating their usefulness. As Weingard states in her book, *Future-Driven Library Marketing* (1998), " . . . marketing is defined in the literature in the language of promotion or of public relations. This misperception is unfortunate because as important as the promotional function is to the marketing process, it is only one part of the total effort–one of the final parts. When a librarian's attention is limited to just this one portion of the entire marketing process, marketing is not truly taking place." While it is important to realize that promotion is not the entire marketing process, this article focuses on the role of the reference librarian in the promotion and on how the flow of information from the reference staff to the marketing team–in both directions–can have a major impact on the overall success of the library's marketing endeavors.

While the development of the marketing strategy by upper management can be an effective way of developing a blueprint for library services, in the long run it will not work unless everyone who works in the library is on board. Unless your staff knows what services and programs the library is promoting, they will not be able to effectively inform their patrons. Stop to think about it. Who sees the most of the library patrons? The reference librarians and the public service staff in your library. The staff who meet and greet the public every day. These employees are the windows on the institution and if they are not outstanding employees, fully aware of all the aspects of your organization, it will reflect poorly on the institution as a whole.

In an article (1998) for the *Missouri Library World*, Duckworth discusses how the Springfield-Green County Library implemented marketing consultant Faith Popcorn's ideas on marketing and forecasting customer behavior. One of the first steps the library took in this process was to involve the full staff–everyone from pages to custodians to reference librarians was introduced to the concepts of looking for customer trends. Duckworth shows the value of taking this step by stating: "Even more valuable than the ideas generated, though, was the beginning of a paradigm shift for many staff who participated. If staff are our greatest resource (and they are!), then this was time well spent if for no other reason than to inform us all that we are moving into uncharted territory for library service and that 'thinking outside the box' is called for in formulating how to respond to our communities' unique needs."

It is therefore up to the Head Librarian, the Head of Public Service, and/or the team developing the marketing strategy, to make sure that all public services staff are fully informed of the long-range goals of the library and what services and promotional events the library is planning. Communication sounds simple, but many times everyone assumes that the staff is aware of everything that goes on in the library. In reality, this is not the case. Often, staff are the last ones to learn what is going on in an organization as management simply assumes that someone else has passed along the information. Poor communication is usually the culprit, but there are some dysfunctional organizations in which people tend to hoard knowledge in an attempt to feel superior or to try to protect themselves. This invariably leads to a complete breakdown in communications and poor public service. If you are in such an organization, you can work to improve the situation, but if the problem resides in upper management, the best option may be to start scouting out other job opportunities. However, if the organization simply suffers from poor communication, there are several steps that can be taken to loosen the communication logjam.

COMMUNICATION TOOLS

There are many different ways to ensure that the lines of communication stay open in your library including the following: newsletters, meetings, internal listservs, and informal communication in staff rooms and offices. All of these options will take time and some of the library's limited resources, but if there is poor communication within the library as a whole, it will be difficult, if not impossible, to maintain a high level of service and supportive clientele.

Newsletters

Although many libraries create newsletters for their public as a method of outreach and communication, unless staff are directly involved in the entire process, they do not always read these newsletters–even if they contribute an article or two. One way to help encourage staff members to read the library's newsletter is to treat staff as if they were library users and put them on the mailing list. This way each member of the staff receives a copy and can read it at her leisure. Although this may seem like an unnecessary added expense, it is worth it to keep your staff up-to-date and connected to library issues. Routing a copy of the newsletter is an acceptable alternative for those libraries that simply cannot afford the extra photocopying costs, but anytime materials are routed, there is a major risk of having the publication sit on someone's desk for an extended period of time.

Another effective method of communication for larger libraries is internal newsletters. Developing a staff newsletter can take some time and effort, but once it is operational it can be used to share biographies of new and old staff members; reiterate library policies; share information about new databases or materials in the collection; outline major issues affecting the library; and contain a calendar of upcoming events, meetings, and promotions within the library. Newsletters can also be a good place to share professional development materials such as library URLs and articles.

In this age of desktop publishing and e-mail distribution, it is easy to create a basic newsletter and then modify it to fit different user groups. Structuring your publications to fit user groups can create an effective way of promoting your library, both internally and to your customers. One thing to consider, according to Weingard, is that " . . . it is also essential that a feedback loop be built into the process so that the audience's response to the message can be determined" (Weingard, 1998). Newsletters, both internal and external, are not useful if they are not being read. Reference staff can be one resource in helping to determine content and usefulness. The reference staff knows what the readers are reading and what types of materials they are requesting. The staff can also tell you if a book that was reviewed in the newsletter suddenly became more popular. If it did not, why not?

The service desks are the best places to distribute newsletters and to have sign-up sheets for those who want to be put on the mailing list. One of the jobs of the service staff is to promote all of the library's services, so staff should be trained to offer to add people to the mailing list if they see someone looking at the newsletter. By constantly offering services to patrons, even if no formal reference interview is occurring, the library will gain a reputation for being friendly and helpful.

Meetings

No one likes to have meetings. They are time-consuming and often nothing much of value is disseminated. A properly-run meeting, however, can provide attendees with valuable information about new library services and policies, as well as allow for discussions of problems and concerns within the library. It is critical that the reference staff provide the management team with feedback on how the new programs and services are working. Do the users really *use* the new service? Does the new web interface cause confusion? Are users asking for different products or services? Do they hate the new signage? Libraries often spend a lot of time and money doing user surveys trying to determine what their patrons want and need, but they fail to talk to the group that could provide insight into the daily requests of the users–the service desk staff.

Ongoing feedback from the service desks is critical, and if the library does not have a structure in place to provide librarians with an easy forum, the marketing team may lose out on many good ideas. As Duckworth (1998) outlined in his article on developing a new marketing strategy for his library, involving the staff was critical: " . . . over 50 staff ranging from pages to custodians, from materials processors to reference librarians, were introduced to the concept of the trends. Within 45 minutes, each group had a creative list of ideas for programs and services. Administrative staff took these ideas and refined them."

E-Mail

E-mail is a wonderful communication tool, both for the outside world and for internal users. Many libraries do not fully utilize this form of communication. It can, however, be a wonderful promotional tool and an excellent distribution medium for library staff. Libraries could consider developing an electronic newsletter to share news about upcoming programs, policy changes, new databases and resources in the library, and Internet sites of interest. Making e-mail one of the primary forms of communication within the library system allows library management to keep in touch with all staff–even if they are at a branch facility. It provides the librarians with a strong sense of community. Using e-mail on a regular basis will help improve overall computing skills and may encourage staff members to share problems and concerns that might otherwise have gone unvoiced.

SERVICE POINTS

Physical Location

Unless you are in the process of building a new library–and sometimes not even then–the reference staff will have little say in where the desk is located. However, the reference staff can ensure that the desk is easy to approach, friendly, and well-marked. Poor signage, lack of good lighting, piles of work on the reference desk, and difficulty reaching the service desk will all lead to a negative impression of the library and its services, even if the user receives the information needed.

Signage

One of the roles the reference and service desk staff can play is informing management about the effectiveness of the signage in the library. These are the people who answer directional questions all day and can accurately assess how easy it is for patrons to navigate throughout the library. Service desk staff should constantly be noting repeat questions and looking to see where signs could be placed to help patrons locate information. This knowledge should then be passed along to administration. It is critical that management pass along the results of their discussion on the topic to the staff members. It is possible that no new signs will be put into place for a number of reasons, but unless this information is conveyed to the staff, they will simply feel that their suggestions are being ignored and will stop making the effort to participate in improving library services.

Access

How accessible are the library's service desks and how welcoming is the staff? At times all library service desks can become quite hectic, but it is critical that staff are trained always to acknowledge newcomers. Even if the reference librarian is on the phone or in the middle of another transaction, she should look up and smile at the newcomer. Simply making eye contact will help to reassure the user that he exists and staff will be ready to assist him shortly.

How is the visibility from the reference desk? Can the librarians see into the computer area? Can they see incoming patrons? Is there room for patrons to maneuver easily about the desk? All of these things should be taken into consideration when designing a desk, and once built there is little that the staff can do to change the layout, but if there are design flaws, all staff should be aware of them and work to help overcome them. For example, if visibility is a problem, perhaps getting taller chairs might help patrons see that there is a librarian at the desk. By constantly striving to improve the atmosphere and ease of access around the service points, the librarians are promoting their services by increasing their visibility.

Brochures

One of the primary means that the library has of communicating with the public is through the use of brochures and other publications. All service desks should be fully stocked at all times with maps of the library, a brochure outlining the general services and policies of the library, a brochure on the library's electronic resources if there are enough to warrant a separate publication, and flyers detailing the training schedule and upcoming events in the library. Having the reference staff develop a monthly calendar of events for library users can be useful–both in informing the users of upcoming events and keeping the staff alerted to upcoming programs.

The reference staff should create all of these publications since they are the ones who interact most with the library users. The service desk staff needs to pay close attention when interacting with the public to determine what questions are not being answered by the brochures. This can be difficult, as many times people do not read the material while they are standing at the desk; however, some feedback may be obtained simply by observing users. Staff should also track what questions are being asked on a regular basis by patrons–both in-house and phone users so that the answers to those questions can be incorporated in the library's informational literature.

When creating publications to sell the services of your library, it is important to place contact information on the material. Nothing is more frustrating then getting a brochure home and not being sure where it came from or whom to contact for more information. The name of the institution should be predominately displayed, followed by contact information including: main phone number, address, web page address, and e-mail address. There should also be a notation indicating the last update for the publication.

TRAINING

Wonderful! There is good communication throughout the library, the staff is aware of all of the services the library has to offer, there are clear and informative brochures and signs throughout the library directing people to where they need to be, and the library has invested a considerable amount of time and money into making the new services available. Only one problem–none of the library's users know how to use the new databases, computers, photocopy machines, or other new gadgets of the day. Users will need to be trained and the people who are going to need to do the instruction are the service desk staff. In order to train someone on a new piece of equipment or a new database, however, the staff is going to have to know how to use the resource. While this seems obvious, it is often a piece of the puzzle that is overlooked. Librarians are very good at making do and teaching themselves what they need to know. On-the-job training with a user breathing down your neck is not the first time you want to be searching. What if this particular vendor hid the print key or if searches require using an asterisk or the exclamation point as the wild card operator?

Once the staff has been made aware of all of the options and services in the library, it is critical to train the reference librarians how to convey this information on the service desks. Nothing is more frustrating than listening to another staff member simply answer a patron's question without going the extra step and offering the patron the alternatives the library can offer. For example: A patron walks up to the reference desk and says: "Do you have the *Encyclopedia Britannica*?" The librarian replies, "Yes, in aisle 2 on the other side of the library." This is technically an accurate response, but what if the library also has this material in electronic form? The patron could have done a keyword search and printed or downloaded the materials. Many times the librarians will simply not tell patrons about the electronic resources. This is a major error and one that will hurt the library in the long run. Part of it is that librarians may be afraid of the response to the statement that the materials are also available in electronic format. Users may then expect to be trained on the new resource, leading to an extra burden on the reference staff, but it is pointless to spend money on resources that people are not aware of and are not being trained on.

In an article for *Computers in Libraries,* Carpenter (1998) states: "In order to be able to market our libraries through technology, we first need to make the technology itself usable and friendly. We need to provide people with know-how, so they can use these new services effectively and without frustration . . . One of the ways in which we can improve customer service is to take ownership of the technological environment we have created and make it easy for the customer to use. Involve your customers in their use of the library and take responsibility for training them in how to use it."

Management needs to be scrupulous about providing their staff with training on the new materials well before these services hit the floor. Many of the vendors are willing to come in and do training on their products and might even be convinced to hold a few public training sessions. This is where good negotiating skills can come into play: By convincing the vendors that if they come in and train, more people will be likely to use their product and the library will be more likely to continue the subscription or obtain an additional license. This strategy can work wonders when trying to get training for your staff and the public. Without training, the library's expensive new products will not be used, and customer satisfaction with the library as a whole may decrease if users are constantly met with new materials they cannot use and the staff cannot effectively train them how to use.

One of the greatest sins on the reference desk is allowing the staff's frustration with a new database or system or policy to be conveyed to the library users. There have been far too many instances on the reference desk where librarians simply will not help the patron use the new materials because they do not like the new resource, or more likely, do not know how to use the new tool and are afraid of looking foolish in front of a user. If the library's new on-line system just "ate" 5,000 records, staff are not fully trained on how to print from it properly, marking a list of materials takes three steps more than before, and the user is standing there complaining–all of this makes it very easy to criticize the system and outline the flaws. While it may appear that you are giving the patron what he wants, i.e., agreeing with his point of view, all that is being accomplished is that the user is getting the idea that the library management does not know what it is doing and that staff do not know how to use the services. This is the message that will be sent, even if the librarian is ultimately successful in providing the user with the requested materials. A far better approach is to let the person rant, agree with part of his statements, explain how the new system or service is better for the library, and offer to walk the user through how to use it. This is where the calm, soothing tones of the experienced reference librarian can really make a difference. It is amazing what a difference tone can make when dealing with a library user. By validating the person's dissatisfaction with the new system, staff are defusing the situation. The user was right to be annoyed, the new computers can be a little confusing, but instead of feeding into this dissatisfaction and allowing it to continue, a skilled librarian, who has been properly trained on the products, can turn this into a situation to sell the patron on both the new product and the library as a whole. This type of approach can be difficult to master, but once the staff has been trained, it can make a world of difference. Librarians who criticize new computers and agree with angry and frustrated users may initially receive positive feedback from them, but although the patron might not go away completely frustrated and angry, he still is left with a negative impression of the library and no way to effectively access the information the next time he uses the library.

CONCLUSION

Promoting library services is critical to the ongoing success of the institution. Gone are the days when the library can simply assume that everyone thinks that the library is a good and wonderful thing. Librarians must be prepared to promote all their services to every person that walks into the library–and to actively go out and seek new users. The reference staff is best suited to making sure that once in the library, the patron receives the highest level of service. Staff must be trained on how to use all resources available in the library, and should be active in helping to develop new products.

BIBLIOGRAPHY

Arant, Wendi and Charlene K. Clark (1999), "Academic Library Public Relations: An Evangelical Approach." *Library Administration and Management* 13 (Spring), 90-95.

Carpenter, Beth (1998), "Your Attention Please! Marketing Today's Libraries." *Computers in Libraries* 18 (September), 62-69.

Cihak, Herbert E. (1997), "Marketing CD-ROM and Other Electronic Library Services." *Computers in Libraries* 17 (June), 73-76.

Duckworth, Paul (1998), "Tapping into the Trends." *Missouri Library World* 3 (Winter), 12-14.

Gorcheles, Linda M. (1995), "Trends in Marketing Services." *Library Trends* 43 (Winter), 494-509.

Norman, O. Gene (1995), "Marketing Reference Services." *The Reference Librarian* 49/50, 45-60.

Rozum, Betty and Kevin Brewer (1997), "Identifying, Developing, and Marketing Library Services to Cooperative Extension Personnel." *Reference & User Services Quarterly* v. 37, no. 2 (Winter), 161-169.

Weingard, Darlene E. (1998), *Future-Driven Library Marketing.* Chicago: American Library Association.

Weingard, Darlene E. (1995), "Marketing of Library and Information Services." *Library Trends* 43 (Winter), 289-309.

Whitlatch, Jo Bell (1995), "Customer Service: Implications for Reference Service." *The Reference Librarian* 49/50, 5-24.

Wolpert, Ann J. (1998), "Services to Remote Users: Marketing the Library's Role." *Library Trends* 47 (Summer), 21-41.

The A, B, Z's of Bibliographic Instruction: Using Real-Life Analogies to Foster Understanding

Naomi R. Sutherland
C. M. Winters

SUMMARY. Actively seeking connections between real life and information retrieval concepts will not only keep students' interest but will also improve their ability to recall key principles when faced with the next research assignment. This article defines analogies and highlights their role as a practical bibliographic instructional strategy. It further presents the use of analogies in the larger context of instructional de-

Naomi R. Sutherland is Reference/Instruction Librarian, Lupton Library, University of Tennessee at Chattanooga, 615 McCallie Avenue, Chattanooga, TN 37403-2598 (E-mail: Naomi-Sutherland@utc.edu). C. M. Winters is a doctoral student, School of Information Studies, Florida State University, 244 LSB, Box 175, Tallahassee, FL 32306 (E-mail: cww7236@garnet.acns.fsu.edu).

The authors wish to thank K. R. Johnson for editorial advice on the draft of this article as well as each librarian who contributed to the analogy survey.

[Haworth co-indexing entry note]: "The A, B, Z's of Bibliographic Instruction: Using Real-Life Analogies to Foster Understanding." Sutherland, Naomi R., and C. M. Winters. Co-published simultaneously in *The Reference Librarian* (The Haworth Information Press, an imprint of The Haworth Press, Inc.) No. 73, 2001, pp. 293-308; and: *Doing the Work of Reference: Practical Tips for Excelling as a Reference Librarian* (ed: Celia Hales Mabry) The Haworth Information Press, an imprint of The Haworth Press, Inc., 2001, pp. 293-308. Single or multiple copies of this article are available for a fee from The Haworth Document Delivery Service [1-800-342-9678, 9:00 a.m. - 5:00 p.m. (EST). E-mail address: getinfo@haworthpressinc.com].

sign, followed by survey results consisting of actual analogies currently used in libraries across the United States and Canada.

KEYWORDS. Analogy, analogical connections, bibliographic instruction, comprehension, conceptualization, metaphors, theoretical framework, transferable information skills

The library tour starts in thirty minutes! You have an inkling that this session could conceivably be as unexciting as the tour you took as a freshman. Desperately seeking pizzazz, you remember Freud: "Analogies decide nothing, that is true, but they can make one feel more at home." That's it! Create a bridge between familiar and unfamiliar concepts using analogies.

The role of an instruction librarian can be compared to that of a coach. A coach is usually a veteran of the sport who explains and demonstrates for the players how to utilize talent and ability to compete and excel. Likewise, a librarian is trained to guide users through ulcer-inducing amounts of information while imparting skills necessary to self-sufficiency. One of the keys to successful teaching is the ability to present ideas in an involving, memorable, yet simple way.

Actively seeking connections between real life and information retrieval concepts will not only keep students' interest but will also improve their ability to recall key principles when faced with the next research assignment. This article defines analogies and highlights their role as a practical bibliographic instructional strategy. It further presents the use of analogies in the larger context of instructional design, followed by survey results consisting of actual analogies currently used in libraries across the United States and Canada.

WHAT IS AN ANALOGY?

A broad survey of educational, psychological, scientific, and library literature yields various interpretations of what an analogy is or should be. As one educator acknowledged, "The term analogy still means different things to different people" (Zeitoun, 1984). The following are samples of these definitions. An analogy is a "comparison between two items not normally considered to be alike which relates new and potentially meaningful knowledge to highly similar knowledge" (Davis and Davidson, 1994; Reigeluth, 1983). Used in instruction, it is considered "an explicit, nonliteral comparison between two objects, or sets of objects, that describes their structural, functional, and/or causal similarities" (Newby et al., 1995). For example, a zero can be compared to a bookmark because neither has value except as a placeholder. This illustrates the cross-contextual application of knowledge inherent in the definition of an analogy. One educator builds on this application by stating that an analogy is "a process of utilizing knowledge from one domain in another" (Suzuki, 1994).

For the purposes of this article, an analogy is defined as the comparison of one thing to another on the basis of some resemblance between the two. It highlights a partial rather than a complete likeness.

Using analogies involves the comprehension of concepts: taking what is known about an area and applying it to another. It is not surprising, then, to find multiple references to analogies used as educational aids. Analogies can be simple (single layer to enhance a concept; e.g., the Library of Congress Subject Headings are like the Yellow Pages) or complex (multiple layer to enhance a complete concept; e.g., the human eye/camera comparison, which has multiple similarities) (Iding, 1993). The kind of analogy chosen to illustrate a principle, concept, or theory depends on a number of factors, including the age of the audience and the general level of familiarity with the basic ideas being discussed.

You likely would not relate finding information in an index to using a crosswalk at a busy intersection when addressing a second grade library tour on the topic of which books to use for their upcoming report on pet adoption. A high school or college audience, on the other hand, would remember their parents teaching them what a crosswalk is and how it works (including the need to look both ways). They would more readily understand the connection between stopping and assessing the street situation each time and the need to make similar evaluative judgements about the citations they retrieve.

"Analogies are useful instructional tools because they make abstract concepts concrete and therefore easier to remember, and they facilitate the exchange of ideas by providing a common terminology and framework" (Halpern et al., 1990). For instance, one reference librarian/instruction coordinator uses the concept of fishing nets to illustrate keyword and controlled vocabulary searching in his library instruction sessions. He says that keyword searching is "like tossing out a very large net with small holes: you get everything from plankton to dolphins." On the other hand, controlled vocabulary searching is "like using a smaller net with larger holes: it lets the unwanted small fry escape, and gets you close to the size fish you want; even if you get a few unwanted specimens, at least you [have] eliminated the bulk of the unwanted stuff" (Amodeo, 1999).

WHEN ANALOGIES FAIL

If, as Freud asserted, analogies can help a person feel more at home, then they must also be clearly presented. Clarity and balance help ensure that the listener does not mistakenly carry the comparison beyond the bounds dictated by the instructor. Another concern involved in overcoming misconceptions is the possible use of unfamiliar analogical components. Relating an analogy that compares things that are familiar to the student is important. Otherwise, the student may be confused rather than helped (Reigeluth, 1980).

Imagine that during the course of a library instruction session the Internet is compared to a large shopping mall. One of the class members is from a village in a developing nation and is so new to the United States that he has not yet visited a mall. That person is likely to lose the analogical "thread" and instead begin wondering what a shopping mall is. In other words, the student fails to make use of an analog due to his failure to understand its applicability. This scenario is reinforced by Hassan Zeitoun who developed his own nine-step plan for devising analogies, discussed later in this article (Zeitoun, 1984). He mentions further limitations to using analogies. Two of these are using weak comparisons and trying to incorporate analogies when the student already knows enough about the topic.

Preventing false analogical connections involves vigilant examination of whether the differences between the concepts being compared are greater than the similarities. If the differences are greater, it is best not to use the analogy rather than risk confusion. Analogies infrequently constitute a *complete* comparison. Pointing out areas that do not match helps prevent over-generalization (Reigeluth, 1983; Davis and Davidson, 1994). Set the limits of the analogy as necessary by defining what things are as well as what they are not.

PRACTICAL BIBLIOGRAPHIC INSTRUCTIONAL STRATEGY: USING ANALOGIES

The term *bibliographic instruction* has been used increasingly since the mid-1970s in reference to teaching strategies designed to empower learners in locating and using information. Computer-assisted instruction, lectures, small group work, discussions, demonstrations, and self-guided workbooks are among the methods librarians and other instructors use to strategically impart information. Analogies can be effectively employed using any of these. The final measure of success, however, is determined by the actual presentation (Wilson, 1995; Warnken and Young, 1991).

Librarians, like coaches, have theories upon which to base the advice and the guidance they give their students. The *active learning theory* can be applied in both instances. It assumes that personal and active involvement are required for learning to begin. The current theory of bibliographic instruction "draws extensively from tenets of active learning in the attempt to 'redefine content' to include skills and understanding, as well as information" (Dyckman, 1995). Focusing on developing an effective bibliographic instruction session, Carolyn Sanford also employs the active learning theory. She describes an environment where analogies could be easily incorporated into the presentation and student interaction periods (Sanford, 1991).

If it is so important to maintain students' active involvement, then using attention-getting analogies is one strategy for hooking and keeping students' interest. Describe the analogy before introducing new knowledge and then refer to it at various times throughout the lesson. Actively engage the students in their own learning process; don't allow them to be casual observers. Ask follow-up questions related to the analogy. Think of how you would process the analogy as an inexperienced information searcher. Delivery is also important to the success of an analogy. Each piece should be clearly described as well as the connection between them (Reigeluth, 1983; Smith and Montanelli, 1999). A creative analogical presentation approach may involve demonstrations, games, moveable models, pictures, or graphs. Finally, use a sense of humor and be enthusiastic. Smile!

One instructor illustrates Boolean logic by using a roomful of students. She first introduces a scenario (extras on a movie set) and then asks the students to imagine that they are asked questions whose answers are entered into a database record with many fields. The first field searched to determine eligibility for the "extra" spots is the clothing field. Two database searches then require a student to stand up and remain standing as long as she matches the search criteria: (a) Stand up if you are wearing running shoes OR you are wearing blue jeans; (b) Remain standing if you are wearing running shoes AND you are wearing blue jeans. The instructor reports that this exercise "seems to be quite memorable for the students" and the only "peril" for the instructor is to make sure the clothing terms are present in sufficient numbers for the scenario to work well (Growe, 1999).

As the above example illustrates, effective analogies used in bibliographic instruction should be practical in nature. If they are too theoretical, the intended connection may be missed. Understanding Boolean logic and selecting the right Internet search tool can be intimidating to the novice researcher. "It takes mental effort for library users to adopt a librarian's way of thinking and deciding–but without these skills they are denied access to wanted information" (Nahl-Jakobovits and Jakobovits, 1990). Analogies can answer questions such as "How can I feel at home in a library environment? How do I navigate across widely different tools?" Some of the analogies highlighted at the end of this article help answer these fundamental questions.

The delivery components of a practical and effective bibliographic instruction analogy can be summarized in three functions. The first function is stabilizing the abstract idea (e.g., Boolean logic) with the help of concrete terms (e.g., salad with oil AND vinegar; salad with vinegar NOT oil). Secondly, provide organization of information by giving the analogy structure (e.g., a steak house menu is like an index because it shows what that restaurant offers, grouped by food category; then explain how this relates to using an electronic periodical database which also uses "index" terms). The final function is helping students assimilate the new information so that students can relate and integrate it into previously recognized structures (e.g., searching the Internet can be like going to the grocery store).

The use of analogies in bibliographic instruction began with the shift at the end of the 1970s from "tool-based instruction" toward "concept-based instruction." Librarians began to recognize that introducing students to specific tools was not always broadly applicable over the course of an undergraduate sojourn, for example. This realization spurred them to experiment with how to teach students to use a search strategy to identify, locate, and evaluate information. Lizabeth Wilson notes librarians also discovered that users learned "transferable" information skills more easily when "using conceptual frameworks and a cognitive approach to research skills instruction" (Wilson, 1995).

The conceptual approach to bibliographic instruction grew in popularity during the 1980s, resulting in teaching principles rather than specific tool-based methods. Current instructional design and learning theories were recognized as a solid foundation for emerging bibliographic instruction strategies. The underlying theme of the transition to concept-based teaching was providing learners with the knowledge to function in a broad range of information situations and environments.

The 1990s have continued to solidify the use of concept-based teaching as an effective bibliographic instruction strategy. The number of electronic indexes and databases advances monthly, if not weekly. If librarians are admittedly hard-pressed in maintaining a firm grasp on which automated tool to use in a particular reference encounter, imagine what the students do when faced with a list of twenty or thirty databases? They often use the one left open by the previous user, not stopping to consider whether it might be the best option for their own search. Analogies such as the earlier cited interactive Boolean "blue jean" example can imprint the importance of how to construct a search that survives multiple database interfaces, focusing on the commonalities rather than the differences.

REVIEW OF THE LITERATURE

Bibliographic instruction (BI) librarians and researchers from a host of other academic disciplines will likely agree that an analogy can be an effective instructional aid. Differences of opinion arise, however, when people from various disciplines explain *why* an analogy is effective, *how* one knows an analogy is effective, and how one can *consistently produce* the best analogy to bridge the gap between the familiar and the unfamiliar.

One of the few recurring concepts that appeared in the literature is that analogies possess a power to create similarities between otherwise difficult-to-understand material and something that the student already understands or finds easy to understand. Rutherford's solar system model of the hydrogen atom (in which the familiar concept of the solar system is used to describe similar properties of an unfamiliar concept, the atom) is perhaps the most famous example of a scientific analogy. The scientific teaching community has used analogies for many years to great effect (Zeitoun, 1984; Thagard, 1992; Baker, 1995; Eflin, 1995). Educators and psychologists have also acknowledged success with analogies (Halpern et al., 1990; Zook and Di Vesta, 1991; Iding, 1993; Davis et al., 1994; Newby et al., 1995; Glynn, 1996; Holyoak and Thagard, 1997). Library science, and particularly bibliographic instruction, continues to experiment with incorporating analogies, as the survey results found near the end of this article attest. Overall, analogies are a "success story."

The roots of contemporary analogy use can be traced to such trailblazers as Mary Hesse, a philosopher whose 1966 treatise on analogy in science "argued that analogies are powerful forces in discovery and conceptual change" (as cited in Gentner and Holyoak, 1997). Gentner and Holyoak are psychologists whose review of the literature concludes with what they see as an emerging consensus on many issues concerning this topic.

They state that the approach to analogical thinking can be "decomposed" into several basic processes to which all current theories of analogy are in some way connected. These processes include setting up the analogy by beckoning to the learner's mind a familiar idea which can then be connected to a "target analog" (the unfamiliar idea that needs to be understood); and identifying "systematic correspondences," thereby "aligning" the similar parts of each idea. The process continues as the instructor points out the inferences to be made about the target analog, inferences which then plug the "holes" in the learner's understanding of the new topic. Afterwards, the student is lead to evaluate the inferences and, in the "aftermath of analogical reasoning," takes away new knowledge and a better assessment of the new idea than they might have otherwise gained.

The belief that a successful analogy takes into consideration how the brain perceives, remembers, and judges (the basis of cognitive science) is found in discussions of cognitive science instructional design concepts (West et al., 1991) and in literature focusing on designing effective learning events (Discian Group, 1999). Research by Timothy Newby and his colleagues used empirical data to affirm the effectiveness of analogies on undergraduate students (Newby et al., 1995). Students in the research sample were divided into two groups. The first group received instructions that contained analogies; the second group did not receive analogies. Test scores of the two groups were compared and results showed "significantly higher scores" for the first group. This project weakened research prior to 1995 which reported no conclusive evidence that analogies work to increase retention and comprehension.

The single exception is Marie Iding's research using undergraduate psychology students. She placed the analogy in a science text and her study concluded that an analogy in a science text is effective when the learning goal is to have students apply the information. The theoretical framework for Iding's study was Mayer's *Theory of Assimilative Encoding* (Mayer 1985, 1987, as cited in Iding, 1993). Mayer's theory states that people process textual information in two ways. These processing methods were labeled "assimilative encoders" and "addition encoders." An assimilative encoder reads a text as an incoherent list of details, resulting in fragmented recall. An addition encoder reads a text as a coherent list of details, resulting in "an overall conceptual representation."

Cognitive science instructional design concepts are also discussed in Holyoak and Thagard's *Theory of Analogical Thinking.* They explain how it is possible to develop an effective analogy. First, pragmatically, the purpose of the analogy must be understood. Then, semantic correspondence must be present between the target and source (the familiar idea used to explain the target) analogs–i.e., terminology remains consistent. Finally, the structure of the analogy must insure that both the target and source analogs fulfill their role and do not become intertwined beyond their desired similarities in the students' minds.

Three methods of developing and/or teaching analogies emerge from the literature and are briefly presented here in an effort to help the reader develop his own effective analogies. The *Teaching with Analogies (TWA) Model* is a six-step approach designed to show people how to construct and use an analogy (Glynn et al., 1995; Glynn, 1994, 1991 as cited in Glynn, 1996). The first step is introducing the target concept/analog to establish the main idea of the analogy. Facilitating recall of the source analog is the next step. For example, approach use of electronic databases (the target analog) by describing a supermarket quest for coffee filters (source analog). The third and fourth points of Glynn's model are pointing out and connecting (i.e., mapping) the distinctive features of the target and source analogs. The fifth step is cautionary, pointing out the differences between the two. For example, students can help decide that coffee filters are usually found in the coffee/tea aisle or in the paper goods aisle. The point can then be made that electronic databases allow the item to "exist" in both aisles at once since the access points are much more varied than the supermarket or a print index. The sixth and final step advises restating the main idea, making reference to the analogy presented. The teacher could finish the example by saying "This analogy helps us think about how someone decides to construct a database, just like someone has to decide in which aisle to place the items found in a supermarket."

The *3C Model* is a more recent and descriptive approach to identifying the steps necessary to develop and present effective metaphors and analogies (Discian Group, 1999). The 3C model is Create, Connect, and Combine. Creation involves identifying where you want to use the analogy, writing down the general elements of the course area on which you want to focus the analogy, and asking yourself "How would you teach these general elements to an 8 to 10-year-old?" Then pick a couple of blossoming ideas that exude energy. Connection is a quick step which involves finding the similarities and differences between your course elements and the ideas (analogs) you just identified. The key question here is "Can you use phrases from the analogy to describe steps or parts of your [course] content?" The final important step is determining where and how to incorporate your new metaphor or analogy into the instruction session. Do you want to introduce it as the theme for the class to provide an advance "mental framework?" What visual aids would reinforce the connection between your course and the analogy? How can you best reinforce the analogy when concluding your remarks or even during follow-up with individual students?

The most theoretically-based blueprint for teaching analogies precedes the previous models by more than a decade. *The General Model of Analogy Teaching (GMAT)* proposes a model for teaching scientific analogies (Zeitoun, 1984). Zeitoun provides a thorough theoretical framework for the model before outlining nine stages ranging from measuring the students' reasoning ability and visual imagery skills to evaluating the outcomes of using the analogy in teaching. The 3C and GMAT models contain some similarities in that both call for analysis of the topic to be presented before finding analogies to match. The GMAT model takes this idea one step further by suggesting that the teacher discover whether or not the topic material contains "built-in" analogies. Additionally, all three models for developing and teaching analogies contain either an implicit or explicit call for determining the appropriateness of the analogy to be used. They also ask for an instructor's judgement regarding the level of student familiarity with the source and target analogs, and they stress the need to make an explicit "connection" between the source and target analogs.

Ultimately, analogical models should help instructors create and use analogies that provide comparisons which "can explain something difficult to understand by pointing out [the] similarities to something easy to understand or already understood" (Zeitoun, 1984). The following survey stresses *creating* good analogies that can be applied in a variety of library instruction situations. The *connections* and *combinations* may vary with each future instructor who seizes them to enlighten students and enliven his or her own library instruction sessions.

ANALOGY BEST-PRACTICES

A recent inquiry asked librarians to share their best-practice experiences with using analogies as an instructional aid. Thirty-three librarians responded. Most used analogies to either facilitate conceptualization or moderate temperament. Conceptualization lent itself to either application of a skill or understanding of a concept relevant to library science (39%), databases (38%), the Internet (15%), or library materials/resources (8%). Moderating learning experiences seemed more like administering information therapy to reduce anxiety, adjust learning expectations, or alleviate predisposed or displaced knowledge. The leading analogies relied on sports, shopping, food, and driving experiences to create word pictures. Below are samples of the analogies submitted.

Understand a Database Concept

- "The analogy . . . I use in describing the results of a LIST search . . . or a BROWSE search is that of a telephone book. That is, the search gets you to an alphabetical list of terms in the index searched (e.g., names, titles, subjects, call numbers) where the search you entered would file–sometimes it's there and sometimes it isn't."–Miki Goral, University of California-Los Angeles (UCLA)
- "One analogy I use is for helping people understand that the database vendor, e.g., Ovid or SilverPlatter, is not the database itself, e.g., MEDLINE, Periodical Abstracts. I tell them to think of Ovid as the mall and the individual databases as the stores. So, if they said they bought a shirt at the mall, it doesn't help . . . as much as saying that they bought a shirt at the mall from J. C. Penney's . . . " –Rebecca Graves, University of Missouri-Columbia
- "One analogy I use is to compare LCSH to the yellow pages. Both have controlled vocabularies that require you to be crafty in thinking about alternatives to your first subject (i.e., in both LCSH and the yellow pages, you can't find information about doctors under that everyday term–you have to use physicians) . . . "–Meg Atwater Singer, University of Evansville

Apply a Database Skill

- "My favorite analogy is for teaching citation indices . . . I explain that it's like a family: sometimes by looking at a child, you can find information or a resemblance to a parent or vice versa. Therefore, by looking at who a person cites–or who cites a given person–you can reconstruct the 'family tree' of a concept, or at least have a view of interlocking relationships."–Sarah G. Wenzel, Boston University
- "To demonstrate the ability to transfer skills I like to ask students what [do] they do when they get behind the wheel of a car they have never driven before . . . . what [do] they look for. Usually, they respond with lights, gas pedal, windshield wipers, and radio! Then I translate that to using new databases or print resources. A database probably has a controlled vocabulary somewhere, the ability to search by author, title, keyword, etc., ability

to print, and so on . . . "–Celia Rabinowitz, St. Mary's College of Maryland

Understand a Library Science Concept

- "I use an analogy to teach Boolean operators. I use salads for the analogy. I want a salad with oil and vinegar (has to have both or I won't eat it). I want a salad with oil or vinegar (I don't care as long as there is something on it for flavor). I want a salad with vinegar NOT oil (I'm on a diet–can't have all that fat) . . . I use overheads with pictures showing all of this."–Donna Jurena, Doane College
- "When I'm teaching students about controlled vocabulary for subject searches, I use the example of grocery shopping at a supermarket . . . In most markets that provide signage to guide shoppers, if you went looking for a sign that said 'spaghetti,' you would look at every aisle without finding it, and you might conclude that the store didn't sell 'spaghetti.' The truth is that you're looking for the wrong sign–you have to look for a sign saying 'pasta' or 'noodles' because the store has shelved spaghetti under that category. I then compare this spaghetti shopping example to the attempt to find results in an on-line catalog by using subject headings that aren't established by LC (or, in the case of a database like the Religion Index, the database's own thesaurus of headings) . . . "–Steve Kuehler, Westin Jesuit School of Theology

Apply a Library Science Skill

- "I always use the 'street address' analogy when talking about how important it is to record the *complete* call number. Example: Ref. PN1564 .A21 1997. I tell them the call number is like a street address. Without the preface, 'Ref.', it's like having the street address without the city–we know the position on the shelf, but not what collection it's in. Without the 'PN,' it's like knowing the city and street number, but not the name of the street. And without the '1997,' it's like having the complete address except [for] the specific apartment number. It seems to work, especially when I ask them (rhetorically) how many cities in the U.S. have a '620 Main Street.'"–Laura Ewald, Murray State University

Apply an Internet Skill

- "My favorite way to explain an Internet directory like Yahoo is to describe it as a shopping mall. I explain that if they had decided to buy a piece of jewelry for grandma, they wouldn't be very efficient if they wandered from store to store. Rather, they should check the directory located in the mall. It lists types of stores and the locations, much like the links in Yahoo."–Christine Godin, Northwest Vista College

Moderate Expectations of a Resource

- "For starting research with an encyclopedia-type source (print or online): Using a pyramid diagram, I say that, though many other newer pieces have fallen apart, the pyramids still stand . . . [T]hey have a broad base that supports the material on top. Just so, reading broader, encyclopedia-like materials gives you a broad base of knowledge. [T]hat serves as a strong foundation upon which to build your research, and your paper will 'hold-up.' It also helps you pick the right building blocks, because it gives you definitions, names, dates, and the vocabulary of the field."–Tony Amodeo, Loyola Marymount University

Moderate Expectations of Library Skills

- " . . . came up with an analogy for trying to explain to groups why it is we even try to teach them! It has to do with comparing learning how to use the library (a skill) with learning how to play sports. Some of the easy stuff (typing, finding books, running to first base) you can pick up on your own. But the strategies are what you want to learn from experts . . . "–Laurie Sabol, Tufts University
- "I do have one analogy that I use when teaching the library resources introductory class. I tell students that our survey is similar to taking a city bus tour. We will zip by a number of places, I'll point out some landmarks, they'll wish they had more time at each stop, and that they'd been able to stop and look at some of the sights more closely. Like the city bus tour, I'm giving them a sweeping overview; when they are done, at least they will have some ideas as to what they would like to revisit in more detail on their own time."–Loring Prest, California University of Pennsylvania

CONCLUSION

In this article, grounded in the research of others and our personal experience, we have sought to explore the definition of an analogy and what the library profession says about the use of analogies as an effective bibliographic instructional strategy. We found that analogies are not well covered in the field of library instruction. They have been used successfully for decades, however, to aid understanding in other fields including mathematics, science, computer programming and problem solving, philosophy, education, and psychology. From these fields, we draw the framework for our own use of analogies as a means of clarifying new ideas, concepts, and principles. The best-practice analogies generously provided by fellow librarians bear witness to the fact that this method of instruction is being used to coach students to become the competent, self-reliant information searchers of tomorrow.

REFERENCES

Amodeo, Tony (1999), "Re: survey participation requested." Personal e-mail (6 July).

Baker, William P. and Anton E. Lawson (1995), *Effect of Analogic Instruction and Reasoning Level on Achievement in General Genetics*. Springfield, VA: EDRS Reproduction Service. ED 390713.

Davis, Patricia M. and Gayle V. Davidson (1994), "Language Is Like the Human Body: Teaching Concepts Through Analogy." *Educational Technology* 34 (5): 27-32.

Discian Group (1999), *Training Success: Special Report: Creating Metaphors and Analogies to Use in Training and Other Learning Events.* At: <http://www.discian.com/resources/resources/Trainingreports/report5.htm>. Accessed July 15.

Dyckman, Lise M. (1995), "Beyond 'First You Push This Button, Then . . . ': A Process-Oriented Approach to Teaching Searching Skills." *The Reference Librarian* 51/52: 249-265.

Eflin, Juli (1995), "Educating for Science Literacy." *Journal on Excellence in College Teaching* 6: 31-43.

Freud, Sigmund (1933), *New Introductory Lectures on Psychoanalysis*. New York: W.W. Norton.

Gentner, Dedre and Keith J. Holyoak (1997), "Reasoning and Learning by Analogy." *American Psychologist* 52 (1): 32-34.

Glynn, Shawn (1996), "Teaching with Analogies: Building on the Science Textbook." *Reading Teacher* 49: 490-492.

Growe, Judy (1999), "Analogies Request." Personal e-mail (11 August).

Halpern, Diane, Carol Hansen, and David Riefer (1990), "Analogies as an Aid to

Understanding and Memory." *Journal of Educational Psychology* 82 (2): 298-305.

Holyoak, Keith and Paul Thagard (1997), "The Analogical Mind." *American Psychologist* 52 (1): 35-44.

Iding, Marie K. (1993), "Instructional Analogies and Elaboration in Science Text: Effects on Recall and Transfer Performance." *Reading Psychology* 14: 5-18.

Miller, Marian I. and Barry D. Bratton (1988), "Instructional Design: Increasing the Effectiveness of Bibliographic Instruction." *College and Research Libraries* 49: 545-549.

Nahl-Jakobovits, Diane and Leon A. Jakobovits (1990), "Learning Principles and the Library Environment." *Research Strategies* 8 (2): 74-81.

Newby, Timothy, Peggy A. Ertmer, and Donald A. Stepich (1995), "Instructional Analogies and the Learning of Concepts." *Educational Technology Research and Development: ETR&D* 43: 5-18.

Reiguluth, Charles M. (1983), "Meaningfulness and Instruction: Relating What is Being Learned to What a Student Knows." *Instructional Science* 12 (3): 197-218.

Sanford, Carolyn C. (1991), "The Census in One Hour?: The Development of an Effective One-Shot BI Session." *Research Strategies* 9 (Fall): 202-205.

Smith, Stephen J. and Dale S. Montanelli (1999), "Toward Self-Sufficient Users: Helping Patrons Learn to Use Information Resources Independently." In *People Come First: User-Centered Academic Library Service,* edited by Dale S. Montanelli and Patricia F. Stenstrom. Chicago: American Library Association, 131-141.

Thagard, Paul (1992), "Analogy, Explanation, and Education." *Journal of Research in Science Teaching* 29: 537-544.

Warnken, Paula N. and Victoria L. Young (1991), "Application of Training Principles and Techniques for Successful Library Instruction." *Reference Services Review* 19 (4): 91-96.

West, Charles K., James A. Farmer, and Philip M. Wolff (1991), *Instructional Design: Implications from Cognitive Science.* Englewood Cliffs, NJ: Prentice Hall.

Wilson, Lizabeth A. (1995), "Instruction as a Reference Service." In *Reference and Information Services: An Introduction,* 2d ed., edited by Richard E. Bopp and Linda C. Smith. Englewood, CO: Libraries Unlimited, 152-184.

Zeitoun, Hassan H. (1984), "Teaching Scientific Analogies: A Proposed Model." *Research in Science and Technological Education* 2 (2): 107-125.

Zook, Kevin B. and Frances J. Di Vesta (1991), "Instructional Analogies and Conceptual Misrepresentations." *Journal of Educational Psychology* 83 (2): 246-252.

Wake Up That Back Row! Interactive Library Instruction Without Hands-On Student Computers

Joan E. Conger

SUMMARY. A review of education literature reveals a pedagogical shift away from linear, step-by-step, instruction toward a fostering of critical thinking and information literacy through active student participation. This conceptual change reflects advances toward cooperative and participatory learning in education. In addition to the students learning more when they are engaged and thinking, we are invigorated as instructors and our tendency toward burnout is reduced or alleviated. This article discusses how those bibliographic instructors who only have one teaching computer in the instruction room can involve the students in their own learning. The author shares ways to conduct a fifty-minute bibliographic instruction session in which all of the students are intellectually engaged in the research process, actively participate in the problem solving of on-line searching, and have fun in a library. Once the students are given agency in the bibliographic instruction session, they begin to develop the critical thinking skills essential to mastering the tools and methods of library research. *[Article copies available for a fee from The Haworth Document Delivery Service: 1-800-342-9678. E-mail address: <getinfo@haworthpressinc.com> Website: <http://www.HaworthPress.com> © 2001 by The Haworth Press, Inc. All rights reserved.]*

KEYWORDS. Bibliographic instruction, teaching methods, active learning, student-centered learning, cooperative learning, critical thinking, computer based instruction, information literacy

---

Joan E. Conger is Database Performance and Assessment Librarian, Main Library Reference, University of George Libraries, Athens, GA 30602 (E-mail: jconger@uga.edu).

[Haworth co-indexing entry note]: "Wake Up That Back Row! Interactive Library Instruction Without Hands-On Student Computers." Conger, Joan E. Co-published simultaneously in *The Reference Librarian* (The Haworth Information Press, an imprint of The Haworth Press, Inc.) No. 73, 2001, pp. 309-322; and: *Doing the Work of Reference: Practical Tips for Excelling as a Reference Librarian* (ed: Celia Hales Mabry) The Haworth Information Press, an imprint of The Haworth Press, Inc., 2001, pp. 309-322. Single or multiple copies of this article are available for a fee from The Haworth Document Delivery Service [1-800-342-9678, 9:00 a.m. - 5:00 p.m. (EST). E-mail address: getinfo@haworthpressinc.com].

The bibliographic instruction (BI) session is the primary activity of my professional life. Other responsibilities, such as evaluating and ordering electronic databases, authoring web pages, and collection development are secondary. The hard fact, though, is that bibliographic instruction is by far the most stressful part of my job. I have been a full-time librarian for three years. For two years the introvert in me cringed in fear of the groups of new faces that I confronted several times a day. Despite the fact that instructors began to request me specifically for the content I delivered, I knew that the students and I were missing something. After each session I retained nightmarish after-images of bored faces, uninterested body language and deadly silence. I began to look toward each new class with dread and walk away from them disheartened. I did not want to make a career of this.

Last year, my third year as a professional librarian, I attended a "quality learning" seminar taught by David Langford (1995). Colleagues and administrators at my college recommended the seminar, but quality principles in general have always struck me as just plain common sense and thus time best spent elsewhere. To my surprise, the seminar ranked in the top five most pivotal experiences of my life. I learned a principle called "active learning" and a technique called "cooperative learning" which have changed my approach to bibliographic instruction. I now eagerly anticipate the next BI session and receive rewarding responses from instructors *and* students.

WHAT NEEDED CHANGING?

Library schools are notorious for not teaching new library professionals how to teach (Oberman, 1998). Indeed, university teachers in many fields have no formal training in pedagogy or learning theory. As instructors, we frequently use the one method that our teachers used, the lecture. As our education progressed, pleasant memories of learning shapes, colors, letters and numbers with paint pots, smeary smocks, scissors and construction paper faded. Our teachers increasingly expected us to sit quietly and listen to presumed experts pontificate on a subject about which we knew little and they knew a great deal. These teachers expected us to absorb this knowledge by osmosis and replicate it fully formed on demand.

In a 1997 study, Linda Shirato and Joseph Badics (1997) compiled data on library instruction practices from 631 college and university libraries. Their study showed that 94% of all respondents use the lecture in their instruction delivery. In the lecture, we, the experts, stand in front of the room and impart knowledge of the library and the research process to rows of students who very likely have a research assignment to complete within the weeks to follow. We do this with the profound awareness that we are not only preparing these students for their assignment; we are also teaching these students a skill they will use the rest of their lives. Because of this awareness we conscientiously pack as much information as we can into the fifty-minute sessions. Interestingly enough, despite the prevalence of the lecture format, respondents to the Shirato and Badics study also listed lecture as one of the least effective methods of instructional delivery.

Students share this ambiguity about the efficacy of passive learning such as reading or listening. Katherine Strober Dabbour (1997) presents the case study of a library instruction program in which students ranked very high the activities of working in small groups and using computers to complete exercises, and gave low marks to reading from the textbook and classroom discussion. In another case study, Carroll Varner et al. (1996) found that for each of six bibliographic instruction modules, students consistently expressed low confidence due to little or no direct interaction with the resource. As much as we use it, the lecture is not working.

ACTIVE LEARNING

In the lecture the student is a passive recipient of imparted knowledge. Active learning requires that students engage themselves in the learning process and become responsible for their own learning. Active learning is not new in pedagogy. The classic Socratic method requires students to construct their own knowledge by responding to the guiding questions of a teacher. John Dewey and Jean Piaget both reject the view that a successful student can be a passive participant (Dewey, 1963; Piaget, 1973). Piaget goes so far as to say that learning only takes place when the student constructs the knowledge for herself out of personal experience (Piaget, 1973). In their 1991 ASHE-ERIC survey of educational research on active learning, Charles Bonwell and James Eison found that active learning helps students go beyond the mere receipt of information to engage in the higher order thought processes of analysis, synthesis and evaluation. In doing so, students explore their own perceptions rather than observing those of an expert distanced from them at the front of a room. Robert Gagne's learning theory draws a connection between active learning and student success by showing that newly introduced knowledge will remain in short-term memory unless the learner processes the information in some way (cited in Piette, 1995).

The underlying concept of active learning is student-centered learning, the idea that the instructor is no longer center stage. The instructor shifts power to the students, encouraging them to be more actively engaged in acquiring the knowledge. Not only does the teacher step out of the limelight, she creates a student-centered classroom in which the students use cognitive skills to construct knowledge for themselves. According to Mary Ellen Weimer (1996), a leader in instruction improvement, "students don't learn by listening or reading. They learn by seeing and doing. To learn they must be actively engaged, involved." Weimer further asserts that effective teaching is not measured by the density of matter covered but by what the students actually learn.

Teachers, in other words, are not filling up empty heads. All students come to learning with preexisting ways of understanding the world. The teacher's role is to guide the link between the students' existing knowledge constructs and the constructs we, as experts, know they will need as they encounter more complex tasks. Cognitive research defines this conceptual organization of knowledge as the major characteristic of expert proficiency, the ability to use abstraction and generalization to create self-sufficiency and original thought in a field of knowledge (Romance, 1999; Ridgeway, 1989; Weinstein, 1996). Students, for example, are not going to remember all Boolean operators listed in one BI session. What they will remember is the differences an instructor asked them to describe between an unsuccessful single keyword search and one in which Boolean operators were used.

HANDS-ON COMPUTER LABS ARE NOT NECESSARY

Before I had a name for it, I intuitively knew that the concepts behind active, student-centered learning were true. As an audience member I frequently came out of my listening trance when the lecturer asked us our thoughts on a topic. I mentally rejoined the class. I applied this experience in my early BI lectures by incorporating ways to get passively listening students refocused toward thinking and explaining. I asked students to call out what came next or explain why I used one technique instead of another or to share experiences using various library resources. Although I often sensed a glimmer of response, I sometimes faced classes that shared little or nothing of their inner thoughts. Silences would stretch from uncomfortable to excruciating.

In my experience, these silences disappear in an active, student-centered classroom. When students own the knowledge and develop skills rather than memorize lists, they accept responsibility for their learning process. The teacher does not disappear. She is simply another member of the team, contributing her expertise to the process that the group controls. The results in my classroom have been extraordinary.

The most obvious way to provide active learning is to provide a hands-on computer lab in which students interact with the electronic resources they will use in research. The biggest drawback to this is that computer labs are prohibitively expensive. Many schools cannot afford to install thirty computers in a classroom, and if they can afford it, many schools do not have the space. My "modest proposal" is that these labs, while nice, are not necessary for active learning to take place. Active learning occurs within the student, not within the computer.

Richard E. Clark has caused great stir by insisting that media does not substantially contribute to improved learning (Clark, 1994). Successful learning, he says, relies solely on the method of teaching. Computers and other gadgets are superfluous. While that is a debate for another day, he does raise an interesting point. The learning takes place not because the student is sitting in front of a computer, but because she is intellectually engaged with the problem before her. The computers are not necessary; the engagement is.

Lecture does not engage intellectually. Computers in and of themselves do not engage intellectually. Indeed, instances are documented of students wandering off on tangents of their own during hands-on library orientations, of which Furlong (1998) and Jafari (1996) cite examples. The student engages intellectually with knowledge when she is in an environment constructed to promote this engagement. The intention is not to say that hands-on labs are ineffective. These labs can be very valuable to a BI program. My assertion is that single-computer teaching rooms can be just as effective. The common denominator to successful learning is the inclusion of the student in the teaching method. Students in front of computer screens can walk away having learned nothing. Students with no computers can learn a great deal by problem solving with an instructor who acts as facilitator. The learning method comes not from touching computer keys but in actively making the decisions of what resources to choose and how to use them (or what to type) when one gets there.

COOPERATIVE LEARNING

The method that I use to promote active learning is cooperative learning. The most extreme form of this type of teaching method is collaborative learning. Students collaborate with each other to outline what they need to learn in a given subject, how they will learn it, and how they will show that they have learned it. Students as a group, with the teacher as a consultant, design the syllabus for the class and create ways to show that they have mastered each part. Collaboration at that depth is usually not feasible within the confines of a fifty-minute session.

In cooperative learning, the teacher facilitates group and individual cognitive exercises and engages the student in meaningful and memorable learning. Cooperative learning creates an environment in which students and teacher work together to define and solve a complex problem. Using tools such as brainstorming and group strategizing, students work as a group through the steps of knowledge acquisition and application. This process transfers the active cognitive processes from the instructor planning a lecture to the students who find the answers with the guidance of the instructor. The instructor facilitates the brainstorming and the subsequent sense-making of information gathered, but the students are the agents in this learning process.

Robert Slavin (1995) compared numerous studies of cooperative learning. He found that 64% of the studies strongly favored the technique, and only 5% of the studies significantly favored control groups. Clark Bouton and Russell Garth (1983) state that while students do not accurately replicate a lecture in their memory, collaboration allows the students to reconstruct the knowledge for themselves, to own it. When David Johnson et al. (1991) reviewed the literature, they found overwhelming evidence that collaborative learning is of greater benefit to the student than competitive or individualistic learning. In Katherine Strober Dabbour's study cited previously (1997), the students themselves gave some of their highest marks to working in small groups.

An interesting finding by Shane Darke puts cooperative learning into perspective. Darke's study, affirming other research results, found that "high anxiety subjects have less residual working memory capacity than their low anxiety counterparts" (Darke, 1988). In my experience, students who are working with their classmates and are in control of their work environment exhibit the relaxed body language of eyes bright and body forward. Absent is the closed body language of crossed arms and slouched spines that students exhibit while letting a lecture wash over them.

The correlation between low anxiety and high working memory may contribute in part to the success of cooperative learning. Including students in the learning process by treating them as valid contributors not only promotes cognitive engagement in the subject matter, but also allows students to contribute to the dialogue in the classroom within the protection of the group. I have had several teachers say that in my class their students have spoken far more than is normal during a class period. I now rarely experience the awkward silence.

PRACTICAL APPLICATION

When I realized that the student was responsible for learning, not me, I saw that *I* was what was wrong with my fifty minutes of bibliographic instruction, not the students. I still have the four main goals for my BI session that I have always had. Now I ask the students to discover this knowledge for themselves. I use two basic techniques in different ways and with varying frequency based on the responsiveness of a class and my own feelings at that particular time.

The primary technique is the cooperative brainstorming session. This exercise takes time, but it is by far the best ice-breaker I have ever seen because it is sincere. The students take on equal status from the beginning of the class. Students begin by breaking up into groups by rows, moving their chairs into circles, taking control of their environment. I ask for a volunteer to be timekeeper, and each group appoints a scribe. I give them one minute (sometimes two if the students speak English as a second language) to come up with all the resources they would use to do research. One group gets to ask me to join them; one group gets the instructor. This ensures that at least my group has all the things I think are important. (I rarely have to say anything at all beyond the occasional well-placed question.)

After the student timekeeper calls time, they turn to face the blackboard. I record their responses beginning with the scribe for the group in the first row. Each subsequent scribe only gives those items we have not named yet. I organize their responses using a fishbone diagram. From a line drawn horizontally across the board (backbone), I draw four to six widely spaced vertical lines (ribs) to form a fishbone diagram.

Each time a scribe gives me a resource, I ask the class to tell me if it is a way to get to information (librarian, library catalog, article database, Internet, etc.). If it is, I write it along one of the vertical lines, or ribs. If the class tells me the resource contains information (reference books, books, articles, web pages, etc.), I ask if there is a way that is already listed to get to that resource. If so, I draw a branch from the appropriate "rib" and write in the resource. If a way to get to that resource is not listed, I draw a branch from a blank "rib," write in the resource and ask how they would get to that information. For example, the class says the first item, librarian, is a way to get to information and that this goes on a "rib." The second item, an encyclopedia, they say contains data, and should be placed on a line drawn out from "librarian." The next item is a magazine article. The class decides that the librarian is not the best way to get to a magazine article, and they tell me to place this item off of a blank "rib." After some discussion, the class decides that article databases are the best way to get to articles and instruct me to write this on the blank "rib." (I, of course, contribute to this discussion with well-placed questions.) Each subsequent scribe only calls out items that are not already on the board. By the time the third and fourth group is reached they rarely have many new resources to add.

When I taught using the lecture format, I would show that a good researcher uses four basic tools (librarian, library catalog, article databases, and the Internet) to retrieve four basic resources (reference books, books, articles, and web pages). In the approximately eighty times that I have completed this new brainstorming exercise, the class has created for themselves the very notes I put on the board during my old lecture. The students, as a group, know the information. I am simply guiding their sense-making of what they see as a mountain of resources.

Now that the basics are organized with the fishbone diagram, I ask questions that start class discussions of the validity and desirability of the various resources. Examples include the following: Why would I still want to use an encyclopedia, something I used in the third grade? What is the difference between books and articles? If you could only choose one of these four resources, which would you choose? Why? Why did some choose books and some choose articles? Why didn't anyone say the Internet? What process do people have to go through to publish on the Internet, get an article published, get a journal article published, get a book published? What does this mean for the quality of the information you are presenting to your reader? Why is it good to have researched books and articles before finding things on the Internet?

Guiding the conversation takes work. I have to constantly keep in mind my basic goals. As a rule, the conversation will quickly elicit these goals and students will frequently come up with much more believable reasons than I could ever espouse. Sometimes the conversation will not go in the direction I want and that is the challenge. I must remember that my ultimate goal is to get them to discover the value of critical thinking.

Once the class has described research resources and how they fit together, I take a vote student by student of what tools make them the most uncomfortable to use. Regardless of what the winning tool turns out to be, I can always demonstrate Boolean logic, explaining that this technique can be used in any of the research tools. Instead of constantly divulging my own cognitive processes, I ask for advice on how to execute searches. I ask for reasons why different searches worked out the way they did. I ask for possible ways to improve searches, divulging what I know about Boolean at appropriate moments. I start discussions with questions such as: How many results will a student's topic probably retrieve? Why did I use the "and" in this second search? Why did I use the "or" in this third search?

OBJECTIONS TO COOPERATIVE LEARNING

Before practicing cooperative learning techniques in their classroom, instructors may offer two objections. The first objection argues that in a cooperative learning environment the instructor will not be able to cover all the material she may have outlined for her lecture. The second objection points out that cooperative learning gives control of the classroom to a group of people who are not supposed to know anything about the subject for which they are gathered to learn.

In response to the first, I agree with Gillian Gremmels (1996) that just because we cover a comprehensive list of excellent theories, techniques and skills does not mean that the students will learn them. As passive receptors of knowledge students will not automatically learn what we are teaching well enough to apply this list of skills to each new research situation. Students need to experience the cognitive processes for themselves before integrating that knowledge into their existing skill set.

In the classroom I can create an environment in which the students create a list of all the resources they feel they would use in research, organize those resources into useful groups, and discover why different resource groups are better for different purposes in the research process. I can get them to discuss why Boolean logic seems to give the searcher better control over search results. I can get them to discuss the relative merits of journal articles and the Internet. These student activities cover all of my objectives, but I do not *tell* the students anything unless they ask me as the resident expert. I have taught close to one-hundred classes, including many English as a Second Language classes. All but one very shy class contributed the vast majority of the information that I used to cover alone at the front of the room.

At the reference desk I can teach concrete ideas easily. Based on the specific information needs of an individual student, I can discuss which database is best, how to find a book on the shelf, and how to phrase a Boolean search. What I cannot do in that five to fifteen minutes is encapsulate the entire research process. In this situation, the student does not need a long list of facts but a set of cognitive skills that help her willingly navigate each new twist in the research experience. The BI classroom is the best place for the students to discover the research process as a whole while I act as knowledgeable facilitator. These cognitive skills can only be passed on if, in the BI session, the student is actively outlining what she already knows, integrating that with new information she discovers from others, and restructuring her knowledge into higher levels of use than those to which she has previously put them.

The second objection usually raised is that the students are there to learn, not to teach. As shown above, cognitive research, beginning with Piaget, has found that learning requires either sense-making within knowledge structures already in place with the learner or building of schemata from the knowledge presented. Any one individual may not have the knowledge structures in place to figure out the intricacies of the research process, but a group of students will always come from varied backgrounds and together will invariably have all the important pieces of that process. The instructor is not absent from this group. Instead of speaking to them, she works with them to tease out all of these pieces and contribute her considerable expertise to helping the students make sense of them. Using the cooperative method to brainstorm what students know allows them to get the sense that they already own this information. This sense of ownership reduces the barriers to learning new things about the research process. Instead of treating everything as new, students discover their existing knowledge and build from this foundation.

As experts, our job is to facilitate the collection of these myriad experiences, to give the experiences names and guide the cognitive restructuring and application of these experiences to the complexities of academic (and real world) research. The research process requires constant evaluation of sources, research direction, and credibility. For research to be successful students must perceive themselves as the active agent in this recursive process, rather than the passive, uncritical receivers of information. By delivering bibliographic instruction in an active cognitive environment, we will model, and therefore reinforce, the very information literacy skills we are trying to pass on. Active evaluation of situations and information is difficult to teach in a passive, uncritical, listening environment. In cooperative learning students stop thinking of library resources as an unmanageable mountain of resources. They discover that it is an integrated system that can be used to fill their information need according to the dictates of amount, quality and type of information. By inviting the students into a cooperative learning environment, we are taking them from the position of passive non-expert to active problem solver.

I am basing my assertions in this paper on anecdotal evidence from successful students and instructors and on my personal observations both in and out of the BI classroom. Further empirical research is certainly required to quantify the effectiveness of the cooperative learning methods in the acquisition of library research methods.

CONCLUSION

In my cooperative learning class I try to follow these basic principles. (1) Group knowledge is usually comprehensive. What an individual does not know the group can provide. (2) Present the knowledge that the group collects in a meaningful way by organizing large amounts of data into an understandable system. Use a diagram or other tool to organize data listed by the group. (3) Discuss as a group what their discoveries mean in a larger context. I apply these principles within a basic structure of what I feel the students should know about research. In cooperative learning students are discovering these points themselves, applying these skills within their own knowledge sets, and gaining the tools to think critically of the research process as they will work through it in the future. Each class will be different and will focus on different things. This variation means that I am finally responding to the students' learning needs rather than imposing my own, often unheeded, knowledge structures.

Active learning is the only way that students achieve a true understanding of a body of knowledge. Without a computer lab, creating an active learning environment takes ingenuity and courage. Cooperative learning provides the structure to promote both the instructor's goals for the class and the students' cognitive engagement in the material. I still have much to learn about teaching, but cooperative learning strategies have freed the students and me to interact with one another to more deeply explore the knowledge I would like them to gain. BI used to mean the exhaustion and drudgery of pulling class after class of unknown faces into the light of good research technique. With cooperative learning I now experience the exhilaration of seeing faces light up, bodies lean forward, and minds engage the knowledge directly. I now look forward to a long, exciting career in bibliographic instruction.

BIBLIOGRAPHY

Bonwell, Charles and James Eison (1991), *Active Learning: Creating Excitement in the Classroom,* ASHE-ERIC Higher Education Report 1, Washington, DC: George Washington University.

Bouton, Clark and Russell Y. Garth (1983), "Students in Learning Groups: Active Learning through Conversation," in *Learning in Groups,* eds. Clark Bouton and Russell Y. Garth, New Directions for Teaching and Learning, 14, San Francisco: Jossey-Bass, 73-82.

Clark, Richard E. (1994), "Media Will Never Influence Learning," *ETR&D,* 42(2) 21-29.

Dabbour, Katherine Strober (1997), "Applying Active Learning Methods to the Design of Library Instruction for a Freshman Seminar," *College & Research Libraries,* 58 (July) 299-308.

Darke, Shane (1988), "Anxiety and Working Memory Capacity," *Cognition and Emotion,* 2(2) 145-154.

Dewey, John (1963), *Experience and Education,* New York: Collier.

Furlong, Katherine and Franklin D. Roberts (1998), "If You Teach It Will They Learn? Information Literacy and Reference Service in a College Library," *Computers in Libraries,* 18 (May) 22-25.

Gardiner, Lion F. (1994), *Redesigning Higher Education: Producing Dramatic Gains in Student Learning,* ASHE-ERIC Higher Education Report 7, Washington, DC: George Washington University.

Gremmels, Gillian (1996), "Active and Cooperative Learning in the One-shot BI Session," *New Ways of "Learning the Library" and Beyond: Papers presented at the 23rd National LOEX Library Instruction Conference,* eds. Linda Shirato, Elizabeth Bucciarelli and Heidi Mercado, Ann Arbor, MI: Pierian Press, 85-91.

Handy, Charles (1998), "A Proper Education," *Change: The Magazine of Higher Learning,* 30 (September/October) 13-19.

Jafari, May and Anthony Stamatoplos (1996), "Promoting Active Learning in the Electronic Classroom: Making the Transition from Presentation to Workshop," *New Ways of "Learning the Library" and Beyond: Papers presented at the 23rd National LOEX Library Instruction Conference,* eds. Linda Shirato, Elizabeth Bucciarelli and Heidi Mercado, Ann Arbor, MI: Pierian Press, 107-112.

Johnson, David W., Roger T. Johnson and Karl A. Smith (1991), *Cooperative Learning: Increasing College Faculty Instructional Productivity,* ASHE-ERIC Higher Education Report 4, Washington, DC: George Washington University.

Langford, David P. and Barbara A. Cleary (1995), *Orchestrating Learning with Quality,* Milwaukee, WI: ASQC Quality Press.

Oberman, Cerise (1998), "Why We Need a National Information Literacy Institute," *Theory and Practice: Papers presented at the 25th National LOEX Library Instruction Conference,* eds. Linda Shirato and Elizabeth R. Bucciarelli, Ann Arbor, MI: Pierian Press, 1-7.

Piaget, Jean and Barbel Inhelder (1973), *Memory and Intelligence,* New York: Basic Books.

Piette, Mary I. (1995), "Library Instruction: Principles, Theories, Connections, and Challenges," *The Reference Librarian,* (51/52) 77-88.

Ridgeway, Trish (1989), "Integrating Active Learning Techniques into the One Hour Bibliographic Instruction Lecture," in *Coping with Information Literacy: Bibliographic Instruction for the Information Age,* eds. Glenn E. Mensching, Jr. and Teresa Mensching, Ann Arbor: Pierian, 35.

Romance, Nancy R. and Michael R. Vitale (1999), "Concept Mapping as a Tool for Learning: Broadening the Framework for Student-Centered Instruction," *College Teaching,* 47 (Spring) 74-79.

Shirato, Linda and Joseph Badics (1997), "Library Instruction in the 1990's: A Comparison with Trends in Two Earlier LOEX Surveys." *Research Strategies,* 15(4) 223-37.

Slavin, Robert (1995), *Cooperative Learning,* 2nd ed., Needham, MA: Allyn and Bacon.

Varner, Carroll, Vanette M. Schwartz and Jessica George (1996), "Library Instruction and Technology in a General Education 'Gateway' Course: The Student's View," *Journal of Academic Librarianship,* 22 (September/October) 355-59.

Weimer, Maryellen (1996), "The Challenges of College Teaching," *New Ways of "Learning the Library" and Beyond: Papers presented at the 23rd National LOEX Library Instruction Conference,* eds. Linda Shirato, Elizabeth Bucciarelli and Heidi Mercado, Ann Arbor, MI: Pierian Press, 1-7.

Weinstein, Claire Ellen (1996), "Strategic Learning: The Merging of Skill, Will, and Self-Regulation," *New Ways of "Learning the Library" and Beyond: Papers presented at the 23rd National LOEX Library Instruction Conference,* eds. Linda Shirato, Elizabeth Bucciarelli and Heidi Mercado, Ann Arbor, MI: Pierian Press, 9-17.

The Development of a First-Year Student Library Instruction Program at Duke University

Tracy L. Hull
Kelley A. Lawton

SUMMARY. In 1995, the Duke University Libraries began an instructional program designed to reach all first-year students. Starting as a general library orientation, this program, through trial and error, has evolved into a two-session program, which incorporates many library instruction techniques, including active learning exercises, and consistently receives high marks. Based on the Duke University Libraries' experience, the authors propose strategies for developing a successful bibliographic instruction program for freshmen. *[Article copies available for a fee from The Haworth Document Delivery Service: 1-800-342-9678. E-mail address: <getinfo@haworthpressinc.com> Website: <http://www.HaworthPress.com> © 2001 by The Haworth Press, Inc. All rights reserved.]*

KEYWORDS. Bibliographic instruction, freshmen, first-year students, teaching, college, university

INTRODUCTION

The Duke University First-Year Library Instruction Program has its origins in a collaboration between Lilly Library and the University

Tracy L. Hull is Communications Liaison/Reference Librarian, Pullen Library, Georgia State University, 100 Decatur Street SE, Atlanta, GA 30303 (E-mail: tlhull@gsa.edu). Kelley A. Lawton is Electronic Access Librarian, Duke University, Lilly Library, Box 90725, Durham, NC 27708 (E-mail: kla@duke.edu).

[Haworth co-indexing entry note]: "The Development of a First-Year Student Library Instruction Program at Duke University." Hull, Tracy L., and Kelley A. Lawton. Co-published simultaneously in *The Reference Librarian* (The Haworth Information Press, an imprint of The Haworth Press, Inc.) No. 73, 2001, pp. 323-336; and: *Doing the Work of Reference: Practical Tips for Excelling as a Reference Librarian* (ed: Celia Hales Mabry) The Haworth Information Press, an imprint of The Haworth Press, Inc., 2001, pp. 323-336. Single or multiple copies of this article are available for a fee from The Haworth Document Delivery Service [1-800-342-9678, 9:00 a.m. - 5:00 p.m. (EST). E-mail address: getinfo@haworthpressinc.com].

Writing Program. Beginning simply as a librarian-led tour, the program has expanded to two class sessions. Through expansion and the refinement of the information presented, the library has been able to develop a highly efficient and effective instruction program, which provides students with a solid foundation to start the research needed for their coursework. It is through these experiences that we hope to provide others with ideas for planning a successful library instruction program for first-year students.

LITERATURE REVIEW

For academic bibliographic instruction librarians, first-year students remain the primary recipients of library instruction. These students are obvious candidates for library instruction, not only because they are often unfamiliar with researching in an academic library, but also many universities and colleges require certain first-year classes. The freshman seminar, "with the goal of introducing students to a particular academic program" (Dabbour, 1997), has been a popular forum for exposing students to library research methods. Other librarians have taken first-year instruction to another level by offering semester-long, for-credit library research methods courses (Blakeslee, 1998). The most typical vehicle for bibliographic instruction to first-year students, though, still remains the freshman writing course, as demonstrated by a survey conducted in 1991-1992 (Barclay and Barclay, 1994).

While the goal of reaching first-year students has remained constant, the strategies for providing the instruction have not. As the literature underscores, the area of library instruction is constantly evolving. From the beginning, library orientation, defined as an "introduction to the library facilities, the physical plant, the staff, the departments, and a few very commonly used resources" (Rice, 1981), has been very much a part of most academic libraries. There is no question that the traditional library tour approach still has its uses. For many librarians, however, this cursory introduction to library resources is not sufficient for meeting students' informational needs. The literature chronicles the ongoing search to find a better instruction method.

Library instruction takes many forms. The reference tool approach is characterized by the discussion of how to use library resources for research projects (Tuckett and Stoffle, 1984). Another method advocates a move away from resource-based instruction to the teaching of "critical thinking skills and research strategies" (Pastine and Wilson, 1992). Active learning, with its emphasis on applied learning techniques such as small group discussions, in-class exercises, and role-playing, has gained many adherents (Meyers and Jones, 1993).

The evolving nature of library instruction is well illustrated by the First-Year Instruction Program created by the staff of Duke University's Lilly Library.

STARTING OUT–YEAR 1

In 1994, Lilly Library, located on Duke's East Campus, found itself facing a new challenge. In December, the Board of Trustees unanimously passed President Nannerl Keohane's residential plan, the most dramatic feature of which was the establishment of Duke's smaller East Campus as the primary residence for first-year students (Stuebe, 1994). As the main library on East Campus, the staff of Lilly knew the residential change would have a profound impact on the library and its services.

Changes to Lilly Library's mission are not without precedent. From 1927 to 1972, East Campus served as the home of the Woman's College, when the Lilly Library was known as the Woman's College Library. Its collection was based on the "required readings for courses to be taught on the women's campus and general books to supplement their work" (Young, 1978). With the merger of the men's and women's undergraduate colleges, the library became known as the East Campus Library, serving the new coed population of East Campus. In the early 1990s, the library was renovated and acquired the Lilly Library name. With the renovation came a refocusing of Lilly's collection on the fine arts, the performing arts, philosophy, and film and video. The clientele overwhelmingly became faculty and graduate students working in these disciplines. Lilly Library was facing another change with the arrival of an all first-year campus in the fall of 1995. Staff knew changes had to be implemented to meet the needs of East Campus's future residents.

Throughout the spring of 1995, a committee of librarians from Lilly and other campus libraries proposed a number of changes including the following: extended reference hours, development of a reference collection geared toward a first-year population, and the creation of an

Undergraduate Library Advisory Board. The committee also discussed the possibility of implementing a library instruction program designed for first-year students.

This last suggestion was ambitious considering Lilly's staff size. For a branch library, Lilly's staff is adequate. At the time of these discussions, there were only three professional librarians on staff, as well as the branch head. To provide library instruction to an average first-year class of 1600 to 1700 students, though, more help was needed. Also, the building housed no computer training facilities. Despite these obstacles, staff decided to explore the possibility.

DESIGNING THE PROGRAM-YEAR 1

A 1991-1992 survey revealed that 39% of students who participated in bibliographic instruction sessions did so through a freshman writing course (Barclay and Barclay, 1994). Lilly Library decided to take the same approach. As the University Writing Course (now entitled Academic Writing) is the only required class for first-year students, this was considered the most effective way to reach a majority of students. Fortunately, the Director of the University Writing Program was enthusiastic about the idea. A partnership was formed between the staff of Lilly and the University Writing Program in the spring of 1995 with the goal of developing an instruction program.

With the support of the University Librarian, the Head of Lilly immediately began investigating the possibility of hiring someone to head up this program. A comprehensive library instruction program did not exist at Duke University, and library administration believed the idea was worth exploring. Approval was given for a temporary, one-year appointment.

Some program development was accomplished before the Resource Education Librarian was selected, but the detailed planning really started with her arrival in late summer. With less than two months until the start of school, the ambitions of the programs had to be scaled down. Due to staffing constraints and lack of adequate classroom space, the instructional sessions could not be offered during actual class times. Instead, the library had to offer sessions at a variety of times during the day and evening. Students were to be encouraged by their instructors to stop by the library and sign up for a session at their convenience. The maximum number of students per session was set at 15.

The lack of classroom/computer training space constrained the organization and content of the instruction sessions. Hands-on instruction was not feasible, so the sessions consisted of: a walking tour of the building, a brief lecture on Library of Congress Subject Headings and Boolean logic, and a demonstration by a librarian of the online catalog and Information Access' (now Gale Group) *Expanded Academic Index*. Each student was also given a folder containing mostly preexisting handouts covering such topics as remote access to the library, Boolean Logic, and Library of Congress Subject Headings.

RESULTS/CONCLUSIONS

The Director of the University Writing Program strongly encouraged his instructors to send their students to the library, and as a result, attendance was approximately 50%. Though 50% was adequate for a first attempt, all involved in the program wanted to see 100% participation. The organization and content of the sessions also needed much work. The Lilly sessions fit neatly into the definition of library orientation, but we wanted to move beyond this basic level to more sophisticated bibliographic instruction.

Gathering a group of 15 students around one computer monitor for a demonstration proved difficult. The students in the back of the group could not see or hear the demonstration. Furthermore, because students could come to any session, there was no class cohesiveness and often no instructors present to reiterate the importance of learning to use library resources. If this program was to be continued, major changes needed to take place. Changes proposed for fall 1996 included the following: hands-on sessions for the students, sessions scheduled during assigned class times with instructors present, a newly designed instructional booklet, and the inclusion of such topics as advanced searching skills.

Though these initial sessions for the most part represented what we did not want to do in the future, there was enough satisfaction in the program for it to be continued in the fall of 1996. If nothing else, the first year had brought about a successful partnership between Lilly Library and the University Writing Program.

A MOVE INTO THE CLASSROOM–YEAR 2

With fall of 1996 ten months away, the staff of Lilly and the University Writing Program began working on the proposed changes. The biggest hurdle was the creation of an electronic classroom. As the writing courses require research-based papers, the library orientation model of instruction was not sufficient to meet the information needs of the students. For a more in-depth discussion of library research methods and resources, classroom space was needed, and one equipped with computers would be ideal for hands-on instruction. There is much anecdotal evidence about the benefits of hands-on instruction. Moreover, an empirical study conducted at the University of Wisconsin-Whitewater showed that students who receive guided hands-on instruction performed better on a post-test than students who receive information via a lecture and demonstration (Bren et al., 1998). The move to hands-on instruction was considered essential.

Though money was certainly an issue, space for the classroom was also a concern. As a branch library, Lilly Library had little available space for an electronic classroom. The only option was a seminar room currently being used for lectures and meetings as well as an art exhibition space. The staff regretted the loss of the seminar room, but all agreed that an electronic classroom would have benefits beyond filling the needs of the First-Year Instruction Program. This space could be used for other library instruction sessions throughout the year. Also, during times of inactivity, the room could be opened to provide students access to additional Internet terminals. Fortunately, Lilly Library received a donation, which funded the construction of the room. Although budget constraints meant that the room could not have all the "bells and whistles," the space was well equipped with 16 student stations, one instruction station, and a projection system.

The next undertaking was the creation of an instructional booklet. Two librarians, along with the Director and Assistant Director of the University Writing Program, wanted to develop a booklet that could be used as an aid to doing research at the Duke University Libraries, not only in the first year but also throughout the students' career at Duke. The decision-making process of what to include in the booklet was not always an easy one. As with any group, there existed competing visions for the program. Arguments were made for a strictly practical guide to doing research, as well as for a booklet that not only covered the how-to aspects but also discussed the Duke University Libraries in the larger historical context of academic libraries. The resulting booklet was a compromise between the practical, historical, and theoretical approaches. The booklet also covered topics and issues that are unfamiliar to many first-year college students, such as Library of Congress Subject Headings, Boolean logic, and the differentiation between scholarly and popular periodical literature.

To utilize fully the new classroom space, the structure of the classes was brought to a more rigorous level. Demonstrations of the on-line catalog and *Expanded Academic Index,* and discussions of Boolean logic and Library of Congress Subject Headings, were retained from the previous year's classes. New additions included discussion of popular versus scholarly resources, and an in-class exercise on searching in subject-specific databases. The instruction sessions were now to take place during class time with instructors present. This change made it possible for the sessions to be tailored to address the research needs of the individual classes. While all these developments were positive, the plan of bringing students to the library in classes increased the total number of sessions to over one hundred. In addition, a decision was also made to team-teach the classes, so that one librarian would always be available to assist with questions and address computer problems. With Lilly's small staff, the scheduling of teachers for these classes was difficult. The situation was somewhat relieved by the hiring of a temporary reference librarian and the recruitment of volunteers from other campus libraries, but the majority of classes were still taught by three Lilly librarians.

RESULTS/CONCLUSIONS

These modifications in the second year of the program, and the encouragement of the Director of the University Writing Program, helped the participation rate soar to over 95%. The new sessions were seen as a tremendous improvement over the previous year, and were very well received. Instructors loved the new electronic classroom as much as we did. While the classroom created terrific teaching opportunities, it also presented challenges as well. We were so enamored of our new classroom and its capabilities that, as often happens with one-shot library instruction sessions, we tried to convey too much information for the time allotted (Ragains, 1995). Rather than eliminate any information, we decided to explore in the coming year the possibility of adding another session, which would take place in the main campus library, Perkins.

Outside of the one in-class exercise, which was often left out due to time constraints, the sessions were still firmly rooted in the reference tool approach. In the fall 1997 sessions, we wanted to introduce the overarching concepts of doing research in an academic library rather than focusing exclusively on searching a particular on-line product. While the teaching involved with these classes was time consuming, we were committed to the program and wanted to see additional improvements in fall 1997.

BRANCHING OUT: A SECOND SESSION–YEAR 3

The instruction staff ended up covering information very similar to that addressed in the previous year. The on-line catalog was still the primary focus. The discussion of advanced searching skills was retained, as were the discussion of how to differentiate popular from scholarly resources and the demonstration of *Expanded Academic Index*. The only major addition was the brief treatment of web resources, which was in response to the increasing prevalence of web resources in academic research.

The most significant change in the third year of the program, fall 1997, was the format. Although the goal of teaching students about the on-line resources was being met, the staff believed that the students also needed to attend a session at Perkins, the main library, since that is the location where they would perform much of their research during their college careers. Another reason for the additional session was that students from previous years often commented in evaluations that too much information was covered in the first session. After considering both of these issues, the staff expanded the format to two sessions. The bulk of the instruction still took place in the first session at Lilly Library.

The second session, primarily devoted to working on a library assignment related to the students' individual research projects, occurred within a week of the first session. The role of the librarian at the Perkins Library sessions was mainly to answer questions. Having the students work on an assignment during the second session helped reinforce the information learned in the first session. The latter half of the second session consisted of a librarian-led tour of Perkins, the main library.

RESULTS/CONCLUSIONS

The new format was in many ways a success, especially in light of the fact that this was the library's first attempt to coordinate two instructional sessions. The second session, at the Perkins Library, however, did not work as well as hoped. As we discovered, students, as well as their writing instructors, needed a more structured environment, one that provided more centralized instruction and less work on individual projects.

The other drawback to this work-in-class approach had to do with the fact that the assignment was tailored to the students' research projects. Since many of the sections came to the library early in the semester, the students often had not yet decided on a research topic, making it hard for them to complete the assignment. Focusing on research topics was thus premature in many cases, causing the exercise to lack that "point-of-need" quality so essential to student motivation. As Dewald discusses in her article on web-based instruction, motivation is essential for learning, and this aspect is lacking if the assignment does not relate to a real-life need at the time of the exercise (1999). Other scholars concur, arguing that if the assignment does not relate to a specific research assignment or class interest, students will treat it as mere busy work (Parks and Hendrix, 1996).

A DIVISION OF RESPONSIBILITY-YEAR 4

The classes in the fall of 1998 maintained the two-session format, with more structure added to the Perkins curriculum. Rather than trying to cover all the essential topics in the first session, the information was more evenly divided. Lilly Library continued to provide a discussion of the on-line catalog and advanced searching techniques, but all of the information regarding periodicals was shifted to the second session. This allowed for more time in the first session to be devoted to searching for web resources, and to add a section on evaluating web sites. Finally, to serve as a segway to the second class in the main library, the class completed a short exercise that required them to locate journal titles in the on-line catalog.

The second session still ended with a walking tour of the main library, but the classroom portion now included a significant teaching component on how to search for journal articles. In the past, such instruction was limited to a demonstration of *Expanded Academic Index*. This year we decided to address the subject specific databases, where many of the scholarly items that students need are likely to be cited. Consistent with the findings of a study on student use of print indexes at the seven regional campuses of Kent State University, we discovered that students often have difficulties with these databases, especially when it comes to identifying the information necessary to locate the article within the library (Kunkel, Weaver and Cook, 1996). By spending an entire class period on this topic, we hoped to better prepare students for this important research task.

One final change was the conversion of the printed guide to library research to an electronic format. When the printed guide was incorporated into the program in the second year, it was considered a great improvement over the folder of handouts that we had previously distributed, but keeping the guide up-to-date was both costly and time consuming. As any research librarian knows, something printed one day can be outdated the next (Ury and King, 1995). Putting the guide on-line solved this problem, because we could now continually update and revise it. This move also enabled us to make the resource more visually appealing, produce it at a significantly cheaper cost, and offer it to a wider audience. The Duke University Libraries *Guide to Library Research* (http://www.lib.duke.edu/libguide/) has been a great asset to the program and its usage continually increases, according to the library's web statistics.

RESULTS/CONCLUSIONS

This two-tiered approach of covering the on-line catalog and other basics in the first session and periodical searching in the second worked fairly well. The students indicated in their evaluations that the information was thoroughly covered and was not as rushed as in past years when everything had to be addressed in the first class session. Reference statistics suggest that the students have retained the information better, hopefully reducing the number of times reference librarians have to answer such questions as "How do I find this article?" The sessions appear to be headed in the right direction, and this two-tiered approach will be continued in subsequent years of the program.

Despite dramatic improvements, there have also been some minor problems with the second session. The second session has received fairly positive reviews, but one standard complaint is that it lacks continuity with the first. The major difference between the two sessions is that the first session is team-taught and the second is not. The team-taught approach used in the first session allows for uniformity in delivery and coverage of the information. If one person forgets something, the second person is right there to catch the omission. This helps ensure that the sessions meet the important goal, discussed by Furlong and Roberts, of conveying a common set of skills (1998). Having two librarians teach a session can also make the session a bit livelier and can help break up the monotony by having two presentation styles. The final major benefit of having two librarians teach the classes is that it greatly reduces what some librarians have termed the "distraction factor" (Martorana and Doyle, 1996). The second person is there to assist those students who fall behind, have computer difficulties, or do not understand a concept, as well as to prevent students from surfing the web.

The assignment was the only feature of the new format that received negative reviews from the students. Evaluation responses regarding the assignment varied, but the majority felt the assignment required too much time, and many viewed it as busy work. Based on these evaluations, the staff concluded that the assignment should be dropped for the following year.

TEAMING UP–YEAR 5

The previous year's approach of splitting the information between the two sessions worked well and will be maintained. The only significant change in the first class at Lilly will be the addition of an active learning exercise, which will help emphasize the importance of evaluating web sites. As much of the literature in the field indicates, active learning is an optimal approach to conveying information to students. Dabbour makes the case for active learning in her article on instructing students in a freshman seminar program (1997). Her helpful review of the literature emphasizes the importance of many active learning strategies, including hands-on worksheets and small-group work that encourages students to develop their skills for synthesizing and evaluating information.

The staff will also make significant changes in the second session in the upcoming year. We plan to take a more global approach to teaching the periodical databases. Rather than picking one database to focus on, we will give an overall perspective on the structure and function of databases. As was discovered in the Kent State University study, most incoming students already understand that indexes are the appropriate resource to locate periodical articles, but many do not know the specific content of the databases and thus cannot determine which one is appropriate for their research (Kunkel et al., 1996). Emphasis will lie on the subject-specific databases, since these index most of the scholarly articles that the students will need. Students will also be taught a variety of ways for searching these databases (i.e., author, title, subject, etc.). By stressing issues and features common to all databases, we hope to better prepare students for the task of navigating unfamiliar databases. Finally, the session will teach students features of the citation that are essential for locating the article within the Duke library system.

The other change that we are looking forward to is using the team teaching approach in the second session as well. While team teaching was an addition to their workload, the reference staff agreed to give it a try for a year. If this technique proves to be as beneficial at the Perkins session as it has been at Lilly, we may propose the hiring of additional staff.

The walking tour of the main library will be eliminated from the Perkins session in order to create more time for instruction, and a virtual library tour has been created to take its place (http://www.lib.duke.edu/libtour/). Virtual tours are available for both Lilly and Perkins Libraries with two tour options. One option lets the user choose departments or locations from a floor map or drop-down menu. The second option, which was designed with the first-year students in mind, is a prescribed route highlighting important features of the library.

CONCLUSION

Today's first-year students have very different research needs from first-year students of even five years ago. Any instruction program designed for these students must reflect the continually evolving nature of library research and availability of resources. Incoming college students are computer savvy. In the United States, the number of public schools providing Internet access rose from 35% in 1994 to 78% in 1997 (Smith and Phillips, 1999). Few students, however, have a firm understanding of how to use efficiently today's academic library. The staff of Lilly Library in partnership with the University Writing Program have worked to develop a program which is flexible enough to meet the information needs of today's first-year students.

REFERENCES

Barclay, Donald A. and Darcie Reimann Barclay (1994), "The Role of Freshman Writing in Academic Bibliographic Instruction," *The Journal of Academic Librarianship,* 20 (September), 213-217.

Blakeslee, Sarah (1998), "Librarian in a Strange Land: Teaching a Freshman Orientation Course," *Reference Services Review,* 26 (Summer), 73-78.

Bren, Barbara, Beth Hillemann, and Victoria Topp (1998), "Effectiveness of Hands-On Instruction of Electronic Resources," *Research Strategies,* 16 (no. 1), 41-51.

Dabbour, Katherine Strober (1997), "Applying Active Learning Methods to the Design of Library Instruction for a Freshman Seminar," *College & Research Libraries,* 58 (July), 299-308.

Dewald, Nancy H. (1999), "Web-based Library Instruction: What is Good Pedagogy?" *Information Technology and Libraries,* 18 (March), 26-31.

Furlong, Katherine and Franklin D. Roberts (1998), "If You Teach It, Will They Learn?" *Computers in Libraries,* 18 (May), 22-25.

Kunkel, Lilith R., Susan M. Weaver, and Kim N. Cook (1996), "What Do They Know?: An Assessment of Undergraduate Library Skills," *The Journal of Academic Librarianship,* 22 (November), 430-434.

Martorana, Janet and Carol D. Doyle (1996), "Computers on, Critical Thinking Off: Challenges of Teaching in the Electronic Environment," *Research Strategies,* 14 (Summer), 184-191.

Meyers, Chet and Thomas B. Jones (1993), *Promoting Active Learning: Strategies for the College Classroom.* San Francisco: Jossey-Bass Publishers.

Parks, Joan and Dana Hendrix (1996), "Integrating Library Instruction into the Curriculum through Freshman Symposium," *Reference Services Review,* 24 (Spring), 65-71.

Pastine, Maureen and Linda Wilson (1992), "Curriculum Reform: The Role of Academic Libraries," *The Evolving Educational Mission of the Library,* 90-108.

Ragains, Patrick (1995), "Four Variations on Drueke's Active Learning Paradigm," *Research Strategies,* 13 (Winter), 40-50.

Rice, James (1981), *Teaching Library Use: A Guide for Library Instruction.* Westport, CT: Greenwood.

Smith, Charles and Chris Phillips, "Are Our Academic Libraries Ready for the

Internet Generation?" *CAUSE/EFFECT,* 22 (no. 1). Available on the World Wide Web: http://www.educause.edu/ir/library/html/cem991a.html

Stuebe, Alison. "Trustees Unanimously Pass New Residential Plan," *The Chronicle* (1994, December 12). Available on the World Wide Web: http://www.chronicle.duke.edu/chronicle/1994/12/12/1anal.html

Tuckett, Harold W. and Carla J. Stoffle (1984), "Learning Theory and the Self-Reliant Library User," *RQ,* 24 (Fall), 58-66.

Ury, Connie J. and Terry L. King (1995), "Reinforcement of Library Orientation Instruction for Freshman Seminar Students," *Research Strategies,* 13 (Summer), 153-164.

Young, Betty Irene (1978), *The Library of the Woman's College Duke University 1930-1972*. Durham, NC: Regulator Press.

The Professional Development of Reference Librarians: Implications of Research, Publication, and Service

Gary W. White

SUMMARY. Professional activities can have a profound impact on the professional development of reference librarians in all types of libraries. This article discusses the positive impacts that research and publication, conference attendance and presentations at professional association meetings, and service activities have on the professional development and growth of reference librarians. Also included are practical tips and strategies for becoming more involved in these professional development activities. *[Article copies available for a fee from The Haworth Document Delivery Service: 1-800-342-9678. E-mail address: <getinfo@haworthpressinc.com> Website: <http://www.HaworthPress.com> © 2001 by The Haworth Press, Inc. All rights reserved.]*

Gary W. White is Head, Schreyer Business Library, The Pennsylvania State University, 309 Paterno Library, University Park, PA 16802 (E-mail: gww2@psu.edu).

The author would like to thank Daniel Mack for editorial assistance and Matthew Harris for research assistance.

[Haworth co-indexing entry note]: "The Professional Development of Reference Librarians: Implications of Research, Publication, and Service." White, Gary W. Co-published simultaneously in *The Reference Librarian* (The Haworth Information Press, an imprint of The Haworth Press, Inc.) No. 73, 2001, pp. 337-350; and: *Doing the Work of Reference: Practical Tips for Excelling as a Reference Librarian* (ed: Celia Hales Mabry) The Haworth Information Press, an imprint of The Haworth Press, Inc., 2001, pp. 337-350. Single or multiple copies of this article are available for a fee from The Haworth Document Delivery Service [1-800-342-9678, 9:00 a.m. - 5:00 p.m. (EST). E-mail address: getinfo@haworthpressinc.com].

KEYWORDS. Professional development, research, presentations, professional associations, service

Professional development is a concept that has long been espoused by the library profession and its professional associations. The Association of College and Research Libraries (ACRL) of the American Library Association (ALA) lists that its number one goal is to "provide development opportunities for academic and research librarians and other library personnel that enhance their ability to deliver superior services and resources" (American Library Association, 1997). In addition, the Reference and User Services Association (RUSA), also of ALA, recognizes the importance of professional development for reference librarians and lists two of its specific responsibilities as the "conduct of activities and projects within the association's areas of responsibility" [primarily the delivery of reference/information services] and "encouragement of the development of librarians engaged in these activities" (American Library Association, 1997). A number of other professional associations, including the American Medical Association (AMA) and the National Education Association (NEA), contain similar statements (American Medical Association, 1999; National Education Association, 1999).

What does "professional development" entail? Julia Gelfand, former chair of RUSA's Committee on Professional Development, states that it "is commonly defined as activity to enhance one's ability to perform work-related functions" (Gelfand, 1985). She goes on to give such examples as attending relevant workshops and seminars at local, national, or international meetings; participating in continuing education courses and programs; enrolling in academic courses; and "availing oneself of professional literature."

Irene F. Rockman gives a broader list of activities, including "active involvement with association work; presentation of papers; publication of books, articles, reviews, abstracts, and bibliographies; grant writing; consulting; research and study leaves; staff exchanges; and other contributions which enable one to perform at a higher level of proficiency" (Rockman, 1989). She goes on to explain that these types of professional development activities are increasing in importance among academic librarians who are "now expected to engage in scholarly pursuits to gain reappointment, tenure, and/or promotion." An article by G. Charles Newman, Amy L. Dibartolo, and Levirn Hill

(1991) agrees with Rockman's lists of activities, stating that professional development programs could consist of "several components, including advanced degrees in a subject discipline, personal research, numerous short-term courses, seminars, workshops, and extended programs." Therefore, it appears that there is some variation in defining professional development, with some librarians viewing it as encompassing specific training/educational opportunities and others looking at professional development as activities which are requirements, or aid in the attainment, of specific academic or faculty rank.

This paper will outline professional development activities as they relate to the reference librarian, with a special focus on research, publication and service. Included will be a discussion of the positive impacts of these areas and practical strategies for reference librarians wishing to become more involved in these professional development activities. Attendance and participation in conferences, which can fall under the research or service categories, will also be addressed.

LITERATURE REVIEW

While the literature on professional development for librarians is quite abundant, there is little written especially for the reference librarian. Johannah Sherrer (1996), in an article outlining the competencies needed by contemporary reference librarians, writes that "library schools need to impart to their graduates that responsibility for continued professional growth and development is as much a personal responsibility as an institutional one. The importance of self-directed learning and the ability to grow and evolve in the practice of reference work are the distinguishing characteristics that mark successful reference librarianship."

Other studies look at the professional development of reference librarians from the perspective of continuing education. Leslie M. Kong (1996) states, "Reference librarians should avail themselves of continuing education opportunities, especially those focused on electronic resources." She also encourages reference librarians to develop their critical thinking skills as these are required for the "continuing process of evaluating information resources in the provision of effective reference services." Gary E. Strong (1996) advocates educational opportunities for training reference librarians for the library of the future, adding that managers must allocate resources for this function.

Most studies of professional development are of academic librarians, and are not limited to reference librarians per se. W. Michael Havener and Wilbur A. Stolt (1994) study the impact of institutional support on professional development activities of academic librarians. By correlating institutional support measures, including release time and financial support, with successful professional development activities, such as publication activity, professional meetings attended, workshops, professional association involvement, and reading of professional literature, the authors find that a "supportive organizational climate has a major positive impact on a librarian's professional development activities," a sentiment the authors found expressed in an earlier article by Grace Saw (1989).

Dennis K. Grumling and Carolyn A. Sheehy (1993) describe the professional development program developed and implemented at Northwestern University, the University of Chicago, and the University of Illinois at Chicago. This cooperative program is designed to "address concerns about integrating younger, newer professional staff members into the complex structure of large research libraries and about encouraging them to look broadly at the issues facing these libraries." Librarians with less than seven years of service were selected to participate in programs which consisted of a series of seminars led by experienced librarians. Surveys of program participants and program administrators indicate that the program achieved its goal of integrating newer professional staff into the research library structure.

The integration of new library professionals into large academic libraries was also the focus of a series of case studies published in the *Journal of Academic Librarianship* (Clemens and Trevvett, 1991). The Council on Library Resources offered grants to a number of large research libraries, including Columbia University, Northwestern University, the University of Chicago, the University of Illinois at Chicago, the University of Georgia, and the University of Missouri-Columbia. Each of these articles outlines the institution's program, its participants, evaluation methods, and conclusions. Each program differed in its offerings, but most offered some form of mentoring and seminar structure. All of the participating institutions reported that they viewed the programs as successful. Peer-coaching is the focus of an article by Levene and Frank (1993) on professional development programs. The authors examine peer coaching as a tool for professional development and growth among instruction librarians. Peer coaching differs from mentoring in that the "participants are at the same hierarchical level."

Professional development as reflected through participation in library associations is outlined by Donald J. Kenney and Gail McMillan (1992). They surveyed all fifty state library associations to gather information on the professional development and continuing education of their members. Forty out of forty-one responding libraries offer continuing education and professional development opportunities and all reported offering "skill-enhancement" workshops.

An article by Darrell L. Jenkins, M. Kathleen Cook, and Mary Anne Fox (1981) looks at development in the other major area for academic librarians, research and publication. They acknowledge the increased number of academic librarians with faculty status or tenure requirements and the resulting increased pressure to conduct research and publish. The authors recommend a professional development program consisting of such items as graduate assistants and release time.

PROFESSIONAL DEVELOPMENT AND REFERENCE LIBRARIANS

The literature on professional development strongly indicates that these activities are useful to the individual and, ultimately, to the profession. Albritton (1990) writes, "In order to function effectively as a professional, one must have continuing learning experiences to reinforce his or her formal education. Due to rapid growth in new knowledge and technology, it is estimated that within 10 to 12 years of receiving their formal professional education, most librarians will become approximately half as competent as they were upon graduation to meet the needs of their profession." While this may be difficult to substantiate quantitatively, the sentiment that professional development is necessary is apparent.

An important issue, however, is whether professional development activities are the responsibility of the individual or of the institution to which the reference librarian belongs. Clearly, there has to be some individual initiative for successful professional development. However, there must also be encouragement and support at the institutional level to motivate employees to seek such opportunities. The Association of Research Libraries (1982), writes that "current evidence suggests that libraries and their parent institutions are assuming greater responsibility for planning, encouraging, and facilitating (professional development) programs." ARL suggests that increased pressures for productivity as well as organizational and operational changes are reasons for this change. Newman, Dibartolo, and Hill (1991) agree, stating, "The profession has begun to assume greater responsibility for the provision of adequate programs of continuing education for its members."

For academic librarians, the importance of professional development activities, especially those of research, publication, and service, are implicitly tied to performance and success factors related to faculty status, reappointment, and promotion and tenure. A study by Emily Werrell and Laura Sullivan (1987) states that 79 percent of academics have some form of faculty status and, therefore, must pursue activities such as research, publication, and professional service. A more recent survey of research, doctoral and master's level institutions shows that 54.3 percent have tenure-track librarians (Mitchell and Reichel, 1999). The literature is abundant with articles on issues related to publishing and tenure, including Janet Swan Hill's article on librarians as faculty members (1994); W. Bede Mitchell and L. Stanislava Swieszkowski's article on publication requirements and tenure approval rates (1985); Robert Boice, Jordan M. Scepanski and Wayne Wilson's publication on coping with pressures to publish (1987); and Bradigan and Mularski's analysis of publication requirements for tenure and promotion (1996). In another vein, Lynne E. Gamble (1989) has written on the importance and value of university service for academic librarians. John N. Olsgaard (1984) looked at "success" among academic librarians, including such items as publications, professional activities and participation in service organization.

For public and other non-academic librarians, there is usually not as strong a mandate, if any, to participate in such activities in order to retain employment or professional status. In addition, there is often not as much institutional support for such activities. Also, as mentioned earlier, the types of activities considered to fall under the umbrella of professional development tend to consist of continuing education programs or workshops. As indicated above, these activities undoubtedly can be very useful in terms of gaining new skills and knowledge. However, as this paper attempts to show, participation in other activities, which are typically conducted primarily by academic librarians, can also yield great benefits to the non-academic librarian.

POSITIVE IMPACT OF RESEARCH AND PUBLICATION

In academic libraries, the growth of faculty status over the years has yielded a number of positive benefits. First, librarians in many institutions have achieved the position as members of the faculty, allowing librarians to serve on governing bodies and to participate in the same educational activities as their teaching counterparts. The increased publication output in the field of librarianship, primarily accomplished by academic librarians, provides a second benefit of increased visibility among all disciplines in the academic arena and an increased sharing of knowledge throughout the library profession. The increased status that comes with sharing the same rank as teaching faculty heightens the reputation of the library profession and the importance of scholarship in the field.

The benefits of research and publication are not limited to academic librarians. Research and publication increases the professional reputation of the author and fosters an acknowledgement of subject expertise among professional colleagues. Subsequently, it also increases the reputation of the institution to which the author belongs, as well as the author's status within the organization. Publication constitutes a contribution to the scholarly discipline of librarianship, an endeavor in which all professional librarians should participate. Other personal benefits to the author include an increased understanding of trends and research in the field; an opportunity to develop further research projects; and increased marketability if seeking a promotion or new position elsewhere.

STRATEGIES FOR BEGINNING RESEARCH

There are many strategies that reference librarians, particularly beginning librarians, can adopt to embark on a research project. Probably most important is to read the professional literature in librarianship. Most research projects are in areas that have previously been covered; they build in some way on past research. Reading and analyzing current studies can often prompt researchers into thinking of a research project which builds on the study. Reading the guidelines for author submissions to professional journals provides the scope of the journal, the types of articles that are accepted, and formal procedures to follow.

Another important area is mentoring. Golian and Galbraith (1996) give two definitions of mentors, including "someone senior to you in the field who actively works for your advancement, or anyone who enhances, enriches, and encourages the professional development of another member of the profession." Beginning researchers should seek the advice and assistance of experienced researchers who can provide assistance and recommendations. Mentors can also assist with data collection; provide information on appropriate journals for submission; and proofread and critique writings. Mentors do not necessarily have to belong to the same institutions; some could be professional colleagues located elsewhere. Beginning researchers can also team up with a mentor on a research project. Collaborating with an experienced researcher will make the research and publication process less intimidating.

Listening to patrons and colleagues, especially in the provision of reference service, is also a tool to develop research ideas. Daily interactions and discussions can yield extremely valuable and interesting research questions. Ideas can also be generated by attending conferences and listening to presentations, or just by interacting with colleagues from other institutions. Subscribing to relevant discussion lists can also produce ideas. What information are your colleagues looking for? Chances are if one person wants some type of information, then there are also many others who are seeking the same thing.

Reading the professional literature in other fields can also produce ideas. Librarians can take a research project in another discipline and apply it to libraries, or they can look for related types of studies such as citation studies or studies of journal rankings. The methodology used in these studies can sometimes easily be adapted for librarianship. Another area is to look for publishing opportunities such as calls for papers or for conference presentations. These "calls" will provide information on the subject matter the editor or organizer is looking for. Beginning librarians may find it useful to develop papers or projects from their library school program. Finally, many reference librarians write about innovations that they have developed in their own libraries. Writing about such projects, and discussing their context in the literature of librarianship, is a good place to start for beginning researchers. A useful tool to use is simply to keep a list of possible research topics as the activities above are performed. This listing acts as a prompting device so that the researcher is on the alert for new ideas and will remember ideas previously generated.

Those who are not familiar with research methods and tools for data analysis will want to familiarize themselves with this information. Depending on whether it is totally new subject matter or simply a refresher, librarians can take a course or workshop or simply obtain a research methods book for reference. Also, writing, like most things, becomes easier the more it is done. Finally, rejected publications, while disappointing, can also be very useful. Reading the reviewer comments can point out methodological errors and provide tips for producing higher quality work for revisions and for future works.

POSITIVE IMPACT OF CONFERENCE ATTENDANCE AND PRESENTATIONS

Professional conferences can be one of the most intellectually stimulating activities available. Conference presentations typically cover the most cutting-edge topics and research that have not yet been published. Attending a conference has many positive aspects. It is probably the best way to learn about innovative practices, new resources, and new research areas. Attending conferences provides a forum for interaction with colleagues, and can serve as a place to develop new ideas for research and for new programs and practices.

Presenting a paper at a conference provides many of the same benefits as publishing a journal article. It increases visibility of authors and promotes their professional reputation and that of their institution. Paper presentations are a great method to present research findings in a timely fashion and to gain immediate feedback from the audience. Information garnered from audience interaction can prove to be useful information when preparing a manuscript for publication. These questions can also serve as a springboard for further, related research. Finally, many conferences publish proceedings, which is another avenue for publication for prospective authors.

STRATEGIES FOR CONFERENCE ATTENDANCE AND PRESENTATIONS

Attending conferences can often be quite expensive. Registration costs, travel, lodging, and meals can make conference attendance prohibitively expensive. Prospective attendees should seek out funding opportunities from their institutions. If this is not possible, grants or awards are given by some organizations, especially for those still in a library graduate program. Attending local or state events is not usually as expensive and can provide many of the same benefits as attending a national conference. Many institutions will, however, fund the cost of conferences if a paper is being presented.

Beginning presenters may wish to pair up with a mentor, preferably an experienced conference presenter. This is a valuable method for properly preparing a presentation and coping with other potential problems such as stage fright. Generating ideas for conference papers is probably best done through reading the call for proposals. Most conference organizers initially require an abstract and title; if the paper is accepted, the author is expected to prepare a paper for presentation. Prospective presenters should not be too hesitant since proposals are not too lengthy and should not take an inordinate amount of time to prepare. Also, the worst thing that can happen is that the proposal is rejected.

POSITIVE IMPACT OF SERVICE

Service in librarianship usually refers to service on local, state or national committees, usually those related to the profession. Serving on local committees, such as institutional or regional committees, allows the reference librarian to have a direct voice and impact on local operations in their own community. As with research and conferences, service also increases the visibility and status of librarians and library-related issues. Reference librarians interact with many different constituents in the community and therefore may be in the very unique position of being aware of different facets of local issues. This knowledge makes reference librarians valuable assets as committee members.

State and national organizations allow librarians to have a broader impact on the profession. Committees at the state and national levels often engage in educational activities and programs to benefit members, and committee members influence what is offered. Service on committees at these levels also provides increased professional status and visibility and allows for the interaction with colleagues from other institutions. These professional linkages continually prove to be useful for a variety of purposes, such as learning about new resources, programs, potential research, or for use as a professional reference. Membership in professional associations provides voting privileges and, subsequently, a voice in how the organization operates.

STRATEGIES FOR BEGINNING SERVICE ACTIVITIES

The best advice for becoming involved with service activities is to volunteer. There are many opportunities for reference librarians to become involved and many committees are searching for members. At the local level, it is probably best to attend meetings as a visitor and to participate if possible. If appropriate, visitors can also place relevant items on the agenda for discussion. Contacting the committee chair, or talking with him before or after a meeting, to volunteer services, is a method that is usually quite successful. Attending meetings is also a valuable experience for those who do not have previous committee experience. Watching the proceedings, listening to the interactions, and learning parliamentary procedure will prove beneficial.

Volunteering at the state or national level can be more involved. First, it usually involves some kind of time commitment, often for two years or more. Potential volunteers should make sure they have the proper authorization from their parent institutions for the time commitment and the financial means to attend the meetings. An extremely useful technique, and similar to that described for local committees, is to investigate ahead of time what the committee does, and to attend the meeting as a visitor. For example, the American Library Association publishes the annual *ALA Handbook of Organization,* which describes all of the committees and lists the current members. Potential volunteers can identify committees that interest them and contact the committee chair for further information or to find out whether there are volunteer opportunities. Another technique is to attend executive committee meetings as a visitor. In addition to gaining valuable information about how the organization works, visitors also get to know the leaders and can learn of possible volunteer opportunities.

Newer librarians, or those still in graduate school, should investigate opportunities such as the American Library Association's New Members Round Table. This committee has the mission to "help those new to the library profession and those who have been association members for less than ten years to become actively involved in the association and the profession." Many other committees will allow inexperienced committee members or current students to serve as interns. Another valuable resource are experienced librarians at the same, or nearby, institutions. These librarians will often provide advice and give recommendations for committee membership.

CONCLUSION

Professional development can take the form of many different activities, including continuing education courses, workshops, research and publication, and service. There is a consensus within the library profession that professional development activities are beneficial and desirable. However, there is some disparity as to whether the responsibility falls to the individual or the institution. Research suggests that there is a greater institutional responsibility and commitment for professional development activities, at least among academic libraries.

Research, publication, and service are three activities that are of particular importance to librarians, especially those in academic libraries with faculty status or tenure. However, the benefits of these activities can prove equally useful for librarians from non-academic institutions. The benefits are multifaceted and bring rewards to the individual reference librarian, the parent institution, and the library profession as a whole. Personally, reference librarians who engage in these professional development activities will gain a more prestigious position within the profession. Also, these activities assist in the performance of reference activities because they facilitate an increased awareness and knowledge of new, innovative resources and services. The strategies for becoming involved in these activities will vary by the individual reference librarian's interests, needs, and organizational commitment and support. Perhaps if administrators at institutions not providing professional development support can be convinced of their utility and potential benefit to the organization, reference librarians at these institutions may be able to broaden their involvement in professional development activities.

REFERENCES

Albritton, Rosie L. (1990), "Continuing Professional Education: A Management Development Approach," *The Reference Librarian* 30, 237-255.

American Library Association (1997), *ALA Handbook of Organization,* 1997-98. Chicago: American Library Association.

American Medical Association (1999), AMA Key Objectives and Strategies. Chicago: American Medical Association. Retrieved July 6, 1999 from the World Wide Web: http://www.ama-assn.org/about/objectiv.htm

Association of Research Libraries (1982), *Professional Development in ARL Libraries,* SPEC Kit 86. Washington, DC: Association of Research Libraries.

Boice, Robert, Jordan M. Scepanski, and Wayne Wilson (1987), "Librarians and Faculty Members: Coping with Pressures to Publish," *College & Research Libraries* 48 (November), 494-503.

Bradigan, Pamela S. and Carol A. Mularski (1996), "Evaluation of Academic Librarians' Publications for Tenure and Initial Promotion," *Journal of Academic Librarianship* 22 (September), 360-365.

Clemens, Bonnie J. and Melissa Trevvett, eds. (1991), "Integrating New Professionals into Large Academic Libraries: A Symposium," *Journal of Academic Librarianship* 17 (May), 68-78.

Gamble, Lynne E. (1989), "University Service: New Implications for Academic Librarians," *Journal of Academic Librarianship* 14 (January), 344-347.

Gelfand, Julia (1985), "Professional Development for Reference and Adult Services Librarians," *RQ* 24 (Summer), 403.

Golian, Linda Marie and Michael W. Galbraith (1996), "Effective Mentoring Programs for Professional Library Development," *Advances in Library Administration and Organization* 14, 95-124.

Grumling, Dennis K. and Carolyn A. Sheehy (1993), "Professional Development Program: Training for Success within Academic Librarianship," *College & Research Libraries* 54 (January), 17-24.

Havener, W. Michael and Wilbur A. Stolt (1994), "The Professional Development Activities of Academic Librarians: Does Institutional Support Make a Difference?" *College & Research Libraries* 55 (January), 25-36.

Hill, Janet Swan (1994), "Wearing Our Own Clothes: Librarians as Faculty," *Journal of Academic Librarianship* 20 (May), 71-76.

Jenkins, Darrell L., M. Kathleen Cook, and Mary Anne Fox (1981), "Research Development of Academic Librarians: One University's Approach," *Journal of Academic Librarianship* 7 (May), 83-86.

Kenney, Donald J. and Gail McMillan (1992), "State Library Associations: How Well Do They Support Professional Development," *RQ* 31, 377-386.

Kong, Leslie (1996), "Academic Reference Librarians: Under the Microscope," *The Reference Librarian* 54, 21-27.

Levene, Lee-Allison and Polly Frank (1993), "Peer Coaching: Professional Growth and Development for Instruction Librarians," *Reference Services Review* 21 (Fall), 35-42.

Mitchell, W. Bede and Mary Reichel (1999), "Publish or Perish: A Dilemma for Academic Librarians?" *College & Research Libraries* 60 (May), 232-243.

Mitchell, W. Bede and L. Stanislava Swieszkowski (1985), "Publication Requirements and Tenure Approval Rates: An Issue for Academic Librarians," *College & Research Libraries* 46 (May), 249-255.

National Education Association (1999), Code of Ethics of the Education Profession. Washington, DC: National Education Association. Retrieved July 6, 1999 from the World Wide Web: http://www.nea.org/info/code.html

Newman, G. Charles, Amy L. Dibartolo, and Levirn Hill (1991), "Fostering Professional Growth in Academic Libraries: A Case Study for the 1990s," *Library Administration & Management* 5 (Winter), 41-44.

Olsgaard, John N. (1984), "Characteristics of 'Success' Among Academic Librarians," *College & Research Libraries* 45 (January), 5-14.

Rockman, Irene F. (1989), "Promoting Professional Development: A Local Approach," *College & Research Libraries News* 50 (November), 902-904.

Saw, Grace E. H. (1989), "Staff Professional Development in Libraries: The Organisation's Role," *Australasian College Libraries* 7 (March), 17-25.

Sherrer, Johannah (1996), "Thriving in Changing Times: Competencies for Today's Reference Librarians," *The Reference Librarian* 54, 11-20.

Strong, Gary E. (1996), "Toward a Virtual Future," *The Reference Librarian* 54, 153- 161.

Werrell, Emily and Laura Sullivan (1987), "Faculty Status for Academic Librarians: A Review of the Literature," *College & Research Libraries* 48 (March), 95-103.

"Be All That You Can Be": Developing and Marketing Professionalism in Academic Reference Librarianship

Sarah Brick Archer

SUMMARY. Library school provides librarians with a good background in library science, but to be a professional reference librarian, continuous improvement must be sought. Professionalism can include developing basic employee skills, supporting library standards, participating in university and library functions; presenting papers; and publishing. Being sensitive to communication skills can impact how a librarian is perceived by library users. Image does play a role in the effectiveness of the library professional.

Professional reference librarians must market themselves by being visible on campus, in the community, and on the Internet. Being a professional librarian is an opportunity for personal growth and educating the public about a very exciting discipline. *[Article copies available for a fee from The Haworth Document Delivery Service: 1-800-342-9678. E-mail address: <getinfo@haworthpressinc.com> Website: <http://www.HaworthPress.com> © 2001 by The Haworth Press, Inc. All rights reserved.]*

KEYWORDS. Homepages, home pages, image of librarians, Internet, marketing, professional communication, professional development, reference librarianship, Web

---

Sarah Brick Archer is Assistant Professor of Library Services and Reference Coordinator, Reference Department, John Vaughan Library, Northeastern State University, 711 North Grand, Tahlequah, OK 74464-2398 (E-mail: archersa@cherokee.nsuok.edu).

The author would like to thank her family, Dr. and Mrs. Samuel E. Brick, Steve and Rachel Archer; Dr. J. Richard Madaus; Victoria Sheffler; and Linda West.

[Haworth co-indexing entry note]: "'Be All That You Can Be': Developing and Marketing Professionalism in Academic Reference Librarianship." Archer, Sarah Brick. Co-published simultaneously in *The Reference Librarian* (The Haworth Information Press, an imprint of The Haworth Press, Inc.) No. 73, 2001, pp. 351-360; and: *Doing the Work of Reference: Practical Tips for Excelling as a Reference Librarian* (ed: Celia Hales Mabry) The Haworth Information Press, an imprint of The Haworth Press, Inc., 2001, pp. 351-360. Single or multiple copies of this article are available for a fee from The Haworth Document Delivery Service [1-800-342-9678, 9:00 a.m. - 5:00 p.m. (EST). E-mail address: getinfo@haworthpressinc.com].

INTRODUCTION

In library school, students are taught the necessary research skills to answer reference questions correctly, but in order to succeed as reference librarians, they must also engage in the continuous process of growing as professionals. Both aspects are important to a librarian in the stimulating process of learning to develop to her full potential. "Being all that you can be" is a career-long mission of developing as a professional reference librarian and using marketing skills to educate the public as to what reference librarianship is all about.

In addition to expertise in librarianship, it is important to identify activities that constitute professionalism. It is also useful to recognize elements that are a hindrance to projecting a professional image. Once professionalism has been defined and barriers removed, skills (e.g., communication) can be enhanced to project a more positive image. In marketing a professional image, it is important for the reference librarian to spread the word outside of the library in order to educate the public as to what reference librarians do. One marketing approach is through an effective homepage on the web. It is through understanding and education that the image of the librarian can be altered, and this alteration will ultimately improve the effectiveness of the librarian.

PROFESSIONALISM

In order to grow as a professional, it is important to understand activities that can aid in this endeavor. Of course, having a good background in librarianship is essential. There are certain competencies that all employees must have to be successful on the job. The University Libraries, University of Nebraska–Lincoln lists the following core competencies:

> Analytical skills/problem solving/decision making; communication skills; creativity/innovation; expertise and technical knowledge; flexibility/adaptability; interpersonal/group skills; leadership; organizational understanding and global thinking; ownership/accountability/dependability; planning and organizational skills; resource management; service attitude/user satisfaction. (Giesecke and McNeil, 1999)

Additional attributes include good self-esteem, a positive attitude, and a challenging plan for career development. All of these elements are necessary for success in reference librarianship.

Professionals in all fields adhere to standards. For librarians, that adherence entails upholding the principles of librarianship, such as supporting the American Library Association's *Library Bill of Rights* (Barker, 1998). It also means following the Association of College and Research Libraries' model statements for issues such as faculty status and collection maintenance. Examples of applicable model statements include personnel issues, such as *Model Statement of Criteria and Procedures for Appointment, Promotion in Academic Rank, and Tenure for College and University Librarians* (ACRL, 1997) and general statements such as *Standards for University Libraries* (ACRL, 1997).

Being a professional also means planning a career with continuous improvement as the goal. It is important to try new things as a reference librarian and to volunteer for committees or take on new projects that might enable the librarian to develop additional skills. Reference librarians should analyze their strengths and weaknesses and plot a course that will encourage growth. Served on reference department committees? Volunteer to serve on state, regional, or national committees. Taught classes? Try writing an article or presenting a paper. After exploring different venues, find a niche. Finding that niche can be a fun and rewarding journey. Become an expert in that narrow area; for example, within library instruction become an expert on active learning.

Dare to be innovative and support change. Go beyond a job description. Special interests or hobbies can be used to add a unique dimension to a job. For instance, if a reference librarian is interested in acting or photography, he could use those skills on the job by doing displays or graphics work or offering workshops incorporating acting skills in librarianship. Always strive to find ways to add value to the reference department.

Find a mentor with comparable goals and style. The one-on-one tutoring and experience of working with a mentor can be a career-altering and enhancing experience.

Be positive and open to new ideas and learning. Be responsible and dependable. Compromise when necessary. Network. Be in contact with the world outside of the library. Have a sense of humor (Boies, 1992).

Participate actively in all levels of library associations. Professionals always support and give something back to the organization. Finally, it is important to have a sense of pride in all endeavors. As Patricia Glass Schuman stated in her paraphrase of John Gardner, "librarianship is not just a job, but a way of life" (Schuman, 1990).

Professionals are not afraid to get actively involved with their clients. Librarians have been hesitant to make recommendations to their users without basing it on a verifiable source. Reference librarians should consider getting more involved with library users by offering educated opinions and by acting as consultants. According to Joan C. Durrance, one element that has contributed to the librarian's image problem is "persistently eschewing the creation of a strong relationship with clients" (Durrance, 1990).

BARRIERS

The traditional librarian stereotype may interfere with how library users perceive the librarian's professionalism. No library user wants to ask a question of an academic reference librarian who does not appear capable of answering it. Besides affecting credibility, presenting a professional image can impact status, salaries, and level of respect. "Perhaps one of the reasons librarians are so concerned with their image is our recognition that what people think of us not only limits our status and salaries, but also the growth of our profession and the funding and use of libraries" (Schuman, 1990).

Presenting a professional image can actually help promote both the librarian and the library. Instead of just promoting reference service, try promoting the librarian. Patricia Glass Schuman states, "Some of our image problems stem from the fact that our profession usually promotes the library, and not the librarian" (Schuman, 1990). In academic libraries a lot of time is spent promoting collections and services, but not the skills of the reference librarian to serve the information needs of the user. "It's the people who make the experience a positive one–not your collections, databases, or services" (Abram, 1996). In 1990, the American Library Association had a campaign to promote the librarian. "The marketing activity of delivering effective information while highlighting our personal qualities and professional attributes is key to promoting ourselves" (Abram, 1996). It is important to remember, however, that librarianship is not the only profession that has been stereotyped.

Another solution to dealing with the stereotype comes from within. Instead of dwelling on the image problem (which many professions have), laugh about it, and emphasize providing excellent service. "How people think librarians look is unimportant. What they think librarians do is crucial" (Schuman, 1990).

COMMUNICATION SKILLS

Dress

First impressions are important in any communication transaction, and the first impression that a patron will have of the reference librarian is based on the librarian's appearance. A librarian must outwardly demonstrate professionalism. It is important for a reference librarian to be aware of the message that her attire is sending. There is no rigid dress code that will ensure a successful reference interaction. However, attire should be clean, neat, easily identifiable, and consistent. Do the shoes go with the outfit? Does the hair seem appropriate? A formal suit with big jewelry or dishelved hair would not project a professional image.

Consider what type of apparel is worn by other professionals, such as business people or attorneys, and emulate it with modifications to maintain individualities. It is important to project an air of intelligence, confidence, and authority, and yet still be approachable. According to Lisa A. Wolfe, "People will perceive your library in a much more positive light if they see staff who care about their appearance. Patrons will believe that they are in an important place–because the people who work there think it is important" (Wolfe, 1997).

Nonverbal Signals

Imagine the message that is sent when a patron walks up to the reference librarian, who is seated at a low desk looking at a computer screen, and the librarian doesn't look at the patron while asking, "May I help you?" Patrons will believe nonverbal signals over verbal signals every time. Most patrons would not believe that the librarian is interested in helping. To be successful, reference librarians must be approachable. It is important to appear physically open by making eye contact with the patron, and perhaps, even standing to meet the patron. Standing with wide-open eyes and with relaxed arms will indicate a willingness to assist the patron. Practicing good posture and projecting an air of confidence reassures the library user that the reference librarian is capable of effectively assisting him.

An alternate approach to sitting at the reference desk is to roam the reference floor asking library users if they need help. The reference desk can serve as a barrier to patrons, so getting out from behind the desk and going to the patron can be a very effective way to serve the public. This is especially true with shy patrons who would not feel comfortable approaching a librarian at a reference desk.

Smiling sounds simple, but such a nonverbal signal can ease the discomfort that many library users feel in approaching the reference librarian. Maintaining eye contact and nodding as the user speaks indicates a high interest level.

Listening Skills

A professional also practices good listening techniques. It is important to really listen to what the patron is saying. Do not interrupt, but let the patron thoroughly explain the question. Ask for clarification or restate the question, if necessary. Be certain to wait for an answer after asking a question. Nod or indicate attentiveness (Ross and Dewdney, 1989).

Practicing good customer service and reference interview techniques, can improve the likelihood of a successful patron interaction. Always remember to follow up on users' questions to make certain that their needs were met.

Verbal Skills

It is important that the library user understands what the reference librarian is saying. Speak slowly enough to enunciate all words, but not so slowly that the IQ of the reference librarian can come into question! Speak loudly enough to be heard; speak with authority. Include inflection and modulation in speaking.

All of the techniques to improve communication can be useful for interacting with staff or teaching a class. Projecting a professional image in attire, gestures, and speech is a good way to be taken seriously, which will increase the librarian's effectiveness.

MARKETING: TAKING YOUR MESSAGE ON THE ROAD

No longer can librarians sit placidly at the reference desk waiting for people to come to them. Information is available from other competing sources. Librarians have concentrated on making library users self-sufficient. "Perhaps we have done our self-service concept in libraries too well: it has been made so easy for patrons to use libraries that there is no reason for them to suppose that librarians have any particularly special expertise to offer" (Kies, 1989). Also, anyone who does a job well can make it look too easy. Both of these concerns can increase the need for the librarian to promote herself. Marketing is about understanding our own attributes, identifying our users, and communicating with our users. Kies states that "successful marketing is based upon the *identification of need*" (Kies, 1989).

The purpose of marketing is not for self-glorification, but for self-preservation and for educating the public. According to Kies, "the purpose of 'marketing' the librarian is not to enhance our status, per se, but to help create a better understanding of how libraries work, and to increase the value which is placed upon libraries by society and our various constituencies" (Kies, 1989). Through marketing, librarians can create powerful library advocates in faculty and students. It can be more effective to have classroom faculty requesting the university administration to increase library funding than hearing the same message from librarians.

Being a professional reference librarian also means taking our message on the road by being involved in projects outside the confines of the library. "This means public relations, it means coalition building, it means full participation in the intellectual and political life of campus and the community" (Schuman, 1990). Librarians can market themselves simply by their actions and by increasing visibility both on campus and in the community. Participate actively in Faculty Senate meetings and volunteer to be an officer. Serve on university or community committees–and not just in a library capacity.

The more the reference librarian is visible in the community projecting a good image and intelligently adding to the university or community organization, the more highly librarians will be viewed and valued. Don't limit activities to traditional "library-related" endeavors. Volunteer to participate in teacher portfolio projects. Other faculty will be surprised to see the reference librarian on the committee and be impressed with what the librarian has to offer. At the same time, the teaching faculty will be educated as to what librarianship is all about.

Remember to submit any information about workshops presented or articles published to any campus newsletters, newspapers, or web sites. Librarians need to let the rest of the university community be aware of their professional activities. This is not the time to be meek, but a time to be assertive and realize that it is necessary to toot one's own horn.

To help with marketing, ask a marketing professor to recommend students to assist with a marketing plan. Always emphasize what the librarian can do to benefit the patron. "Marketing and selling a professional means building and maintaining a mutually beneficial relationship" (Wallace, 1989). Inform the university administration of how the librarian's efforts benefit the organization. "Librarians seem to have failed to define their contribution to institutional success . . . " (Martin, 1998).

MARKETING: TAKING IT ON THE WIRE

Many librarians are actively involved with the web. They teach classes and are listed in library personnel directories on the web. But how many librarians have personal homepages on the web that include the same kinds of details as other teaching faculty on campus? This is another good opportunity to market the professionalism of the reference librarian. Think of the homepage as a working portfolio and a public relations opportunity.

How can this be done? Look at the personal web pages of classroom teaching faculty to determine what to include. Tailor this to the expertise of the reference librarian.

For instance, on a personal homepage include contact information, such as snail mail and e-mail; phone and fax numbers; office and reference desk hours; internal links to relevant reference department and library pages; external links; and list the date the page was created and updated. Included on the homepage could be a vita listing education, work experience, tenure received, articles published, awards received, workshops presented, etc. On the homepage, include any PowerPoint or Presentations software presented at workshops. List committees and organizations and include hot links to these sites. For reference librarians, who are also instruction librarians, connect all instruction pages to the librarian's personal homepage. Include course syllabi where applicable. Philosophical and mission statements could be included, as well as future goals.

If creating subject pages for specific disciplines, link the subject pages to the academic departments. This will be a service to the academic department and a good marketing tool for the librarian. If developing an extensive personal homepage, consider including a dedicated search engine to make finding information easier.

Of course, presentation is also important with the homepage. The basic mechanics of homepage design should be followed with appropriate type fonts, type size, colors, and graphics that load quickly. It is crucial that the homepage be kept current and that links be checked frequently and outdated links removed.

CONCLUSION

The best way to improve and promote librarianship is for each librarian to develop to his full potential. This involves having a good library science education, adhering to standards, participating actively in library organizations, publishing, projecting a professional image, and marketing the librarian's skills outside of the library. Professionalism is an exciting career-long journey that requires continuous improvement and growth on the part of the librarian. Developing professionally can keep a reference librarian from getting bored or burning out. It combines creativity, imagination, applying personal strengths, research, and drive. As if that isn't enough, the professional reference librarian must constantly take her message on the road and educate her users as to what reference librarianship is all about. "Being all that you can be" is an exciting opportunity to grow as a professional as well as a person.

REFERENCES

Abram, Stephen (1996), "Marketing Your Valuable Experience," *MLS (Marketing Library Services)* 10 (October/November), 4-5.

Association of College and Research Libraries, *Model Statement of Criteria and Procedures for Appointment, Promotion in Academic Rank, and Tenure for Col-*

lege and University Librarians, Online. 1997 [Available: http://www.ala.org/acrl/guides/criteria.html] 25 June 1999.

Association of College and Research Libraries, *Standards for University Libraries: Evaluation of Performance,* Online. 1997 [Available: http://www.ala.org/acrl/guides/univer.html] 25 June 1999.

Barber, Peggy, and Hodges, Gerald G., eds. (1998), *ALA Handbook of Organization 1998-99.* Chicago: American Library Association.

Boies, Kay (1992), "Learning to Be a Library Leader," [excerpted from audio tape *Learning to Be a Library Leader*] *Oklahoma Librarian* 42 (September/October), 55.

Durrance, Joan C. (1990), "Librarians: The Invisible Professionals," in *The Bowker Annual: Library and Book Trade Almanac,* 35th ed., edited by Filomena Simora. New York: Bowker, 92-99.

Giesecke, Joan, and McNeil, Beth (1999), "Core Competencies and the Learning Organization," *Library Administration and Management* 13 (Summer), 158-166.

Kies, Cosette (1989), "Marketing the Librarian: The Weakest Link in the Chain," *Catholic Library World* 61 (July/August), 25-30.

Martin, Murray S. (1998), "Who Are We?" *Technicalities* 18 (March), 4-5.

Ross, Catherine Sheldrick, and Dewdney, Patricia (1989), *Communicating Professionally: A How-To-Do-It Manual for Library Applications.* New York: Neal-Schuman.

Schuman, Patricia Glass (1990), "The Image of Librarians: Substance or Shadow?" *Journal of Academic Librarianship* 16 (May), 86-89.

Wallace, Linda (1989), "Tips From a Pro on Promoting the Pro," *American Libraries* 20 (January), 24. (Reprinted from the *PR Activity Report,* 1988, Chicago: ALA Public Information Office.)

Wolfe, Lisa A. (1997), *Library Public Relations, Promotions, and Communications.* New York: Neal-Schuman.

Service to the Profession: Definitions, Scope, and Value

Candace R. Benefiel
Jeannie P. Miller
Pixey Anne Mosley
Wendi Arant-Kaspar

SUMMARY. For academic librarians with faculty status, service to the profession often forms part of the requirements for promotion and tenure. Considering the concept of professional service raises questions as to what specific activities qualify; what is their weight, both within the service requirement and also as compared with other requirements, such as research and publication; and how are service activities best documented. Examination of ARL Standards and selected promotion and tenure documents revealed inconsistencies between institutions and great flexibility in interpretation by most. *[Article copies available for a fee from The Haworth Document Delivery Service: 1-800-342-9678. E-mail address: <getinfo@haworthpressinc.com> Website: <http://www.HaworthPress.com> © 2001 by The Haworth Press, Inc. All rights reserved.]*

KEYWORDS. Service, tenure, promotion, academic librarians, faculty

Candace R. Benefiel is Senior Humanities Reference Librarian (E-mail: candace@tamvm1.tamu.edu); Jeannie P. Miller is Director, Science/Engineering Services (E-mail: jmiller@tamu.edu); Pixey Anne Mosley is Head, Access Services (E-mail: pmosley@tamu.edu); and Wendi Arant-Kaspar is Coordinator, Electronic Reference Services (E-mail: warant@tamu.edu). All are affiliated with the Texas A&M University General Libraries, College Station, TX 77843-5000.

[Haworth co-indexing entry note]: "Service to the Profession: Definitions, Scope, and Value." Benefiel, Candace R. et al. Co-published simultaneously in *The Reference Librarian* (The Haworth Information Press, an imprint of The Haworth Press, Inc.) No. 73, 2001, pp. 361-372; and: *Doing the Work of Reference: Practical Tips for Excelling as a Reference Librarian* (ed: Celia Hales Mabry) The Haworth Information Press, an imprint of The Haworth Press, Inc., 2001, pp. 361-372. Single or multiple copies of this article are available for a fee from The Haworth Document Delivery Service [1-800-342-9678, 9:00 a.m. - 5:00 p.m. (EST). E-mail address: getinfo@haworthpressinc.com].

For academic librarians with faculty status, service to the profession often forms part of the requirements for promotion and tenure. The requirements are based on the premise that participation in professional service activities has beneficial effects for the individual, the institution, and the profession as a whole. The definition, scope and weight of service activities vary widely from institution to institution. The concept of professional service raises questions as to what specific activities fall into the area of professional service; what is their weight, both within the service requirement and also as compared with other requirements, such as research and publication; and how are service activities best documented. Lack of definitive information on this topic affects not only untenured librarians as they make decisions on directing their efforts towards tenure and promotion, but also can affect tenure committees as they seek to provide consistent guidance and objective evaluation of the tenure cases of faculty members. In addition, it has implications for the perception of the validity and value of tenure for librarians with comparison to other disciplines.

The novice librarian, attempting to navigate a course through the shoals of professional duties and tenure and promotion requirements, which may seem to conflict, is in need of definitions. Without a grasp of what weight is given to various activities, or even a specific idea of what activities "count" as service, it is difficult to choose what activities to pursue, and what activities should be postponed until after tenure is granted. What guidance on this matter can be found in tenure and promotion documents? The ACRL "Model Statement of Criteria and Procedures for Appointment, Promotion in Academic Rank, and Tenure for College and University Librarians" (Association of College and Research Libraries 1994) gives several examples, but does not suggest relative weight and does little to reconcile the often-conflicting documents.

Many questions come up in mentoring discussions with tenure-track faculty. What is the definition of service? What is the value of service to the profession to the individual? What weight attaches to service in tenure and promotion evaluations? What is the value of participation in subject-oriented associations outside of librarianship? Are work-related committees given a different value than general committees? Is a Social Responsibilities Round Table committee as valuable as one in the English and American Literature Section? Is activity in New Members Round Table as valuable as work in the

Library Instruction Round Table? Are nominations committees as valued as program or publications committees? What are the relative values of elected and appointed committees? How are verbal invitations for presentations, facilitation, etc., documented?

The answers to these questions can have a significant impact on how individuals map out their goals and objectives in seeking appropriate service to the profession. There is the potential for a corresponding functional impact on library governance and professional organizations. If there is unanimous agreement regarding the value of one level of service over another, the committee perceived as less valuable with regard to tenure requirements might find it difficult to recruit quality membership. While a mentor or colleague will usually have opinions on these issues based on personal experience or observations of past tenure cases, the opinions may be incorrect, or at best reflect personal biases. Referral to the local promotion and tenure document may be equally uninformative, as these issues may not be explicitly addressed in a document.

In addition, broader questions need to be answered. What is the value of service to the profession to the organization? What is the perceived attitude of administrators (library and/or university) toward service by librarians? What financial support is available for service activities? And how is it justified? What is the value of committee work to the profession? Does any consistency on the value of service exist in the documents formulated by research libraries with faculty status for librarians?

LITERATURE REVIEW

Faculty status for librarians, in almost every aspect, is one of the most-discussed issues in the library literature. Faculty status for librarians is often questioned, while the status of teaching faculty is seldom at issue. This dilemma is compounded by the inability of the library profession to define itself and its contribution to the profession and to academia with regard to tenure and promotion, the distinctive mark of faculty. Over the last 40 years, literally hundreds of articles have been written on the topic, from opinion pieces on the validity of the whole concept to studies on specific requirements and surveys on the rate at which librarians are tenured. The issue is still attracting vigorous debate. Krompart (1992) and Werrell and Sullivan (1987) have attempted to survey the literature on faculty status, while DeBoer and Culotta (1987) have reviewed surveys on faculty status throughout the 1980s, updating Krompart and DiFelice's (1987) similar coverage of the 1970s. And yet, among the avalanche of writings, very little deals with the topic of service to the profession.

Service to the profession is a common requirement for faculty-status librarians, and indeed for college and university faculty generally. Richard I. Miller, in his book *Evaluating Faculty for Promotion and Tenure* (1986), defines professional service as "activities such as participating or holding office in professional associations and societies," but goes on to state, "The relative weights of various activities in this category are difficult to determine because little attention has been given to the matter in higher education literature." Nevertheless, Miller indicates that for faculty members across disciplines, effectiveness of professional service is an important factor in the assessment of faculty for tenure (1986).

In the Association of College and Research Libraries' "Standards for Faculty Status for College and University Librarians" (1992), the statement is made, "Librarians should be promoted in rank on the basis of their academic proficiency and professional effectiveness (job performance, service and scholarship)," and also notes, "The standards should be consistent with the campus standards for faculty." Similarly, the ACRL "Model Statement of Criteria and Procedures for Appointment, Promotion in Academic Rank, and Tenure for College and University Librarians" (1994) also speaks of "contributions to the advancement of the profession: for example, active participation in professional and learned societies as a member, as an officer, as a committee member, or as a committee chairperson." Clearly, the ACRL expects faculty status for librarians to parallel that of faculty in other disciplines. And this brings up an interesting point: If librarians are unsure of a specific definition of service activity and its relative weights, they are not alone. Lowry (1993) found that approximately 74% of academic libraries in a survey had some form of faculty status, and over 90% of those institutions either used the same criteria or a slightly modified version of criteria used to evaluate teaching faculty, including the requirements for research, publication, and service to the profession.

Park and Riggs (1991), discussing a 1989 national survey of tenure and promotion policies, note that service is frequently mentioned as a criterion, but also allow that "its impact as a criterion is not clear." In a later study, Park and Riggs (1993), surveying tenure and promotion practices, found that service was "the second most frequently mentioned criteria included in the review process," with 87% of responding institutions listing service. The survey also inquired into what activities were considered service, with responses ranging from university committees and regional/national committees down to community, civic and religious activities. It does seem significant that more institutions cited service than publication as a requirement for tenure and promotion.

When the service component of tenure and promotion evaluation is mentioned, it has generally been viewed as a positive activity. For example, Horenstein's (1993) study correlating faculty status and job satisfaction found that while librarians who have faculty status do not actually participate more in service activities than other librarians, they perceive themselves as being more professionally involved.

Some suggestions have been put forward for changing the traditional, teaching faculty model for academic faculty-status librarians. McGowan and Dow (1995) have put forth a clinical model, which translates the clinical model of patient care into a close parallel to librarian/user interactions. Under this model, professional service remains important and deserving of recognition in the evaluation process. As McGowan and Dow state, "Professional service is also an area that separates academic library faculty from most of their teaching faculty counterparts. Because information policy is at the forefront of national politics, academic librarians have the expertise and the mandate to guide many of these debates. All of this requires time and commitment, both of which often go unrecognized during evaluation."

In writings on faculty status and tenure and promotion criteria for librarians, the vagueness encompasses both the definition and the weight of service activities. Carol Cubberly, in *Tenure and Promotion for Academic Librarians: A Guidebook with Advice and Vignettes* (1996) writing on service activities, offers a laundry list of activities, along with a few hints on breaking into committees, but gives little guidance on the importance of such activity. Her generic tenure and promotion criteria suggest that service may be considered on a par with the areas of professional development and publishing, and "Successful candidates for tenure and promotion . . . will be expected to achieve a high level of performance in . . . two of the three . . . categories" (1997).

The most provocative article, and the one which focused most specifically on service, was "An Exercise to Test Perception of Expectations for Tenure and Promotion" (Grumling and Sheehy, 1991). The exercise involved librarians from three Illinois academic libraries ranking various service activities as to their perceived importance in the evaluation process. The authors assert that use of this exercise "may help build staff and administrative consensus regarding the value of professional activities."

From a survey of available literature, it seems evident that more study on the nature and importance of professional service is warranted. A comparison of statements from a number of ARL libraries should yield an idea of the nation-wide standard criteria for service to the profession. The present survey of academic research library tenure and promotion documents is not the final word on the subject, but may add to the body of knowledge on promotion and tenure issues for librarians.

METHODOLOGY

A list of activities that might be classified in the arena of service was developed following consultation of ACRL Standards and a review of pertinent literature. The list, provided in Appendix A, included a wide range of activities that might be classified as service. These included many options, from internal committees to university service and from community/local service to national professional organizations. The participation levels were broken out, ranging from simple membership to chairing committees or holding officer positions at the organization level. The list also included activities that are sometimes considered more relevant to the research and publication process, such as conducting workshops or making presentations.

Promotion and Tenure Documents of selected ARL libraries were obtained either through the World Wide Web or from ARL Spec Kit 182 (1992). The documents from the 32 ARL member libraries, listed in Appendix B, were reviewed to determine the types of service activities that are specified and what, if any, weight is assigned to these activities, both generally and specifically. This information was then compared with the compiled list. In looking for trends, other criteria examined included whether librarians have faculty or academic status and if librarians earn tenure or an equivalent rank, such as long-term contracts.

DATA SET

Out of the 32 ARL Library documents examined, 22 were tenure based; 8 were non-tenure; and 2 had dual track systems. There was significantly more emphasis placed on service activities for the tenure institutions, although the definition of service did vary widely. The only area of service mentioned regularly at the non-tenure institutions were the roles of Library Committee Member and Library Administrative Role, and only 50% of the institutions encouraged this. All other service activities from the checklist were either not mentioned at all or only mentioned by 1 or 2 non-tenure track institution documents. Obviously, institutional support of service to the profession is heavily dependent on tenure-track institutions.

According to the data, most of the promotion and tenure documents examined took a broad interpretation of service by including many of the activities from the compiled list. The documents often used very general language, such as "evidence of service may include" (Indiana University Bloomington <http://www.indiana.edu/~libpers/promotions.html>) or "makes significant contributions to the profession through some or all of the following" (University of Oregon <http://libweb.uoregon.edu/admnpers/faceval.html>). Then the documents go on to provide examples of acceptable service activities. Most of these examples would themselves be vague with no evidence of ranking or weighting and used words such as "participation in," "membership in" or, as found in one document, "Service to the Profession and Discipline (State, National, International level)" (University of Colorado <http://www.cusys.edu/~policies/Personnel/implemtenure.html>). Some documents indicated a preference for committee service through statements such as "Active participation and leadership in committee work in the Library, elsewhere in the University, or in state, regional, or national organizations" (University of Tennessee–Knoxville <http://toltec.lib.utk.edu/~lss/lpp/criteri2.html>) or "holding office or committee membership in national, regional, state, or local professional or learned societies" (University of Illinois at Urbana–Champaign <http://www.library.uiuc.edu/committee/promo/PTA.asp>). The most frequently cited activity, which appears to be a standard measure of service, is participation in professional societies at the committee member level or above. More than 90% of the libraries surveyed indicated that this was the quintessential service activity.

Even given the vagueness of some documents, it is obvious that some activities are consistently NOT mentioned in the promotion and tenure documents as a part of professional service. Only 18% of the documents from tenure track institutions considered continuing education in the service part of the document. Similarly, less than 50% allowed conference/workshop attendance and public/community appearances and public relations to be considered service to the profession.

The documents generally avoided a discussion of the justification of the service component. Benefits to the profession as a whole, the professional organizations, home institution, and individual were implied obliquely rather than stated directly or explained in detail. In the documents reviewed, some regarded service activities as a part of professional assignment, and some regarded publication and research as a part of service to the profession.

In looking at the value of service relative to other performance measures, those documents, which did address the issue, tended to state that given the three traditional areas of evaluation (professional assignment, publication and research, and service), professional assignment was the most important. In fact, 86% of the tenure-granting university libraries and 63% of the non-tenure university libraries indicated that professional assignment was the primary consideration with regard to advancement within the organization. Several put an equal weight on all three areas. Only two academic libraries specifically ranked their criteria for promotion and tenure in quantitative detail.

CONCLUSIONS

Service as a component of tenure criteria for librarians (and indeed for academics generally) is not well defined, either in the literature or in tenure and promotion documents. Most tend to imply that the definition of service is unnecessary since, as Supreme Court Justice Potter Stewart said in 1964, in speaking of pornography, " . . . I know it when I see it." The promotion and tenure documents examined in this study appeared to be written to allow for great flexibility, so that individuals are not forced into a mold, but in their flexibility they often did not give much guidance as to what activities "count," and how various types of activities factor into tenure and promotion decisions. Flexibility is an admirable quality and highly desirable in academic environments where academic freedom is "sacred"; however, when flexibility borders on ambiguity the results can be disastrous, or at least disconcerting, to librarians in pursuit of tenure and to the status of the profession as a whole.

BIBLIOGRAPHY

Academic Status for Librarians in ARL Libraries. ARL Spec Kit 182 (1992), Compiled by Jack Siggins and Ronald P. Naylor. Washington, DC: Association of Research Libraries, Office of Management Services.

Association of College and Research Libraries. Academic Status Committee (1992), "Standards for Faculty Status for College and University Librarians," *College and Research Libraries News* 53 (May): 317-18.

Association of College and Research Libraries. Academic Status Committee (1994), "Model Statement of Criteria and Procedures for Appointment, Promotion in Academic Rank, and Tenure for College and University Librarians," in *Academic Status: Statements and Resources (2nd ed.*), edited by Susan Kroll. Chicago: Association of College and Research Libraries, 11-24.

Association of College and Research Libraries. Academic Status Committee (1994), "Guidelines for Academic Status for College and University Libraries," in *Academic Status: Statements and Resources (2nd ed.*), edited by Susan Kroll. Chicago: Association of College and Research Libraries, 9-11.

Cubberly, Carol W. (1996), *Tenure and Promotion for Academic Librarians: A Guidebook with Advice and Vignettes*. Jefferson, NC: McFarland.

DeBoer, Kee and Wendy Culotta (1987), "The Academic Librarian and Faculty Status in the 1980s: A Survey of the Literature," *College and Research Libraries* 48 (May): 215-23.

Grumling, Dennis Keith and Carolyn A. Sheehy (1991), "An Exercise to Test Perception of Expectations for Tenure and Promotion," *College and Research Libraries News* 52 (May): 300-1.

Horenstein, Bonnie (1993), "Job Satisfaction of Academic Librarians: An Examination of the Relationships Between Satisfaction, Faculty Status, and Participation," *College and Research Libraries* 54 (May): 255-69.

Indiana University Bloomington (Approved by the Library Faculty April 1998). Criteria For Librarian Promotions. Retrieved April 20, 1999 from the World Wide Web: *http://www.indiana.edu/~libpers/promotions.html*

Krompart, Janet and Clara L. DiFelice (1987), "A Review of Faculty Status Surveys, 1971-1984," *The Journal of Academic Librarianship* 13 (March): 14-18.

Krompart, Janet (1992), "Researching Faculty Status: A Selective Annotated Bibliography," *College and Research Libraries* 53 (September): 439-49.

Lowry, Charles Bryan (1993), "The Status of Faculty Status for Academic Librarians: A Twenty-year Perspective," *College and Research Libraries* 54 (March): 163-72.

McGowan, Julie Johnson and Elizabeth H. Dow (1995), "Faculty Status and Academic Librarianship: Transformation to a Clinical Model," *The Journal of Academic Librarianship* 21 (September): 345-50.

Miller, Richard I. (1987), *Evaluating Faculty for Promotion and Tenure,* The Jossey-Bass Higher Education Series. San Francisco, London: Jossey-Bass Publishers.

Park, Elizabeth and Robert Riggs (1993), "Tenure and Promotion: A Study of Practices by Institutional Type," *The Journal of Academic Librarianship,* 19 (May): 72-77.

Park, Elizabeth and Robert Riggs (1991), "Status of the Profession: A 1989 National Survey of Tenure and Promotion Policies for Academic Librarians," *College and Research Libraries* 52 (May): 275-89.

University of Colorado (Effective Date: February 8, 1983), University of Colorado Administrative Policy Statement: Implementation of Tenure Policies for Librarians. Retrieved April 20, 1999 from the World Wide Web: *http://www.cusys.edu/~policies/Personnel/implemtenure.html*

University of Illinois at Urbana-Champaign (Approved and adopted by the University of Illinois Library Faculty at the June 17, 1994 meeting). Statement on Promotion, Tenure, & Appointments to the Library Faculty at the University of Illinois at Urbana-Champaign. Retrieved April 20, 1999 from the World Wide Web: *http://www.library.uiuc.edu/committee/promo/PTA.asp*

University of Oregon (Last revised: October 1996). OU Library Policy on: Faculty Evaluation Procedures. Retrieved April 26, 1999 from the World Wide Web: *http://libweb.uoregon.edu/admnpers/faceval.html*

University of Tennessee-Knoxville (Reprinted 1995). Promotion and Tenure Criteria: Guidelines for Library Faculty. Retrieved April 20, 1999 from the World Wide Web: *http://toltec.lib.utk.edu/~lss/lpp/criteri2.html*

Werrell, Emily L. and Laura A. Sullivan (1987), "Faculty Status for Academic Librarians: A Review of the Literature," *College and Research Libraries* 48 (March): 95-103.

APPENDIX A. List of Possible Service Activities

University Committee Member
University Committee Chair
University Administrative Role
Student Government Committee Member
Student Government Advisor
Library Committee Member
Library Committee Chair
Library Administrative Role
Departmental Committee Member
Departmental Committee Chair
Departmental Administrative Role
National/International Committee Member
National/International Committee Chair
National/International Association Officer
National/International Association Member
State/Regional Committee Member
State/Regional Committee Chair
State/Regional Association Officer
State/Regional Association Member
Local Committee Member
Local Committee Chair
Local Association Officer
Local Association Member
Continuing Education
Public Relations
Community Appearances
Educational Consultancy/Committees
Corporate Consultancy/Committees
Government Consultancy/Committees
Consultancy/Committees
Conference/Workshops Presentation
Conference/Workshops Facilitation
Conference/Workshops Attendance
Conference/Workshops

APPENDIX B. ARL University Libraries Documents Reviewed

Brigham Young University
Colorado State University
Cornell University
Duke University
Indiana University
Indiana University–Purdue University–Indianapolis
Louisiana State University
New York University
Pennsylvania State University
Rice University
State University of New York–Buffalo
Texas A&M University
University of Alabama
University of Alberta
University of Arizona
University of British Columbia
University of Chicago
University of Cincinnati
University of Colorado
University of Florida
University of Georgia
University of Hawaii
University of Illinois–Urbana Champaign
University of Nebraska
University of Oregon
University of Pittsburgh
University of Southern California
University of Tennessee–Knoxville
University of Texas
Washington State University
Yale University
York University

Index

Page numbers followed by t indicate tables; those followed by f indicate figures.

